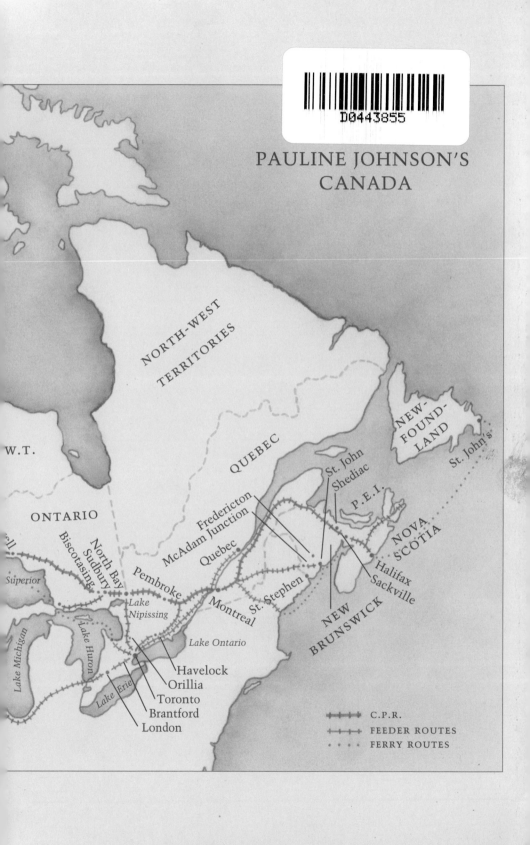

PAULINE JOHNSON'S CANADA

NORTH-WEST
TERRITORIES

QUEBEC

NEW-
FOUND-
LAND

W.T.

St. John
Shediac

St. John's

P.E.I.

ONTARIO

Fredericton
McAdam Junction
Quebec

NOVA
SCOTIA

Biscotasing
North Bay
Sudbury

Halifax
Sackville

Superior

Pembroke

Lake
Nipissing

Montreal
St. Stephen

NEW
BRUNSWICK

Lake Michigan

Lake Huron

Lake Ontario

Lake Erie

Havelock
Orillia
Toronto
Brantford
London

├┼┼┼┼┤ C.P.R.
├┼┼┼┤ FEEDER ROUTES
•••• FERRY ROUTES

FLINT & FEATHER

CHARLOTTE GRAY

FLINT
&
FEATHER

THE LIFE AND TIMES OF
E. PAULINE JOHNSON,
TEKAHIONWAKE

Harper*Flamingo* Canada · 2002
A PHYLLIS BRUCE BOOK

Flint & Feather : The Life and Times
of E. Pauline Johnson, Tekahionwake
Copyright © 2002 by Charlotte Gray.
For information address:
HarperCollins Publishers Ltd.,
55 Avenue Road, Suite 2900,
Toronto, Ontario,
Canada M5R 3L2

www.harpercanada.com

HarperCollins books may be purchased for educational, business,
or sales promotional use. For information please write:
Special Markets Department,
HarperCollins Canada,
55 Avenue Road, Suite 2900,
Toronto, Ontario,
Canada M5R 3L2

First edition

National Library of Canada Cataloguing in Publication

Gray, Charlotte, 1948–
Flint & feather : the life and times of E. Pauline Johnson,
Tekahionwake / Charlotte Gray.

"A Phyllis Bruce book."
Includes bibliographical references and index.
ISBN 0-00-200065-2

1. Johnson, E. Pauline, 1861–1913.
2. Poets, Canadian (English) – 19th century – Biography.
3. Mohawk Indians – Canada – Biography.
I. Title.

PS8469.O283Z6 2002   C811'.4   C2002-902402-1
PR9199.2.J64Z6 2002

DWF 9 8 7 6 5 4 3 2 1

Printed and bound in Canada
Set in Trump Mediaeval

CONTENTS

For George

1

THE ROMANCE
OF CHIEFSWOOD

WHEN the young Pauline Johnson stood in the hallway of Chiefswood, the family home on the Grand River, on a summer's afternoon, she had the happy certainty that she was in the centre of her own small universe. All around her flowed the sounds of the busy Johnson household. From the study on her left seeped the growl of discussion as her father, George Johnson, held court with various neighbours. From the drawing room on her right came the *plink* of awkward chords as her older brother Beverly picked out the latest dance tune on the Heintzman piano. Breathy chatter flowed from the parlour, where her sister Eva helped the maid set out the silver tea service. Allen, the brother closest in age to Pauline, was probably in the kitchen garden, gorging himself on the last raspberries of the season. If Pauline glanced up the elegant staircase, she could see her mother, Emily Johnson, carefully adjusting her tea gown before she descended to the ground floor.

Even on the hottest July day, the hallway's dark walnut panelling and high ceilings kept the house cool. Pauline loved to lean against the hand-turned railing, close her eyes, run her finger along a slippery brass stair rod and breathe in the aromas of fresh-cut flowers, newly baked bread and furniture polish. She adored Chiefswood, the creamy stucco villa her father had built in 1855, six years before she was born. She spent her days wandering its grounds amidst the majestic old walnut, oak and elm trees, watching squirrels scampering among the branches and crows wheeling overhead. In early spring, violets

The graceful symmetry of Chiefswood, built by Pauline's father in the
1850s, reflected the ideal of harmony for which the family strove.

bloomed in the shadows. In late summer, pungent walnuts crunched underfoot. In the evening Pauline often ran down to the riverbank, her little dog, Chips, scampering alongside, to watch the mauves and golds of the sunset reflected in the water. And at night she would lie on the grass, gazing up at the brilliant stars twinkling in the inky vastness above her. Wisps of the romantic poetry that her mother read to her each afternoon drifted through her mind. She silently repeated to herself some of her favourite lines, almost intoxicated by the emotions of longing and loss that drenched the languorous verses about blossoms, clouds and seasons.

Maybe Pauline's idyllic world occupied only a trackless patch of pink on the margins of the far-flung British Empire. Maybe Queen Victoria, whose stern likeness hung in Chiefswood's dining room, would never visit this isolated outpost of her mighty realm, let alone encounter her North American subjects on their own land. Even the name of the region in which Pauline lived, a vast and largely unexplored forest stretching from the Great Lakes northward, was uncertain and fluid. Its residents usually called it "Upper Canada," the name it had been given by the British in 1791, but in 1861, when Pauline was born, it was officially "Canada West" (part of "the Province of Canada"), and six years later at Confederation it would be retitled "Ontario." But Pauline's surroundings were all that she knew and, she assumed with childish confidence, all that she needed to know. Most important, she understood even as a child that Chiefswood itself reflected her parents' larger universe, which blended two distinct traditions: the Mohawk heritage of Pauline's father and her mother's British roots.

Like many houses of the period, when travel along waterways was more comfortable than along rough roads, Chiefswood had two front doors. As Pauline sat on the bottom stair, she could hear, beyond the large oak door ahead of her, the sound of horse-drawn carriages travelling along the dusty rutted track that led to Brantford, twelve miles (nineteen kilometres) away. Pauline occasionally accompanied her mother along that track when Emily Johnson visited the bustling manufacturing town to buy fabric and trimming for her own and her daughters' gowns. If Pauline peered around the newel post to the other heavy front door, which was usually left ajar, she could look through the wooded parkland towards the sinuous, slow-moving Grand River. Her father loved to walk out of this door, stroll down to the riverbank and chat with friends waiting for ferryman Jessie Green to winch the old wooden boat along its chains from the opposite bank. George Johnson's youngest child often joined him there, slipping her small hand into his and admiring the dugout canoes of her Iroquois relatives as they skimmed across the water. The creak of the ferry's rusty old cogwheel and the splash of the heavy chains in the water haunted Pauline's dreams all her life.

Whether visitors arrived by road or by water, Chiefswood's two front doors welcomed them. The house's symmetry, with its matching French windows and elegant hipped roof, reflected the ideal of harmony that Pauline's parents were determined to embody. Throughout her life, Pauline extolled her parents' rapport: "They loved nature—the trees, and the river, and the birds. They loved the Anglican Church, they loved the British flag, they loved Queen Victoria. They loved music, pictures and dainty china. . . . They loved books and animals, but most of all, these two loved the Indian people, loved their legends, their habits, their customs." They also loved to demonstrate, to an impressive procession of visitors, that European settlers and "the red race," in the parlance of that era, could live side by side in peace. Chiefswood was as graceful a mansion as could be found in any newly settled British community in Upper Canada, but it was firmly situated within the reserve of the Six Nations Indians. Pauline's parents were determined that their sons and daughters would reflect credit on their mixed heritage. The children, Pauline later wrote, "were reared on the strictest lines of both Indian and English princi-

Pauline Johnson, aged 3: all her life, Chiefswood haunted her dreams.

ples. They were taught the legends, the traditions, the culture and the etiquette of both races to which they belonged."

Yet it was a curious education. George Johnson passed on to his children the legends and history of his Mohawk people, but he never taught them to speak the language fluently, so that they never felt they belonged on the Six Nations Reserve. His sons never went through the Mohawk initiation rites that their father had undergone, and his daughters never wore Indian costume. For her part, Emily Johnson had a horror that her children might be considered "plebeian." Through sharp reprimands and disapproving frowns, she instilled in them a need to please her and an acute English sensitivity to what others might think of them. So her sons and daughters grew up prim and inhibited, unable to relax completely with anybody outside the cocoon of their own family. Only Pauline would learn to move with ease in European-born society.

Though the Johnsons were a close-knit family, love and a shared sense of purpose could not obliterate the tension under the tranquil surface. Emily and George Johnson wanted to protect their children from the kinds of stress that each of them had suffered—the loneliness felt by a rejected child, the confusion of a young man caught between two value systems, prejudice against an interracial marriage. Perhaps the best illustration of the pressures that made Chiefswood an emotional fortress comes from an unpublished memoir by Evelyn (Eva) Johnson, Pauline's older sister. One day, wrote Evelyn, her brother Beverly brought home a puppy and insisted he was a purebred fox terrier. Pauline, the scrappy younger sister, insisted he was not purebred and took the puppy to Mr. Glasgow, the dog fancier, to prove her point. She returned at dinnertime and triumphantly reported that Mr. Glasgow agreed with her. Beverly snapped that Mr. Glasgow knew nothing, that the dog was a purebred fox terrier.

"None of the rest of us said anything," Evelyn later wrote, "and the argument waxed hot. Finally Allen, who had not spoken before, said, 'Well, he belongs to a mongrel family, anyhow,' and calmly went on eating his dinner."

Dead silence enveloped the table after Allen's blunt words; the children stared nervously at each other. Evelyn began to laugh hysterically. Her mother went white and said, "Eva, stop that screaming." She turned to her son, and said, "Oh, Allen, how can you talk like that?"

Evelyn did not record how Pauline reacted to this exchange. But for the rest of her life Pauline Johnson struggled with the legacy of Chiefswood. She yearned for the security her childhood home had provided—a security that none of the Johnson children would know in their adult lives. She embraced the ideal of harmony Chiefswood embodied—an ideal that would prove both oppressive and elusive. And in poetry, prose and performance, Pauline tried to straddle the gulf between two worlds, as her parents had done. But as her country evolved from a pioneer society to a self-assured nation, those two worlds drifted further and further apart.

2

THE EDUCATION OF EMILY HOWELLS JOHNSON

1824—1845

I T was largely thanks to Pauline Johnson's mother, Emily Susanna Howells, that Chiefswood was an emotional fortress as well as a happy family home. Emily was a devoted mother, but she was also an intense and brittle woman. The roots of her neuroses are not difficult to find: she had the kind of childhood that appalls a modern reader but that was not uncommon two centuries ago.

Emily was born into a devout, law-abiding and ostensibly well-established British family in 1824. Her father, Henry Charles Howells, was a Welshman who started life as a tinsmith. By the time Emily was born, however, he had risen in the world: he ran a small school for the children of the wealthy in Bristol, one of the largest ports in England. Situated on the west coast at the head of the deep cleft between England and Wales known as the Bristol Channel, Bristol was prosperous and smart. It was only nine miles from Bath, the spa fashionable amongst those exhausted by the dissipation of Regency London or by the boredom of county life. There was plenty of traffic between the two cities, although their populations were very different. Bath was a city of fops and flirts living off family fortunes. Bristol was a city of merchant-adventurers earning their money from trade.

From the Roman conquest of Britain onwards, Bristol had been a major entry point into England. By the start of the nineteenth century, the port was groaning with nautical activity. Schooners, brigantines and sloops from all over the world sailed up the Bristol Channel into the mouth of the River Severn, then nosed their way between the limestone cliffs of the Avon Gorge towards Bristol's crowded wharves. Once the vessels were moored, sailors unloaded the wealth of the British Empire—Canadian lumber and furs, Newfoundland salt cod, animal pelts from the Arctic, precious stones and silk from India, South African gold. Hoarse-voiced merchants completed their complicated transactions by the four bronze pillars of Bristol's imposing Exchange Building. At the wharves, the ship's captains oversaw the loading of the human cargo that filled their holds on the outward journeys: the massive outflow of impoverished labourers from all over the British Isles, hoping to make a new life in the colonies.

Teaching the classics to the young sons of the merchant class had propelled Henry Howells, Emily's father, into the comfortable ranks of the Bristol bourgeoisie. Bristol was a good city for a man of education. The city hummed with literary activity: in the 1790s the Bristol bookseller Joseph Cottle had started publishing the works of a young, brilliant and wild group of local poets, including Robert Southey, Samuel Taylor Coleridge and Robert Lovell. Henry Howells must have been well acquainted with the works of these men, and of their friend William Wordsworth; he probably had opportunities to meet them. He would also have been familiar with the novels of the period, particularly Jane Austen's exquisite depictions of Bath society. The popularity of literature in Regency England fired Bristol's progressive-minded merchants to give their children more education than they themselves had received. Schools for both boys and girls were established. One of Bristol's better-known educators was Hannah More, a pioneer of female education who ran her own ladies' academy. Henry Howells flourished, first as the principal of the Kingsdown Preparatory Boarding School (which advertised itself as a "classical and commercial academy" for boys) and then as head of the West Bank Academy in the wealthy suburb of Cotham.

For all his learning, however, Henry Howells appears to have been narrow-minded and insensitive. He had been raised a Quaker but had been forced out of the Society of Friends when he married Mary Best, an Anglican, in 1805. Nevertheless, the austerity and self-discipline of his Quaker upbringing remained with him—combined with a most un-Quaker-like temper and an autocratic disposition. It made him a tyrant of a father. During her lifetime, Mary Best may have managed to soften her husband's harshness. She was undoubtedly a loving mother to the thirteen children she bore him (of whom at least seven survived). But Mary died when her youngest surviving child, Emily, was only four. Emily's earliest recollection, she later told her own children, was of her own terror at the cacophony of shrieks and wails made by hired mourners at her mother's funeral. Memories of that clamorous grief, and of her father's ear-splitting rages, instilled in Emily a horror of emotional outbursts.

In 1830, when Emily was only five, Henry married again. His second wife, Harriet Joyner, was soon too busy having children herself to pay much attention to her husband's first family. Emily was barely six when her father and stepmother packed her off, along with her sisters Maria and Eliza, to boarding school in Southampton, a day's journey away.

Worse was to come. One day in 1832, little Emily and her sisters were summoned to their school principal's office and told to pack their bags. The girls were to be taken directly from their school to the Bristol docks, to board a ship in which they would sail to New York. Their father had decided to uproot his family and cross the Atlantic. The ostensible rationale for this abrupt move was Henry Howells's determination, as a God-fearing Christian, to join the fight to abolish slavery. But there were, undoubtedly, other reasons for the Howellses' emigration. Perhaps Henry Howells's penchant for ill-treating children caused a drop in enrolment in his academy for young gentlemen. Perhaps Pauline Johnson's grandfather was influenced by the rest of his large family. In the late eighteenth century, Henry's father had made two visits to America to sell woollen cloth, and had been introduced to President George Washington; as a result, he became a big booster of the New World. Two of Henry's brothers had already emigrated, along with Henry's eldest daughter, Mary, and her husband, the Reverend Robert Vashon Rogers, an Anglican clergyman. Or perhaps Henry was simply caught up in the tremendous enthusiasm that swept Britain in the 1830s, to escape a crippling agricultural depression and a rising tide of social unrest. Between 1831 and 1841, 655,747 people sailed away from British shores, nearly three times the number that had emigrated in the previous decade. The year that the Howellses crossed the Atlantic was also the year that Susanna Moodie and Catharine Parr Traill, two sisters who would achieve fame as writers in Canada, made the same journey. Whatever the reason for Henry Howells's departure, his leave-taking was hurried. The only memory that Emily retained of the city of her birth was the poignant peal of bells summoning parishioners to evensong in Bristol's parish churches as the ship weighed anchor and set off towards the setting sun.

The voyage was dreadfully long; their vessel was becalmed for days, and drinking water ran low. The Howellses were protected from the worst deprivations of the crossing because they were cabin passengers, which meant they dined with the captain and shared his supply of beer and Madeira wine. But they could hear from below decks the groans of the dehydrated, seasick and crowded steerage passengers. Relief swept through the ship when, after thirteen long weeks at sea, the forests, potato fields and water mills of Long Island came into view. Mr. and Mrs. Henry Howells, their large brood and their maidservant Hannah Kell were the first passengers to step ashore onto the passenger ship docks at the southern tip of Manhattan. So many boxes, trunks, packing cases and valises, all labelled "Howells," were unloaded from the ship's hold that the porters assumed these new arrivals from the Old Country were planning to open a furniture store. The contents of the crates included a library of books and two pianos. Henry was going to make a fresh start in life, but he was sufficiently rich that he didn't have to start from scratch. After a few nights in New York City, he planned to travel west to Ohio, a centre of the anti-slavery movement. There he intended to rent a large mansion, with a dining room in which he would put the best piano for his own use and a nursery in which his flock of children could practise their scales on the second piano.

Pauline Johnson used her mother's life history as the basis for a four-part series of semi-fictional articles she wrote in 1908 for *The*

Mother's Magazine, an American publication. Wallowing in every miserable detail with Dickensian fervour, Pauline described her grandfather as "a very narrow religionist, of the type that say many prayers and quote much Scripture, but he beat his children—both girls and boys—so severely that outsiders were at times compelled to interfere. For years these unfortunate children carried the scars left on their backs by the thongs of cat-o'-nine-tails when he punished them for some slight misdemeanor. They were all terrified at him, all obeyed him like soldiers but none escaped his severity. . . . [The stepmother] was of the very cold and chilling type of Englishwoman. . . . She took no interest in [her stepchildren], neglected them absolutely. . . . [S]he saw that all the money, all the pretty clothes, all the dainties, went to her own children."

Pauline described a particular incident when the second Mrs. Howells accused Emily, who was about ten years old, of stealing a cookie. When Emily denied the charge, her father gave her a brutal beating and sent her to her room. Emily was evidently a spunky little girl—"high-tempered," in her own phrase. On her release, she stuck to her story that she had not stolen the cookie. Her father beat her again, although his wife urged him to aim his blows at the child's body rather than her head. Still Emily insisted on her innocence, so her father gave her a third beating. Finally Harriet Howells said magnanimously, "Don't whip her any more; she has been punished enough."

This tale of assault has a ring of truth to it, although how much Pauline Johnson exaggerated the Cinderella details of her mother's life is open to question. "Spare the rod and spoil the child" was a popular maxim in nineteenth-century homes, and Pauline's older sister Eva did not mention any severe beatings in her own account of Emily's life. Moreover, Eva deplored Pauline's approach to family history, insisting that Pauline "never got history accurate" because "she always branched out into thoughts of her own [and] . . . always developed a story to suit herself." Both Pauline and Eva ignored another aspect of their grandfather's behaviour. Henry Howells was a schoolmaster, with an ample library and a commitment to education. In addition to the beatings, he gave his children a love of learning. He ensured that his children had a knowledge of the classics of English literature, including the poetry that had been so fashionable in the England he had left behind. Emily was an avid reader, and well acquainted with Romantic poets such as Wordsworth and Byron. She bequeathed to both her daughters, especially Pauline, her own attachment to early-nineteenth-century English verse.

Nevertheless, it is clear that Emily Howells was a forlorn child. In the classic pattern of abused children, she blamed herself for both her mother's death and her father's neglect, presuming that she was unloved because she was unlovable. She learned to hold her tongue and keep a tight rein on her own feelings. "She conquered her temper very early in life—completely subdued it," Pauline noted. "I can never recollect having seen her more than 'irritated' or 'annoyed.'" Instead, she began to sink into melancholy, which exasperated her parents further. So she learned to show the outside world the façade of a quiet, well-read, self-possessed young woman with beautiful English manners. Inside, however, she was a churning mass of insecurity. Emily never came to terms with her own sense of abandonment, or with her anger at the cruel cards that fate had dealt her. Throughout her adult life, she was incapable of spontaneity or the clear expression of her own emotions.

As a young woman,
Emily Susanna Howells was
frequently lonely and unhappy.

During these years, the ever-growing Howells family lived first near Columbus, Ohio, and later in Pittsburgh, Pennsylvania. It is possible that Henry Howells also took his family back to Bristol for a few years before finally settling in Eaglewood, New Jersey. He appears to have supported the household by setting up schools wherever he lived, but his daughter recalled most vividly his efforts in Ohio to help slaves. For all his cruelty to his own children, his Christian conscience was deeply troubled by the practice of slavery, and by the assumption that one man might own another. He sternly admonished his children to pray for the blacks and to pity the poor Indians, although his compassion did not preclude the view that his own race was superior to others.

Henry's Christian outrage at the practice of slavery was shared by the majority of Americans in the industrialized states of the northern United States. The pressure to emancipate American slaves was swelling rapidly during the 1830s and 1840s. Slavery had been abolished in Britain in 1807, and in British colonies in 1833, and political leaders on both sides of the Atlantic decried its continuation in the Old South. Both Columbus and Pittsburgh were strongholds of abolitionists and important way stations on the escape route to Canada, the one known as the Underground Railroad. Once a slave reached Canada, he or she was beyond the reach of American law. Henry took considerable risks in aiding and abetting runaway slaves: at one time he had twenty-one slaves hidden in his attic. Emily's older brother Thomas would dress up as a labourer and drive a cart, on which was piled old furniture, across Columbus. Slaves would hide in the armoires and chests and in the drawers of bureaus. In later years Henry Howells made much of his abolitionist courage, in a tone that suggests his granddaughter Pauline inherited her gift for hyperbole from him. "Mobs composed of hundreds attacked my house by night and day with rails, tar and feathers and weapons of death to take me," he wrote.

When Emily Howells was at home, she was treated as little better than a kitchen maid in a household in which babies were more plentiful than cash. In February 1842, when Emily was seventeen, her stepmother, Harriet Joyner Howells, died, having borne Henry at least another six children. Within a year, Emily's father had taken as his third wife Hannah Kell, the maid who had accompanied the family from England ten years earlier and who had nursed Harriet on her deathbed. Hannah would have five children, bringing the total of Henry Howells's progeny to twenty-four.

By now, fortunately, Emily had discovered a few avenues of escape. She went to stay for extended periods with three of her older sisters, each of whom was married to a clergyman. Her sister Maria had married a Reverend McCandlish of Wooster, Ohio. Her sisters Mary and Eliza were across the border in Canada. Mary's husband, the Reverend Robert Vashon Rogers, had settled in Upper Canada. The Rogerses lived for a few years in the rough little lumber town of Bytown (renamed Ottawa in 1855) before moving to the much more dignified city of Kingston around 1836. Eliza, the sister closest in age to Emily, also married a clergyman. In 1839, Eliza Howells became Mrs. Adam Elliott and joined her husband in Tuscarora, Upper Canada, where he was an Anglican missionary with the Six Nations on the Grand River Reserve, south of Brantford.

The routes Emily took on visits to her sisters were well travelled. Traffic flowed back and forth across the US border with the briefest stop at customs; nobody was required to produce any kind of travel document. Many families, both of native and of European origin, had relatives on both sides of the border. Stagecoaches made regular stops at inns for refreshments and changes of horses and to deliver mail. Sailing vessels offered the opportunity to admire distant shores and enjoy lake breezes in the scorching summers.

Nevertheless, the journeys of several hundred miles from her father's house to her sisters' homes must have unnerved young Emily. She had to spend the first day in a stagecoach rattling over the dusty road from Pittsburgh to Erie, on the south shore of Lake Erie, and the second day on the lake, where ships were frequently caught in vicious storms and driven onto sandbars. In 1848, the first bridge was built across the Niagara River, allowing Emily to make the whole journey by stagecoach. But stagecoaches were cramped, uncomfortable vehicles; a shy young woman could easily get crushed into a corner as the coach lurched in and out of the ruts on the road. And penniless Emily would have to provision herself for a two- or three-day journey before she left home. Once she arrived in Upper

Canada, her route varied according to which sister she was going to see, but it always involved at least a day's further travel along rough roads. Eliza Elliott was closest, and therefore the Six Nations Reserve was the most frequent destination.

Emily made her first visit to her sister Eliza when she was about sixteen, soon after the latter's marriage in 1839. Eliza Howells had always been Emily's friend; only five years older than Emily, she had done her best to protect her younger sister from parental wrath. To reach the Elliotts' parsonage on the Six Nations Reserve, Emily took the stagecoach to Brantford, then took a local conveyance from Brantford through the forest. This was Emily's first sight of the uncleared bush which, once the shoreline of the Great Lakes was left behind, stretched for miles in Upper Canada. Although the triangle of land bounded by Lake Huron and Lake Erie was the most densely populated area in Upper Canada in the 1840s, settlements were small and scattered. Acres of virgin forest remained to be cleared. The ten-mile (sixteen-kilometre) journey to Tuscarora through ancient elms and maples took three hours. The horse-drawn cart trundled slowly along the corduroy track, in which tree trunks were laid side to side to counter the heavy mud that jammed the cartwheels every spring and fall. Staring up at the dense foliage that arched over her, Emily imagined she was travelling down a splendid English avenue to some great estate. When she arrived at her destination, she was surprised to see not some magnificent house, but a small frame cottage with green shutters, a shady verandah and neat flowerbeds filled with marigolds and roses. Nearby was St. John's, the little white clapboard church in which the Reverend Elliott ministered to his parishioners. The only other buildings that Emily could see in the distance were a few scattered one-room shacks with untidily tended vegetable gardens next to them.

Once the cart had come to a full halt, Emily clambered awkwardly down, her gait unsteady after the bone-rattling drive. Her sister Eliza rushed out of the house and hugged her tightly. Close behind Eliza came the Reverend Adam Elliott, a tall grey-haired man who was nineteen years older than his wife.

Then a third person emerged from the house: a young Mohawk man smartly dressed in European clothes. With obvious pride, Adam Elliott introduced his church interpreter, Mr. George Johnson, to his sister-in-law, and explained that Mr. Johnson lived in the Elliotts' parsonage. George shook hands politely with the new arrival and enquired in faultless English whether her journey had been comfortable.

In Pauline Johnson's description of the first meeting between her parents, Emily was immediately smitten by twenty-nine-year-old George. The "lithe, clean-limbed, erect, copper-coloured" young man was "Indian to his finger-tips, with that peculiar native polish and courtesy, that absolute ease of manner and direction of glance, possessed only by the old-fashioned type of red man of this continent."

The naïve English girl struggled to match this sophisticated figure before her with her mental image of Indians, culled from books about noble savages written by armchair travellers in London. According to Pauline, "She thought all Indians wore savage-looking clothes, had fierce eyes and stern set mouths." Now Emily was face to face with a mild-mannered man dressed in the same outfit—cloth pants, wool shirt, dark jacket—worn by the European immigrants she had seen milling around the coaching inn in Brantford. George's eyes, she had to admit, were "narrow and shrewd," but at the same time, she noted that they were also "warm and kindly, his lips were like a Cupid's bow, his hands were narrower, smaller than her own: . . . his deportment . . . was correct in every detail."

That evening, the Elliotts, George Johnson and Emily Howells took their seats in the dining room for a formal dinner. The Elliotts' maidservant brought in a delicious game pie, which contained partridge and venison shot by George that day. Emily could barely keep her eyes off the man who would become her husband. According to her daughter's highly romanticized account, Emily found that his manners equalled any she had seen in the most aristocratic of European families: "He ate leisurely, silently, gracefully; his knife and fork never clattered, his elbows never were in evidence, he made use of the right plates, spoons, forks, knives; he bore an ease, an unconsciousness of manner, that amazed her." Her own British-born brother-in-law had no such grace: he clumsily dropped his knife, ate with an open mouth and was awkward and shy in conversation. Compared to Reverend Elliott, George Johnson "gleamed like a brown gem."

George Johnson was, without question, a graceful and handsome man. But it was his self-possession, rather than his good looks, that impressed Emily Howells. What took her breath away was not the exotic appeal of an Iroquois, but the gallantry and warmth of his greeting. George's poise suggested an individual who enjoyed everything that Emily had always lacked—loving parents, a happy childhood, a sense of his own worth, a belief that the world was a friendly place. He was the product of a family background rich in history, pride and tradition: he was a member of the Mohawk nation, which had always considered itself the aristocracy of North American Indians. To a young woman intimidated by a tyrannical father, short on self-esteem and entirely lacking any sense of where she belonged, George Johnson was an irresistibly attractive figure.

"Pity the poor Indians," Henry Howells had instructed his daughter. In later years, Emily's son Allen used to tease his mother that she had pitied one particular poor Indian so much that she had married him. However, there was absolutely nothing to pity about George Johnson. It was Pauline Johnson's mother, Emily Howells, who was the pathetic creature. George Johnson rescued her from an uncertain future. But Emily brought into her marriage the neuroses and needs of an unhappy childhood.

3

THE LEGACY OF SIR WILLIAM JOHNSON

1738—1845

W H E N Pauline Johnson was growing up on the Six Nations Reserve, many of her parents' friends had European names, like Moses, Hill or Buck, alongside traditional Iroquois names. Sometimes families took European names when they were baptised as Christians; in other cases, the names were the result of intermarriage with a non-native, or to accommodate the European immigrants' notorious inability to pronounce unfamiliar tongues. But the Johnson name was special. It originally belonged to a man who, almost alone amongst the non-natives of his time, accorded to the Iroquois the respect that was their due. Sir William Johnson lived in eighteenth-century colonial America. Pauline Johnson's pride in "the red race," as she liked to call Indians, owed much to the story of this exuberant character who is often described as "one of the greatest frontiersmen of all time."

In his day, Sir William Johnson was one of the wealthiest men in the colonies, thanks to his shrewd investments in the fur trade and the settlement of present-day New York State. However, he was not remarkable because he was rich—the New World was easy pickings for Old World strategists bent on acquisition. What sets him apart from his contemporaries is that from the moment he stepped on American soil in 1738, he treated the continent's indigenous inhabitants as fellow human beings. He was one of the few Europeans who mastered the Mohawk tongue, and his friendships with the Iroquois peoples were based on mutual benefit rather than his own self-interest. The

Sir William Johnson (1715–1774) was known to the Iroquois as "Warraghiyagey," which means "a man who undertakes great things." Boisterous and blunt, he did not appreciate the way that fashionable painter John Wollaston deliberately "improved" his figure in this 1751 portrait.

Mohawks, amongst whom he was best known, returned his friendship and respect. They adopted him as a Mohawk and named him "Warraghiyagey," which means "a man who undertakes great things."

Perhaps William Johnson's sympathy for native Americans, who were gradually being pushed away from their ancestral lands, reflected his own humble origins. He too was born on the social and geographical margins of British power, and he had watched his family callously brushed aside because of their poverty and strange accent. He was born just outside Dublin in 1715 into a shabby genteel Irish family who depended on rich relatives to give them a helping hand. Young William was lucky: he had a distinguished uncle, Peter Warren, a Royal Navy officer who had acquired land in the American colonies. In 1738, Warren commissioned his twenty-three-year-old nephew to cross the Atlantic and develop his land holdings, which lay along the Mohawk Valley between Lake Ontario and the Hudson River.

Johnson's uncle had never set foot himself on the 14,000 acres (about 5,500 hectares) he had bought. All Peter Warren knew about his land was that it was on the edge of the wilderness and that it supported some hardscrabble German tenants. The cocky little sea captain assumed, however, that it was like the New England seaboard or the hinterland of New York City, which by the mid-eighteenth century were prosperous lands thickly populated by European immigrants. Cities like New York and Boston were still rough; the houses were mostly jerry-built clapboard affairs on ill-laid foundations, and stray drunks and livestock roamed the streets. Nevertheless, there was a rising middle class of citizens building brick homes and founding gentlemen's clubs. Captain Warren blithely told his nephew to establish a "plantation," and promised to send him several slaves as labourers. He himself remained on active duty; in 1745, he was made Governor of Louisbourg after leading the successful siege of the French port on the tip of Cape Breton.

As William Johnson left behind him the thriving seaport of New York City, where he had landed, and made his way northwest, he quickly discovered that the European veneer on the New World in the late 1730s was, in fact, paper-thin. The thriving markets and welcoming inns quickly faded out. William rode alone along rough tracks, ducking to avoid the treacherously low branches of huge oaks, maples and firs. The impenetrability of the surrounding thick bush was a revelation. Occasionally the trail rose and he found himself in a clearing at the top of a hill, from which he could gaze out at an unending panorama of dark forest. Bird calls and the noise of animals rustling or crashing through the undergrowth were all that broke the silence.

Such a gloomy vista would only have depressed anyone accustomed to the stimulation of London society or Dublin's literary circles. But William Johnson, a refugee from Irish poverty who knew he must make his own way in the world, embraced the challenge. His uncle's commission was a spur for his own ambition. The large, lumbering young man realized that the key to future wealth was control of the lucrative fur trade. In addition, he soon saw that his most important potential allies in the region were not the indigent Germans, scratching a living from the land, or the arrogant Dutch burghers in Albany, cheating Indian hunters by exchanging shoddy European goods for their lustrous harvest of furs, pelts and hides. The people who really understood the vast landscape of thickly wooded hills and fast-flowing rivers were the Indians.

The first glimpse of Indians for most Europeans was usually of the most helpless representatives of tribal society: the beggars hanging around the forts and towns built by newcomers to the New World. Like beggars anywhere, they were an unimpressive sight. William saw men sitting motionless in the sunshine, wrapped in dirty blankets and covered in bear fat, with their greasy hair cut in strange styles. Obscenities characterized their broken English, since they had learned the language from foul-mouthed traders. "Some of them wear a bead fastened to their noses with a thread hanging down to their lips," sniffed a British army officer who visited the Mohawk Valley. The women wore men's shirts and blankets impregnated with bear grease, and worked bare-breasted in the fields with their babies strapped to their backs on cradleboards. Most of the Indians took little notice of Europeans except to pester them for food and drink. Europeans had quickly learned that if they plied the Indians with rum and brandy, the natives became so drunk that, ignorant of the consequences, they would sign away title to their ancestral lands.

William Johnson, however, did not judge by appearances and was not blinkered by cultural prejudices. In later years he acknowledged that the only way to understand Indians was through "a long residence amongst them, and a desire of information in these matters superseding all other considerations." Within months of building his own log cabin in the Mohawk Valley, he had moved beyond superficial impressions. He made the effort to get to know the leaders of the various Iroquois peoples who travelled across his uncle's land. He learned that five related Indian nations made up the Iroquois nation and that they had established for the thickly wooded central valley of the continent a sophisticated system of government. Some time during the sixteenth century, two hundred years before Johnson's arrival, the five nations had established a formal federation. Known as the Iroquois Confederacy, the federation viewed its territory as a longhouse (the traditional home for several families in Iroquois culture), with each nation occupying a room around its own fire. In the east, the door of this metaphorical longhouse opened on the Hudson: the Mohawks were the keepers of this door. Next, as the trails wove westward through the thick bush, came the Oneidas, the Onondagas, the Cayugas and, at the other door on the Genesee River beyond the Allegheny Mountains, the Senecas. By the time that Johnson arrived, a sixth nation had joined the Confederacy: the Tuscaroras. Compared to most of the dozens of different native groups scattered over the northern half of the continent, the Iroquois peoples were cohesive, well organized and unusually sedentary. The economic and political stability of the Iroquois Confederacy, now often called the Six Nations, had given its members some resilience against the greedy incursions of French and British armies and settlers. They were effective forest fighters and highly skilled traders. Henry Wadsworth Longfellow's famous poem about the Onondaga hero Hiawatha, written in 1855, reflects the European view that the Iroquois peoples were the elite of the New World. The Mohawks, who occupied the most eastern parts of the territory and were the first native people Johnson encountered, were regarded as the leaders of the Confederacy.

Johnson set about earning the trust of his Mohawk neighbours. He broke the monopoly on the fur trade that merchants in New York and Montreal had managed to establish, and which had depressed the prices paid to the Iroquois. He lent the native peoples money, gave them generous gifts in their own manner, enjoyed their feasts and their friendship. He threw himself into their rituals: he danced at their weddings and appeared at the conferences of the Iroquois Confederacy dressed and painted like a warrior himself. He founded schools so that they would learn English as well as their own languages, and he built churches in which they could practise the rituals of the Church of England. He translated the Anglican prayerbook into a phonetic version of their language, and he paid for the education of Mohawks so that they could have their own priests.

Johnson's energy and enthusiasm made him irresistible to those around him. A great bear of a man by the time he was middle-aged, he dominated every event he attended. One such event was a tribal gathering on the shores of the Niagara River in the summer of 1758, when an Anglican priest officiated at the baptism of babies born the previous winter. Of course Johnson was there, decked out in Mohawk finery. A young Mohawk woman, Mary Tekahionwake, came forward with her newborn son for baptism. At the point in the ceremony when the priest asked Mary her child's name, the young mother hesitated for a moment. A loud voice boomed out: "Give him my name!" It was none other than Johnson, who also insisted on being the child's godfather. So the priest made the sign of the cross on the child's forehead and gave him a name that enfolded within its noble rhythms two cultures: Jacob Tekahionwake Johnson. Pauline was his great-granddaughter.

Back in England, the periwigged officials of the court of King George II were less enthusiastic about Johnson's friendship with the New World's native peoples. Most Europeans simply couldn't comprehend a truly open relationship with Indians. They didn't trust the "noble savages" from whom they had purchased the land for their colonies and with whom they conducted sporadic and bloody territorial squabbles. They were uneasy about the power base Johnson had built in the Mohawk Valley. However, government officials had to admit that Johnson's warm relationship with the Mohawks in pre-revolutionary America worked to their benefit. The settled regions of the North American continent regularly erupted in skirmishes between French and English troops and their native allies. Johnson's friendships amongst the Iroquois never undermined his diehard loyalty to the monarch back home, and his links with them guaranteed their equally firm attachment to British interests. The alliance that Johnson created between Iroquois and British would have long-lasting consequences.

During the years that the youthful William Johnson was establishing his kingdom in the wilderness, he defended British interests against constant incursions from *les Canadiens* in New France, north of the St. Lawrence River, and their Algonquin allies. In 1755, French troops had crossed the St. Lawrence River and tried to invade the British-held Mohawk Valley. Thanks to Johnson's Mohawk allies, the invaders were turned back at the Battle of Lake George. This victory effectively shut the French out of the northern American colonies. News of this victory "echoed through the colonies, reverberated to Europe" and, according to a jealous rival of Johnson's, "elevated a raw, inexperienced youth to a kind of second Marlboro." (The first Duke of Marlborough had been the victor of the decisive Battle of Blenheim, fifty-one years earlier.) The colonial rulers in England knew they must reward this patriotic frontiersman, even if he was a little too wild for British tastes. He was appointed Superintendent of Indian Affairs north of the Ohio Valley, and made a baronet—one of only two Americans during this period who were so honoured. (The other one was William Pepperell, who in 1745 had led a large army of New Englanders to help Johnson's uncle, Peter Warren, capture the French fortress of Louisbourg in Nova Scotia.)

In his later years, Sir William Johnson lived in a ménage that sounds like a cross between a gentlemen's club and a summer camp. Peacocks strutted in the garden of his spacious Georgian mansion, five miles (eight kilometres) north of the Mohawk River and thirty miles (forty-eight kilometres) west of Albany. Iroquois and European friends were always welcome. It was a non-stop open house at Johnson Hall, according to contemporaries who lavished praise on his hospitality, books and fine furnishings. "The freer people made, the more happy was Sir William," wrote Thomas Jones, a New York judge who was a frequent visitor.

> After breakfast, while Sir William was about his business, his guests entertained themselves as they pleased. Some rode out, some went out with guns, some with fishing tackle, some sauntered about the town, some played cards, some backgammon, some billiards, some pennies, and some even at nine-pins. Thus was each day spent until the hour of four, when the bell punctually rang for dinner, and all assembled. He had beside his own family, seldom less than ten, sometimes thirty. All were welcome. All was good cheer, mirth and festivity. Sometimes seven, eight, or ten, of the Indian sachems [chiefs] joined the festive board.

Johnson's own appetites were legendary: he loved carousing until dawn and was rumoured to have fathered 700 children. There were plenty of light-skinned babies with Sir William's pale eyes in the communities surrounding Johnson Hall. Pauline's great-grandfather, Jacob Johnson, was sometimes assumed to be Sir William's illegitimate son as well as his godson and namesake.

By the time Sir William Johnson died in 1774, he was famous throughout British North America. He had huge land holdings: 600,000 acres (about 24,000 hectares) of what is now New York State. His Iroquois friends had proven to the British that they were crucial military allies who could defend British territories overseas. And Sir William had shown his Iroquois allies that it was possible for Europeans and Indians to live in harmony. Sir William Johnson's strong commitment to the equality of nations shaped Iroquois attitudes to the British for the next century. On the Six Nations Reserve in 1861, the year Pauline Johnson was born, the Iroquois still clung to the assumption that they could happily co-exist with Europeans.

The harmony between colonists and Crown crumbled during Sir William's later years, however. And within three years of his death, the first skirmishes of what would become the War of American

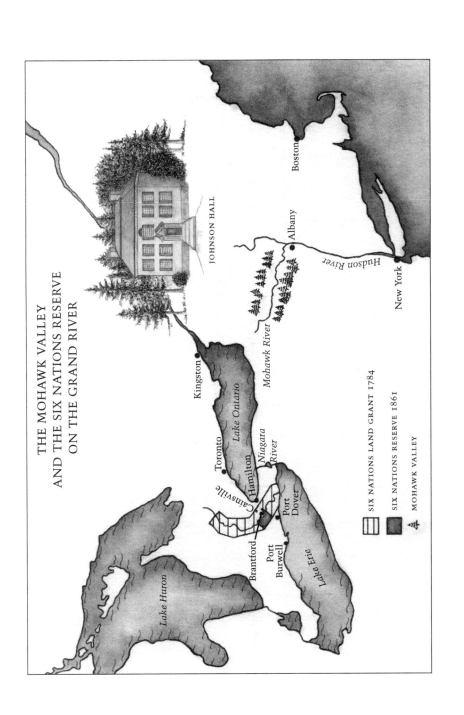

THE MOHAWK VALLEY
AND THE SIX NATIONS RESERVE
ON THE GRAND RIVER

JOHNSON HALL

Kingston

Lake Ontario

Toronto

Mohawk River

Hamilton

Niagara River

Cainsville

Brantford

Port Burwell

Port Dover

Lake Erie

Lake Huron

Albany

Boston

Hudson River

New York

SIX NATIONS LAND GRANT 1784

SIX NATIONS RESERVE 1861

MOHAWK VALLEY

Independence had broken out. Sir William's power lingered on mainly in the person of Molly Brant, sometimes known as Mary Brant, who had lived with Sir William for fifteen years. Molly was a full-blooded Mohawk, whose name in her own language was Gonwatsijayenni, meaning "someone lends her a flower." She became Sir William's second wife (in an Iroquois rather than Christian ritual) in about 1759, bore him eight children and was the formidable chatelaine of Johnson Hall.

Molly Brant straddled two worlds in the same way that Pauline Johnson would a century later. She carried in her person the self-respect of a native woman who belonged to a matriarchal society where women had considerable status. "One word from her is more taken Notice of by the five Nations than a thousand from any white Man without Exception," wrote William Claus, a Pennsylvanian whom Johnson had befriended. At the same time, Molly moved easily in colonial society. She displayed real flair in the way she combined European and native dress, wearing, for example, green velvet leggings below a well-cut wool jacket from London fastened with the silver brooches specially exported from Britain as trade items for Indians. Her wardrobe included both silk-lined wool cloaks and Hudson's Bay blankets; sometimes she wore leather shoes, and at other times she preferred beautifully sewn moccasins decorated with quillwork. She could move silently through the forest, and she would also ride sidesaddle like an aristocratic Englishwoman.

Most important, Molly Brant emerged from her husband's shadow to become a leader of the Mohawks in her own right. Together with her younger brother Joseph, she urged her fellow Mohawks and the rest of the Six Nations peoples to remain loyal to the Crown. This time, though, the enemy was not the French settlers and their Algonquin allies north of the St. Lawrence River, but the American revolutionaries pushing up from the south. Molly's loyalty was an invaluable asset for the British, who depended on the Iroquois to hold the territory north of the Mohawk River. She became the chief conduit between the British authorities and the Iroquois. But as revolutionary troops overran the Mohawk settlements in 1777, she was forced to admit she had chosen the losing side. She fled northward from the lands of the Iroquois longhouse, where her family had lived for generations, taking her children and her black slaves. For years, she hoped she would be able to return to the splendour of her old life in the Mohawk Valley, but her lands were seized by American revolutionaries while the ink on the Declaration of Independence was still wet.

Molly Brant finally settled in Kingston, on the north shore of Lake Ontario, in a house built for her by the British government. She was much better off than most of the Loyalists forced to move north when their lands were occupied by the Revolutionary army. An annual pension of 100 pounds was settled on her "in consideration of the early and uniform fidelity, attachment and zealous Services rendered to the King's Government by Miss Mary Brant and her Family." She was a frequent guest of General John Simcoe, who became the first Lieutenant-Governor of Upper Canada in 1791, and his wife Elizabeth. Her six daughters, of mixed Irish-Mohawk parentage, were each regarded as a "catch." Of the five who married, three became the wives of British army officers, one married a physician, and one wed John Ferguson, member for Kingston in the Legislature of Upper Canada.

Jacob Tekahionwake Johnson—Sir William Johnson's godson and Pauline's great-grandfather—was as loyal to the British Crown as Molly Brant, and like her, he suffered for it. In the late 1780s, Jacob, then about thirty years old, was one of 448 Mohawks, alongside about 1,200 other Iroquois, who followed Molly Brant's younger brother, Joseph, and fled north to escape the American revolutionaries. A long, sad line of Iroquois, bearing as many of their possessions as they could, slowly snaked out of the Mohawk Valley towards those territories that the British had managed to hold on to. In a flotilla of small boats, the Indians crossed the Niagara River. But the example of Sir William Johnson lived on: the British Crown gave the same generous welcome to these refugees as it had given to Molly Brant. A huge tract of land had been purchased from the Mississauga people and was now granted to "His Majesty's faithful allies . . . the Mohawk Nation and such other of the Six Nations as wish to settle in that quarter to take possession of and . . . enjoy for ever." The Grand River grant to the Six

Nations consisted of nearly 570,000 acres (230,000 hectares) of prime agricultural land; twelve miles (nineteen kilometres) wide, it stretched from the source to the mouth of the river.

Over the next hundred years, the Six Nations Reserve provided a solid economic base for the 1,700 Iroquois who had elected to move north. (Another 4,000 had made peace with the Americans and stayed in the Mohawk Valley.) Since the original grant was far more extensive than the Iroquois required, it gradually dwindled in size. Joseph Brant sold chunks of it to raise funds for his followers; the British government bought more acres to ensure land development by European settlers. But the Iroquois never forgot that the reserve was their reward for military services rendered rather than their ancestral hunting ground. The King had treated them the same way as he had treated others on whose military services the British depended. Other Loyalists from the American colonies who arrived in the 1780s, and British officers who had been pensioned off after the end of the Napoleonic Wars in Europe in 1815, were also offered free land in Upper Canada as a reward for services rendered.

Little is known of Jacob Johnson's years in Upper Canada, other than the fact that in 1792 he became the father of a boy, whom he named John after the only legitimate son of his godfather, Sir William Johnson. But John Johnson, Pauline's grandfather, was an important figure in her childhood. In the military tradition of the Mohawk people, he became a fierce warrior in defence of British interests. He was only twenty when he followed Joseph Brant into battle during the War of 1812 and fought the ragtag American army at Queenston Heights, Lundy's Lane and Stoney Creek. John Johnson never flinched from taking enemy lives or from risking his own, and in later years his grandchildren loved to hear of his exploits. "Have you killed many men, grandfather?" Pauline, as a child, would ask as she leaned against the old man's knee. With a toothless grin, he would reply, "No, not many, baby, not many, only four or five." His youthful bravery verged on recklessness. His grandchildren's favourite tale concerned the time when, under cover of darkness, he and another young man from the reserve silently paddled across the swiftly flowing Niagara River, crept ashore on the American side and set fire to the ramshackle lakeside town in which enemy troops were billeted. Amongst his contemporaries in the Six Nations on the Grand River Reserve, he was known as the man who razed Buffalo.

John Johnson had a certain aura about him that both his own people and the British recognized. The colonial government, always eager to cultivate its Indian allies, was smart enough to see that it could use this wiry young warrior to cement ties with the Iroquois. The Johnson family had no special standing on the reserve, but the British pushed the Iroquois Council to elevate John's status.

The Council leaders were not averse to being pushed. They too recognized the potential of a young man who was committed to his own people as well as to British interests. John Johnson might be a loyal British subject, but he was no sycophant. In 1840, at a historic assembly of Ontario native peoples, he encouraged his fellow Indians to cooperate in demands for land title. He also urged the Ojibwa to refer to the British governor as "Brother" rather than "Father" to promote a relationship of equality. Moreover, John was skilled in the traditional Iroquois art of oratory. In the oral culture of the Iroquois, eloquence was the people's literature: its metaphors painted the skies and the forest; its cadences were their music. When John Johnson rose to speak at public gatherings, a deep hush would fall as he lifted his voice in a spellbinding singsong rhythm that mesmerized listeners.

The Mohawk elders knew that young Johnson, who had mastered the English tongue as well as most of the languages of the Iroquois, could be as valuable to them as to the British. They consented to make him a "pine-tree chief," which meant he was appointed for life only. He became the speaker of the Six Nations Council, with the name Sakayengwaraton. The name translates as "the haze that rises from the ground on an autumn morning and vanishes as the day advances." It didn't take Johnson's colleagues long to shorten this splendid appellation to the nickname "Smoke," or to refer to the great orator, behind his back, as "the Mohawk warbler."

John "Smoke" Johnson was canny. With a pine-tree chieftaincy under his belt, he made an advantageous marriage. His wife, Helen Martin, belonged to one of the fifty noble families of the Iroquois Confederacy, the families which held hereditary chieftaincies. Helen's mother, Catherine, had her own intriguing history. She had been born Catherine Rolleston, daughter of Dutch settlers near Philadelphia, but as a young girl she had been captured by Mohawks during a skirmish in the War of Independence and had been adopted by a chief. Although her parents came from Holland and she spoke English, Catherine had no interest in emulating Molly Brant and straddling two worlds. She married a young Mohawk named George Onhyeateh Martin, and appears to have been happily absorbed into the Mohawk nation. During the long trek from the Mohawk Valley to the Grand River Reserve in the late 1780s, Catherine Rolleston Martin hid in the bundle on her back the silver communion service sent by Queen Anne to the Mohawks in the early years of the eighteenth century. She passed on neither a hint of her Dutch upbringing nor a word of English to her daughter Helen, who became Pauline Johnson's grandmother.

John "Smoke" Johnson and Helen Martin Johnson had six children. The childhood of these youngsters differed little from that of their parents and grandparents. They ran barefoot through the woods and learned to hunt and paddle as their ancestors had done in their lost lands to the south since time immemorial. The Six Nations Reserve, established less than thirty years earlier, was still for the most part uncleared wilderness. Tall forests of white pine and oak, and thick scrub of tamarack and muskeg, were rich in game—white-tailed deer, passenger pigeons, quail, woodcocks, wild turkeys—to supplement the diet of cornmeal and berries. Over-hunting had almost wiped out the beaver population around the Great Lakes, but there was plenty of other quarry for hunters who wanted to sell pelts to the Europeans—black bear, muskrat, fisher and marten.

The Iroquois peoples planted corn and root vegetables in the cleared patches of earth around the scattered settlements of roughly built wooden houses. Willow trees lined the banks of the Grand River, and porcupines snuffled through the undergrowth, allowing women to continue the traditional crafts of basket-making and quillwork. Trading links developed fast between the reserve and the steadily growing immigrant settlements in the surrounding areas. Mohawk and Onondaga women arrived at the markets of Hamilton, Brantford, Port Dover or Port Burwell to trade cornmeal, embroidered moccasins and baskets for products shipped in from England, including iron pots, cloth and silver trinkets. Iroquois men would appear with venison, freshly caught salmon or muskrat pelts, and barter them for guns, gunpowder and whiskey.

Although European and Iroquois settlers did not mingle socially, there was plenty of room for all in the 1820s and 1830s, and it was an easy co-existence. Outside Kingston and Toronto, both natives and immigrants in Upper Canada relied on the land for their living. Most of the British were at least as poor in worldly goods and formal education as the Iroquois; there was little difference between the two groups in their living conditions. Almost everybody lived in wooden houses with smoky fireplaces, root cellars and sleeping lofts. European settlers respected their native neighbours' local know-how. Most were eager to copy their hunting and trapping skills and to learn from them about medicinal plants and vegetable dyes. They adopted their means of travel: snowshoes in winter, canoes in summer. Besides, shared loyalty to Church and Crown united these diverse British subjects. Every Sunday, John "Smoke" Johnson would take his children along to the little whitewashed Mohawk Chapel near Brantford, where he would read the Ten Commandments to the congregation. As one of the few Iroquois who spoke English fluently, he often interpreted the sermon, given each Sunday by a cleric who had been sent across the Atlantic by the missionary association called, with the arrogance of imperialism, the "Society for Converting and Civilizing the Indians." While John "Smoke" Johnson translated the clipped English phraseology into the melodious singsong of the Mohawk tongue, his children would gaze at the shiny silver communion service that their grandmother had carried to Canada all those years ago.

The second child of John "Smoke" Johnson and Helen Martin Johnson was born on October 7, 1816, and named George after the British monarch, King George III. When George Henry Martin Johnson was still a boy, it was evident that he had inherited many of his father's finer qualities. Straight-backed and self-assured, he had an easy grin and a quick wit. He also had a gift for languages, so his parents sent him away to school in the neighbouring town of Brantford, where he boarded with another Mohawk family. Soon he spoke English well enough to substitute for his father as interpreter at the Mohawk Chapel.

George Johnson's Brantford sojourn allowed him to make valuable connections with British authorities. When the firebrand William Lyon Mackenzie led a rebellion against the colonial government in Upper Canada in 1837, there was no question where Mohawk loyalties lay. George Johnson stood proud beneath the Union Jack and was recruited as a despatch rider to Allan Napier MacNab. MacNab, a Hamilton lawyer, was amongst the most zealous in the suppression of the uprising. (For a brief period in the 1850s, MacNab was Premier of the United Canadas.) George Johnson's reputation as a young man to watch shot up. The Cayugas, one of the six nations of the Iroquois Confederacy, presented him with a tomahawk inlaid with silver, as a token of their admiration for him.

In 1838, when George was twenty-two years old, a new minister arrived at the white clapboard mission church at Tuscarora. The Reverend Adam Elliott was a tall Scotsman of devout intent and impossibly shy disposition. At first, he was uncertain how to treat the young Mohawk who translated his sermons so gracefully. But George's easy manner and quiet self-assurance soon put Elliott at ease. He invited George Johnson to stay with him at Tuscarora parsonage, and despite Adam Elliott's reticence, a father–son relationship blossomed between the gawky Scotsman and the lithe young Indian. Together they criss-crossed the reserve, visiting the separate communities of Mohawks, Oneidas, Onondagas, Cayugas, Senecas and Tuscaroras. Each people still spoke its own language (although the tongues were sufficiently similar that they could understand each other). George would switch effortlessly between the native tongues and English as he translated the clergyman's words of comfort to the sick and dying or spread the gospel to those who still resisted baptism (the Onondagas, in particular, had not abandoned their traditional beliefs). Duty done, the two men would then stick to English as they tramped along the rough corduroy roads, discussing Christian doctrine and Canadian politics until they reached the next needy soul. George seemed to have a special gift for comforting anybody afflicted with smallpox. Most people shrank from contact with the killer disease, but George showed no fear. He would shake hands with sufferers, even though his skin often stuck to their suppurating sores. His fellow Indians were awed; they did not know that while in Brantford, George had been vaccinated (or "salivated," as it was then known) by a London-trained physician.

Adam Elliott's friendship with George Johnson was unaffected by the parson's marriage to Eliza Beulah Howells in 1839. Soon Eliza was as fond of her husband's protegé as Adam himself was. The Elliotts' first child, Mary Margaret, was born in 1840; three years later, Henry Christopher arrived. The Mohawk boarder was a boon to Eliza. George had none of the British male's discomfort with bawling infants, and was always ready to take a fractious toddler off her hands for a slow, soothing stroll through the woods.

By now, George Johnson knew how to move smoothly through European society. He wore European clothes, spoke English flawlessly and modelled his behaviour and values on those of his mentor, Adam Elliott. Nobody could find fault with George Johnson's manners. The combination of a charming personality and the manners of a British gentleman won him almost complete acceptance in the larger world. George's position and income meant that, unlike many of the young men in pioneer townships, he could afford a wife and family.

With the birth of her third child, Charles O'Reilly, in 1845, Eliza was more than happy to welcome her shy little sister Emily, who arrived from Pittsburgh to live at the parsonage and help Eliza with the growing family. Soon Emily was joining the two older children and George for their strolls in the woods. George's courtesy and gentle manner continued to attract Emily, who was nine years his junior. Given Eliza Howells Elliott's own fondness for George Johnson, the minister's wife cannot have been in the least surprised to watch the steady growth of affection between him and her younger sister.

A few months later, George caught typhoid fever. The sound of his retching and groaning terrified Adam Elliott, who knew that his wife's health was frail and his young children were vulnerable to such a devastating infection. So he asked Emily, who was much sturdier than her sister, to nurse the young man. It was a situation made for romance: as Emily bent solicitously over George, he stared up at her pale skin and blue eyes and fell in love. In later years, Emily's daughters revelled in the story. This was the "real beginning of the love match between my mother and father," Eva recorded in her memoirs. Safe within the four friendly walls of the Tuscarora parsonage, George and Emily failed to recognize that their romance might horrify both their families.

4

FOR RICHER,
FOR POORER, FOR
BETTER, FOR WORSE

1845—1861

As both Molly Brant and Catherine Rolleston had demonstrated, marriages between Europeans and Indians were neither unusual nor unacceptable in eighteenth-century North America. For Europeans, the rigid conventions of class-ridden societies back home evaporated once they were settlers in frontier communities. The Iroquois, for their part, had successfully absorbed into their peoples any number of non-Indian women captured during skirmishes. And the Mohawks had a very particular status within Upper Canada. Valuable military allies and beneficiaries of a huge land grant, the heirs and followers of Sir William Johnson and Molly Brant had every right to consider themselves equal to the other Loyalists who had streamed north half a century earlier.

Nevertheless, when George Johnson's parents heard he wanted to marry a non-Mohawk, they were taken aback. Their objection centred not on any feelings about race but on a much more tangible issue: power. George's mother, Helen Martin Johnson, had inherited through her own mother and grandmother one of the most important positions on the Six Nations Reserve: she was a hereditary clan mother of the Wolf Clan of the Mohawks within the Iroquois Confederacy. All members of the Iroquois Confederacy belonged to the Wolf Clan, the Tortoise Clan or the Bear Clan. These clans crossed tribal lines and were an essential element in the harmony between peoples. As a clan mother, Helen Martin Johnson participated in discussions within the clan and among the Iroquois peoples on land allotments, disputes, public games, welfare of the elderly and sick, and compensation for crimes. The clan mothers decided who should be pine-tree chiefs and which hereditary chiefs should be the leaders of the ruling Confederacy Council. Helen Martin Johnson had the right to address the ruling Council when it met in the Six Nations Council House at Ohsweken. Council members paid attention to her words. Her hereditary position gave her far more status and authority than George's father had in his role as pine-tree chief—a position he could not pass on to his children.

George Johnson's mother made little impression on those who did not know her well. Unlike her husband and son, she had not adopted European ways. Small and unsmiling, her black eyes expressionless, she made no effort to learn English and she still wore the traditional leggings and tunic of her people. In the market square in Brantford, or on the porch of the Tuscarora parsonage, she would sit cross-legged on the ground, a blanket pulled tight around her shoulders, staring silently at those around her and smoking a small carved pipe.

Her own family, however, knew she was a woman to be reckoned with. She had already faced down her fellow leaders in the community in order to secure an important role for her son George on the reserve. When her brother died in 1843, she had stood up amongst all the Iroquois chiefs and proposed her son to replace him as a member of the Iroquois's top decision-making body, the Council.

The chiefs objected that as an official interpreter, George Johnson's primary loyalty was to the colonial government, and that this responsibility compromised any claim he might make through his mother's family. They argued that a salaried official of the colonial government would be in conflict of interest if he also assumed the responsibility of a chief. The position of interpreter gave George a lot of influence: though he was still in his twenties, he already acted as liaison between the colonial authorities and the Council. He represented the colonial government at the semi-annual distribution of gifts from the British government to the Six Nations. Moreover, his eagerness to speak at meetings did not sit well with the non-Mohawk chiefs. He was too keen to play a prominent role at ceremonial events (he looked magnificent in the fringed buckskin tunic and leggings stitched with countless quills that he wore for these occasions, and he knew it). The chiefs were uncomfortable with the fact that George's father, John "Smoke" Johnson, was already a pine-tree chief. As a rule, sons never succeeded fathers on the Council, because they were likely to vote as a block. If George combined the roles of official interpreter and Council member, they argued, excessive power would be concentrated in Johnson hands.

But Helen Martin Johnson had stood firm. She told Council members that they could depose a chief in the event that he did something wrong, but they could not refuse to appoint someone for fear he might do something wrong in the future. Eyes blazing, she warned them that if George Johnson was not appointed, they would end up with no member: she refused to appoint a substitute. The Council members shifted uneasily on their seats; they murmured amongst themselves. They knew that she would not budge. So they accepted her son as a chief. Amongst his fellow chiefs, he was known as "Onwanonsyshon."

After this victory, Helen Martin Johnson turned her mind to the question of whom her son should marry. The choice was important politically: after her own death, her daughter-in-law would inherit the powerful role of clan mother. Helen selected a young woman from another Mohawk family who would bring credit to the Johnson name. But her careful plans were wrecked by George's announcement that he wanted to marry Emily Howells rather than his mother's candidate. Helen had no particular feelings about Emily, but George's choice appalled her because a non-native woman could not become a clan mother.

Sixty years after the event, Pauline Johnson published her own fanciful description of the encounter when George announced his choice of bride. Helen Martin Johnson, according to Pauline, exclaimed incredulously, "But your children, your sons and heirs—they could never hold the title, never be chief!" George winced, but held his ground as stubbornly as his mother had held hers in the Council on his behalf. He insisted he was going to marry Emily. Then he quietly left his parents' house and walked back along the forest path to the parsonage, back to the "fair young English girl whose unhappy childhood he had learned of years ago, [with her] lips that were made for love they had never had." Meanwhile, continues Pauline's account, George's mother "folded her broadcloth about her, filled her small carven pipe and sat for many hours smoking silently, silently, silently." The breach between mother and son appeared unbridgeable.

Even allowing for Pauline's taste for melodrama, this account captures the emotional intensity that had developed between the Mohawk youth and the shy young English immigrant. The intensity was enough to make George betray his family.

George and Emily could not get married straightaway, because in the next few months a series of tragedies hit the Elliott household. Between November 1847 and August 1848, an epidemic of scarlet fever swept through the community. Despite Emily's tireless nursing, Adam and Eliza's three youngest children all died (a fourth child, Emily, had been born after Emily came to live at the parsonage). The following year Emily's skills as a nurse were again called into service when tuberculosis, the scourge of nineteenth-century Canada, struck her sister Eliza. Within months, Eliza Howells Elliott had joined her children in the Tuscarora graveyard. The following year, the devastation of Adam Elliott's family was complete. Tuberculosis also took the life of his only remaining child, his eldest daughter, Mary.

At this point, it became inappropriate for the rector's unmarried sister to be living in the parsonage with him and his Mohawk interpreter. The moment had arrived for George and Emily to announce their engagement. But Emily quickly discovered that in the eyes of some members of her own family as well as the citizens of Upper Canada's small towns, she was betraying her British blood as recklessly as George Johnson had broken faith with Mohawk tradition.

By the mid-nineteenth century, attitudes were changing in Upper Canada's small towns—although the roads remained unpaved and cows often wandered down the main streets. Successful merchants, lawyers, factory owners and brewers, who rarely saw a non-European face and had never known the grinding hardships and hunger faced by earlier pioneers, thronged the marketplaces and meeting halls. In the backwoods, families scratching a living on pioneer farms were still knit together by mutual need, but townsfolk picked their friends carefully. The well-furnished parlours of those born in England or Scotland and now living in Belleville, Brockville or Hamilton welcomed only those with similar origins. Prejudices spawned in the Mother Country crept across the Atlantic. Few Catholics, Jews or French Canadians were invited to join exclusive male clubs such as the Freemasons, the Odd Fellows or the Orange Order. Everybody despised the destitute Irish who were arriving in waves up the St. Lawrence River. Indians who spoke strange languages and clung to unfamiliar traditions were increasingly unwelcome. And nobody was more alert to social nuance and respectability than Emily Howells's sister Mary and her husband, the Reverend Robert Vashon Rogers, comfortably ensconced within the elite of Upper Canada's largest city, Kingston.

Kingston was a city of imposing limestone buildings and stuffy pretensions. It had served as provincial capital between 1841 and 1843. One legacy of its brief pre-eminence was the largest city hall in the province, with a magnificent green dome. Its most important citizens gathered each Sunday under the slender steeple of Kingston's oldest church, St. George's, which in 1862 would be elevated to the status of cathedral. There, members of Kingston's *crème de la crème* would sing solemn hymns and admire each other's outfits. Emily's brother-in-law, Robert Rogers, took his position in Kingston society very seriously. As rector of St. James Church, headmaster of the Midland District School and chaplain of the Kingston penitentiary, he moved in the best circles. His wife, Mary, kept his house and garden immaculately. His son Robert was already a respected lawyer in Kingston, regularly hobnobbing with the rising young politician John A. Macdonald and doing much of the work for the Anglican Diocese. The Reverend Robert Rogers, a short, chubby man with a fussy manner and darting eyes, bore an uncanny resemblance to an obsequious cleric in a Trollope novel as he strolled down King Street, raising his hat to his fellow citizens.

In the summer of 1853, Emily Howells arrived at the Rogerses' home. It had been many months since Emily's previous visit, and Mary Rogers was surprised by her twenty-nine-year-old sister's cheerful good health. Mary knew that the Elliott household had lurched from crisis to crisis, and she had made known her concern about the propriety of Emily's remaining at the Tuscarora parsonage with her widowed brother-in-law. Adam Elliott might be a man of God, but he was still a man. Never one to resist gossip herself, Mary didn't want tongues wagging about her own sister. Besides, she thought a young woman of Emily's accomplishments could do quite well for herself in a garrison town like Kingston. Emily had all the makings of a colonial lady, despite her tendency to be tongue-tied in a crowd. She was well-versed in literature and nimble-fingered at embroidery, and she played the piano with refinement. She would make some lucky officer a delightful wife.

As Mary escorted her sister up the stairs to her bedroom, she caught the flash of emerald and diamonds on Emily's engagement finger. Surprised, Mary asked where the ring came from. A joyful Emily immediately told her sister her news: George Johnson, of the Six Nations Reserve, had asked her to be his wife. Emily expected Mary to be as pleased by the tale of her great love affair as Adam Elliott—and Eliza before her death—had been. She naïvely believed that Mary and Robert Rogers would be happy to organize her wedding in St. George's Church. Instead, her news was received even more coldly than George Johnson's announcement to his parents that he wanted to marry Emily. Mary's face froze. "An *Indian*," she stuttered.

At first, according to her daughter Pauline's account of the episode, Emily misinterpreted her sister's reaction. "Yes," she laughed. "Handsome, noble and the kindest man who ever lived. Wait till you meet him tomorrow." But this time, the look on Mary's face was unmistakeable. Mary was horrified that a "girl of your upbringing" would dream of marrying a non-European. In the Kingston of 1850, marriages to Indian women were frowned on but reluctantly accepted; the notion of marriage to an Indian man, however, triggered a torrent of nasty stereotypes about helpless females corrupted by savages. Emily, taken aback, protested that George's family was equally shocked because he was marrying a non-Indian, but this just added to Mary's outrage. Mary was furious that any "wretched Indians" should consider themselves too good to marry someone born in England—someone, moreover, whose sister had married one of the leading churchmen of the colony. How *could* Eliza Howells Elliott have allowed an Indian to flirt with her little sister? Mary had no time for any talk of Indian titles or chieftaincies. Her voice grew even shriller as she anxiously anticipated what the Reverend Robert Vashon Rogers would say.

When Robert Rogers returned home, Mary's fears proved justified. The news propelled her husband into a frenzy of outraged Victorian respectability. He retired to his study, then issued a summons to his sister-in-law to appear before him. Drawing himself up to his not-very-impressive height, he ordered Emily to pack her things, leave his home and never darken his door again. He spat out his disgust at the idea of a union between a woman such as her and "the red race." "And if you have children," he added, "they shall never associate with mine." Emily Howells was unceremoniously bundled out of St. James's parsonage. Mary tried to cushion the blow by pressing several yards of beautiful lace into her sister's hands. Emily, white-faced and trembling, added it to her parcels and walked away down the street.

On previous visits to Kingston, Emily had become acquainted with Jane Harvey, wife of a regimental quartermaster. Jane was as generous as the Rogerses were snobbish. When Emily gave a tremulous knock on the Harveys' door, Jane opened it immediately. She swept the weeping Emily up in a warm embrace, issued a series of oh-lordy-lordy clucks when she heard how the Rogerses had behaved and promised the young woman that she and her "young Hiawatha" would have a lovely wedding and a cosy wedding breakfast. The following day Jane Harvey made the arrangements for a marriage ceremony to take place in the little limestone church of St. Mark's, on a hilltop in Barriefield, across the Cataraqui Creek from Kingston. Then she sent her brother to meet George Johnson, due on the Toronto steamer at Kingston docks that afternoon, and to steer him away from the parsonage and towards a hotel for the night.

George Johnson and Emily Howells were married on August 27, 1853, in front of the Harveys and several of their friends. Emily, a

George Johnson and Emily Howells obviously enjoyed sitting
for their wedding portrait: George always loved to dress up,
while Emily clutched a ceremonial tomahawk and glowed
with happiness at her new domestic security.

few brown curls peeping out from a demure white bonnet, looked like a mouse as she lifted her dark wool skirt to step through St. Mark's Gothic doorway and into the church's cool interior. In contrast, George Johnson strutted like a peacock under the vaulted roof. White gloves in hand, he was dressed in a frock coat of pale grey broadcloth with grosgrain trim, a starched collar and silk cravat, a silver sword and a tasselled sash. Earlier that morning, a man had accosted him outside his hotel and told him that an Indian chief was rumoured to be getting married in Kingston that day; did this well-dressed stranger know where the ceremony was to take place? The

Kingstonian obviously hoped for an exotic parade of buckskinned and feathered Indians wielding tomahawks; he may not even have realized that he was speaking to a Mohawk. George courteously directed him to St. George's Church, "where the ceremony," he told the enquirer, "was expected to take place." Then, chuckling at his own careful deployment of the truth (he had, after all, expected to be married at St. George's), he himself made his way to Barriefield.

As George and Emily stood in front of the altar of St. Mark's Church, the minister supervised their exchange of vows and then offered some bland advice that was probably his standard sermon for weddings. "A married couple must pull together like a yoke of oxen," he intoned. If each pulled in a different direction, the load would never be drawn forward, he warned. Did the newlyweds need such advice? Hardly. Both were outcasts. Already shunned by their own relatives, they knew they probably had only each other to rely on in the years to come. Their marriage meant that George's family had lost its claim to a hereditary title and Emily had lost her status as an Englishwoman. From now on, she and her children would be classified as Indians, although they would never be accepted on the reserve as Mohawks. Emily clung to George with the feverish dependence of a woman bruised by too many rejections. George lovingly stroked her hair, torn between happiness that at last they were wed and sadness that his parents were not there to see it.

News of the interracial marriage, and the displeasure of the bride's relatives, rippled through Upper Canada's close-knit elite. By the time the steamer on which George and Emily were travelling from Kingston reached the docks at Toronto, a crowd had gathered. Many of the gawkers wished the young couple well; a group of women presented Emily with a bracelet made from the braided locks of their own hair, fastened with a cameo. George, as usual, was gracious and poised before the crowd. But Emily climbed as quickly as possible into the carriage that was to take them home to Tuscarora.

For the first two years of their marriage, the Johnsons remained with Adam Elliott at Tuscarora parsonage. George was determined that Emily's life should be no different than if she had married a European man. His first gift to her was the epitome of middle-class British taste: a silver tea service, including teapot, coffee pot, sugar bowl, milk jug and slop bowl, which had been displayed in the Crystal Palace at the Great Exhibition, held in London that same year. Adam Elliott presented Emily with initialled silver spoons, pearl-handled knives and forks, and a dress length of brown satin. Like her husband, Emily Howells Johnson was determined to pre-empt her critics by outdoing them in any display of manners; she would entertain in the same dainty style as any of Brantford's young wives. Only the set of placemats made of doeskin and embroidered with the tribal designs of the Six Nations in porcupine quills suggested an additional dimension to the Johnson marriage.

Eleven months after the wedding, Henry Beverly Johnson was born. The birth of the Johnsons' first child prompted an important reconciliation. A small figure wrapped in a Six Nations blanket—white, with a black stripe at each end—appeared at the front door of the parsonage. Helen Johnson wanted to see her grandson. She bent silently over the cradle, scrutinizing the baby's thick black hair, pale brown skin and grey-blue eyes. She gave an approving nod, then spoke to her son in Mohawk. George's face split into a wide grin as he told Emily that his parents now recognized her as their daughter. Helen presented Emily with the tiny moccasin that had been her own child's first shoe. In Pauline Johnson's account of the reconciliation between her mother and grandmother, the moment throbs with emotional significance: "For a second the two women faced each other, then Emily sat down abruptly on the bedside, her arms slipped about the older woman's shoulders, and her face dropped quickly, heavily—at last on a mother's breast." All the other women important to Emily had either died or rejected her; finally, a maternal figure embraced her. Helen's initiative reassured the young couple that the fiercest critics of their controversial marriage might eventually embrace them. There is no evidence, however, that Emily ever renewed contact with her own father. Henry Howells died in New Jersey in 1854.

George had begun planning his own mansion even before his wedding. Across the fields from the parsonage, he had bought 200 acres (80 hectares) of wooded land situated between the Grand River and the Brantford-to-Caledonia road. The house, with its two arched entrances and its broad walnut stairway, gradually took shape during George and Emily's first two years of marriage. It was solidly built: the planks were laid horizontally, rather than vertically, and three tons of iron nails were used in its construction. There were four rooms on each of the two main floors, and a roomy attic lit by skylights. The main rooms all had fireplaces and there were five chimneys on the roof. A local cabinetmaker constructed walnut lintels, trim and mantelpieces, as well as a large sideboard for the dining room. The house had the most modern conveniences of the 1850s: pulleys for the sash windows, folding doors between the dining room and parlour, and a system of bells linking each room with the kitchen. The slope between the house and the river was cleared of many of the old elms and walnut trees to allow a view of the water. Separate barns for cows and horses were constructed behind the house, a double-walled ice house was built near the river and a vegetable garden was planted near the summer kitchen.

A century and a half after its construction, Chiefswood remains an inviting home. Although it has been neglected and derelict during periods of its history, its clean lines and beautiful walnut woodwork have retained their dignity. Its double front doors pique a visitor's interest in its past. When the Johnsons lived there, it exuded the cosy warmth of any Victorian family household. George and Emily chose heavy red curtains and a black carpet with roses for the parlour, and imported wallpapers for all the rooms. Engravings of Indians and of George's hero, Napoleon Bonaparte, and photographs of Johnson relatives hung on the walls. Two carved ottomans covered in green silk and a large walnut rocking chair stood in the parlour. Little china ornaments, Indian quillwork and arrangements of dried flowers cluttered every mantelpiece and table top. And George shocked his friends with his extravagance by purchasing a big square rosewood piano for the parlour, so that his beloved could accompany herself as she sang his impossibly sugary favourite English song, "Oft in the

Stilly Night." George could afford such purchases, thanks to his earnings from the colonial government plus his income as a chief.

By the time the Johnsons moved into the house in 1855, Beverly had been joined in the nursery by Eliza Helen Charlotte Johnson, who was always known as Evelyn or Eva. Three years later, Allen Wawanosh was born, and in 1861, Emily Pauline completed the Johnson family.

5

THE MODEL FAMILY
1861—1876

E MILY was thirty-seven when Pauline was born. The stress of her courtship was far behind her, and she had developed enough feistiness to display a touch of irony about reactions to her marriage. "All my friends are delighted to see me," she wrote to George while visiting relatives elsewhere in Upper Canada. "They say I look as well as ever and 'just like old times.' . . . I do not see that I am *treated* with the least *disrespect* because I am the *wife of an Indian Chief.*"

The Johnsons settled happily into a busy family life, and into the mythology of their own marriage. Deeply devoted to each other, Emily and George were determined to show the world that an interracial union could work.

Emily encouraged her children, who were born on Indian land and were wards of the British government, to take pride in their Indian heritage and in "that copper-tinted skin which they all displayed." When they were little, the children frequently visited their Johnson relatives on the reserve. Wide-eyed, they sat quietly at their grandmother's kitchen table, listening to stories about spirit-healers, medicine men, faith-keepers and ghosts. Most conversation was in the Mohawk tongue; although Emily and George's children never learned to speak their father's language, they did learn to understand its soft rhythms and guttural sounds.

A deep spiritualism suffused the reserve, and the Johnson children unconsciously absorbed it. The Mohawks were devout members of the Anglican Church, and the Johnsons regularly attended the little church close by in Tuscarora where Uncle Adam Elliott remained rector. A few Sundays each year, they would travel by carriage the ten miles (sixteen kilometres) to the Mohawk Chapel when their father was asked to read out loud the Ten Commandments in his own tongue. But not all the Iroquois had been converted to Christianity. The traditional rituals still current amongst some of their neighbours fascinated George Johnson's children. They nagged their grandparents to describe again the "false face" masks that the Tuscarora used in their celebrations. They gazed with fearful curiosity at the longhouses where the Onondaga people gathered for their twelve festivals marking the seasons of the year. Each February when the Onondaga celebrated the "Dance of the White Dog," many of the children on the reserve—including the occasional Johnson—hid nearby. They listened to the wild beat of the drum and to the dance rattlers, and they tried to catch a glimpse of the dead white dog that would be carried in, decorated with wampum, beads and porcupine quill embroidery.

When she was still small, Pauline watched a medicine man treat a neighbour with a high fever. The medicine man, wrapped in a buffalo skin and wearing a carved wooden mask, moved slowly around the sickroom, swaying from side to side and chanting with "a peculiar nasal intonation." Then he tossed a shovelful of ash over the patient and turned the man's family and friends out of the room. Within hours, the man had recovered. Pauline was deeply moved by such sights. "The practice of employing these men," she wrote years later in an article for the *Dominion Illustrated*, "is not by any means confined to the Pagan: the belief in charms and witchcraft is a prevalent one among many of the educated as well as civilised Indians. Love charms, medicine charms—they all exist in the faith and imagination of a people whose greatest charm lies in their exquisite beliefs, their seeing of the unseen and their touch of the poetic nature."

At the same time, Emily schooled her children in the rigid comportment of well-brought-up British children. Self-doubt and inhibition were never far from the surface with Pauline's mother, whose own upbringing had left the scars of abuse and a residue of British prejudice. She was so determined that her own children would never give anyone cause to reject them that she insisted on flawlessly correct behaviour at all times. Her green eyes held within them an infinite capacity for stricture: she chastised not with sharp words, but with a piercing gaze. She impressed upon her children that they were a blend, as Pauline wrote, "of the better qualities of . . . the two great races from whence" they came. But she did not teach her children to defend themselves: "My mother's philosophy was, 'If I lose my place by the selfish crowding of others, I at least have the higher satisfaction of knowing that I have not been the selfish one.'" Such training laid the foundation for a corrosive passivity in three of her children.

Just as George Johnson moved easily amongst settlers by becoming more British in style than a British immigrant, so Emily wanted her children to outdo in refinement and self-control any other children they met. She hated, recalled Pauline, "hypocrisy, vulgarity, slovenliness, imitations." This was a high standard to set in the rough-and-tumble society of Upper Canada 150 years ago, where most people were illiterate, a piano in a home was a rarity, and breweries and distilleries outnumbered churches and schools. In neighbouring Brantford, for example, there were 53 liquor outlets for a population of 4,000, and homeowners paid in beer for the services of the volunteer fire brigade. It was easier, the children found, to stick to each other's company. "As a family," Eva recorded in her memoirs, "we were clannish and loved to be among our own people, where we were understood. We had all the reserve of the British and the reticence of the Indian."

Beverly and Eva, the two older Johnson children, were particularly affected by their mother's insistence on correct behaviour. Both were suffocatingly shy; incapable of spontaneity, neither made friends easily. When other children came to visit, the two Johnsons would stand motionless,

Beverly Johnson was musical, athletic, but painfully shy.

Brantford's Mohawk Institute was one of the first residential schools for Indian children in Canada: from the start, there were stories of beatings and cruelty.

staring at the newcomers and refusing to join in their games. Emily Johnson appears to have forgotten how much she had suffered under harsh discipline when she was young. With gritted teeth, she refused to spare a rod or spoil a child. Minor crimes such as stealing apples or telling untruths merited both a whipping and a few hours' isolation.

Beverly was sent away to Brantford's Mohawk Institute, one of the first residential schools set up by the British government to "civilize" native children by immersing them in Christianity and the English language. When the schools were founded, their purpose was regarded as entirely benevolent. Nobody discussed the long-term impact of removing children from their families, languages and cultures. In Westminster, the thinking seems to have been that if boarding schools worked for the elite of Britain, surely they would be of enormous benefit to Imperial subjects elsewhere. In theory, Beverly Johnson should have been able to adapt to the Institute better than most of his fellow students. He was already baptised, he could read and write with ease, and because English was his first language the ban on speaking a native tongue was no hardship for him. But the harsh discipline and the insidious contempt for Indian ways displayed by the

Institute's staff unnerved the sensitive youngster. He ached with
homesickness and wept whenever
he saw his parents. Nevertheless,
Emily and George refused to let
him leave until he was in his mid-
teens because they felt he should
set an example to other children
on the reserve whose parents were
reluctant.

From the Mohawk Institute,
Beverly was sent to Hellmuth Collegiate in London, sixty miles
(about ninety-five kilometres)
away. At the same time, Eva was
enrolled at its counterpart, Hellmuth Ladies' College. There was

*Evelyn (Eva) Johnson inherited
her mother's self-discipline
and subdued dress sense.*

none of the us-and-them approach of the Mohawk Institute at these
smart private schools. Most students and teachers came from prominent London families, amongst whom Emily was happy to see her
own children making friends. When Bev and Eva invited the children
of London's *haute bourgeoisie* to visit Chiefswood, the young guests
brought with them the British habits and loyalties of their parents—
reverence for royalty, the ritual of dressing for dinner—which were
part of Emily's own life.

But the rigour of their upbringing appears to have left Beverly and
Eva prisoners of good breeding for the rest of their lives. "Ever correct,
dignified, aristocratic," an acquaintance said of Eva when she was in
her sixties. "Even after the strangeness of first acquaintanceship had
worn off and warmed, [she] seemed to cling with Indian tenacity to
this correctness. Sometimes I could not understand, and felt
aggrieved. . . ."

The younger two children, shielded from their parents by their
elder siblings, were more extroverted. Allen was a bumptious little
boy who was his father's favourite because he loved to dress up and
play at soldiers. Only Emily's opposition had prevented George

*From an early age, Allen
Johnson demonstrated a
talent for amateur dramatics.*

Johnson from naming his elder son after his hero, Napoleon Bonaparte, and he always called Allen "Kleber," after Napoleon's general. (He also nicknamed Beverly "Boney.") George roared with laughter when he caught six-year-old Allen stealing out of the front door with his father's gun, powder and shot bag. But like Beverly, Allen was sent off to the forbidding brick Mohawk Institute, with its freezing dormitories and scratchy grey wool uniforms. Like Beverly, he hated it. Less malleable than his elder brother, Allen ran away to his grandparents' house on the reserve, knowing that the kindly old couple would let him stay. By now, however, his mother had mellowed slightly; when she discovered him hiding in her mother-in-law's kitchen, she told him he could come home to Chiefswood.

Pauline, the baby of the brood, was named by her father after Napoleon's favourite sister, Pauline Borghese (subsequently Duchess of Guastalla). From birth, Pauline Johnson was her mother's favourite. Emily was particularly protective of Pauline because her younger daughter's health was precarious, and because as soon as she began to speak, she demonstrated a taste for poetry. She was four before she finally graduated from the black walnut cradle next to her parents' bed. Emily, who had watched her sister Eliza's children die, fretted over every cold and earache. Pauline was indulged in a way the older children never were. Each night her mother sang her to sleep, and she was allowed to keep a pet chipmunk (in a cage), as well as her terrier, Chips, and a kitten called Mitten. There was no question of a residential or boarding school for her. Until she was fourteen, her skimpy education was gleaned from her mother, a couple of non-native governesses (the second, Emily Muirhead, was the daughter of the Mayor of Brantford) and two unsatisfactory years in the little school on the reserve. By this point, Pauline was too far ahead in reading, and too fastidious in her behaviour, to mingle easily with the other Mohawk children. So she came home and worked her way alone through her parents' library of Milton, Scott, Longfellow, Browning, Tennyson, Keats and Byron. She particularly enjoyed stories about the nobility of Indians written by her favourite authors. In later years, she often recommended to others both Canadian-born John Richardson's *Wacousta*, the 1832 novel about an Englishman who assumes Indian identity, and *The Song of Hiawatha*, Longfellow's epic poem about the mythical Ojibwa peacemaker.

But Pauline's fascination with Indian culture and folklore was essentially literary: she saw native myth through the eyes of non-native writers. Her grandmother, Helen Martin Johnson, had died when Pauline was five. George Johnson felt the loss of his mother deeply, both emotionally and politically; she had been an important ally in his role on the reserve. With the loss of the clan matriarch, his own family had begun to drift away from their Mohawk relatives. Increasingly, the only link was George's father, John Johnson, who spent long periods at Chiefswood. The old man had plenty of time for his grandchildren, and he was always happy to take Pauline's hand and walk down to the river with her. If she pressed him, he would tell her stories out of his own past and the Iroquois legends that his mother had told him. But Pauline was still too young to pay much attention, particularly if Chips had raced off into the undergrowth after a squirrel.

The Johnsons enjoyed a standard of living that was unusually high amongst both Indians and settlers. They were sufficiently well-off to employ two or three servants when Pauline was young, so the children were expected to perform only "character-training" chores. A quarter of a century after she left Chiefswood, Pauline remembered that, for thirty minutes each morning before lessons with the governess, Eva had to clean the oil lamps, and that she had to sweep the stairs. "How endless those stairs were!" she recalled. "I can count them yet—nineteen horrors, with mahogany coloured velvet carpet, so difficult to

*John "Smoke" Johnson, Pauline's grandfather, passed on the
Iroquois legends he had learnt as a child.*

dust, a strip of linen in the centre, so gloriously easy to slide over, and
broad, polished brass rods, perfect demons for holding the 'fluff' from
the velvet." The little girl would frequently give up around the tenth
stair and wait with a woebegone face, hoping that Milly the nurse or
Jane the cook would relieve her of the stiff brush and finish the job. But
her mother rarely let her get away with such behaviour: finishing the
job was "something whereby you can help Milly and Jane." *Noblesse
oblige* required Pauline to reach the bottom stair.

Except for that one morning chore, the children were free to roam over the Chiefswood grounds, exploring the ravines, gathering morel mushrooms and picking anemones, violets and tiger lilies. In the spring, they watched a tenant farmer plough and plant the land between the house and the road. In the summer, they were enthusiastic spectators for the pickup lacrosse games that boys from the reserve organized on the grassy flats near the river. In the fall, they gathered butternuts, walnuts and hickory nuts. In the winter, they helped their father cut ice from the river. The two girls took turns riding Marengo, a little black pony that their father had named after Napoleon's favourite horse.

In family photographs, the Johnsons appear the epitome of Victorian respectability as they sit, straight and silent, before the lens. Small boys all over the British Empire played with drums similar to the one on which Allen Johnson's feet rest. The pattern for Eva's dress, with pretty bows on the sleeves, probably came from an illustration in a British magazine. In their black button boots and starched petticoats, the children could be the offspring of any moderately prosperous churchgoing family in Montreal, Manchester or Melbourne. The olive skin and dark eyes suggest a different parentage, but it is a subtle difference. The boys' hair is brown, not black, and only Allen has inherited his father's swarthiness.

The two Johnson boys were good athletes, the stars of local lacrosse teams. But there were no such physical outlets for the girls; even the newly popular game of tennis, considered a suitable activity for ladies, was banned from Chiefswood by Emily Johnson. Emily passed on to her daughters her own phobia about social intimacy. Visitors were never allowed to kiss the little girls; by the time she was three, Pauline had learned to bestow only distant handshakes on boys and men. Since kissing games were popular in this period, Pauline was quickly branded as standoffish. In later years she recalled an incident in the summer that she was eight, when some children from Brantford came to visit a Chiefswood neighbour:

A laughing-eyed boy of nine or ten suddenly developed a teasing tendency. "I'll kiss all you girls and make you cry!" he shouted, waving his arms like a windmill, and rushing toward the biggest girl, who took to her heels, screaming with laughter and calling back: "Georgie, porgie, pudding and pie, kiss the girls and make them cry." Of course, he caught her, kissing her a half-dozen times; then he chased and captured several others, and finally made a rush for where I stood, my little back fortified against a tree trunk, my face sullen and sulky. "Run, he'll catch you!" shouted the others, but I never stirred, only stood and glowered at him, and with all the indignation my eight years could muster, I shouted at him. "Don't you dare insult me, sir!" The "sir" was added to chill him and it did.

On this occasion, and all subsequent ones, she was left alone.

Both Eva and Pauline appeared to recall their childhood with nostalgia, but theirs was an upbringing that was stiflingly inflexible by today's standards. There wasn't a dainty rule of conduct that Emily Johnson didn't enforce. Never reach in front of a person, but ask for what you want. Don't make a noise with your lips when you are taking soup. Never say a person is sick; say he is ill. At dinner always break your bread, never bite it. Always put your hand over your mouth whenever it is necessary to sneeze, cough or yawn. Never tip your soup plate to get the last of the contents or drink the last of a cup of beverage; always leave a little at the bottom of a cup. . . . Sometimes the catalogue seemed endless. The children were never permitted to eat in the kitchen, or to take a slice of bread and butter or cake unless they were sitting properly with a plate and napkin in front of them. And gossip was never permitted, no matter how much Pauline longed to discuss with her sister the rumour that a local clergyman was too fond of a tipple.

Emily Johnson's strictures worked. The reputation of the Johnsons as a model Victorian family rippled throughout Brantford and beyond, as did the renown of Chiefswood as a home of refinement. George Henry Johnson and Emily Howells Johnson were themselves the kind of attractive couple of whom everybody wanted to believe the best. Both were slim and good-looking, and fastidious dressers. Whether George Johnson was dressed up in buckskin as an Indian chief or wearing his everyday starched collar and broadcloth jacket, he made sure that his buckles shone and his dark hair was oiled smooth. Day-time callers at Chiefswood always met Emily in an immaculate after-noon dress, with freshly laundered lace collar and cuffs, her side curls neatly pinned up. The Johnsons entertained frequently. There were musical evenings, with family and friends grouped around the piano. There were games of croquet on the lawns. There were lavish Sunday teas, at which the best linen, silver and china were set out, and Emily gracefully received local dignitaries.

George Johnson's reputation as a skilful mediator between Indian and European interests was also spreading. Thanks to his dual respon-sibilities as both George Johnson, government interpreter for the Six Nations, and Onwanonsyshon, member of the Six Nations Band Council, he found himself the reserve's de facto chief executive offi-cer. He was simultaneously paid by the government in Ottawa to enact its laws and empowered by the Council to enforce its rules and regulations. He often found himself in a difficult position, straddling two systems of government and uncertain how secure his position was with either of them. This balancing act was a source of stress and, at times, danger.

Trouble first erupted one evening in January 1865, when Pauline was only four. Emily was just lighting the parlour lamps when George lurched through the door with blood pouring from his head and mouth. The children stared in horror at him until their mother shooed them upstairs and sent the stableman to Brantford for the doc-tor. George stammered that he had been attacked in a local village by two men while walking home; then he passed out. When the doctor arrived, he quickly ascertained that both George's jaws were broken and his head wound was serious. He and the stableman carried the injured man upstairs, while the terrified children peeped out from behind their bedroom doors. For three weeks, Emily scarcely left her husband's side as he lay in bed, at first delirious with fever, then rigid with pain.

The attack on George had been perpetrated by two non-native boot-leggers, infuriated by his efforts to stop Indians illegally selling reserve timber in return for rotgut whiskey. For several months, George Johnson and the Indian Superintendent, Lieutenant Colonel

Gilkison, had pursued the illicit whiskey traders with prosecutions, fines and imprisonment. Johnson's zeal had made him a marked man. Now he was scarred by the wounds, which had been inflicted by a heavy lead ball on a piece of elastic, and for the rest of his life he suffered bouts of neuralgia. His children never forgot the sight of their father covered in blood, or the sound of his groans.

George and Emily were determined to carry on as if nothing had happened. The underlying stress remained, but the incident was rarely mentioned; George continued to combine the jobs of Council member and government interpreter. His enjoyment of ceremonial occasions was undiminished. It was George Johnson, alongside his father, John "Smoke" Johnson, who stood beside Arthur, Duke of Connaught, on a momentous occasion in October 1869. In an elaborate ceremony, Queen Victoria's third son stood on a scarlet blanket and was inducted as a chief of the Six Nations. Soon George was styling himself the "Warden of the Reserve" and receiving invitations to address both the provincial assembly in Toronto and the Dominion Parliament in Ottawa.

One day, a tall young engineer whom George had met in Brantford came to call. Alexander Graham Bell had arrived with his elderly parents from Scotland in 1870, after the family had suffered a double tragedy: the deaths from tuberculosis of both Alexander's brothers. Throughout the nineteenth century, Canada was promoted in Britain as a land of good health, and the Bells had decided that they must flee Edinburgh's germs. Alexander's mother was very deaf, and the children were fascinated by her ear trumpet. Pauline was even more intrigued when Alexander, asked to say grace before the meal, said the prayer in sign language.

The Bells were so impressed with the Johnson ménage that a few days later, they returned the invitation. In later years Pauline loved to tell the story (an anecdote that also signalled to her audience the prestige of her family's friends) of her father's visit to Tutelo Heights, the Bells' sprawling home with its lacy gingerbread trim outside Brantford. George Johnson was invited to help test a new invention. He found Alexander Bell walking towards the house, tacking stovepipe wire to

*Tutelo Heights, the Bells' home outside Brantford, where
Alexander Graham Bell rigged up the first telephone system.*

every tree and fence post he passed. George took off his coat to give
him a hand. After Bell had connected the wire to a strange device in his
study, he and George joined a group of Brantford worthies in the dining
room for lunch. When the meal was finished, the party returned to the
study and Bell explained that the wire stretched between his workshop
and the Great Western Telegraph office in Brantford, two and a half
miles (four kilometres) away. He spoke into a mouthpiece, then
watched with delight the expressions on his guests' faces as they heard
clearly the voice of Walter Griffin, the telegraph operator in Brantford,
replying. Each took turns speaking to Griffin, who heard every word
perfectly. But when it was his turn, George Johnson opted to speak
Mohawk. "*Sago, ghasha*," he said, whispering to those around him
that this meant "How do you do, my cousin."

There was silence at the other end, then Griffin said, "I couldn't get
that; repeat it please." George repeated the Mohawk greeting; Griffin
again was stumped. After a couple more exchanges, Griffin said in

exasperation, "Well, all I can say is, Professor Bell's champagne must have been very heady!"

Another prominent neighbour who turned up at Chiefswood was a tall young man from Doon, several miles up the Grand River. This was the painter Homer Watson, who arrived with a party of teachers from Berlin (now Kitchener) High School. Watson, a self-taught artist, loved to depict the hills, valleys, trees and cattle of Southern Ontario as though it were a rural British scene. ("The Canadian Constable!" Oscar Wilde exclaimed several years later when he caught sight of one of Wat-

By the time she was fourteen, Pauline Johnson knew by heart large parts of Longfellow's The Song of Hiawatha.

son's canvasses.) The artist was captivated by the Georgian architecture of Chiefswood, by the copses of old elms in the grounds and by Emily's English manners and gooseberry preserve. "The Chief and his cultured wife made us welcome," he wrote to a friend. "Pauline and her sister sang duets, and then Pauline, a slight, striking-looking young girl, recited some of her verses, which showed much talent."

By the mid-1870s, all Emily's fears that her family would be outcasts had proven groundless. The Johnsons were acknowledged as a leading Canadian family. An envelope addressed simply to "Chiefswood" would be delivered promptly by the Brantford post office from anywhere in the province. Distinguished travellers from as far afield as the southern United States angled for invitations to this showpiece house. And in Ottawa, the newly built capital of the Dominion of Canada, successive Governors General were urged to call in at Chiefswood on their vice-regal tours. In 1874, Lord and Lady Dufferin arrived at the Six Nations Reserve to visit the Mohawk Church and watch a war dance. George Johnson was their interpreter, and he played the role of Indian chief for all it was worth. Lady Dufferin noted he was "a clever, fine-looking man . . . beautifully-dressed in well-made, tight-fitting tunic and breeches of deerskin, with silver ornaments. He looked magnificent on horseback." The vice-regal party went on to Chiefswood for "a great luncheon and some excellent tea." Thirteen-year-old Pauline found herself curtseying to a debonair figure who inspected her through his monocle and to a slender woman in a marvellously fashionable hat. Five years later, there was a repeat performance of the war dance, curtseys and an excellent tea at Chiefswood for Dufferin's successor, the Marquess of Lorne and his wife, Princess Louise, daughter of Queen Victoria.

George Johnson could never resist an opportunity to dress up—sometimes in native dress, other times in his well-cut European-style suits—and mingle with the mighty. On one occasion, he travelled to Montreal to have his photograph taken by William Notman, the Scots-born photographer who captured all the celebrities of the time with his lens. On another occasion, George attended a theatrical performance in New York City in full Indian costume, decorated with several large medals. At least half the audience was convinced that

The nineteenth-century ethnographer Horatio Hale (1817–1896), who wrote several articles about the Six Nations Reserve, was a close friend of the Johnson family.

this splendid figure sitting in a private box was the Czar of Russia. George was also a frequent guest at Rideau Hall, in Ottawa, where his exquisite manners impressed whichever British aristocrat held the position of Governor General of Canada.

Horatio Hale, a Canadian ethnographer of the later nineteenth century who made a special study of the Six Nations Reserve, was impressed by the reception tendered Johnson: "He was often sent by his people as a delegate to bring their needs, and occasionally their remonstrances, to the attention of the government. If not in all cases successful in such missions his appearance and address always secured him attention and respect. Governors and statesmen received him with courtesy and interest." And George relished every opportunity to join the exclusive clubs established by British immigrants. By the time of his death, in addition to being a Freemason, he was a member of the Conservative Party, the Order of Odd Fellows and the York Pioneers, and frequently added the letters UE (United Empire Loyalist) to his name.

With the leading statesmen and scientists of his day treating George Johnson so respectfully, it is no surprise that his youngest daughter idolized him. Pauline's attitude to her father was always one of unconditional admiration. His frequent absences from home, and the way he left child-raising entirely to Emily, meant that he had the additional mystery of distance. George Johnson could do no wrong in his family's eyes. He presented an example of manhood which his sons felt they could never live up to and which his daughters looked for, and failed to find, in their beaux.

Emily never accompanied her husband to grand events in Toronto, New York or Ottawa, although George urged her to do so. She had found her role: she was the angel in the house. In Pauline's magazine article "My Mother," she quotes Emily as saying, "My babies need me here, and you need me here when you return, far more than you need me on platform or parade. Go forth and fight the enemy, storm the battlements and win the laurels, but let me keep the garrison— here at home, with our babies all about me and a welcome to our warrior husband and father when he returns from war."

Pauline's account could be read as a description of the self-effacing behaviour of the model nineteenth-century mother. Emily would seem to fit the stereotype of ideal maternity as laid out in an article by Elizabeth Lynn Linton in the August 1870 edition of the British magazine *Saturday Review*. Mrs. Lynn Linton decreed that the woman at home should be "the careful worker-out of details and the upholder of a sublime idealism," her maternal influence being "the real bond of family life." But a more modern interpretation of Emily's conduct suggests an almost pathological fear of the outside world, and a determination to remain in her "garrison," where she had complete control. Pauline described her mother as "abnormally sensitive, prone to melancholy." Agoraphobia probably lurked close to the surface of Emily's reclusive tendencies and of the suffocating restrictions she put on her four children. The brutal attack on her husband in 1865 would only have exacerbated her neurosis.

As the children grew older, they came to recognize the shortcomings of their stifling upbringing. In her memoirs Eva Johnson wrote, "We were brought up quietly, played amongst ourselves in our own grounds and garden, and knew little of the outside world. For each of us the first peep at it was a great novelty, and consequently the first love of each of us was unworthy." Pauline, as usual, was more outspoken than her sister. "An inherited sensitiveness was a perfect bane in our childhood," she recalled in a magazine article. "We were all shy, which mother conquered in us by having us assume a dignity far beyond our years. We learned from her to disguise our wretched bashfulness with a peculiar, cold reserve, that made our schoolfellows call us 'stuck-up,' and our neighbours' children mock us as 'proudy.'"

However, Emily Johnson deserves credit for achieving her goal. The Johnsons were living proof that Indians and European settlers could live together in style and harmony. The family photograph album, a heavy volume covered in green leather with an elaborate brass clasp, was filled with the *cartes de visite* of all those distinguished guests. Bewhiskered gentlemen, frock-coated bishops, haughty women in full-skirted gowns stare out of the small, stiff photographic visiting cards that were wildly popular in the late-nineteenth century and played the role of business cards today. Even Emily's own sister, Mary Rogers from Kingston, had swallowed her misgivings and now consented to visit. Only a few un-Christian curmudgeons, like the Reverend Robert Vashon Rogers, still shunned the Johnsons. The Reverend Rogers snorted angrily when his younger son, Mansel, decided to spend some months living at Chiefswood in order to learn farming—but he did not stop him.

6

SPREADING
HER WINGS
1876–1885

Chiefswood, August 8, 1881

My dear Lottie, I received your very kind letter asking me
to go and visit you. . . . I am pleased to have such a prospect
[and to] accept your hospitality and kindness. I am going up
to Goderich the latter part of this week for a very short visit
to some friends there. . . . I have just written to Katie asking
her when she is going up to London which I suppose depends
on when you return from Burlington. I hope you are having
ever such a nice time there—tho' I believe it is rather quiet
there. . . .

I F there was one thing that twenty-year-old Pauline Johnson found
difficult, it was too many "rather quiet" intervals in her own life.
As she sat at the table in her Chiefswood bedroom gazing out at
her mother's kitchen garden on a sticky summer afternoon, she
thought with envy of her friend Charlotte Jones's life in London,
Ontario. She was impatient to take up Lottie's kind invitation. Lottie
could walk out of her front gate on Maitland Street and within minutes be window shopping on Dundas Street. On a sunny afternoon,
Lottie could stroll down to the River Thames and listen to the strains
of Souza marches wafting from the ornamental bandstand nearby.
When Pauline was staying with her, Mrs. Jones might take the two
young women to the newly opened Grand Opera House, at the back of

the massive Masonic temple, to see whichever travelling theatre company was putting on *Uncle Tom's Cabin* this year.

Pauline, in contrast, was stuck deep in the country, with absolutely *nothing* to amuse her. Her mother was fussing in the kitchen and her father, as usual, was away. Pauline's only relief came from visits to friends and cousins who lived within a few hours' train journey of Chiefswood. She particularly enjoyed such visits if, as in Lottie's case, there was a good-looking brother in the house as well: "I wish you would tell your brother I am in a good humour now. Please Lottie dear, write to me soon. I am so lonely down here in the country and your letters always cheer me up."

Pauline had grown into a very attractive young woman. Slim and petite, with bronze glimmers in her thick mane of curly brown hair, she glowed with health these days. There was always a spring in her step and a smile hovering around the corners of her full lips. In public she could seem as aloof and cool as ever, but amongst friends her deep-set grey eyes sparkled with life and her throaty voice dominated conversation. She was very conscious of her appearance: she knew that delicate blues and pinks flattered her complexion, and she spent hours sewing tight-fitting blouses, trimming hats and pressing satin skirts. Her mother's lacquered jewellery box was an irresistible source of hatpins, bracelets and brooches. She particularly liked the Indian-trade silver brooches bequeathed by her Mohawk grandmother; she wore them at her neck to fasten the high-fitting fichus and ruffs which were all the rage at the time and which set off her heart-shaped face to such effect. It was, though, her physical grace as much as her dainty appearance that struck observers. She was at home in her skin in a way that few of her contemporaries were. "She even lies upon the ground with more grace and ease than any other woman," commented Peggy Webling, an English visitor to Brantford. There was "no touch of self-consciousness in the stretch and curve of her lithe body, the arms and throat sun-kissed to the colour of bronze."

Emily often wondered where her younger daughter's spirit and self-confidence came from. During Pauline's early teens, it had been a different story. At fourteen, Pauline seemed too timid and frail to be sent away to school in London like Beverly and Evelyn. Beverly and Allen had already demonstrated to their parents their unhappiness at the Mohawk Institute. So George and Emily decided to send their two youngest children to Brantford Central Collegiate on Sheridan Street, an imposing brick building which was the largest of the town's public schools. Allen and Pauline would be almost the only children from the reserve at Central Collegiate, and since Brantford was too far from Chiefswood for them to journey back and forth each day, the two youngsters would have to spend the weeknights with family friends near their new school. Pauline stayed in the household of David Curtis, a customs inspector, who had three unmarried daughters and ran a boarding house for students.

During Pauline's first weeks in Brantford, she didn't make many friends. At fourteen, she was a prim little thing with her thick hair scraped back into a tight braid and a suspicious expression on her face: "My mother knew I had every evening to myself [and] that young men boarded in the same house; but the one coat-of-mail which she clasped about me when she left me in the city was, 'Allow no liberties; it is not aristocratic.' Consequently I was a very lonely, isolated girl . . . away from home for the first time, for I carried this creed with me as far as women were concerned as well as men, and even women don't care for a chilling, haughty, reserved young miss, who is continually on the lookout to snub them for approaching intimacy."

But it wasn't in Pauline's nature to be Miss Goody Two-Shoes for long. Up until then, she had never spent much time with girls her age who shared her interests. She found the experience intoxicating. The shy, frail newcomer with the "aristocratic" façade soon blossomed into a lively and clever young woman who loved the limelight. She shone at English and history, and was a star attraction in school recitals and plays. It was a different story in mathematics, which she never mastered, but she didn't care—she was too busy making classmates laugh. The graffiti in her school poetry reader suggests a mischievous wit: an "Ode to Duty" has been retitled "Darn the Ode to Duty," and "Labour," the title of another poem, has become "Labour is Devilish."

It wasn't simply the inhibitions instilled by Emily's strictures that evaporated. So did the wariness with which Pauline's classmates initially approached this stranger from the Six Nations Reserve. Pauline was soon surrounded by a circle of close girlfriends who called her "Paul" or "Pauly." Prominent within this circle were Jean Morton, a pretty brown-haired girl, and Emily and Mary Curtis, daughters of Pauline's host. Most of these girls had grown up in the solid white-brick mansions on Brantford's tree-lined streets; their fathers were successful merchants, lawyers and newspapermen, and their mothers organized church suppers and Sunday school picnics. Pauline often invited them out to Chiefswood for weekends, where they mingled with Eva's and Beverly's friends from similar backgrounds in London and (once Bev got a job there) Hamilton. By the time Pauline left Central Collegiate in 1877, she had escaped from her mother's domination. She had also put a distance between herself and the Six Nations Reserve. Although she loved playing the "Red Indian" to her Anglo-Saxon girlfriends (she brandished her father's tomahawk in a war dance for them on one occasion, then recited a monologue on the life of Pocahontas), none of her friends was Iroquois.

Late-nineteenth-century Brantford boasted a handsome town hall and formidable civic pride.

In later years, Brantford would seem suffocatingly small and sleepy to Pauline Johnson. In her teens and early twenties, however, she was dazzled by the prosperity and sophistication of this little town sixty miles (ninety-five kilometres) southwest of Toronto. Canada had established its new nationhood only a few years earlier, at Confederation, but since 1867 the young country had surged towards industrialization. Brantford was in the forefront of this surge. In 1877, it achieved city status, and its population had doubled since Confederation to more than 10,000. Thanks to the city's ease of access, by rail and water, from Toronto, Hamilton, Buffalo and Detroit, its economy was booming. Its foundries, factories, mills, potteries and distilleries attracted a new class of immigrant: blue-collar workers from the northern United States and the British Isles, eager for steady work and steady wages. Loyalty to the Mother Country was combined with Yankee know-how and capital. "Made in Brantford" was stamped on goods that were sent to every corner of the British Empire: Massey-Harris mowers and reapers; Tisdale's iron stoves; Brant Forde Brand wool blankets woven at the Slingsby mills; Lily White Gloss Starch from the Brantford Starch Works; T. J. Fair cigars.

Brantford had a boosterish mentality even before its Chamber of Commerce was founded. Along with the neighbouring Six Nations Reserve, it was always on the itinerary for any tour of the colony by British royalty, and it was always ready with brass bands and bunting. In 1860, when Edward, Prince of Wales, came through town, he was served a sixty-dish luncheon at the Kerby House Hotel, on the corner of Colborne and George streets. The Kerby House had been billed as the largest hotel in Upper Canada when it opened in 1854, and His Royal Highness (no slouch as a trencherman) remarked he had never seen such a gargantuan feast. His brother Prince Arthur, the Duke of Connaught, followed him in 1869, and was greeted by the 38th Brantford Battalion and by the local volunteer fire brigade's hook-and-ladder cart bedecked in flags and ribbons. Five years later, Governor General Lord Dufferin and his wife were met by "guards of honour, both foot and horse, a band and a great crowd." In 1879, when Dufferin's successor, the Marquess of Lorne, arrived, an enthusiastic school choir sang a special welcome song.

Brantford boasted two daily papers (the *Brantford Courier* and the *Daily Expositor*), its own rail link to the States (the Buffalo and Brantford Railway, opened in 1854), a Philharmonic Society *and* a Mendelssohn Society, and its own wine-making business, which claimed to be Canada's first winery (Major J. S. Hamilton, proprietor). There were plenty of other thriving little manufacturing towns located on land once owned by the Iroquois in the Grand River Valley—Elora, Waterloo, Berlin, Galt, Paris, Guelph—but Brantford was confident that it was biggest and best, and it didn't care who knew it.

Pauline was not particularly interested in the factories on the edge of town, with their chimneys belching out smoke night and day. She could not care less about the prosperous professional men who discussed accounts payable and receivable over roast beef in the Kerby House. But she was extremely interested in the plate-glass windows (newly installed at the astronomical cost of $300 per store) of the merchants along Colborne and Dalhousie streets. At Frank Cockshutt's Dry Goods Store, Pauline could gaze at soft silks, woollens, cottons and linens; if she ventured inside, she might try on gloves and bonnets. At Lester's Candy Store, she could buy 5 cents' worth of snowflake marshmallows or handmade lollipops. At Robertson's Drug Store, she and Jeanie Morton debated the merits of Pompeiian beauty powder (60 cents a packet) or "bloom"—a rouge that cost 60 cents for a small pot. She could buy her mother a small jar of Dr. Chase's nerve food, with a picture of snowy-haired Dr. Chase on the lid. At Hawthorne's Sporting Goods, she could point out her brothers in the prominently displayed photographs of winning lacrosse teams. And she regularly called in at Mason and Risch's Music Shop to pick up sheet music for Bev. He was particularly fond of the newest dance tunes.

Pauline spent only two years at Brantford Central Collegiate; even by late-Victorian standards of girls' education, her schooling had been skimpy. In 1877, she triumphantly graduated from the school— and then came down to earth, and to Chiefswood, with a bump. Once she had left ink-stained desks and chalky blackboards behind, she no longer had any excuse to linger on weekday afternoons in Brantford. She was now expected to spend her days helping her mother at home, making only occasional forays away from her family. But Chiefswood began to seem more like a cage than a haven; she hankered after the hissing gas lamps and colourful bustle of the Market Square. The traditional way of life of her father's people and the quiet harmony of her parents' home lost their charm. Most of Pauline's Mohawk cousins still lived in simple wooden houses with dirt floors; none of her Brantford schoolfriends came from such humble dwellings. The Johnson relatives on the reserve continued to eat a diet of corn soup supplemented by roasted guinea fowl, rabbit or squirrel—the same diet that immigrant pioneers had once enjoyed. But middle-class Brantford families turned up their noses at such fare. They preferred stuffed partridge followed by English custards at their Sunday lunches after church. Several of the girls Pauline had known at the little school on the reserve were already mothers; they all wore drab woollen gowns rather than satin and lace. None of them pored over the photogravures in *Canadian Illustrated News* to see what Queen Victoria's daughters were wearing, as Pauline and her friends did. Pauline knew that the only women other than herself from Six Nations whom her Brantford friends might meet were the pipe-smoking Cayuga elders selling live chickens, apples and corn in the market, or the unsmiling Oneida women who went door to door in the more affluent parts of town selling tin pails of wild raspberries.

Consciously or unconsciously, Pauline realized that the Six Nations Reserve, including Chiefswood, was being left out of the booming growth visible in places like Brantford, London and Hamilton. In the rest of southwestern Ontario (as Upper Canada had been named in 1867), European- and American-born entrepreneurs were building manufacturing plants on credit, expanding their businesses on borrowed money and shipping goods south into the States or east to the Mother Country. But there was no such commercial explosion amongst the Six Nations, largely because of new laws that remoulded relations between non-natives and Indians. In 1857, the legislature of the Province of Canada had passed the Gradual Civilization Act, which had the express purpose of absorbing native peoples into European-settler society and culture. Traditional communal land-holding practices were modified. Indians had to demonstrate their capacity for British citizenship by proving themselves debt-free and of good moral character (a test many British settlers would not have passed) before they would be entitled to hold land freehold and to enjoy other rights of citizenship. In the meantime, Indians would have "protected" status, which meant that they were treated as wards of state, like children. Native leaders had made it clear that they did not welcome the Gradual Civilization Act, but worse was to come. In 1860, Britain transferred jurisdiction over Indian matters to the legislatures of its British North American colonies. Responsibility for native affairs was now in the hands of a land-hungry settler society rather than the lofty (but ostensibly impartial) rulers of Imperial Britain. Sir William Johnson's ideal of harmonious cohabitation had been overtaken by a policy of assimilation.

The assimilation approach was strengthened by an avalanche of further Indian Acts, whose primary goal was to speed up settlement in the north and west of Canada. The Dominion government was eager to convert nomadic peoples like the Cree and the Blackfoot to Christianity, settle them on reserves and teach them to farm (and, incidentally, to release land on which new immigrants might homestead). The policy was unpopular with native peoples throughout the Dominion. It made no sense at all for the Six Nations, who had been farming alongside non-native neighbours ever since they had arrived within the past century. The new legislation throttled enterprise on the Grand River Reserve, which by now had shrunk to one-tenth the acreage of the original land grant. Thanks to the various new laws, Indian self-determination was eroded. Pauline's Iroquois relatives, and Pauline herself, were now non-citizens, under the supervision of an Indian Agent—usually a spit-and-polish military type who treated his charges like irresponsible conscripts. The heirs of Joseph Brant were locked into subsistence farming because their new legal status denied them access to capital.

Relations between native and non-native communities deteriorated as rapidly as the native standard of living. The last threat of an American invasion had fizzled out with the collapse of the 1866 Fenian raids. From then on, the Six Nations had no value as military allies for politicians in Westminster, Ottawa or Toronto. Nor had the Iroquois retained the novelty value of being "noble savages." Thanks to intermarriage and the adoption of European dress, many of the reserve's residents were indistinguishable from other Canadians. The Six Nations' Indian Agent had to issue special certificates of identity so that they might claim their right to travel half-fare on the railways.

Leaders of the two communities maintained cordial relations: George Johnson continued to be treated with respect by the Mayor of Brantford, and the chiefs of the Six Nations, in ceremonial dress, always participated in royal parades and banquets. But in less exalted circles, a gulf yawned. Brantford girls would no longer come out to Chiefswood as maids or governesses, because European immigrants would no longer work for Indians. New immigrants, still pouring into the area, greedily eyed the undeveloped, well-forested lands within reserve limits. Violence flared. At one point, a group of Iroquois attacked with pitchforks a newly arrived British family who were squatting on the eastern bank of the Grand River, close to Chiefswood. Intimidated by the simmering hostility, in 1883 the parishioners of Adam Elliott's old church, St. John's, decided to move their place of worship from the Tuscarora village to the centre of the reserve lands, across the river. The old church was torn down; the fittings were sold and a black walnut *prie-dieu* that George Johnson had given the church in Adam Elliott's day ended up at Chiefswood.

Struggling to find their own footing in society, the four Johnson children uneasily watched what was happening. Even without the tension, they would never have been content to remain on the reserve, stuck within a slow-moving farming community. It is hardly surprising that all four, and particularly Pauline, initially opted for the non-Indian world. They could see that a stigma was increasingly attached to having native blood, and they heard people of mixed blood contemptuously dismissed as "breeds" (for "half-breeds"). But all the Johnson children continued to take pride in their Mohawk heritage. None of them would ever dream of deliberately "passing for white," although Beverly and Pauline, in particular, could easily have done so.

As the four Johnson children reached adulthood, they remained a tight little group, although the differences between them became more obvious. Bev was a tall, good-looking young man—"the handsomest man in all of Canada," according to his sister Eva. After he graduated from Hellmuth College, he got a job with the Mutual Life Insurance Company in Hamilton. His colleagues there were often unaware of his Mohawk blood, since his skin was pale, his eyes grey-blue and his thick hair brown rather than black. In company Bev was awkward, but when he was at a piano or on a stage he shone. He could play any tune, from Chopin to Sullivan, and he loved to take the male lead in productions by the Garrick Dramatic Club in Hamilton. Girls flirted with Beverly,

As adults, the Johnson siblings (L to R: Pauline, Beverly, Allen and Eva) formed a close-knit group as they navigated between two worlds.

but even his sisters found him remote. He was secretive about his family to colleagues and about his social life to friends.

Evelyn seemed remote to people outside the family, too. She tended to hunch her shoulders, press her lips together and keep her own counsel. She dressed in starchy white or dull black gowns, and always disappeared in a crowd. She never found it easy to make new friends. Her family knew that Eva's cool exterior came from lack of confidence and an obsession (instilled by Emily) with the need to be "proper." Eva played the organ at church each Sunday and helped Emily provide dainty teas for visitors to Chiefswood. Unlike her siblings, she made an effort to keep in touch with old friends on the reserve, such as the Styres and Buck families. She knew that people found her pleasant but stuffy compared to her extroverted younger sister; she once overheard an acquaintance remark, "You'll like Eva, but Pauline you'll love."

As the two girls entered their twenties, the truth of this remark became painfully obvious to Eva. She had one intense relationship with a young native man, but she broke off their engagement when she heard a rumour that her fiancé was too fond of the bottle. Nobody else ever proposed to her. Meanwhile, male admirers—Indian and immigrant—flocked round her younger sister. Pauline once quipped, "Eva is like the sun, she dazzles the men. I am like the moon, I drive them crazy." The young men who congregated at Chiefswood these days always seemed more interested in going crazy than in being dazzled. Eva tried not to resent Pauline's looks and popularity, but she was sensitive to every slight and never forgot a grudge. Her sensitivity made for a lifetime of prickly relations between the sisters.

Mohawk features predominated in the looks of both Evelyn and her younger brother, Allen: they were dark-skinned and dark-eyed, with what Eva described as "straight black Indian hair." In many ways, Allen was the most easygoing of the four Johnsons. His brother and sisters berated him for his lie-abed laziness; he admitted in a letter to a friend, "Procrastination is one of my worst faults." Peggy Webling, a young Englishwoman who met the Johnsons in the late 1880s, described him as "handsome in his dark, stealthy way, and he danced divinely." He had few ambitions, but luckily his father had useful contacts. When Allen left school, his father managed to get him a job as a cashier in a Hamilton warehouse owned by Senator James Turner, a family friend. Allen immediately joined his brother in the Garrick Dramatic Club and the Hamilton lacrosse club, and took up rowing. He was not as good-looking as Bev, but he was more popular with Pauline's girlfriends because he was more fun. "The Brantford girls," recalled Peggy Webling, "used to call him the Black Prince."

Pauline finally made her visit to her friend Charlotte Jones in London in the fall of 1881. "I do not exaggerate," the vivacious twenty-year-old wrote to her hostess in October, "when I say that of all the visits I have ever made, my first to you will ever rank among the most enjoyable and I only regret that when you come to Chiefswood I will be unable to entertain you as handsomely as I would wish." Over the next few months, Pauline also made visits to her cousin Katie Howells in the

Pretty and vivacious, nineteen-year-old Pauline had plenty of male admirers.

village of Paris, fifteen miles (twenty-four kilometres) from Chiefswood, to relatives in Wingham and Hamilton, and to friends in Goderich, on the shores of Lake Huron. Her brothers, twenty-five miles (forty kilometres) away in Hamilton, often invited their pretty sister to visit. They escorted her to performances at the local theatre, and to At Homes given by the wives of Hamilton's wealthy manufacturers. A sharp observer with a good ear for accents, Pauline would behave beautifully in Hamilton's best drawing rooms, then perform wicked imitations of her hostesses as soon as she was back in her brothers' digs. "My boys are always so good to me," she wrote to Lottie. "They drove me about and took me on the Bay sailing and made me sit for new photos, for which they paid, and otherwise were adorable."

Back at Chiefswood, Pauline persuaded Eva that they both simply *had* to enrol in dancing classes taught by their friends Emily and Mary Curtis, which necessitated new dresses and overnight stays in Brantford. She promised her closest friend, Jeanie Morton, that if Jeanie took the morning train from Brantford to Onondaga station, Pauline would meet her and carry her bags for the mile-and-a-half walk to Chiefswood. She flirted with a succession of young men, about whom she wrote with ingenuous enthusiasm to Lottie. In 1881, she mentioned to Lottie that "We had a fancy Londoner with us for a few days. . . . Hugh Hartshorne—and he was quite taken with the idea of me spending a few days with you and says he lives quite near you."

The following year, she told Lottie that "I hear quite frequently from David and about three weeks ago he sent me his photograph." But David, whoever he was, had competition. Pauline went on to write that "Bert Beddoe is in Toronto . . . and he asked after me. So he has not forgotten the wild girl that made him play 'drink' one night and decorated that little ale bottle of Labatts with a ribbon! I would like to meet him again so much."

There were long periods, however, when Pauline had no excuse to leave home. In the early 1880s she would while away summer afternoons in a canoe, drifting dreamily between the Grand River's willow-lined banks, or surging through its churning rapids. The Grand River was a source of never-ending fascination to her; she loved to spot mink and muskrat along its banks, to gaze up at the hickory and butternut trees arching over the water, to pick wild grapes along the shoreline. She was a skilful canoeist, which gave her an added attraction to any young men who might be around. "I have an engagement to take a young fellow out in my canoe," she wrote Lottie Jones in 1882. "Said boy is a teacher and can only get out Saturday and as he is particularly fond of Nature, he asked me to take him—for I have a habit of going out in my canoe up the river by myself."

Pauline was careful to keep her flirtations secret from her mother. Emily Johnson made it clear to both her daughters that she would tolerate no talk at Chiefswood of "beaux, fellows or spooning." Her attitude to marriage was extraordinarily conflicted, considering her own much-vaunted marital bliss. On the one hand she assumed her daughters would marry—indeed, she shared the widespread assumption that it was the only future for a respectable young woman. On the other hand, she found discussion of the emotional aspects (or even worse, the physical side) of marriage distasteful. She was so determined to keep her daughters pure that she preferred to keep them ignorant. When the family physician, on a social visit to Chiefswood, detected Emily's reluctance to raise the subject and tried to raise it himself, Emily was appalled. "Doctor, you never step into this house but you begin that foolish topic," she snapped at him. "You seem never to talk of anything but love and marriage, love and marriage."

It seems unlikely that Pauline allowed her mother's inhibitions in this area to smother her own curiosity. She had long since learned to rely on books and friends for hard facts. In any case, she was in no hurry to settle down. The boys were a diversion from her not-so-secret ambition: she wanted to be a writer.

With her mother's encouragement, Pauline had always loved reading poetry. Emily Johnson took great pride in telling friends that when Pauline, aged about eight, had been asked whether she would like some candies from Brantford, she had replied, "No, bring me verses." Emily herself, like many educated women in the nineteenth century, had tried her hand at composition. In the Brant County Museum's collection of Johnson papers, there is a fragment on which is written, in a cramped and spidery hand, "To dear George," and which contains the poignant lines,

> Linger not long!
> Though crowds should woo thy staying,
> Bethink thee: can the mirth of friends, though dear,
> Compensate for the grief thy long delaying
> Costs the heart that sighs to have thee here?

Like her mother, Pauline would scribble verse whenever she found herself with pen and paper in hand. She composed poems for family occasions and for her school friends' autograph albums. Pauline's early verses bore the same stamp of Victorian sentimentality, rife with anachronistic language, as did her mother's. When she was eighteen, for example, she wrote a throbbing testament of friendship to Jean Morton, entitled "My Jeanie":

> When thou art near
> The sweetest joys still sweeter seem
> The brightest hopes more bright appear
> And life is all one happy dream
> When thou art near.

At the same time, she kept up her reading in contemporary literature. She still loved the favourites of her youth—Tennyson, Longfellow, Byron and Keats—but her taste now ran to some of the more
florid late Victorians. She declared herself a devotee of the poet Algernon Swinburne, on the strength, one assumes, of his metrical skills
and his association with Pre-Raphaelite artists and writers such as
Edward Burne-Jones and William Morris. She could not have known
that by the time she was old enough to read his verse, this strange little red-haired man was an alcoholic obsessed with incest, lesbianism
and flagellation. Pauline was also addicted to the lush novels of the
period. She admitted to Lottie that on the train home from London, "I
buried my fevered brain and thoughts in *Under Two Flags* and forgot
for a while the existence of anyone but the conductor and Ouida's
hero." This novel, published in 1867 by Louise de la Ramée under her
pen name Ouida, was a melodramatic romance of fashionable life.
Even in her own day, Ouida found her forty-five novels parodied by
critics, but as G. K. Chesterton remarked of her, "It is impossible not
to laugh at Ouida, and equally impossible not to read her." The distinguished Canadian critic Pelham Edgar, who headed the Department of
English at Victoria College, Toronto, from 1912 to 1938, admitted in
his memoirs that as a young man, "I developed great fondness for
Ouida. *Under Two Flags* was a book I could not put down."

Louise de la Ramée had yearned from youth to see her name in print,
and Pauline Johnson was no different. One of Pauline's Brantford
friends was a young man named Douglas Reville, who worked for the
Brantford Courier and who would later marry Jean Morton. Pauline
suggested to him that he should publish "My Jeanie." Douglas said the
poem deserved a bigger readership, so he sent it on to a New York magazine, *Gems of Poetry*. Pauline was ecstatic when the poem, retitled
"My Little Jean," was published. She felt that she had found her métier
when three more of her verses appeared (one under the pseudonym
Margaret Rox) within the next few months. However, the publication
of "My Little Jean" did not provoke a roar of applause for the arrival of
an important new poet. *Gems of Poetry* had a tiny circulation—too
small to pay its bills. In 1885, it would go out of business.

* * *

But Pauline scarcely noticed the demise of *Gems of Poetry*. A far greater crisis had engulfed the Johnsons. The 1865 attack on George Johnson had shown all too clearly that his position as chief go-between for Indians and the civil authorities was fraught with difficulty. Pauline's parents had done their best to smother the memory of George's bloody injuries, but the threats intensified as tensions between the Iroquois and European settlers grew. By the 1870s, unscrupulous residents of both Brantford and the Six Nations Reserve were flouting the law banning alcohol on the reserve with increasing recklessness. And timber prices rose steadily, which made timber merchants greedy for the reserve's stock of black walnut and oak trees.

George redoubled his efforts to catch the criminals who were supplying Indians with whiskey and stealing their lumber. Eight years after the first skirmish, he was again attacked on a lonely road. This assault was more severe: six European men wielding clubs knocked him to the ground, broke his ribs, knocked out his teeth, then shot him and left him for dead. But the bullet only grazed him, and he managed to drag himself to a local farmhouse. Once again, a devoted and terrified Emily nursed him through the long weeks of recovery. From now on, his neuralgia recurred even more frequently and he suffered constant attacks of erysipelas, a virulent staphylococcus infection that caused ugly red blotches on the face and high temperatures. The infection was nicknamed St. Anthony's fire because sufferers were often afflicted with such a burning fever that they felt as though they were being consumed by flames. John Richardson, the Canadian author of *Wacousta*, which was one of Pauline's favourite books, had died of erysipelas in 1852. No remedy existed for the disease before the development of antibiotic medications.

Despite George's health problems, the crusade against the bootleggers obsessed him. He limped along the forest paths for hours, trying to see where trees were being felled or caches of liquor hidden. Wincing with pain, he rose in Council meetings and implored younger chiefs to join him. He knew he could rely on Mohawk support, but he also knew that the Onondaga, Cayuga and Seneca chiefs had started to whisper that he was simply a puppet of the Dominion government. Still, to his children he remained the genial paterfamilias who regretted his frequent absences on important business. Only Emily realized he was a broken man.

Pauline's father suffered a third assault in 1878 when he was walking home from the Council House. This time, the scars from the attack were more psychological than physical—his assailant was an Indian whiskey buyer. George Johnson was now under attack from his fellow chiefs and menaced by European and Indian petty crooks. His health went downhill rapidly. He lost his *joie de vivre* and his appetite for public life. In February 1884, he reluctantly attended a reception in Brantford for the newly appointed bishop, the Very Reverend Baldwin, at Grace Church. When he left the meeting to ride home, a chilly rain began to fall. By the time he reached Chiefswood, he was drenched to the skin and his teeth were chattering. As his fever intensified, he started raving incomprehensibly in Mohawk, the tongue of his birth, then he lapsed into unconsciousness. Within a week, his life was over. He was sixty-eight.

George's two sons had not been given sufficient warning to reach home before he died. The rest of the family—Emily, Evelyn and Pauline—stood by George's deathbed, listening to one of the most haunting sounds of North America echo up and down the Grand River. A young man from the Six Nations Reserve knelt close to the water's surface to sing out the ululating death cry. The wail rippled through the dusk, propelled from one Indian settlement to the next. Chief George Henry Martin Johnson, Onwanonsyshon, was gone.

The funeral was a splendid affair. The casket, covered by a Union Jack and piled high with wreaths, was carried from the Brantford train terminus to the Mohawk Chapel on a black horse-drawn hearse. The three most prominent chiefs from the Six Nations Reserve, along with George's fellow Masons and Odd Fellows, walked slowly behind it, followed by a large crowd of Brantford's citizens. At the graveside, five Anglican clergymen read the funeral service in English from their prayerbooks. The funeral mourners from the reserve then stepped forward and launched into the haunting atonal mourning chants that had accompanied native burials for centuries.

In late-Victorian Canada, a widow rarely attended her deceased husband's funeral. Emily remained at Chiefswood, with Pauline's friend

The Mohawk Chapel, built in 1785, was the first Royal
Chapel in the world belonging to native people, and the
final resting place of both Captain Joseph Brant and
Pauline's father, George Johnson.

Jeanie Morton (by then Reville) keeping her company. In the Mohawk cemetery, Beverly, Evelyn, Allen and Pauline, their faces impassive as they suppressed all emotion, stood a little apart and watched the scene. To an outsider, the shared grief of Indians and Europeans might have suggested that the dreams of Sir William Johnson, John "Smoke" Johnson and George Martin Johnson had been realized, that the two communities co-existed happily, respecting each other's traditions and contributions to community life. But nothing could be further from the truth. George Johnson's funeral marked the death of the old ideal. Canadians of European origin had already adopted the assumption, enshrined in government policy, that the "red race" would quietly, and conveniently, die out.

7

WAVE-ROCKED AND PASSION-TOSSED

1884—1888

ALTHOUGH George Johnson had been in poor health for years, his death was a dreadful shock. Life without him was unthinkable for his widow. The most immediate problem for Emily was the loss both of George's government salary and of any income from the reserve. George had left Emily an annuity, but it was too small to cover the maintenance costs of Chiefswood in the years ahead. A more fundamental issue for Emily was her own ambiguous status. If she had to leave Chiefswood, should she stay on the reserve or move into Brantford? By law she was a registered Indian, and her relations with her husband's family were friendly. Yet she had never felt that she belonged amongst the Mohawk people. She remained relentlessly English in her attitudes and aspirations.

Pauline's brothers had already left home and moved beyond the confines, both physical and psychological, of the Six Nations Reserve. Beverly, now thirty, was making a good career for himself in the rapidly expanding insurance industry. After a few years in Hamilton with Mutual Life, he had taken a job in Montreal with New York Life, as head cashier in the Canadian head office. Allen remained in Hamilton. He too was working in the insurance industry, but at twenty-six he still showed little enthusiasm for his nine-to-five job—he preferred being a man-about-town. Both boys tried to help their mother by sending her any cash they could spare, but it was Pauline's twenty-eight-year-old sister, Evelyn, who took the responsibility of providing her mother with housekeeping funds. Immediately after her father's death, Evelyn asked the local Indian Superintendent for a job in his Brantford office, and she was soon installed there as a filing clerk.

This left Pauline and her mother in unhappy isolation at Chiefswood. There was no longer money for Pauline's jaunts to friends in London and Hamilton, or for lavish entertaining if her friends arrived for a visit. And Emily remained catatonic with grief; her deep-set eyes were permanently bloodshot and ringed in dark shadows, and her blue-veined hands trembled with stress. She was unable to make any decision about her future. Chiefswood was the only home she had ever known.

Pauline was also devastated by the loss of her father, around whom the Chiefswood routines had revolved. But she had the resilience of youth and was eager to get on with her own life. She and her siblings all knew that the Chiefswood idyll was over. Eight months after their father's death, they found a small house in Brantford and persuaded their mother that she and her two daughters would be happier there. A local farmer took an eight-year lease on Chiefswood for $250 a year. Emily accepted the inevitable. But she was still too sad to help with

After Emily Johnson and her daughters left Chiefswood
in 1884, the mansion fell into disrepair.

the packing. While Evelyn and Pauline decided which possessions would accompany them and which must be sold, Emily wandered through Chiefswood's grounds, gathering a bunch of pansies. When everything was finally packed up, she reluctantly climbed into the carriage, the pansies carefully pressed between the pages of her Bible.

As the carriage rumbled down the dirt road towards Brantford, each woman watched in silence as her old home dwindled into the distance. Each was engulfed by the choking sadness that always accompanies departure from a home filled with happy memories. "The last I saw of Chiefswood," Evelyn wrote in her own memoirs, "was the house, dark, lonely and forsaken, the moonlight casting weird shadows on its lightless panes."

The three women settled into a small brick house with gingerbread trim on Napoleon Street, a few blocks from Brantford's Market Square. (The street was subsequently renamed Dufferin Street.) The rooms in the right-hand side of the duplex were poky and dark, with mean little arched windows, but the Johnsons managed to squeeze their most treasured possessions into the cramped new quarters. The

Number 7 Napoleon Street became home to Mohawk heirlooms, Emily Johnson's books and Pauline's ambitions.

rosewood Heintzman piano took up almost the entire parlour; on it was draped the red blanket on which the Duke of Connaught had stood in 1869. Other precious Indian artefacts were given pride of place. George Johnson's scalping knife, with its horn handle and Sheffield steel blade, and the tomahawk presented to him by the Cayugas in 1837 sat on the mantelpiece.

The Johnsons had opted to join the Brantford bourgeoisie as it hurtled towards the prosperity of the twentieth century. But visitors to Number 7 Napoleon Street were left in no doubt that the Johnsons' Mohawk legacy, rooted in the events of the eighteenth century, was just as important to this family as the latest agricultural invention or Toronto fashion. Nevertheless, ties to family and friends on the reserve gradually withered. Pauline's visits to Ohsweken became increasingly infrequent, particularly after the death of her grandfather, John "Smoke" Johnson, in 1886. At ninety-two, Smoke Johnson had been the oldest resident on the reserve, and the only remaining chief who could remember Joseph Brant and the War of 1812. Years later, Pauline acknowledged that she had never paid enough attention to the kindly old man's rambling reminiscences of his childhood: "I shall never forgive myself for letting grandfather die, with his wealth of knowledge, and I did not find out more of what he knew."

Each morning, Evelyn would dress quickly, pull her dark hair into a tight bun and walk briskly out of the front door and down Napoleon Street. She loved the regularity of her office job, her privileged relationship with Jasper Gilkison, the Indian Agent, and the pitifully small wages paid to her each Friday. Her younger sister had no such structured routine. Pauline frittered away much of her time visiting friends like Jeanie or the Curtises, or attending plays and recitals in Hamilton with Allen. She joined the Brantford Players, the local amateur dramatics society, and she was active at Grace Church, where the Reverend Garland Crawford Gordon Mackenzie, a genial bear of a man, was rector. Just as frequently, though, she found herself sitting morosely in her bedroom, craving a more exciting life. Her efforts to compose poetry with a view to publication were frustrated by constant calls from Emily, who needed help with the sewing, baking, dusting, canning, polishing, cleaning, shopping or cooking. These days, the Johnsons could afford only one part-time laundress to help with the endless housekeeping tasks that women of their period faced. Pauline's mood cannot have been improved by the endless chatter amongst her friends about "the New Woman," of which Brantford already boasted a surprising number.

The New Woman challenged every principle of female behaviour embraced by Emily Johnson. At the same time, the New Woman opened Pauline's eyes to revolutionary possibilities. This self-confident archetype believed that she had a right to the same privileges as men—a good education, paid work and outlets for athletic abilities— and to an egalitarian marriage. Heated debate on the justice of these claims filled the magazines and newspapers of British North America. As early as 1873, a citizen of Brantford wrote to the *Brantford Expositor* to uphold the good sense of women who chose not to marry: "all females do not require a male appendage to drag them through the years." Agnes Maule Machar, a well-known poet who happened to be the daughter of a former principal of Queen's University, published a call to arms in an 1879 article in *Rose Belford's Canadian Monthly*, in which she argued that women must stop thinking of themselves as handmaidens to their menfolk—a woman must make her own contribution to society. Miss Machar herself was a small, stern woman who never leavened her message with humour. "There is little doubt," she stiffly informed her readers, "that in the long run women will find themselves permitted to do what-

Agnes Maule Machar (1837–1927) was a poet and essayist who argued that women should make an independent contribution to society.

ever they should prove themselves able to do well." Miss Machar's arguments quickly provoked the outrage of various male commentators, such as the cantankerous Professor Goldwin Smith, editor of *The Week*. Smith had fled Cornell University in Ithaca, New York, in disgust when Cornell started to admit women, and had taken up residence in Toronto. History, however, was on the New Woman's side. Middle-class women were infiltrating not only the universities, but also the professions and the arts, and they were asserting their independence.

Perhaps Brantford was turning out an unusual number of New Women because, as a town on the move, it was always prepared to recognize talent. Or perhaps it was just a coincidence. Whatever the reason, ambitious young women found congenial company in the busy industrial centre on the Grand River. It was the first city to appoint a female school principal, Emily Howard Stowe. Emily went on to obtain a medical degree in the United States in 1867, and then became the first woman doctor to practise in Canada. In 1877, she founded the Toronto Women's Literary Club. Her daughter, Augusta Stowe, achieved equal prominence: she became the first woman to gain a medical degree in Canada when she was awarded her MD from Victoria College, Cobourg, in 1883.

The Stowe family lived in Mount Pleasant, just outside Brantford, where a frequent guest was another of Brantford's female pioneers, Sara Jeannette Duncan. While Pauline was brooding in her bedroom on Napoleon Street, Sara Jeannette Duncan, who was her exact contemporary, had already achieved Pauline's ambition: she was a recognized writer. The daughter of a prosperous Brantford furniture dealer, she had been christened Sarah Janet, and had exoticized her byline and had poems and articles published in several magazines. In 1886 she became the first woman to be employed full-time by the Toronto *Globe*, where she wrote under the pen name Garth Grafton. "Careers, if possible," she wrote in one of her first articles there, "and independence anyway, we must all have, as musicians, artists, writers, teachers, lawyers, doctors, ministers, or something."

Privately, Pauline may with justice have considered her own poetry superior to Sara's, but she recognized that Sara had something she

Pauline's passionate and lyric poetry
reflected her strong will.

herself lacked: the confident presumption (common amongst those, like Sara, with ample family resources) that she would always be taken seriously. The two young women moved in the same Brantford circles, but whenever they met, Pauline was intimidated by Sara's classic good looks, acerbic wit and air of success. Now in her early twenties, Pauline herself was wary of the "New Woman" label. "I hope I am not a 'Woman's Righter' or a masculine Amazon," she wrote to a male friend, "[just] because I sometimes despise the little-nesses that interest other women. I confess a likeness for certain feminine conventionalities such as five o'clock teas or 'hen Parties' . . . but I would everlastingly hate to dine on these things: they are but the peaches and cream that top the roast beef of life."

Pauline had scored her own small successes by the mid-1880s. In 1885, she and Evelyn were included in a delegation of seventeen people from the Six Nations Reserve who attended a ceremony in Buffalo honouring the Iroquois leader Sagoyewatha, also known as Red Jacket. Red Jacket was a fiery Seneca orator who had championed the Iroquois Confederacy and deplored encroachment on Iroquois lands and customs by European immigrants. He had died in 1830, but his remains were scheduled for re-interment fifty-five years later. The two granddaughters of the great Mohawk chief Smoke Johnson received official invitations to the occasion. Pauline immediately put pen to paper and wrote an ode to this "master mind" whose thought was "so vast, and liberal and strong." The ode was a paean of unalloyed admiration for the handsome advocate of Indian rights, but the poem's main thrust was a plea for reconciliation: "Forgive the wrongs my children did to you, / And we, the redskins, will forgive you too." It was not read out at the ceremony, but the Buffalo Senecas liked it enough to include it in a commemorative booklet. And it was probably the cause of an invitation to Pauline from the City of Brantford to write a poem for a similar ceremonial occasion: the unveiling of a statue of Joseph Brant, to stand in Victoria Square.

The Brantford ceremony, which took place in October 1886, began the way that all Brantford ceremonies began, with a parade led by the Dufferin Rifles Band. The city had made every effort to include its native neighbours; Iroquois chiefs and warriors from both Canada and the United States marched behind the band. Alongside the police, the firefighters, the Masons, the Odd Fellows, the Imperial Order of Foresters and the massed choirs of all Brantford's churches, they bowed their heads when the Reverend William Cochrane read the prayers and the 100th Psalm. Twelve of the chiefs assisted the Mayor in unveiling the splendid monument, designed by the famous British sculptor Percy Wood. The figure of Brant himself, and those figures representing the Mohawks, Oneidas, Onondagas, Cayugas, Senecas and Tuscaroras, were cast in bronze from British cannons that had been used at Waterloo and in the Crimean War.

The high point for Pauline and her family, however, came when William Foster Cockshutt, owner of Cockshutt Plough Limited and

Brantford Roofing and a future MP, rose to his feet. "The lines I am about to speak," he informed his audience, "are from the pen of Miss E. Pauline Johnson: they are creditable alike to the young Indian poetess and the race for whom she speaks." A few people began to clap, then the applause swelled as a slim figure, eye-catching in a fur-trimmed suit and hat, was assisted onto the platform of celebrities. Pauline was shown to a seat next to Mr. Cockshutt, who then declaimed, in his booming voice, her "Ode to Brant."

"Ode to Brant" has a darker tone than the Red Jacket poem. Pauline alluded to Brant's role in the Iroquois loss of "their valley home . . . blessed with every good from Heaven's hand" because of Brant's loyalty to Britain. Indians were doomed to extinction as a separate people, her poem implied, reflecting the grim logic of the Dominion government's new policy towards Indians. "Indian graves, and Indian memories," she wrote, "will fade as night comes on." But once again her overriding message was that natives and European immigrants can achieve "one common brotherhood." At this stage, Pauline chose not to challenge the status quo of race relations. Either she didn't see the need to rock the political boat or she was more concerned to establish herself as a literary figure. She certainly knew her mother would be shocked and hurt if she offended the local celebrities on the platform. Her ode ended with a ringing endorsement of British authority, embodied by "the loving hand of England's Noble Queen." When Cockshutt finished reading the poem, the crowd erupted into even louder applause as Pauline rose demurely to receive a bouquet of flowers. At the age of twenty-six, Pauline had made a discovery that she would put to good use in the years ahead: crowds love uplifting patriotism and a great outfit.

The following day, a long article about Pauline appeared in the Toronto *Globe*, written by Garth Grafton. Sara Jeannette Duncan, who had a good nose for a story, had already recognized that the half-Mohawk woman living quietly on Napoleon Street was someone to watch. Like Sara herself, Pauline had recently been discovered by Goldwin Smith's monthly journal *The Week*; despite the editor's wariness of clever women, at least six of Pauline's poems had appeared there in recent months. And Sara knew enough about the

Six Nations Reserve to find the Johnsons' family history intriguing. She resolved, she told her readers, "that all Canadiennes deserve to enjoy" Pauline's acquaintanceship. However, Sara was intent on making Pauline out to be as exotic as possible. Small facts such as the colour of Pauline's hair (brown) and her petite stature (5 foot 2 inches) were not allowed to get in the way of Sara's portrait of a powerful, raven-haired warrior princess: "She is tall and slender and dark, with grey eyes, beautifully clean cut features, black hair, a very sweet smile," Sara wrote, "and a clear, musical, pleasant voice. . . . She has certainly that highest attribute of beauty, the rare, fine gift of expression. She is charmingly bright in conversation, and has a vivacity of tone and gesture that is almost French."

Sara interviewed Pauline in the parlour at 7 Napoleon Street, where she was fascinated by the Indian relics. Pauline showed her George Johnson's scalping knife. The writer knew how to spice the interview with just the right blood-curdling touches for the *Globe* readership:

> "But don't they-didn't-he-I mean isn't it unusual for people who indulge in that kind of amusement to do it with their tomahawks?" I inquired rather delicately, for I wasn't at all sure that their fair descendant would relish this allusion to the peculiarities of her warrior ancestors. My compunctions were unnecessary. "Oh, no!" she laughed. "It would be very awkward to scalp with a tomahawk. You see, this is the way they do it," and she raised some of her own dusky locks and made a mimic circle around it.
>
> "Really!" I said, "Please don't. I always thought that to scalp a person was to deprive him of his hirsute adornment out and out!" "I know most people think that," she responded, "but it is only a single lock and the portion of scalp it grows on. I saw once a scarf of several hundred and fifty Indian scalps, all braided together with beads and things."

"Garth Grafton" ended her article on an upbeat note. Miss Johnson's poems, she suggested, "have a dreamy quality that is very charming, and while she has given us no sustained work as yet, we

*Pauline and her girlfriends (unidentified in this photograph)
frequently picnicked on the banks of the Grand River.*

may doubtless expect it ere long." Pauline was encouraged by Sara's prediction, but it was only half right. Pauline continued to work hard on her literary technique and tone, turning out both poetry and prose that appeared with increasing regularity in the handful of small-circulation literary journals that limped along in Canada. But it would be a while before she had reason to feel that she was taken as seriously as Sara Jeannette Duncan.

Most frequently Pauline found herself described with the kind of patronizing phrase employed by the *Toronto World* reporter who covered the unveiling of the Brant statue. "Miss Pauline Johnson," he told his readers, is "a pleasant looking Indian maiden [who] is the writer of some good verse." Pauline's rebuttal, preserved in her scrapbook, reveals both a quick wit and a thin skin:

Alas! how damning praise can be!
This man so scared of spoiling me
Shook all the honey from his pen
Dipped it in acid, and scribbled then—
"No compliments on her I'll laden
She's but a pleasant looking maiden."

*   *   *

Pauline Johnson was now twenty-six years old. In the next five years, her output consisted largely of poetry—much of it lyric poetry which is rarely reproduced today. Many of the poems share the same theme: nostalgia for a lost lover with whom she spent happy hours in a canoe. Does he remember her? the poems ask. No private diary or personal letters detailing her romances have survived, so the verses themselves are the only clues to what was going on in her heart. The poems are sentimental and unmistakeably erotic; they combine exquisite phrasing, awkward diction and echoes of Swinburne. In 1888, for example, *Saturday Night* published "Unguessed," which includes the lines

> Beneath this tangled bower
> We've idled many an hour
> And tossed away too many tender days—
> I quite content in love
> To watch your face above
> The netted couch, in which you lie, that softly floats and
>   sways.

> Did young Apollo wear
> A face than yours more fair,
> More purely blonde, in beauty more complete?
> Beloved, will not you
> Unclose those eyes of blue
> That hold my world and bless and curse the life they render
>   sweet?

Two years later, Pauline published "The Idlers," a poem of breathtaking intensity in the same metre, and with the same aching sense of impending disappointment:

> The sun's red pulses beat
> Full prodigal of heat,
> Full lavish of its lustre unrepressed,
> But we have drifted far
> From where his kisses are,

And in this landward-lying shade we let our paddle rest.
So silently we two
Lounge in our still canoe
Nor fate nor fortune matters to us now—
So long as we alone
May call this dream our own—
The breeze may die, the sail may droop, we care not when or
   how.

Against the thwart near by
Inactively you lie,
And all too near my arm your temple bends,
Your indolently crude
Abandoned attitude
Is one of ease and art with which a perfect languor blends.

Your costume loose and light
Leaves unconcealed your might
Of muscle so exquisitely defined,
And falling well aside,
Your vesture opens wide
Above your splendid sun-burnt throat that pulses
   unconfined.

With easy unreserve,
Across the gunwale's curve
Your arm superb is lying brown and bare.
Your hand just touches mine
With import firm and fine—
(I kiss the very wind that blows about your tumbled hair.)

But once, the silence breaks,
But once, your ardour wakes
To words that humanize this lotus land,
So perfect and complete
Those eager words and sweet,

So perfect is the single kiss your lips lay on my hand.
Has destiny a bliss,
A counterpart of this
Wild flame your kiss has left upon my palm?
Does heat respond to heat?
Does fire with fervour meet?
Or does a storm tempestuous but image empty calm?

The uninhibited passion of Pauline's love poetry leaps out at the reader. So does the way, unique for the period, that she portrays herself as the active partner in the romance. In most nineteenth-century love poetry, the woman is a delicate, passive flower overwhelmed by her lover's ardour. That is how Emily Johnson expected to be treated. But Pauline is no shrinking violet: in all her poems, she is in charge of the canoe in which the lovers sit ("My arm as strong as steel . . . the boat obeyed my hand") and the momentum of the affair ("My hand still tingles where / It touched your windblown hair"). But who was the object of Pauline's passion? Who was her young Apollo?

"Pauline had many offers of marriage," her sister Evelyn recorded. "Few of these were Indians. I know of eight that she received, but of those she had later when she began to travel, I do not know." There were so many opportunities for Pauline to meet young men—at church, with the Brantford Players, at the canoe meets that she had started attending. Critic Carole Gerson observes that the love poetry falls into two distinct groups, suggesting two chapters to this period of Pauline's life. One group of poems, dating from the 1880s, suggests a liaison with a young man who offers only friendship rather than love and who disappears to England. The second group dates from 1890 and points to another romantic encounter which also ends sadly with the young man's departure. In Pauline's scrapbook at Chiefswood, there is a small, undated, anonymous photo of a handsome young man in a beautiful cedar-strip canoe. A melancholy pervades much of Pauline's verse as she wonders whether a boating companion recalls the days spent "In listless indolence entranced and lost, / Wave-rocked and passion-tossed."

Names flit in and out of Pauline's own correspondence, and of reminiscences of her recorded by others. There was "the fancy Londoner," Hugh Hartshorne, whom Pauline mentioned to Lottie Jones and who remained a family friend. There were two regular canoeing partners, James Watt and Frank Russell. There was Cameron Wilson, who would call at Napoleon Street to talk to Pauline, only to discover that she was out and he had to make polite conversation with Evelyn. There was Archie Chetwode Kains, who was briefly manager of the Canadian Bank of Commerce's Brantford branch in 1888, and with whom Pauline had a lively but chaste correspondence after he moved to New York City.

Many of these suitors treasured a tobacco pouch or handkerchief sachet, hand sewn by Pauline and sent to them with an intimate note. ("I have spent many pleasant hours embroidering . . . pleasant memories into this little sachet," she wrote to Archie. "Of course you have other sachets, but ever selfish, I wish you would use mine, just because I designed it specially for you.") On one occasion, as a group of young people was about to set off on a canoe trip, Douglas Reville ostentatiously pulled out of his pocket a fine leather tobacco pouch on which Pauline had embroidered his monogram. Immediately, five other young men pulled out identical pouches on which Pauline had embroidered their initials.

Maybe there were two particular beaux. Maybe there were more. Maybe there were several lighthearted flirtations and one heartbreaking affair. "I wonder why women think that because you are fond of a person you must necessarily be in love with them," mused Pauline herself in another letter to Archie. "Bless me, if I were in love with Laddie and Jeff and all the boys I am fond of I would never have any appetite left for breakfast and I am painfully healthy."

One particular name, however, spirals down through the years: Michael Mackenzie, son of the Reverend Garland Crawford Gordon Mackenzie of Grace Church.

Michael Mackenzie was a young teenager, and the Johnsons still lived at Chiefswood, when Pauline first met him. Michael's father had arrived in Brantford in 1879 after spending most of the previous ten years as minister in Haliburton and Kincardine. For the rector, the large and growing industrial town was a big switch from rural parishes where most of his congregation still lived in log houses and made their living from the land. But the Reverend Mackenzie quickly made Grace Church, an ugly brick building on the west side of Brantford, the town's leading Anglican place of worship. Filled with the benevolent paternalism typical of leading churchmen of the day, "Maxie," as the good rector was known, threw himself into his work. During the forty years he spent in the parish, he set up a coal and grocery fund for Brantford's poor, got three more Anglican churches built, founded a large (but not always tuneful) choir, and each year organized a summer camp on Lake Erie for boys from underprivileged homes.

The Grace Church rectory, on the corner of Charlotte and Darling streets, was on the other side of town from Grace Church, so the sight of a bulky, black-coated figure striding across Victoria Park, past Joseph Brant's statue and down Nelson or Wellington street soon became familiar to Brantford citizens. The rector's wife, Helen, was a tall, elegant woman, with a ready smile and endless patience for her six children and the gaggle of relatives and visitors who thronged the rectory. Those who dined at the rectory were always amazed at the fare; thanks to relatives scattered through India and the West Indies, the Mackenzies had developed a taste for such exotica as curried fish, melons with black pepper, fruit stewed with ginger, and red peppers liberally used in salads.

The Mackenzie family played a large role in both Brantford and the Johnsons' lives. The Reverend Maxie was on the platform in 1886 when the Brant memorial statue was unveiled and Pauline's ode read out. He served on the boards of all the local institutions, such as the Public Library, the Institute for the Blind and the Brantford Sanatorium. As his granddaughter wrote in a family memoir, "His great social gifts were at his Master's service; he made the humblest household feel that he was happy to be with them." This often meant accepting a cup of tea even though the proffered cup was filthy; he had learned to prefer, in the Scottish parlance of the day, to take his tea "strong enough to trot a mouse." He enjoyed calling on his parishioners, and regularly visited Emily Johnson in the parlour on Napoleon Street. And Pauline would frequently join in the evenings of charades and musical chairs at the rectory, when Francie (the only girl in the Mackenzie brood) would play the upright piano with its blue silk panels, and Norman (the youngest son) would serenade his terrier on his flute. The highlight of the evening usually came when Francie persuaded her father to give a solo performance of his favourite ballad, "When Polly and I Were Sweethearts."

In Evelyn Johnson's unpublished memoir, Pauline and Michael Mackenzie are described as setting off one warm July day on an excursion down the winding Grand River towards the Six Nations Reserve, eighteen miles (twenty-nine kilometres) away. They planned to stay overnight with friends in Onondaga and return the next day. Their parents must have assumed, with the blithe naïveté of middle age, that a canoe was too unstable to allow for much horseplay, so it was

Michael Mackenzie, future professor of
mathematics at the University of Toronto:
was he the young man in the locket that
Pauline wore throughout her life?

perfectly proper for the young couple to paddle off together. Judging by the sensuality of Pauline's poetry, their confidence may have been misplaced.

It is easy to imagine what an attractive couple Pauline and Michael made that day. She would be wearing her favourite "New Woman" canoe outfit: a saucy tam with a red pompom on her head, a white sailor blouse and colourful kerchief, a blue serge skirt and (most significantly) no corset. Michael would be in a close-fitting cotton sweater and flannel trousers, probably rolled up to allow him to dip his feet into the water. They packed a picnic lunch for the following day and tied two bottles of ale to the stern of the canoe to cool in the water. The canoe trip took a surprisingly long time, and the participants were too absorbed in their conversation to notice what was happening behind them. When their thirst finally reminded them of the ale and they hauled up the string, they were surprised to find only the bottle necks on the line. The bottles had smashed miles earlier.

Was Pauline sweet on Michael? Mackenzie family legend holds this to be true. Michael was the kind of handsome youth—a blue-eyed Apollo—for whom Pauline always had a soft spot, and his impeccable Anglican background would have appealed to both Pauline and her mother. He was, unfortunately, five years younger than Pauline (one of her most lighthearted poems from this period begins, "I've been having a whacking flirtation / With a boy not twenty years old: / And although I am five years his senior, / That ugly fact need not be told"). Perhaps this was the reason that, despite the passion evident in Pauline's more serious verses, the friendship never blossomed into anything. Pauline's poetry, as in this passage from "Unguessed," makes it plain that the object of her affections, consciously or unconsciously, chooses not to recognize that her heart is bursting with love:

> I wonder how you rest
> So calmly when my breast
> Is tortured by the efforts that I make
> To strangle love and keep

His ensign from my cheek
To still the passion in my heart just for our friendship's
   sake.

There was no room for serious romance in Michael's life. At eighteen, he had entered Trinity College, Toronto, on the first Dickson Scholarship in Mathematics. By the time he and Pauline were drifting down the Grand River, he had already won two further math scholarships, plus additional awards for physical and natural science and for mental and moral philosophy. A brilliant academic career beckoned as long as he kept winning scholarships and did not get sidetracked. Money was tight in the rectory, where the motto was "Make Do and T'will Serve." On lazy summer afternoons, in the gently rocking canoe, he and Pauline probably discussed their dreams: his ambition to attend a great university in the Old Country; her hope of international recognition for her poetry. For Michael, a flirtation with a published poet several years his senior was a boyish escapade—an hors d'oeuvre to the serious business of life. Her Mohawk blood only enhanced her appeal to him. When Pauline reproached him for his preference for older women, he replied, "If two plates of apples were placed before me, and one contained ripe fruit and the other green fruit, which do you think I should choose?" He revelled in Pauline's attention and enjoyed her lively wit; judging by her poetry, both were swept away by physical passion. But Michael had the ruthlessness of ambitious youth, and, metaphorically at least, he kept Pauline at arm's length.

In 1887, Michael Mackenzie graduated from Trinity with top marks. His family recognized his exceptional abilities: an uncle in England agreed to underwrite his further education. Michael left Brantford that summer to spend the next three years studying mathematics at Selwyn College, Cambridge, England. He graduated in 1890 with a brilliant first-class degree but was apparently in no hurry to come home. Instead, he stayed on in England for a further four years to teach at a school in Folkestone, a town on the south coast. In 1888, Pauline published a poem called "My English Letter," which describes how much she looks forward to "those dear words" on the "folded note" that arrives each month by boat from "the Mother-land." She has never visited Britain, and she is not particularly eager to do so:

> And yet my letter brings the scenes I covet,
> Framed in the salt sea winds, aye more in dreams
> I almost see the face that bent above it,
> I almost touch that hand, so near it seems.

Seven years is a long time to wait, especially when there has been no spoken commitment on either side. While Michael Mackenzie was still at Cambridge, he went to Ireland for a holiday with his second cousins, the Nivens, whose family home, Chrome Hill, was ten miles (sixteen kilometres) west of Belfast, on the banks of the River Logan. There he met Maud, a young woman of twenty-four: soon he was crossing the Irish Sea at every opportunity (once he even attempted to row across). Maud Niven found this young Apollo just as attractive as the girls in Brantford had. By 1893, they were engaged; to their families' satisfaction, Michael and Maud were married on July 6, 1895, in Grace Church, Brantford. Michael Mackenzie went on to teach mathematics at the University of Toronto, ending his career there as a full professor. There is no record of whether he kept in touch with any of his old friends from Brantford, least of all Pauline Johnson.

But some young man, and Michael Mackenzie seems the most likely candidate, left a permanent scar on Pauline Johnson's heart. A poem entitled "Close By," which appeared in *Saturday Night* in 1889, is a haunting elegy for a lost love:

> Once, many days ago, we almost held it,
> The love we so desired,
> But our shut eyes saw not, and fate dispelled it
> Before our pulses fired
> To flame, and errant fortune bade us stand
> Hand almost touching hand.

I sometimes think had we two been discerning—
The bypath hid away
From others eyes had then revealed its turning
To us, nor led astray
Our footsteps, guiding us into love's land
That lay so near at hand.

What then availed the red wine's subtle glisten?
We passed it blindly by,
And now what profit that we wait and listen
Each for the other's heart beat? Ah! the cry
Of love o'erlooked still lingers, you and I
Sought Heaven afar, we did not understand
'Twas then so near at hand.

The following year, Pauline reflected on the pain of unrequited love in a letter to her friend Archie Kains, who had recently moved from Brantford to New York City. "Women don't get rid of these things by putting on their hats and lounging off to the theatre or smoking a consoling cigar," she wrote. "Girls must grin and bear it in silence, and the fun you enjoy may be so serious to her. . . . If it is the man who loves he may and does speak . . . if the woman loves what is there for her but silence, assumed indifference, and desolation?"

Throughout her adult life, Pauline Johnson wore a silver locket. Inside was a photograph of a good-looking young man. She would never part with the locket, nor would she tell her friends the identity of its occupant. We will never know whether Michael Mackenzie was the lost lover. But in 1927, as a distinguished former resident of Brantford, Professor Mackenzie was invited by the *Brantford Expositor* to write some recollections of his boyhood for a special edition marking the fiftieth anniversary of the city's incorporation. He wrote fondly of canoe trips down the river, where there were so "many charming spots for lunch or tea." He singled out for mention, as his favourite companion for such outings, Pauline Johnson.

8

THE CANOEING
CRAZE

1888–1892

LIKE most of their Six Nations neighbours, the four Johnson
children had grown up with paddles in their hands. As soon as
each could sit safely in a small craft, George Johnson had carefully dropped his canoe into the Grand River, then lifted the child into
the bow. The older two children never exhibited much enthusiasm for
paddling, but Allen and Pauline were instantly at home on the water.
While they were still small, they mastered the various paddle strokes
that enabled them to skim forwards or backwards across the river,
carve an elegant curve through smooth water, steer firmly in the middle of the current or surge through the boiling waves of a set of rapids.
Their first solo expeditions, when they were still small, were limited
to the broad, fast-moving stretch of flat water in front of Chiefswood.
Emily would stand on the shore, white-lipped with anxiety. The old
ferryman, Jessie Green, and his passengers were nearby, ready to go to
the rescue in case of disaster, but this had no effect on her fear. She
only calmed down when she was confident that her children were
proficient in and on the water.

By the time Pauline was a teenager, she was a supremely skilful
canoeist. Naturally athletic, she had inherited her father's sense of
style, particularly when anybody was watching. Her bow stroke was
long and quick; when she knelt in the stern, she could turn the blade
of the paddle with a quick twist of her wrist to counteract the canoe's
inclination to move in circles. She knew how to lean forward at the
end of a stroke so that her body did most of the work and her arms

remained stiff. She steered the canoe from either side and either end, with little apparent effort. She could use the gunnel as a fulcrum to lever the paddle out of the water to recover her control. She knew how to angle the canoe against the wind and how to squat flat on her heels so she didn't catch the wind. She had the balance of a ballerina, the strength of a gymnast.

What she most enjoyed, however, were the moments on the water when her adrenalin surged—when she was racing Allen or his friend Hugh Hartshorne, for example, or when whitewater foamed before her. "There is nothing in life that sends me as crazy as a rapid," she once admitted. "My brain goes aflame when I see the distant white-caps, my heart pulses wildly with the first faint music of waters galloping madly over their rocky obstructions, singing, surging, laughing their endless reckless poetry—the world holds no such music for me as the cool calling of waters that my bow will kiss and conquer before the hour is over." The erotic thrill in Pauline's tone is unmistakeable.

Whenever she had a spare hour or two on a bright afternoon,

In her canoe Wildcat, Pauline would often drift
dreamily down the Grand River.

Pauline would paddle off in *Wildcat*, her elegant cedar-strip canoe. "My canoe . . . takes the place with me of a cigar to a man," she wrote Archie Kains, adding coquettishly, "I wish you were here. I would run you down the rapids today and we would put up a sail in the quiet water beyond. It would be perfect." In later years Douglas Reville would recall, "To know her best was during one of the canoeing trips she loved so much."

It was Pauline's good fortune that her skill in the traditional Indian means of travel coincided with the canoeing craze. In the 1880s and 1890s, canoeing was as fashionable amongst the young and affluent as snowboarding is today. There were various reasons for the enthusiasm: the increased wealth and leisure available for the urban middle class; the urge to escape the smog and noise of industrial cities and enjoy the back lakes; the romantic possibilities (as Pauline and Michael Mackenzie had demonstrated) of canoe expeditions. The chief reason, though, was technological. During the 1860s, settlers in and around the Peterborough area of Ontario successfully adapted European boat-building techniques to Indian canoe design. The result was the cedar-strip canoe—easily manufactured, light, sturdy and ideally suited to Canada's lakes and rivers.

When Pauline Johnson was growing up at Chiefswood, most of her father's friends and relatives used canoes as their principal form of transport on the Grand River. Canoes, both dugout and birchbark, had been developed centuries earlier by North American Indians and were the ideal vessel for a vast continent in which the major thoroughfares were waterways. The slender boats, the shape of which has always been some variation on an elongated slice of melon, could be manoeuvred through any type of water—shallow streams, island-studded lakes, fast-flowing rivers. They could be turned upside down and used as shelters at campsites. Birchbark canoes could be lifted out of the water and carried ("portaged," as early French settlers said) past rapids. Native canoes exemplified the skilled workmanship of their makers. They were also art forms that symbolized the harmonious relationship between their creators and the land that supplied the materials.

The type of canoe used depended on where a particular band lived.

Birchbark canoes were made in the regions in which birch trees (*Betula papyrifera*) were common in the forest. The birch belt was an irregular strip of land that stretched from Newfoundland to the lower end of British Columbia and covered the territory of several Indian peoples, including the Beothuk and the Miqmaq on the east coast and the Algonquin nation in the centre of the continent. The canoe-makers began by carefully peeling the paper-like bark from the tree trunk in large sheets, then securing it to skeletons of ribs crafted from roots or branches that had grown naturally curved. The birchbark sheets were pinched together fore and aft and sewn together at the joins. The seams were painted with pitch to waterproof them.

The second type of native canoe, popular in regions outside the birch belt, was the dugout. A large tree (usually pine, cedar or basswood) was hollowed out, then its sides softened with hot water so that strong thwarts could be inserted between them to splay them outwards. Once the sides had been moulded to the desired curvature, the hot water was emptied out and the shell allowed to dry. According to George Johnson, Pauline's father, Iroquois warriors always rubbed the prows of their canoes with the brains of muskellunge because it made them glide through the water even faster in a race. The Haida, Nootka and Coast Salish peoples on the west coast all constructed massive and magnificent dugout cedar canoes, often more than forty feet (twelve metres) long, which were decorated in brilliant colours and were solid enough to face ocean waves. More modest dugouts were in common use in central Canada by the Mississauga Indians. The Iroquois nations were not particularly known for canoe construction; dugouts were the most common craft on the Six Nations Reserve when Pauline was growing up.

Early European settlers acquired both birchbark and dugout canoes from native peoples, and quickly learned to rely on them as Indians always had—for exploration, travel, fishing and hunting expeditions, even recreation. John Moodie, who arrived in the Peterborough area northeast of Toronto in 1834, bought a cedar dugout from the local Chippewa and fixed a keel and sail to it. His wife, the British-born writer Susanna Moodie, described in *Roughing It in the Bush* the pleasant sails they took together on Lake Katchewanooka. She also wrote about the expedition that they made in a birchbark canoe to Stony Lake, several miles distant.

But both dugout and birchbark canoes were laborious to make, and each had serious disadvantages from the European point of view. The dugouts were heavy to lift over portages and often clumsy in appearance; Susanna Moodie's nephew George Strickland admitted that his first attempt "looked more like a hog trough than a boat." The birchbark canoes were much lighter, but they were flimsy because the birchbark skins were easily punctured. "Every bark canoe carried on board a pitch pot and pitch," *The Field*, the favourite magazine of Britain's huntin' and shootin' set, explained in 1880, "and when the paddler struck a sunken rock or snag . . . he had to paddle ashore as quickly as possible, light a fire, melt the pitch and repair the leak. This, to say the least of it, was rather awkward and trying to the temper, especially if it happened while trying to get within shooting distance of a fine large buck." Moreover, the supply of birchbark began to dry up during the nineteenth century as settlers crowded into North America.

One of the first to experiment with new ways to construct canoes was a mill owner in Peterborough. John Stephenson had trained as a blacksmith, and he was proficient with both metal and wood. He was also a keen huntsman who was tired of shouldering a heavy dugout over portages between the lakes around Peterborough. In the late 1850s, he began to experiment with bentwood constructions. It is possible that he got the idea from an unusual bentwood Indian canoe brought from the Pacific Ocean by the great map-maker David Thompson several decades earlier. Or perhaps Stephenson simply started playing around, seeing if he could treat wood like metal. First, he built a mould that looked like an upturned boat, with the exact dimensions of the ideal canoe. Next, he steamed straight strips of hardwood until they were flexible, and bent them over the mould, attaching them with nails, in the same way he attached iron hoops to wooden staves when he was making barrels in his mill. Last, he nailed thin, wide basswood boards lengthwise at right angles to the steam-bent ribs and sealed the seams. When the complete canoe was assembled, it was gradually worked free from its mould and the nails were clenched on the inside.

By 1861, the year of Pauline's birth, Stephenson's board canoes were participating in canoe races around Peterborough, and customers were snapping up every canoe he could produce. Soon other local craftsmen started making bentwood canoes, and the Peterborough region became known for its canoes. Another British immigrant in Peterborough, William English, purchased a mould from Stephenson and went into production. At Lakefield, where the Stricklands lived, a former Quebecer, Thomas Gordon, began building cedar-strip canoes. At Gore's Landing, twenty miles (thirty-two kilometres) south on Rice Lake, a burly young Irish shipwright named Daniel Herald was working on a different prototype for a planked canoe: a double-walled, ribless craft in which a sheet of waterproofed canvas was sealed between two layers of thin planks. By 1880, canoes from Peterborough were turning up all over the world. Various models were sent to exhibitions as far afield as Philadelphia, Paris and Australia; in 1883, one of Dan Herald's Rice Lake canoes won a gold medal at the Fisheries Exhibition in London. During these years, a seventeen-foot (five-metre) "Peterborough" craft would arrive at Whiteley's Department Store in Bayswater or Cordings' Sporting Goods Store in Piccadilly, London, with five progressively smaller "Peterboroughs" nestled inside. Since transoceanic shipping charges were calculated by bulk size, this procedure allowed great savings in costs. On the canoes' arrival, the shopkeepers would fit the decks and thwarts into place.

Alongside the increased availability of canoes, there was a further reason for the late-nineteenth-century canoe craze that swept the United States and British Isles as well as Canada. A wealthy English barrister named John MacGregor fired the imagination of a whole generation with a series of books he published in London in the 1860s and 1870s about canoeing in Europe, the Baltic, Egypt and Palestine. Mac-Gregor called his European-designed craft a "Rob Roy Canoe," but strictly speaking, it was a kayak, not a canoe. The ninety-pound, fifteen-foot (forty-kilogram, four-and-a-half-metre) boat had decks fore and aft, and MacGregor used a double-bladed paddle. But it boasted all the advantages of a canoe: it was sturdy and light, and it allowed its single occupant to navigate any form of inland waterway. MacGregor's books went into countless printings. In common with other Victorian explorers such as David Livingstone, MacGregor was an enthusiastic performer on the lecture circuit, with hair-raising stories of near-death experiences and lantern slide shows of pounding waterfalls and surging rapids.

MacGregor was messianic about the benefits of paddling. He argued that canoe trips allowed true Christian soldiers to renew themselves physically and spiritually before returning to the workaday battle against the world, the flesh and the devil. Such muscular Christianity struck a nerve in Victorian Britain and Canada, where growing consciousness of the cruel impact of capitalism on the urban poor was spawning such movements as the Salvation Army and the Settlement societies. And when MacGregor decided to found a canoe club in London in 1866, he enlisted Edward, Prince of Wales, as co-founder. (Edward had got the canoeing bug during his 1860 trip to Canada, when the Strickland family presented to him a racing dugout finished with French polish.) Thanks to the Prince of Wales's support, the club was renamed the Royal Canoe Club in 1873. With both God and royalty on his side, MacGregor's campaign to promote canoeing could hardly fail.

Back in Brantford, Pauline Johnson may have been aware of the Rob Roy canoe and the Royal Yacht Club. She certainly knew about the revolution in canoe technology and the rising enthusiasm for canoes. Much of her social life revolved around them. In common with most small Ontario towns situated on water, Brantford had its own Canoe Club (founded in 1877). It couldn't rival the Toronto Canoe Club (founded in 1880) for size or sophistication, but like the Toronto club it had a handsome fleet of cedar-strip Peterboroughs and an annual summer regatta in which there were both paddling and sailing races. Only men were allowed to enter the single paddle races at the regatta, but Pauline ran down the river path to cheer on those she had taught to paddle in her own Peterborough canoe, *Wildcat*. Women were allowed to paddle in the bow, with a man in the stern, in the "tandem canoe, ladies and gentlemen half-mile race," and on September 21, 1889, Pauline and Alick Mackenzie, Michael's younger brother, won the tandem trophy.

"The Regatta was the sporting event of the season here," she wrote to Archie Kains that year, "and of course I was in my element." Her friends, she confided, "love to see me in my vagabond clothes . . . my flannel canoeing shirt and tam," and she was thrilled when they called her "the best boy in the crowd." It was always a wrench when the days grew cooler and she had to content herself with Brantford's more conventional social occasions, which required ostrich feathers and evening dresses. Elegant satin gowns, she wrote, revealed "my hideous muscular arms, bare and burnt . . . Oh well, in a few weeks I will get over it, and will handle a fan as readily as a paddle I suppose." But Canoe Club activities lasted all year. During the winter months, Club members threw themselves into amateur theatricals, in which Pauline often took the female lead. One year, she helped organize a performance of William S. Gilbert's *On Guard*, "a little comedy in aid of the canoe fleet." It wasn't only the Canoe Club that benefitted from these performances: Pauline, already a star of the Brantford Players, acquired considerable confidence in front of the footlights as a performer of light verse and comic dialogue.

Racing was only one element in the canoe craze; recreation was another, and Pauline was equally involved with this. In the late 1880s, she was invited by friends to join a camping and canoeing trip to the township of Rosseau, at the northern end of Lake Rosseau in Muskoka. She quickly discovered that "this gypsy life" was the life "I love best of all." She would return to Rosseau each summer for the next few years. The summer camping expeditions provided her with both inspiration and material for her poetry.

On her first trip, in 1888, Pauline and her friends (probably members of the Brantford Canoe Club) disembarked at Muskoka Wharf Station along with several dozen other dusty vacationers from the tri-weekly express train from Toronto. On that hot August afternoon, Pauline gazed in wonder at "this rockbound, fir-covered Muskoka with its exquisite lakes and their myriad islands" stretching as far as the eye could see. Only the *toot-toot* of a steamer's whistle reminded her that she should be helping load luggage (including canoes, sails, tents, fishing rods and iron cooking pots) onto the *Kanozha*, one of the Muskoka Navigation Company's fleet of lake steamers. Once passengers and possessions were aboard, the steamer pulled away from the

*At Port Carling, in the Muskoka region, city dwellers could
rent anything from a small canoe to an elegant steam launch.*

wharf and nosed its way north across Lake Muskoka towards Port
Carling, where passengers would change onto the steamers that plied
the shores of lakes Joseph and Rosseau. Captain Henry, on the bridge
of the *Kanozha*, entertained his passengers by telling them to watch
out for wildlife: black bears, he informed them, could often be seen on
the shore, and one season the *Kanozha* had run down two deer that
were swimming across the lake.

The Muskoka region, 120 miles (193 kilometres) north of Toronto,
had been "discovered" less than twenty years earlier. In the 1860s, the
area around Lake Muskoka, Lake Joseph and Lake Rosseau had been
regarded as wild, inaccessible and far too rocky to attract settlers. But
when the new railroad opened in 1875 connecting Toronto to the
southern tip of Lake Muskoka beyond Gravenhurst, the region
quickly became a fashionable summer playground. It attracted families anxious to escape from the city, sportsmen eager to hunt and fish,
amateur botanists keen to "botanize" and canoeists who wanted to
explore its crystal-clear waters and deep bays. The dramatic scenery of
"The Highlands of Ontario," as its promoters called the region, was
extolled in advertising brochures and newspaper columns throughout

eastern North America, and tourists flooded in. Many were up-and-comers in Toronto's professional class; by the 1890s the published lists of cottage owners, along with weekly reports on who was staying at which hotel, read like a *Who's Who* of Toronto society. But there were plenty of humbler holidaymakers who enjoyed the bathing, berry-picking, sketching and churchgoing summer routines.

On that first trip, Pauline hung over the steamer rail, admiring the cottages and resort hotels scattered along the shores of the three major lakes. Some of the cottages were simple clapboard fishing shacks; others, such as the one owned by the retail king Timothy Eaton, were grand stone buildings with sweeping verandahs and boat-houses full of skiffs and canoes. "One expects to see almost everything in Muskoka—from a palace to a bivouac, from a prince to a pauper," observed Pauline. Once into Lake Rosseau, she was captivated by the scenery: "How different is this stern, rock-girdled lake to our own beloved river—the dear old Grand that purrs away in its nest of velvet hills. . . . These waters and shores are filled with a vastness of character that our own native river can never hope to attain."

Since Rosseau township was the steamer's last call, it was evening by the time the Brantford party arrived there. The sight that met their eyes was enthralling. Despite the fact that of all the Muskoka resorts, Rosseau was the farthest from Toronto's Union Station, in those years it boasted the region's most lavish hotel. Monteith House was a three-storey lodge built in 1886 and boasting a roller-skating rink, a tennis court, extensive stables and accommodation for servants. It was stuffed with animal trophies (including the skin from a 1,600-pound—725 kilogram—polar bear) because John Monteith, the owner, was a passionate hunter. Many of the trophies were displayed in the hotel's "Indian Room," which also featured a birchbark wigwam. On warm summer nights, the gentle glow of Chinese lanterns along the hotel's porch and the tinkle of the piano in the ballroom were magical.

Monteith House, of course, was far beyond the means of Brantford Canoe Club members. The canoeists more likely chose Rosseau because it was also home to the four Ditchburn brothers from England. William Ditchburn was a vigorous Rosseau-booster: he was the village postmaster, his wife headed the Women's Auxiliary and his brothers and sons built, sold and rented rowboats, skiffs and canoes. Until the Ditchburns moved their business to Gravenhurst some years later, Rosseau was a magnet for those who loved messing about in boats. There were plenty of spots along the shoreline, between birches and pines, on which visitors could pitch camp and enjoy the "gypsy life" in this wilderness paradise. Pauline's group camped on a promontory about half a mile (just under a kilometre) from the village, close to a cottage called Camp Knockabout owned by Mr. and Mrs. Walter Wilkes of Brantford, who chaperoned the party. The group would return to Camp Knockabout for all its subsequent Muskoka excursions.

Pauline Johnson had none of the snake-phobic fastidiousness of the stereotypical Victorian lady; she loved life in the outdoors. Not for her the ruffled linen blouses and tea gowns required for a sojourn in a resort hotel. She preferred to cram her bags with the candles, canned meat and coarse grey blankets required for a month of sleeping rough. No repast was more appetizing, in her opinion, than one cooked over an open fire: "The tin coffee-pot may have all the ashes of a thousand camp-fires clinging to its smoky sides, the butter may be garnished with myriads of brown pine-needles, the marmalade may be excavated from its primitive wide-mouthed glass bottle by means of a steel knife-blade, the canned beef may be warm and shapeless, the slices of bread ragged and huge, but ah! the deliciousness of it all, out under the giant forest trees." After dinner, if someone produced a banjo, she was the first to lead the singsong. At night, she was never more content than when under canvas, listening to "the far-off calls of herons winging their late passage through the night, the gentle wash of waves along the stony shore, and the toss, toss, toss of a loosely-moored canoe on the ripples."

At Rosseau, where the Brantford group both paddled and sailed their canoes, Pauline was an enthusiastic athlete. "It is a nice thing to be a lady canoeist," she noted. "All the men in the camp revere you, and if you are a very good paddler they may do the honour of imposing on you. . . . When a long cruise is on the programme, you are sought by every masculine member of the camp, and the honour of your company begged, nay, supplicated for." Pauline was not afraid to flaunt her expertise or to tease male companions when they were ham-fisted. She described how she knelt in the stern "while a handsome, lazy affair in white flannels decorates the bow. He sings, while you shoot through a score of eddies. . . . With a great deal of floundering and bungling he gets the mast up and excavates the sail from under the thwarts. You tell him several times just how to fix the whole business and he does it exactly the opposite way, then you beach the bow and walk up to the deck, stepping meanwhile over his big shoes and telling him he is a great stupid."

She was too smart, though, to forgo all the delights of being the maiden lolling "gracefully in the bow, with all the cushions." She was happy to let some "dear, athletic college boy" take her off in a canoe in which a mast had been erected and a sail unfurled. "Oh! the deliciousness of a sail on a hot August day," she wrote in a newspaper article about one such trip, when someone named Sam held the tiller. "To lie back in utter sloth, and with half-closed eyes watch the canvas fill overhead, while your taut little canoe cleancuts the water, its bow lined with bubbling foam, the cooling swish of water beneath the gunwales that parts to the aggressive little keel. . . . The gale blew steady now. . . . Faster and faster we flew, our bow splitting every wave it caught square. . . . [Sam asked] if I was 'scared.' Not I; I had been in worse things than a Muskoka gale in a canoe."

The Camp Knockabout crowd swam, sailed and fished during their three-week vacations. On Sunday evenings most of them struggled into their cleanest outfits and rowed over to Rosseau's clapboard Anglican church, with its gothic windows and belfry, for evensong. They accompanied Mr. and Mrs. Wilkes on frog-catching expeditions; Mrs. Wilkes produced a sizzling platter of fried frogs' legs for tea, and Pauline asked for a second helping of these "broiled dainties." They explored the woods behind Rosseau, and met some Chippewa Indians from the Parry Sound Reserve. Pauline's description of the encounter suggests she felt no sense of kinship; her reactions could have been those of any member of the Brantford Canoe Club: "[The Chippewas] are selling quaint little bark baskets and canoes embroidered in porcupine quills. They speak very good English, and were most courteous and obliging in filling special orders for us. Of course our host took out his omnipresent 'hawkeye': photographing is as prevalent here as *la grippe* was at home last winter. Someone is always calling us to 'Stand still please.'"

Pauline was a tomboy, but Muskoka also appealed to her solitary, lyrical side. Her picturesque surroundings, she admitted, "calmed me into a reverie that was almost akin to pain." She loved to "luxuriate in the great heart of Nature." She would paddle out alone, drinking in the "velvet air" and silently rehearsing the words that would shape into verse the dramatic scenery and her emotional response to it. Or she would walk off and hide amongst the rocks by the water's edge so she could scribble her thoughts on paper. At home in Brantford during these years, she was writing nature poems which make specific seasons and scenes act as metaphors for larger human experience. Much of this poetry reflects the Muskoka landscape, and the exhilaration that its untamed beauty roused in her.

She wrote about "The pine trees whispering, the heron's cry, / The plover's wing, his lullaby." She wrote a poem called "Moonset," the first line of which is "Idles the night wind through the dreaming firs." In "Bass Lake, Muskoka," she suggests the landscape is too poetic in itself for language: "The littleness of language seems the flower, / The firs are silence, grandeur, soul and power." In "Under Canvas, in Muskoka," published in November 1888, she captures the intoxicating pleasure of an evening in camp, surrounded by wilderness:

Some northern sorceress, when day is done,
Hovers where cliffs uplift their gaunt grey steeps,
Bewitching to vermilion Rosseau's sun,
That in a liquid mass of rubies sleeps.

The scent of burning leaves, the camp-fire's blaze,
The great logs cracking in the brilliant flame,
The groups grotesque, on which the firelight plays,
Are pictures which Muskoka twilights frame.

And Night, star-crested, wanders up the mere
With opiates for idleness to quaff,

And while she ministers, far off I hear
The owl's uncanny cry, the wild loon's laugh.

Pauline's imagination was fired by the grandeur of Muskoka's rocky cliffs, vast starlit skies and empty shores, which dwarfed its human visitors. There are echoes of the Romantic poets, familiar to her since childhood, in these poems, but she also identified deeply with the natural elements: earth, wind, rain, fire. Perhaps it was the sensibility of an exuberant and creative young woman, or perhaps it was her deep roots in the aboriginal tradition of living within the soft rhythms of the land, that prompted her to pen such lines as

Soulless is all humanity to me
Tonight. My keenest longing is to be
Alone, alone with God's grey earth that seems
Pulse of my pulse and consort of my dreams.

One of her most successful poems of this period appeared in *Saturday Night* in 1889. Entitled "Shadow River," it describes Rosseau's famous beauty spot: a hidden creek in which, as an 1886 guide to the area promised, "the surface is as motionless as glass and everything is duplicated in marvellous detail, each leaf and branch having its reflected counterpart even more distinct than it appears itself." Pauline found Shadow River bewitching, and she longed to show it to her closest friends. "I dream and dream the whole day long," she wrote to Archie Kains in 1890, "and sometimes find myself wishing for you as a comrade during my canoe trips up Shadow River." The poem combines close observation of the natural world with respect for a mighty landscape. Pauline begins by painting an exquisite picture of "opal tinted skies" reflected in "the sapphire floor," and of the borderline between water and air so fine that the keenest vision could barely see it. Then she acknowledges that "The beauty, strength, and power of the land / Will never stir or bend at my command." And, in a pattern that was starting to characterize much of what she wrote, she ends on a poignant, personal note:

For others Fame
And Love's red flame,
And yellow gold; I only claim
The shadows and the dreaming.

The Muskoka poems gave momentum to Pauline's reputation. Her verses had been appearing in the Toronto magazine *The Week* since 1885; between 1888 and 1891 at least thirty-seven poems by Pauline (including both nature and love verse) appeared in *Saturday Night*, and other poems appeared in the *Globe*, the New York magazine *Outing* and a Montreal publication called *Young Canadian*. In addition, she began to write prose for a variety of publications. In the summer of 1890, the *Brantford Courier* carried three pieces that she wrote under the pseudonym Rollstone with the heading "Charming Word Pictures, Etchings by an Idler of Muskoka and the Beautiful North." Pauline sold three jaunty articles about Muskoka to *Saturday Night* the same year, and two more in 1891. The *Weekly Detroit Free Press* took a piece from her on canoeing for its July 1891 issue. Mr. Worman, the editor of *Outing* magazine, was obviously quite taken with his "New Woman" contributor: he commissioned her to write a series of columns on "Outdoor Pastimes for Women." (In a slangy and subversive private letter to "My dear Mohawk," *Outing*'s deputy editor warned Pauline not to let herself be exploited: "Never forget that Worman is a Jew heart and soul, and don't allow him to hold you too cheaply. Never be afraid to put a decent price on your articles— they're worth at least $5 per page.") Pauline wrote about canoeing, skating, tobogganing, snowshoeing and women's hockey with breathless enthusiasm, suggesting that outdoor exercise bestowed sex appeal as well as good health on participants: "The girl who can weather the wintry gale . . . will slay more than bears, will bring to her feet rarer game than deer."

Like any neophyte writer, Pauline revelled in her successes. Each Saturday, she waited anxiously for copies of *Saturday Night* to arrive at the Brantford newsagents. She would quickly thumb through the twelve-page newspaper-style weekly. On her first read-through, she scarcely noticed the front page illustrations; the items about the

Cawthra, Kirkpatrick, Mulock and Ross families in "Social Notes"; the sections entitled "Boudoir Notes" and "Varsity Chat"; the reviews of concerts, plays and art shows; the advertisements for Pears' Soap, Carter's Little Liver Pills and Health Brand Undervests. She went straight to the right-hand column on page 6, where each week four or five poems appeared, and ran her eye quickly down the bylines. Would they include the *Saturday Night* regulars, such as Ernest Leigh, Eugene Field, A. L. McNab or Pauline herself? Or had some newcomer caught the editor's eye that week—some potential rival of whom she had never heard?

The muse was working overtime in late-nineteenth-century Canada—a period in which poetry was considered the highest of the literary arts. There were many Canadians with poetic pretensions and names to match: Violet Roberts, Esther Talbot Kingsmill, Ella Maude, Emma Seabury, Jas. A. Tucker. As Pauline read, she kept her fingers crossed. If one of her verses appeared, she knew she could expect congratulations from friends like the Mackenzies—and a cheque for $5 in the mail.

She couldn't help cataloguing all her published work in a jubilant letter to Archie Kains. She knew she was boasting, but she added defensively, "If you could look into my life sometimes when a long ill wind has blown, and see how barren of encouragement are the days that often crowd with worry and work you would forgive my utter childishness when I take a step upward, and add a little space to my range of vision that sometimes sees but clouds."

The most significant step upward in Pauline's career at this point was her appearance in a publication with a longer shelf life than newspapers and magazines. In August 1888, when she returned from her first trip to Muskoka, she found a letter waiting for her from William Lighthall, a Montreal lawyer and author. Lighthall had been asked by a British publisher to put together an anthology of Canadian poetry. It would appear as a volume in the Windsor Series, which was intended to encompass literature from all corners of the British Empire. A volume on Australian poetry had already been published, and all the proposed volumes would include in their frontispiece this drumbeat for Imperial unity:

When men unto their noblest rise,
Alike for ever see their eyes;
Trust us, grand England, we are true,
And, in your noblest, one with you.

Lighthall had sent Pauline, along with several other leading poets, a circular requesting contributions to his proposed anthology, in which he intended to celebrate the young poets of a young nation. The tone, it was clear, would be furiously patriotic.

Pauline was flattered and excited by Lighthall's request. Inclusion in such an anthology vaulted her out of the ranks of Sunday poets and into the literary pantheon. At the same time, however, Lighthall's letter alerted her to the importance of controlling where her verses appeared and of ensuring that she was always paid for them. She was happy to contribute, she told Lighthall, but she wanted to keep the copyright to anything she published. She was nursing the dream of every young writer: to see her own work between hard covers. "My intention," she wrote, "is to publish a book sometime in the future for which I wish to procure and own the copyright myself."

By return of post, William Lighthall reassured her that she would keep the copyright to her verses. Pauline threw herself into the challenge of choosing her submissions. Lighthall had requested material that illustrated "Canada and its life"; he wanted descriptive rather than subjective poems. Pauline sent him four examples of her work. The first, "In the Shadows," she described as "one of my best poems on canoeing, a sport I am fond of." The second, "Cry from an Indian Wife," was one of a handful that she had written that drew on her Indian background. The third, "At the Ferry," described the creaky old ferry across the Grand River. The fourth, "Joe," was about a young Irish boy on a summer's day. "They are the poems," she told Lighthall, "I consider my best and are most of them Canadian in tone and colour." She knew he would give attention to "Cry from an Indian Wife," on account, as she said, "of my nationality," and she promised to send another Indian poem, "The Indian Death Cry," if he wanted more. But she finished her letter, "I request you to particularly notice 'In the Shadows.'"

Lighthall's anthology, entitled *Songs of the Great Dominion: Voices from the Forests and Waters, the Settlements and Cities of Canada*, was published in London the following year, 1889. In his introduction, Lighthall promised readers that they would catch "something of great Niagara falling, of brown rivers rushing with foam, of the crack of the rifle in the haunts of the moose and caribou, the lament of vanishing races singing their death-song as they are swept on to the cataract of oblivion. . . ." The anthology featured 67 poets, whose 164 poems were divided into 9 sections with titles like "The Imperial Spirit," "The Spirit of Canadian History" and "The Voyageur and Habitant." Two of Pauline's poems were included: "In the Shadows" appeared in a section on "Sports and Free Life," "At the Ferry" in the section headed "Places." However, Lighthall did not use Pauline's "Cry from an Indian Wife"; instead, most of the poems in the section called "The Indian" were doleful paeans to past native glories penned by British-born men. Pauline pored through *Songs of the Great Dominion*, puzzled by Lighthall's principles of selection and intimidated by the erudition and skill of the other contributors.

It was exciting to be an up-and-comer in literary circles, but it was also daunting. The more Pauline wrote and read, the more she realized that it was a highly competitive world—and that she, as an ill-educated woman, was at a distinct disadvantage.

9

THE HEIGHTS
OF LITERATURE
1891—1892

O N a chilly March morning in 1891, Pauline Johnson bent down and gathered up the mail from the doormat in the dark hallway of the Johnsons' Brantford house. She felt wretched. A cold that she had caught at Christmas had lingered for weeks, migraines had laid her low on several occasions and her vision was blurry. A doctor in Hamilton told her she had strained her eyesight. Ill health had plunged her into what she called "unutterable gloom," which threatened to "grow and become stronger and finally master one." Moreover, as the winter months dragged on and spring seemed as elusive as ever, her mother had found plenty to complain about too: rheumatism, arthritis in her hands and, like Pauline, problems with her eyesight. Emily, Evelyn and Pauline all knew that more coal and modern gas lighting in their Napoleon Street home would alleviate some of these problems. But such luxuries were out of reach of Emily's minuscule annuity and Eva's modest salary. Beset by depression and financial pressures, Pauline was incapable of producing any literary work, in prose or verse.

Instead, she spent the dark winter months brooding over various reverses she had suffered and over her inability to make a decent living as a writer. Although her work now appeared regularly in Canadian and minor American publications, she had been unable to break into the top end of the American magazine market. Eleven American magazines had turned down her poem "In the Shadows." The editor of *Harper's*, William Dean Howells, had scrawled in the margin, "It will never go. It has no backbone!" Since Howells was her mother's first cousin, Pauline was doubly hurt by this brush-off. Even the poem's inclusion in Lighthall's anthology could not compensate for Howells's rudeness. "No one would expect that a little watercolour of a sunset would have any backbone," she complained. "With a big painting in oils it would be different. That poem was a little water-colour picture."

But on that March morning, Pauline examined an envelope which was addressed to her and carried the postmark of Danvers, Massachusetts. She opened it and pulled out the single sheet of paper inside. A smile spread slowly across her face as she deciphered the crabbed, forward-leaning script that covered it. "My dear Miss Johnson," it read. "I have rec.d. with great pleasure thy poems so kindly sent me. They have strength as well as beauty, and study and patient brooding over thy work will enable thee to write still better."

Some weeks earlier, Pauline had decided to seek out a well-placed sponsor in the American market, who would (in the idiom of the day) "boom" her work. She had sent a selection of her poems and a photograph of herself to John Greenleaf Whittier, the eighty-four-year-old American poet famous for his pastoral evocations of New England farm life. She probably chose Whittier at her mother's urging; like Emily's own father, John Greenleaf Whittier was a Quaker who had fought tenaciously against slavery. It is possible that Henry Howells and John Whittier were known to each other. Now, in March 1891, Whittier had sent a gracious reply praising Pauline's work and suggesting that "There is a splendid opportunity before thee."

Whittier was particularly impressed with a series of poems on Indian themes. The selection would have included some of the long narrative poems that are amongst Pauline's finest work: "Ojistoh," about a Mohawk wife who kills her Huron captor; "As Red Men Die," about a Mohawk chief who dies a proud death on a bed of coals; and "A Cry from an Indian Wife," about the sorrow of both Indian and European settler women as their menfolk fought each other in the 1885 Riel Rebellion on Canada's prairies. The poems were clearly influenced by Longfellow's *Hiawatha*, but the themes were original and the voice authentic. They were full of blood and thunder, rape and murder. "It is fitting," remarked the American poet, "that one of their own race should sing the songs of the Mohawk and Iroquois in the English tongue." He signed his note, "Thy aged friend, John G. Whittier."

Grinning broadly, Pauline read the letter again. A huge weight seemed to have lifted from her heart. She rushed into the parlour, where her mother was sitting, and read out Whittier's comments to Emily. In a letter to Archibald Kains in New York City, Pauline described the effect on her of Whittier's words. They came, she wrote, "like a wreath of bays to me. . . . Ah Archie! You do not know how I love the dear old man now who has penned with his trembling aged hand those dear encouraging words to me. His is such a beautifully simple pure mind and he so loves all races in America that my heart goes out to him, as it did in my childhood to dear dead Longfellow." Pauline treasured Whittier's letter all her life. Years later, she told an interviewer that "I owe to Whittier all I have ever accomplished for he first gave me faith in myself."

Pauline needed such a lift in 1891. She had just passed her thirtieth birthday, and her life seemed stalled. Most of her girlfriends were married, and she knew that she risked being labelled "old maid." Granted, her performances with the Brantford Players had earned her local celebrity, and her poems enjoyed a respectable readership in *Saturday Night*. No less a person than Arthur Hardy, the local Liberal MPP, had sent her a note of congratulation on her verses. Hardy, who would serve as Premier of Ontario between 1896 and 1899, employed Frank Yeigh, a school-friend of Pauline's, as his personal secretary. Frank probably drafted the complimentary letter. The abject gratitude of Pauline's reply to Hardy indicates how low her morale had sunk: "Your kind notice of my little poem I will always regard as an imperishable laurel leaf in my tiny wreath. . . . I can scarcely tell you how often an author requires approbation or how dear is the handclasp of encouragement when it does come. Your praise and approval of my work will lighten many a hard road that I must needs tramp over before I reach the heights of Literature I mean to attain."

Some of Pauline's low spirits were attributable to her dawning recognition that she was ill-equipped to attain those heights of literature. An education that consisted of a few years in the reserve's one-room schoolhouse and two years at Brantford Central Collegiate had left her with a good knowledge of English Romantic verse and a respect for classical metre, but not much else. Most middle-class girls in this period received minimal education because they were destined for marriage, but Pauline's schooling had been particularly hit-and-miss. She knew little of the world beyond southwest Ontario; she was too poor to travel or to buy many books; she was rarely able to rub shoulders with other writers. Friends and acquaintances in Brantford who shared her interests or had a wider world view, like Sara Jeannette Duncan, Michael Mackenzie and Archie Kains, had all moved on to larger cities and bigger challenges. And Pauline knew that "the heights of Literature" that she wished to scale were dominated by a small cadre of poets. She had much in common with these "Confederation Poets," as critics dubbed them fifty years later. They were exactly the same age as she was; they also wrote about the Canadian landscape; they were all represented in William Lighthall's anthology, *Songs of the Great Dominion*. But there were significant differences. The Confederation Poets were well-educated men who shared a cosy, but competitive, intimacy from which she felt excluded.

The most important Confederation Poets were two New Brunswick cousins, Charles G. D. Roberts and Bliss Carman, and two Ottawa civil servants, Archibald Lampman and Duncan Campbell Scott. Three of the four were sons of church ministers (Bliss Carman was the exception); all were steeped in the intellectual rigour common to sons of the manse. Sometimes two more names are included in the "Confederation Poets" galaxy: William Wilfred Campbell and Frederick George Scott, whose work is in a similar vein but not of such fine quality. Thanks to the kind of classical education that Pauline had not enjoyed, these earnest young men were able to articulate and argue about the challenges facing Canadian poets. In her own work, Pauline herself had wrestled with these issues, although she had neither the opportunity nor the vocabulary to express them. How could a Canadian poet steeped in British Romantic poetry, in which nature is used as a metaphor for both God and the human mind, reconcile this tradition with the vast, untamed landscape of the Great Dominion of the North? Could a former colony establish its own literary culture shaped by its own history and geography?

The first of the Confederation Poets to see his work in print was Charles Roberts, a stocky, energetic man with a bristling moustache and a penchant for women and floppy felt hats. In 1880, at the astonishingly young age of twenty, he published a volume entitled *Orion, and Other Poems. Orion* appeared only thirteen years after Confederation, when the newborn nation of Canada still looked to London for its culture. As William Lighthall had discovered while gathering material for his anthology, there were plenty of Sunday poets in the Great Dominion scribbling away about sun-fleck'd fields and babbling streams. But most of the verse finding its way into *Saturday Night* and other publications was ersatz Wordsworth: sentimental, superficial and strangely detached from the dramatic reality of Canadian vistas and seasons. Charles Roberts's poetry, in *Orion* and subsequent publications, was a departure from all that. Although he wrote in classical metre, his verses mingled myth and landscape and were firmly rooted in the apple orchards, potato fields and salt flats of his native New Brunswick.

Roberts's achievement spurred on other aspiring poets. A copy of *Orion* fell into the hands of another twenty-year-old, a frail young man with a broad brow and haunted brown eyes who was enrolled at Toronto's Trinity College (subsequently part of the University of Toronto). Archibald Lampman sat up all night reading and rereading Roberts's vigorous and melodic poems. "Like most of the young fellows about me," he wrote later, "I had been under the depressing conviction that we were situated hopelessly on the outskirts of civilization, where no art and no literature could be, and that it was useless to expect anything great could be done by any of our companions, still more useless to expect that we could do it ourselves. It was like a voice from some new paradise of art, calling to us to be up and doing." He was sleepless with excitement when he finally closed Roberts's slim volume. As the sun rose, he pulled on a sweater and went out into the meadows that surrounded the old Trinity building. He found himself looking at the world with new eyes: "The dew was thick upon the grass, all the birds of our Maytime seemed to be singing in the oaks, and there were even a few adder tongues and trilliums still blooming on the slope of the little ravine. But everything was transfigured for me beyond description, bathed in an old world radiance of beauty. . . . I have never forgotten that morning, and its influence has always remained with me."

Then as now, poetry did not put bread on the table. Both Roberts and Lampman had to earn their living. In 1883, Roberts spent a brief period as editor of *The Week* in Toronto, where he was able to encourage other young poets. In 1885, he returned to the Maritimes to teach English literature at King's College in Windsor, Nova Scotia. Archibald Lampman turned his back on the church, and in 1883 entered the service of the federal Post Office in Ottawa, where he remained a humble, ill-paid clerk for the rest of his life. But both men continued to heed the "voice from some new paradise of art"; both were determined to persevere with the literary "up and doing." And both attracted the friendship of others with similar interests.

Charles Roberts was not the only writer in his family; his cousin Bliss Carman, one year younger, began writing verse while he was still at the University of New Brunswick. Carman had left New Brunswick, first to study in Edinburgh and at Harvard, and then to work in New York as a literary journalist. Carman and Roberts shared more than a common interest in poetry. Like Roberts, Carman liked to dress the part of the literary icon: he always looked slightly dishevelled, in the style common to New York's bohemian set, and he wore his hair unfashionably long. Both men fancied themselves as ladykillers. But "home" remained the Maritimes for Carman; he made frequent visits to his family, and the two poet cousins seized every chance to discuss the literary world and read each other's work. Although a more mystical poet than Roberts, Carman, like his cousin, used the east coast scenes of his childhood as the setting for much of his verse: "The running dikes, the brimming tide, / And the dark firs on Fundy side . . ." His most famous, and much-anthologized, poem was "Low Tide on Grand Pré," a delicate, eerie seascape:

The sun goes down, and over all
These barren reaches by the tide

Such unelusive glories fall,
I almost dream they yet will bide
Until the coming of the tide.

. . . . .

Was it a year or lives ago
We took the grasses in our hands,
And caught the summer flying low
Over the waving meadow lands,
And held it there between our hands?

Meanwhile, in Ottawa, Archie Lampman had established the same kind of supportive relationship with a fellow clerk in the federal public service, Duncan Campbell Scott. As a young man, Scott, like Lampman, was as poor as a church mouse, and he had become a copying clerk in the Bureau of Indian Affairs when he was not quite eighteen. Painfully shy, since childhood he had poured his emotional and creative energies into music. Lampman opened a whole new world to him. "It never occurred to me to write a line of prose or poetry until after I had met Lampman," he later admitted.

The Lampman–Scott partnership was of incalculable benefit to each of them. Lampman himself wrote of his need for stimulating society: "The human mind is like a plant, it blossoms in order to be fertilised, and to bear seed must come into actual contact with the mental dispersion of others. Of this natural assistance the Canadian writer gets the least possible." By the mid-1880s, Lampman and Scott were setting off together into Quebec on long canoeing expeditions that inspired them, as Muskoka inspired Pauline, to watch, dream and write. They immortalized the tranquillity of Canada's natural beauties and the mesmeric rhythms of a canoe, just as Pauline did in her verse. Like Pauline's "Shadow River," Lampman's limpid poem "Morning on the Lièvre" suspends the canoeist between water and sky:

Softly as a cloud we go,
Sky above and sky below,
Down the river; and the dip
Of the paddles scarcely breaks,

With the little silvery drip
Of the water as it shakes
From the blades, the crystal deep
Of the silence of the morn,
Of the forest yet asleep.

*In Ottawa, Duncan Campbell Scott (front left) and Archie
Lampman (seated behind him, wearing a hat) enjoyed the
company of each other and a circle of admirers.*

On winter evenings, when the birchbark canoe had been put away,
Lampman and Scott and a few friends would gather in front of a
crackling fire in the front parlour of Scott's home on Lisgar Street.
They would discuss each other's work, the latest Trollope novel from
England or the capital's most recent political scandal. A frequent visitor was William Wilfred Campbell, a former Anglican minister who
now worked in the Department of Railways and Canals, whose first
book of verse, *Snowflakes and Sunbeams,* had appeared in 1888.
Sometimes Scott and Lampman would walk together across the

Minto Bridges to the village of New Edinburgh, where another poet, Achille Fréchette, lived. Fréchette, who spent his days as a translator in the House of Commons, was the brother of Quebec's Poet Laureate, Louis-Honoré Fréchette. His American-born wife, Annie Howells Fréchette, was related to Pauline: her father and Pauline's mother were cousins. The Fréchettes ran an interesting little bilingual salon at which any literary figure who appeared in the capital was always welcome. And Scott and Lampman delighted each Christmas in sending out to friends and relatives a card containing a poem from each of them.

The names of Roberts, Carman, Lampman, Scott and Campbell were all familiar to Pauline Johnson. On occasion, she had received the Scott–Lampman Christmas card (perhaps Scott had run across the young poet with Mohawk blood through his work at the Bureau of Indian Affairs). It was a rare month when *Saturday Night* did not include verses by at least two of them, and each was represented in *Songs of the Great Dominion*. (The editor, William Lighthall, conferred on Charles Roberts the title of "foremost name in Canadian song" and used thirteen of Roberts's poems, including one of his most mawkish works, a verse entitled "Canada" which begins, "O Child of Nations, giant-limbed.") Their names cropped up in surveys of young poets in both Canadian and American magazines. Critics vied with each other to promote them. Bliss Carman was tagged "the Canadian Tennyson," while Charles G. D. Roberts was "the Longfellow of Canada." Most galling to Pauline, when Archie Lampman published his first book, *Among the Millet*, in 1888, her mother's cousin William Dean Howells (Annie Howells Fréchette's brother) was sufficiently impressed to write that Lampman was as good as any American poet.

Pauline recognized that these poets produced lyric verse to a standard she tried to emulate. But the success of her male contemporaries must have prompted her to ask herself the kind of questions that struggling outsiders always ask when they watch from the sidelines as others triumph. Could she ever aspire to the company of these poets? Was their poetry so much better than hers? Or was it simply that they moved in the right milieu and helped to "boom" each other? How much of Roberts's success was due to the fact that his work had caught the attention of the famous British poet Matthew Arnold? Was *Among the Millet* reviewed so favourably in *Harper's* because of the cosy links between Lampman, Louis Fréchette and Annie Howells Fréchette? Did Charles G. D. Roberts attract notice in New York because his cousin Bliss Carman, who moved in literary circles there, was prepared to show a relative more generosity than William Dean Howells had shown Pauline herself? Could a woman of her background ever reach Parnassus?

There were, to be sure, a handful of women who had made their literary mark. Of the sixty-seven poets included in *Songs of the Great Dominion*, thirteen were women. The editor, William Lighthall, showed surprising discernment when he included seven poems by Isabella Valancy Crawford in the anthology. Crawford wrote in obscurity until she died in 1887 when she was only thirty-seven. Few of her contemporaries recognized the narrative strength of poems such as "Old Spookses' Pass" and "Malcolm's Katie"; their titles alone discouraged fastidious critics, and they contained too much raw passion. Many of the images and themes that occur in her verses also crop up in Pauline's: respect for a living nature, the power of native culture, the canoe as an erotic symbol. With Crawford's early death, however, her poetry vanished. Lighthall had also included in *Songs of the Great Dominion* verses by Agnes Maule Machar, Susanna Moodie and Rosanna Leprohon. But in most cases, only a single poem represented the work of these women, whereas a poet such as Charles G. D. Roberts merited thirteen contributions.

Alone in Brantford, Pauline was far from the world of literary salons and what Lampman had called "the mental dispersions of others." Unlike Roberts and Carman, she had nobody on whom she could rely to publicize her poetry. Unlike Lampman and Scott in Ottawa, she had no kindred spirit with whom to discuss her work. Like Isabella Valancy Crawford, she lived in obscurity. She wrote wistfully to Archie Kains, "There are so few friends I write 'shop' to, so few who think enough of me to bear with my newspaper chatter and my hilarity when I have success." She took what steps she could to promote herself. She commissioned a series of photographic *cartes de visite* in the same way that a musician today might produce a video. Some of these cards were for personal use, but Pauline also allowed them to be sold by newsagents and photographic studios to people who either admired the subject or enjoyed collecting such keepsakes. Pauline told Archie that she was ambivalent about such photos: "I confess it sadly crosses the grain of my own inclinations, to be sold on the street corners for five cents or bought in a shop for twenty. My mother does not mind it as she realises that the road to literary success in this age lies through 'Booming'—and really, I have climbed such a hard hill that I am willing to consent to anything legitimate that will mean success in the end."

But Pauline knew that she had to extend both her intellectual range and her circle of acquaintances if she was going to attain those "heights of Literature." That's where, she realized, Archie Kains could be very useful.

The seventeen letters that Pauline wrote to Archie Kains between 1889 and 1893, now lodged in the National Archives of Canada, trace the course of a relationship that moved, on Pauline's part, from light-hearted flirtation to intimate trust. Since none of Archie's replies to Pauline have survived, it is impossible to say what he expected from his correspondent. The two spent relatively little time together. Archie lived only a few months in Brantford in 1888, working at the Canadian Bank of Commerce. The following year, after his transfer to New York City, he returned for a brief visit. (He went on to a distinguished banking career, culminating in his appointment as Governor of the Federal Reserve Bank of San Francisco.) A stilted correspondence between "Mr. Kains" and "Miss Johnson" was established in early 1889. Within a few weeks, Pauline admitted Archie to the circle of her admirers by sending him a handkerchief sachet embroidered with a Scottish emblem. "The thistle I selected as the fullest compliment I could offer you—your patriotism is so true and strong," she wrote. Archie sent Pauline a photograph of himself, which she placed on her writing desk under the window of her second-floor bedroom.

But Pauline was at pains to appear both demure and popular; Archie's photo, she told him, was displayed alongside those of "one or two [others] whom I have known for years."

The formal relationship metamorphosed into a warm, platonic friendship in late 1889, when Pauline visited Archie in New York City. He may have casually suggested she call on him if she was ever in the city, or he may have urged her to find an excuse to visit the most important cultural centre on the North American continent. Pauline obviously wasted no time in arranging a visit with both personal and professional goals, although the train fare and other costs must have strained her resources. The professional goal was publicity. Pauline had already met the American anthropologist Harriet Maxwell Converse, who knew of the Johnson family from Chiefswood days and who lived at 155 West 46th Street. Mrs. Converse was happy to offer Pauline accommodation since she had followed the young Mohawk poet's career with interest. While Pauline was staying on 46th Street, she and Mrs. Converse had several long conversations. They formed the basis of an article that Mrs. Converse later wrote for the Buffalo publication *Twentieth Century Review*.

The personal goal, of course, was to improve her acquaintanceship with Archie Kains. She spent an inordinate amount of time on her wardrobe for the visit. A friend called at Napoleon Street while Pauline was carefully fitting on a dress form a beautiful gown of rose cashmere and wine velvet. The friend commented admiringly, "How nice you are able to sew; you can make your own dresses when you are married!" Pauline retorted, "When I am married I do not intend to make my own dresses."

Pauline's trip to New York did not culminate in marriage. Perhaps Archie did not have enough time to show Pauline around; perhaps he suffered a bout of the dreadful "glooms," which he mentions in a couple of letters; perhaps, like Michael Mackenzie, he found this intense woman, some years older than he was, too rich for his blood. Archie was a reserved man with deeply conventional views of male and female behaviour, and Pauline was a passionate woman who did not always hide her feelings. He was not as attentive to Pauline during her

Stratford 19th July 93.

My dear Stephen

Pauline poured her heart out to Archibald Kains, an up-and-coming banker, in letters that went far beyond "floating chit-chat."

visit as she had hoped. "I remained in both morning and afternoon," reads a note from Pauline, "and need scarcely tell you, I was disappointed when you did not come. . . . Tuesday evening I will be at home and shall expect you."

Archie did not entirely neglect Pauline while she was at Mrs. Converse's. He took her to the most popular art show of the year, an exhibition at the New Jersey Academy of French paintings of the Barbizon School. He escorted her to a theatrical performance in Brooklyn, which starred Edwin Booth. Booth, said to be the best actor of his generation, was a member of the famous American acting family that included John Wilkes Booth, who had shot Abraham Lincoln. (Edwin Booth's nickname was "the Prince of Players," but he also had to suffer the ignominy of being known throughout his life as the brother of "the President-Killer.") Pauline felt her intellectual horizons expand on these expeditions. Archie quietly explained to her where the village of Barbizon was, and why Jean-François Millet's painting *The Angelus* was so important. The two of them discussed Booth's performance in *Hamlet*, and whether the actor was overdramatic as he delivered the Prince of Denmark's lines. Despite Archie's deliberate disregard of Pauline's sensual charms, he admired her quick intelligence. Each enjoyed the other's company; they were soon on first-name terms. Not for the first time, Pauline skilfully turned an unsuccessful romance into a comfortable companionship.

After Pauline returned to Brantford, she wrote a touching letter of thanks to Archie for the friendship of someone with "that almost divine gift of imparting instruction without permitting one to feel [one's] ignorance. . . . I never object in the least to let [you] see I have no education and comparatively no advantages. . . . It is a happy gift and a rare one, and I often speak of it in connection with you and the generous kindness you showed me in New York." She pinned a sepia reproduction of *The Angelus*, sent by Archie, to her bedroom wall. And she continued to cherish Archie's letters for the education she gleaned from them. "I like a man," she wrote to him in October 1890, "to write on business, commercial or labour topics as you sometimes do. It is one of the most delicate compliments . . . paid me to receive a letter from you and feel while reading it that you have written as to an equal in understanding and intellect." She thanked him for not restricting his letter "to idle nothings or floating chit-chat that so many men think they ought to write and talk to a girl. I hate people to think they must lighten a subject before I have the brain capacity to follow it."

Pauline had other acquaintances besides Archie on whom she relied for new cultural experiences. She was particularly proud of her friendship with the members of Rosina Voke's touring theatre company. Voke was a well-known American actress who had launched her career on the New York stage as a child actress alongside her two sisters in a comedy, *Belles in the Kitchen*, in 1872. She now had her own touring company, specializing in the kind of burlesques and melodramas that late-nineteenth-century audiences loved. Voke was always the star, and she had the critics eating out of her hand. The theatre critic for the *New York Times* enthused about her acting, singing and dancing skills, as well as her "unquenchable vivacity" and "delightful drollery." In 1889, he was euphoric about Voke's performance in the farce *The Circus Rider* at Daly's Theater, New York, which included on stage a "wonderful impromptu exhibition of skill as a bareback rider." Voke's leading man was usually Courtney Thorpe, an old ham of an actor who excelled at playing handsome suitors and English milords.

Pauline's first encounter with Rosina Voke's company was probably in Hamilton in 1886, when her brothers Beverly and Allen regularly took her to whichever travelling shows were in town. Twice a year, the company also spent a week in Toronto and played the Grand Opera House on the corner of Yonge and Adelaide streets. Pauline made every effort to see Voke's company when they were in Canada, and she was soon on friendly terms with Voke herself, as well as with Thorpe and an elderly English actor named Charles Bell. Bell was a minor player in Voke's company, but he was appreciated for his impeccable British accent (his father was the Rector of Cheltenham). In November 1890, he and his Philadelphia-born wife invited the young Brantford poet to join them as their guest at Rossin House, a large hotel on Toronto's York Street. Pauline was overjoyed. Rossin House, a magnificent five-storey building of freestone and white brick, was the height of Victorian luxury. It boasted 180 well-furnished bedrooms, 15 ground-floor stores, a ladies' parlour and gentlemen's baths. However, it was not Rossin House's splendours that thrilled Pauline. It was the opportunity to acquire some stagecraft.

During Pauline's visit, the high point of each day was the evening's entertainment in Toronto's most up-to-date theatre. Rosina Voke's company had brought five productions to the Grand Opera House, all of which had done well in New York: *A Double Lesson, Wig and Gown, A Corsican Legacy, My Milliner's Bill* and *A Game of Cards.* Each night, a different play was performed to sellout crowds in the Grand's 1,750-seat domed auditorium. "You would not have known me, I was so swell," Pauline reported joyfully to Archie. "I had a box at the Grand every night and disported [myself] as a very great snob!" She was intrigued by Rosina Voke's performances, particularly when the actress was portraying society ladies. She watched Voke glide across the stage, carriage erect; she saw how she responded to the audience's laughter, applause or fidgets. Unkind critics sometimes suggested that Voke never acted from the heart; she was too busy parodying either the character she was playing or a more famous actress, such as Sarah Bernhardt. But her audiences didn't care. They loved her beauty, her sense of timing, her coquettish manner and her wit. Pauline drank it all in.

After each performance, the actors recuperated in Rossin House's lounge. Pauline relished the conversation. She described Voke to Archie as "a gleam of intellectual sunshine to poor little me." The New York sophistication of the company was intoxicating. "They are all such thorough ladies and gentlemen, so cultured, well read and with ideas so liberating such as one never hears in a small provincial town." It spurred Pauline to think about her own hopes. "Mr. Bell and Courtney Thorpe did some critiquing of me that will be of great advantage to me in the future. They both recite magnificently and have asked me to write them a semi-dramatic poem for this purpose."

Pauline's mother, Emily, was ambivalent about her daughter's stage friends. There was a stigma of immorality attached to the word "actress," and according to Evelyn Johnson (who thoroughly disapproved of the theatre), "Mother would never consent to [Pauline] becoming an actress." But the whiff of greasepaint and the sound of an audience's applause thrilled Pauline. She was not just star-struck: she hungered to have a public role herself. In a letter to Archie she mused, "I wonder how people without ambition live." She assured the oh-so-proper Archie that she had no interest in a simple "chase for fame." She felt that everyone should want "to better one's self morally and materially through . . . the ambition that means purpose and despises to stand still." She couldn't stand the idea that her life might dwindle to "the purposeless humdrum life of some I know."

The prospect of living like her sister must have appalled Pauline as she watched Evelyn leave home each morning on her way to a routine office job, dressed in her threadbare cloth coat. Modest commissions continued to come Pauline's way; in November 1891, the *Brantford Expositor* asked her to write a story for its special Christmas edition. But Pauline wanted to get out of Brantford and onto a larger stage. The opportunity finally arrived in 1892.

Pauline first met Frank Yeigh when they both attended Brantford Central Collegiate. Frank was a lively, self-confident fellow whose father had begun as a reporter with the *Brantford Expositor* and later moved on to the Toronto *Globe*. Frank followed in his father's footsteps, working in the news department first at the *Expositor* and then at the *Globe*. But he always wanted to be in the centre of the action rather than simply reporting it. He secured the job of personal secretary to Arthur Hardy, the MPP from Brantford who had sent Pauline a note of congratulation on her work. Frank also got himself elected president of the Young Men's Liberal Club of Canada, which boasted over a thousand members. He fancied himself as an author, too; he moved in Toronto's literary set and, along with Pauline, he had been invited to contribute to the *Brantford Expositor*'s Christmas issue.

Like Lampman and Roberts (although without their talent), Frank was captivated by the idea that Canada should have its own national culture. He had read William Lighthall's *Songs of the Great Dominion*, and he was fired by Lighthall's celebration of Canadian verse. He decided to combine his two interests, literature and politics, by staging a flamboyantly nationalist "Evening with Canadian Authors," at which the club's new "Canadianism" policy would be publicized. He knew that he could fill with young Liberals the lecture hall at the Art School Gallery, above the new Academy of Music theatre on King Street West, and he reckoned they would supply their usual rowdy enthusiasm for speakers. He assembled a programme of eight distinguished writers, including Duncan Campbell Scott, William Wilfred Campbell, Agnes Maule Machar, William Lighthall himself—and Pauline Johnson. Frank had dropped Pauline a note only a few days earlier. She was thrilled by the invitation to appear in such distinguished company, but also apprehensive. "I have nothing to wear!" she wailed to Eva.

The "Evening with Canadian Authors" was scheduled for the evening of Saturday, January 16, 1892. That morning, the news from Britain made Frank anxious. There were rumours that seventy-two-year-old Queen Victoria, following the recent death of her grandson the Duke of Clarence, had fallen ill. The news, as the *Globe* itself said, made "every artery of the empire tingle . . . Bombay, Hong Kong, Melbourne, Natal and Toronto." Frank's nerves tingled because if the Queen died, he would have to cancel his event. But by the end of the day, there were no newsboys shrieking out bad news at street corners or selling special black-edged editions of the *Evening Telegram*, the *Empire*, the *Mail* and the *Globe*. The Queen had rallied. Frank walked along King Street and was pleased to see lines for tickets already forming outside the Art School building.

Half an hour before the curtain was scheduled to rise, the hall was packed and young Liberals were scurrying to find more chairs. Sharp January winds whistled down the narrow streets outside, but the temperature inside rose steadily and people shrugged off their heavy woollen coats. Frank scuttled up and down the aisles; the place was as packed, he recalled later, as a "sardine box." The *crème de la crème* of Toronto sat in the front row. There were two of the era's greatest orators: George Ross, Minister of Education for the province, and the Reverend D. J. Macdonnell of St. Andrew's Presbyterian Church. There was Graeme Mercer Adam, the author, editor and close associate of Goldwin Smith, now white-haired but in his day, as publisher of *Rose Belford's Canadian Monthly*, a tireless promoter of Canadian writers.

There was another leading churchman, the Reverend Dr. Dewart, who in 1864 had edited the very first anthology of Canadian poetry, *Selections from Canadian Poets*. The sense of anticipation was almost tangible. Was not the audience about to witness the official inauguration of Canadian literature? Frank Yeigh held a sheaf of letters from those who regretted they could not attend such a significant evening. Writers included Principal George Monroe Grant of Queen's University, Archibald Lampman, William Kirby (whose novel *The Golden Dog*, published in 1877, was still a bestseller) and Louis-Honoré Fréchette, Poet Laureate of Quebec and Achille Fréchette's brother.

The young impresario began the evening with a stirring appeal for cultural nationalism. Canadians must learn to appreciate the growing strength of their own culture, Yeigh said, instead of waiting for American critics to do it for them. It was appalling that, by his estimate, only about "10 percent of intelligent Canadians were aware of the literary feast by home talent" available to them. Unless Canadians learned to appreciate their own literature, Yeigh told his audience, they risked losing their best poets to the United States. Canada could already boast an astonishing national literature for a country so young: "the intelligent life of Canada is keeping pace with its material development."

All those intelligent young Liberals in the hall applauded their President enthusiastically. Then they sat back to listen to the literary lions. But as the evening got underway, the spirits of the students, would-be writers and literary critics began to droop. Frank had made a miscalculation. He was used to dealing with politicians, and somehow, since both politicians and poets deal in words, he had assumed that writers could fire up a crowd in the same way as George Ross, or even the silver-tongued Liberal leader, Wilfrid Laurier.

He was wrong. Reading verse has nothing to do with fiery oratory. The first poem featured was Miss Agnes Maule Machar's "The Mystic Singer." It was received well because it was short and read with gusto by the Reverend Macdonnell, a personal friend of Miss Machar's. But Wilfred Campbell, a poet with a high opinion of himself and a loud, monotonous voice, followed Miss Machar. He read a doleful work entitled "The Mother," which described the corpse of a woman who died in childbirth, and which included such lugubrious lines as "I kenned my breasts were clammy and cold." Next came William Lighthall, who read a lengthy and didactic chapter from his book *The Young Seigneur on Nation-Making.* By now an hour had passed, the heat in the hall was oppressive and less than one-quarter of the programme had been covered. The audience fidgeted and coughed. The chairs at the back of the hall began to empty.

Pauline stood in the wings, listening to Mr. Lighthall. She could see and hear what was happening. Under her white gloves, her palms were damp. But at the same time, her stage training and the lessons from Rosina Voke's actors gave her confidence. She knew what the audience wanted. Unlike Campbell and Lighthall, she knew how to perform. She would not stand there, eyes focussed on the printed page as she read her verse. She would connect directly with the audience by reciting from memory. She adjusted the bodice of her pale grey silk gown and arched her neck. She swept back into place a few stray tendrils of hair that had escaped her chignon and ran her fingers through her carefully curled bangs. She took a deep breath.

Finally, Mr. Lighthall's reading drew to a close, and he walked off the stage to polite applause. As Frank Yeigh appeared before the footlights to introduce the next speaker, those in the wings could hear the sound of more people leaving at the rear of the hall. Pauline Johnson took another deep breath, then glided onto centre stage. Once there, she remained silent, eyes raised to the ceiling, as shapely and motionless as a Greek statue, until every last whisper had died down, every fidget was stilled.

Then she began. She had chosen to recite "A Cry from an Indian Wife," an extraordinarily forceful poem that she had written seven years earlier and offered to Mr. Lighthall for his anthology. It concerned one of the most inflammatory incidents in Canadian history: the 1885 North-West Rebellion that took place on the plains of Western Canada. In 1869 the Métis leader Louis Riel had led an uprising to secure Métis land rights against the aggressive incursions of Ontario settlers. By and large the uprising was successful, although the execution of an Ontario Orangeman by the rebels shocked Anglo-Protestants in Ontario. But in 1885 Riel led a second uprising in support of Métis land rights which involved Métis, Assiniboine and Plains Cree warriors and which ended in disaster. Canadian troops were quickly on the spot, and the uprising rapidly spiralled out of control. Before Dominion authorities had suppressed the trouble, European settlers, rebels and soldiers had been killed. Ottawa then approved the hanging of Louis Riel and eight Indian chiefs. The 1885 Rebellion proved deeply divisive in both Central and Western Canada for years to come. Quebecers were outraged by the execution of Louis Riel; they regarded him as the champion of French-speaking Catholics who had been sacrificed to satisfy Protestant Ontario. Out west, the 1885 Rebellion, which left the Métis and the Indians defeated both politically and emotionally, was regarded as a symbol of Ottawa's arrogant dismissal of native claims. Although the events of 1885 were seven years old when Pauline took to the Toronto stage, the memory had not faded and sensitivities were still raw.

Pauline's poem deals with the uprising from an entirely original point of view—that of the wife of an Indian warrior. Rage ripples through the first half of the poem as the narrator deplores the treatment that Indians have received at the hands of European settlers:

> They but forget we Indians owned the land
> From ocean unto ocean; that they stand
> Upon a soil that centuries agone
> Was our sole kingdom and our right alone.
> They never think how they would feel today,
> If some great nation came from far away,
> Wresting their country from their hapless braves,
> Giving what they gave us—but war and graves.

In the later lines of the poem, there is an abrupt change of pace. The narrator considers the feelings of the "white-faced warriors'" mothers:

> Yet stay, my heart is not the only one
> that grieves the loss of husband and of son;
> Think of the mothers o'er the inland seas;
> Think of the pale-faced maiden on her knees . . .

Pauline lowered her voice as one tragic image followed another. In the hall, most people were at the edge of their chairs. Suddenly, her voice was loud and her arm raised. The words reverberated into the farthest corners of the room as she reached the poem's climax. Every lesson on breath control and voice projection that Rosina Voke had ever taught her was now fully employed.

Pauline had ended the original version of the poem, published in *The Week*, with a fatalistic acceptance of European victory: "God and fair Canada have willed it so." But in later versions, she toughened up the ending to reflect the injustice of the British Empire's treatment of Indians:

> Go forth, nor bend to greed of white men's hands,
> By right, by birth we Indians own these lands,
> Though starved, crushed, plundered, lies our nation low . . .
> Perhaps the white man's God has willed it so.

It was probably this revised version, eloquent with anger, that she used for her 1892 appearance.

"A Cry from an Indian Wife" held the audience in thrall, although few of its members would have shared the poet's views. Many people present that night had read Pauline Johnson's work in *Saturday Night*, but most of her published poems dealt with canoeing, nature or love. Only a handful of people in the hall had already heard her recite or knew she was half Mohawk. Now, her musical voice and intensity of expression mesmerized them. She was both sensuously beautiful and intriguingly exotic. Few people remained unmoved by the emotional pull of a poem which reflected Pauline's own divided loyalties, as she identified with both Indian and European women caught up in the conflict out west.

At the close of the poem, Pauline let her eyes drift down. She turned to leave the stage. There was total silence for a moment, then the audience broke into wild applause. Completely self-possessed, Pauline turned back and gave a deep curtsey as cries of "Encore" began to reverberate around the hall. Frank Yeigh was waiting for her in the wings as she walked off stage; he beamed with relief that she had rescued the evening. After a brief consultation with Pauline, he led his diva back on stage and announced that Miss Johnson would be happy to recite a second, unscheduled work.

There was yet another storm of applause. At the age of thirty-one, after nearly a decade of hard work and regular publication, Pauline had finally been discovered.

10

BEADS, QUILLS, SASHES, SHOES AND BROOCHES

1892–1894

"MISS E. Pauline Johnson's may be said to have been the pleasantest contribution of the evening," the *Globe* reviewer announced two days after the "Evening with Canadian Authors." "It was like the voice of the nations that once possessed this country, who have wasted away before our civilization, speaking through this cultured, gifted, soft-faced descendant."

Pauline smiled as she carefully clipped the review out of the newspaper and stuck the cutting in her scrapbook. The wild enthusiasm that had greeted her first performance in Toronto had been intoxicating. She had always found the applause for her Brantford appearances gratifying, but since she knew most of her hometown audience personally, she took the ovations for granted. The Toronto reception was different. Most of her fellow performers in January 1892 were far better known than she was. The VIPs in the front-row seats were people she was keen to impress. And the throngs of eager young Liberals, whooping at her beauty and passion, made her feel the equal of a Jenny Lind or a Sarah Bernhardt. Who wouldn't blush with pride and pleasure at such a warm response?

But there was an additional reason for Pauline's sense of achievement. The "Evening with Canadian Authors" confirmed her perception that her Mohawk blood was an asset to her career. Lots of Canadians were composing verse about sunsets, canoes and northern skies. A few poets, including Duncan Campbell Scott, who worked in Ottawa's Bureau of Indian Affairs, were writing about native people. But she was the only one with aboriginal ancestry herself who was creating such poetry. Her Indian blood and use of Indian myths and history gave her an edge in the crowded literary marketplace. It also gave her an opportunity to confront the patronizing attitude displayed by some English Canadians to their country's native inhabitants. A self-serving assumption was spreading that native bands were bound for extinction, through disease and assimilation, because they were mentally unfit to survive as separate peoples in the face of superior British "culture." Pauline resented this arrogance. Thoughtless allusions to "Injuns" and "squaws," and the lofty reference in the *Globe*'s review about Indians "wast[ing] away before our civilization," rankled. Although her day-to-day life was that of any Brantford young lady and none of her friends was Indian, she had not lost the pride in her dual heritage instilled in her by her parents. Her new ambition, she told Archie, was to "upset the Indian Extermination and Non-education Theory, in fact to stand by my blood and my race."

Pauline never recorded any instances of prejudice directed against her personally during these years, but she came face to face with dismissive stereotypes of Indians in her reading matter. William Lighthall had turned down the chance to include Pauline's "Cry from an Indian Wife," with its implicit message of two mighty races striving to understand each other, in his 1889 anthology. Instead, nine of the twelve poems in "The Indian" section of *Songs of the Great Dominion* were by non-natives. (The remaining three were pedestrian translations of traditional native songs, two from the Wabanaki people and one from the Mohawks of Caughnawaga.) A chilling assumption threaded its way through the entire section: native peoples were destined to vanish. Phrases such as "fated race" and "poor red children" recurred like drumbeats. One poem, by George Martin, began, "Onward the Saxon treads" and ended with a doleful quatrain on the disappearance of the Ottawa Indians:

I hated for his sake the reckless tread
Of human progress;—on his race no morn,

No noon of happiness shall ever beam;
They fade as from our waking fades a dream.

William Lighthall included one of his own compositions, which spoke of Indians as "dying, dwindling, dying!" And a poem entitled "The Indian's Grave," written by the mid-nineteenth-century Bishop of Montreal, George Jehoshaphat Mountain, sounded a death knell:

Poor savage! In such bark through deepening snows
Once did'st thou dwell—in this through rivers move;
Frail house, frail skiff, frail man!

In Pauline's own experience, this pessimism seemed unwarranted. Granted she had seen the Six Nations Reserve dwindle in size and most of its residents adopt European dress and names. But respect for traditional practices and ceremonies remained strong, despite attempts by government officials to discourage them. Moreover, she had also watched a handful of her fellow Iroquois make decent lives for themselves outside the reserve. Her two brothers were doing well in the insurance industry. One of her Mohawk relatives, Peter Martin, or Oronhyatekha as he was called in his own tongue, had studied at Oxford University, had graduated with a medical degree from the University of Toronto and had then joined the Independent Order of Foresters. By the early 1890s, as Chief Ranger of this fraternal benefit society, he had built the IOF into a formidable North American organization. Another person who grew up on the Six Nations Reserve, John Ojijatekha Sero, was emerging as an articulate spokesperson for Iroquois interests. He gave a talk on the Six Nations at the 1889 Toronto meeting of the American Association for the Advancement of Science.

Pauline was exasperated by a particular aspect of the literature of her day: the treatment of young native women in fiction and verse. Only a few writers took the trouble to explore the character of any Indian woman they chose to feature in their compositions, or to identify her particular features or background. "The Indian girl we meet in cold type," Pauline pointed out, "is rarely distressed by having to belong to any tribe, or to reflect any tribal characteristics. She is merely a wholesale sort of admixture of any band existing between the MicMacs of Gaspé and the Kwaw-Kwliths of British Columbia." There were about 122,000 native people in Canada, in numerous different bands, "yet strange to say . . . our Canadian authors can cull from this huge revenue of character but one Indian girl." The generic Indian heroine never had any education and was described by a variety of clichés, such as " 'dog-like,' 'fawn-like,' 'deer-footed,' 'fire-eyed,' 'crouching.' "

This was not how Pauline saw herself. An 1887 novel called *An Algonquin Maiden*, which the well-known literary critic Graeme Mercer Adam wrote in conjunction with the young Ontario journalist and poet Agnes Ethelwyn Wetherald, particularly riled her. The maiden of the title is Wanda, who is courted by a smart young Toronto beau called Edward Boulton. (Adam was much more interested in getting the non-native details right: his European characters all bore the names of Toronto's real-life Fine Old Families.) Wanda duly falls in love with Edward, and he feels obliged to offer marriage to her. But she shames him with her childlike behaviour and inattention to dress. In a moment of revelation, Edward realizes that Wanda "seemed like some coarse weed, whose vivid hues he might admire in passing, but which he would shrink from wearing on his person." In due course, Wanda drowns after saving Edward's life, releasing Edward to marry the entirely suitable Hélène DeBerczy, a creamy hothouse bloom who has no idea how to paddle a canoe.

"Will some critic," fulminated Pauline, "who understands human nature, and particularly the nature of authors, please tell the reading public why marriage with the Indian girl is so despised in books and so general in real life! Will this good far-seeing critic also tell us why the book-made Indian makes all the love advances to the white gentleman, though the real, wild Indian girl (by the way, we are never given any stories of educated girls, though there are many such throughout Canada) is the most retiring, reticent, non-committal being in existence!"

The "Evening with Canadian Authors" gave Pauline the opportunity to put these questions to Mercer Adam in person. Adam invited the evening's performers to a reception at his home at 196 Spadina Avenue.

It was an invitation for a little-known poet to treasure. In 1892, Adam was one of the Grand Old Men of the young country's cultural life. Born in Scotland in 1839, he had arrived in Upper Canada when he was in his early twenties and immediately became a pioneer in its infant publishing industry. He helped found a series of short-lived literary magazines, joined the staff of Goldwin Smith's influential periodical *The Week* in 1883, edited a series of school readers and wrote travel books, monographs about early explorers and a history of Upper Canada College. Adam knew anybody who was anybody in Toronto; when Pauline met him, he was working on a biographical compilation titled *Prominent Men of Canada* (he gave himself a prominent mention). His reputation had spread into the United States; within months of his encounter with Pauline, he would make his home in the US. A white-haired fifty-three-year-old with a gravelly Scottish accent and a penchant for snuff, Adam held court in his well-furnished sitting room while his wife, Frances, fussed around the guests.

Frank Yeigh, William and Cybel Lighthall and most of the others present on this occasion contented themselves with nodding respectfully at their host as he pontificated about the need for a national literature and the importance of good textbooks in the classroom. But Pauline was not prepared to adopt the dog-like crouch of the generic Indian maiden. She shook his hand, gave him a captivating smile and enquired how much research he had done when he and Miss Wetherald were writing their novel. "I made him confess," she wrote triumphantly to Lighthall, "that he had never met an Indian Girl and knew nothing about them." In retrospect, Pauline felt a little rueful about her bluntness to the revered critic. "I wonder if you thought me rude to dear old Mr. Adam, in differing from him in his own house," she asked Lighthall, "but I confess to you, the dear old gentleman frets me at times. The extraordinary things he made 'The Algonquin Maiden' do are astounding."

Pauline soon had another opportunity to perform in Toronto. In his role as Pauline's manager, Frank Yeigh was eager to capitalize on his new star's January triumph. He hired Association Hall for a second recital on February 19, in which Pauline was the main attraction. Nine days after the *Globe's* glowing review of Pauline's first Toronto

Miss E. Pauline Johnson,
of Brantford, the Indian Poetess, in a series of
Readings of her own poems.

Mrs. Maggie Barr Fenwick,
of Hamilton, Canada's Favorite Soprano, and
Scottish Vocalist.

Mr. Fred. Warrington,
the well-known Baritone

✳✳✳✳✳   Mr. W. S. Jones,
Organist.

TICKETS, 25 AND 50 CTS.   Association Hall,
Reserved Plan opens at Nordheimer's on Tuesday,
February 16th.   Friday Ev'g, February 19th, 1892.

SEE BLANK ORDER FORM ON FOURTH PAGE.

"Miss E. Pauline Johnson," her collar secured by a brooch
in the shape of a snowshoe, was the star attraction
of her second Toronto appearance.

performance, the paper's readers were informed that "Miss E. Pauline Johnson of Brantford, the Indian poetess," would read her own poems in "A Novel and Unique Entertainment." The programme would be filled out with musical selections by Mrs. Maggie Barr Fenwick of Hamilton, "Canada's Favorite Soprano and Scottish Vocalist," Mr. Fred Warrington, "the well-known baritone" and, last and obviously least, Mr. W. S. Jones, who was described simply as "organist." Tickets were 25 and 50 cents.

Once again Pauline travelled up from Brantford alone and made her way to Rossin House, where, she now liked to tell friends, she "always stayed" when she was in Toronto. She carefully dressed her hair and pressed the elegant white satin evening dress that she had sewn herself. Frank Yeigh arrived to escort her along Wellington Street to Association Hall; he knew that punctuality was not Pauline's strong suit, and he wanted to ensure she reached the hall in good time. When she joined him in Rossin House's marbled reception area, he was able to tell her that the recital was sold out. It was a fashionable as well as an intellectual gathering, he added with excitement: members of some of Toronto's first families were present. Frank and Pauline had already discussed which of her works she should recite. Pauline was adamant that unlike most "elocutionists" of the 1890s, who read the works of others, she would speak her own verse from memory. She had just finished a new canoe poem, which she looked forward to including. But her program would consist largely of her Indian work. From now on, she told Frank, she was going to live up to the billing "the Indian poetess."

Frank Yeigh was more than happy to follow Pauline's lead. Once the audience was settled and the last chords of Mr. Jones's overture had rolled through the hall, he straightened his cuffs and strode onto the stage. It gave him enormous pleasure, he announced, to introduce Miss Pauline Johnson, whose ancestors were one of the fifty noble families who helped organize the Iroquois Confederacy in the fifteenth century—a federation, he solemnly explained, which was almost as old as that of Switzerland. Miss Johnson's grandfather, he went on, had fought in the War of 1812, and her father had been a revered chief on the Six Nations Reserve. Coached by Pauline, Frank now came to the climax of this lavish introduction. He pointed out that Miss Johnson, who was steeped in Indian history, life and legend, "wrote as one of their number and not as an onlooker," as too many contemporary authors were wont to do.

Pauline then glided onto the stage, to loud applause. Her composure and gracefulness impressed those in the audience who had no idea what an "Indian poetess" would look or sound like. When she began to recite "A Cry from an Indian Wife," an appreciative ripple ran through the hall; many of those present had also attended the January performance. She followed this with a dramatic monologue entitled "The Avenger," which told of a Mohawk warrior who kills a Cherokee in revenge for his own brother's death. It was splendidly bloodthirsty and allowed Pauline to use her wonderful throaty voice at full throttle. In January, she had barely strayed from centre stage. This time, she paced around, directing her voice first to the left, then to the right, as she built a picture of a powerful and proud people:

"Last night, thou lent'st the knife unto my brother,
Come I now, oh Cherokee, to give thy bloody weapon back
   to thee!"
An evil curse, a flash of steel, a leap,
A thrust above the heart, well-aimed and deep,
Plunged to the very hilt in blood
While Vengeance gloating yells, "The Debt is paid!"

Pauline intended to lighten the atmosphere by reciting next a poem she had written specifically for this recital, and which was to become her most enduring memorial: "The Song My Paddle Sings." The poem combines two of her favourite themes, nature and canoeing, and describes with mounting excitement a journey through foaming whitewater. "West wind, blow from your prairie nest," she began softly, "Blow from the mountains, blow from the west. / The sail is idle, the sailor too; / O! wind of the west we wait for you." The sibilant opening lines of Pauline's celebration of a fearless and skilled female canoeist whispered their way across the hall.

I stow the sail, unship the mast:
I wooed you long but my wooing's past;
My paddle will lull you into rest.
O! drowsy wind of the drowsy west,
Sleep, sleep,
By your mountain steep,
Or down where the prairie grasses sweep!
Now fold in slumber your laggard wings,
For soft is the song my paddle sings.

August is laughing across the sky,
Laughing while paddle, canoe and I,
Drift, drift,
Where the hills uplift
On either side of the current swift.
The river rolls in its rocky bed;
My paddle is plying its way ahead;

Dip, dip,
While the waters flip
In foam as over their breast we slip.

And oh, the river runs swifter now;
The eddies circle about my bow.
Swirl, swirl!
How the ripples curl
In many a dangerous pool awhirl.

And forward far the rapids roar,
Fretting their margin for evermore.
Dash, dash,
With a mighty crash,
They seethe, and boil, and bound, and splash!

But halfway through the poem, Pauline abruptly stopped. Frank, watching from the wings, started to sweat. This was more than a pause between verses. "I vividly recall those awful few moments that seemed prolonged minutes, as she plucked a rose to pieces from a vase on the table," Frank later wrote in a memoir of that evening. "What had happened? The silence of the audience waiting for an explanation was in itself terribly oppressive until she quietly remarked, 'I'm sorry, I've forgotten the words, and if you don't mind, I'll give something else.' . . . Picking up the threads of her work, her memory did not fail her again." Another Indian monologue followed the hiatus: "The Pilot of the Plains," the haunting story of an Indian woman whose paleface lover dies as he struggles towards her through a prairie snowstorm.

Finally, Pauline returned to "The Song My Paddle Sings." This time, her canoe raced unharmed through the rapids to the calm waters of the final stanza:

We've raced the rapid, we're far ahead!
The river slips through its ancient bed,
Sway, sway,

As the bubbles spray
And fall in tinkling tunes away.

And up on the hills against the sky,
A fir tree rocking its lullaby,
Swings, swings,
Its emerald wings,
Swelling the song that my paddle sings.

Within months, "The Song My Paddle Sings" was a staple of campfire recitations at every canoe meet in Canada and the northern United States.

At the end of the evening, the ovations were even louder and longer than those of a month earlier. Frank's fashionable audience found Pauline's combination of passion and vulnerability irresistible. A handful of her listeners even asked Frank whether her forgetfulness was actually a "stage trick" to enlist exactly the kind of sympathy that she had won. Frank protested that the star would never descend to such a ploy. Pauline returned to Brantford the next day, glowing with triumph and eager to perform again. The following Saturday, *Saturday Night* announced, "Miss Johnson is sure of a hearty welcome whenever she may visit Toronto."

Now that Pauline had established her stage presence, she wondered how to improve her act. She was conscious that when reciting her Indian poems, she presented two incompatible images. On the one hand, she appeared as an entirely proper young lady with a fashionable hourglass figure, thanks to a tightly laced corset, and the air of dainty helplessness customary amongst late-Victorian gentlewomen. On the other hand, she was reciting monologues about fearless Indian warriors and women prepared to kill, or urge their sons to kill, in revenge for ghastly crimes.

Pauline cast around in her mind as she tried to decide how to give her act more punch. She had watched her father clothe himself in beads and buckskin when he wanted to impress non-natives with his tribal prestige. She also knew that there was a public appetite for "Wild West shows," in which showmen like Buffalo Bill Cody presented set-piece battles between cowboys and Indians. In 1885, Buffalo Bill had brought the great Sioux chief Sitting Bull to Brantford and Toronto as part of his Wild West Show, which included sharpshooter Annie Oakley, equestrian acrobat Buck Taylor, a cowboy band and an entourage of fifty-two Indians in feather headdresses. The show, which was staged outdoors and advertised as "the Greatest Novelty of the Century," sold out everywhere. Audiences watched re-enactments of some of the clashes, such as Custer's Last Stand at the 1876 Battle of Little Big Horn, that had occurred during the invasion and conquest of the American West in the 1860s and 1870s. From today's perspective, these shows appear to have pandered to the worst kind of stereotyping. The only Indians represented were bare-chested Plains Indians in feathered war bonnets, and the climax of the war-whooping, tomahawk-wielding battle (even as General Custer lay dying) was always a spectacular victory for cowboys, depicted as ambassadors of "white civilization." But Pauline's generation believed that the shows gave them their first glimpse of "the Redman" in his pre-contact state—the state of fierce and distinguished independence that Pauline celebrated in her poems.

The success of the Wild West shows gave Pauline an idea. The ambitious young poet had recently heard again from William Lighthall in Montreal. His anthology *Songs of the Great Dominion* had been well received in England; he enclosed a positive review from the *Athenaeum* by the revered English critic Theodore Watts-Dunton. Watts-Dunton had made special mention of Pauline's poem "In the Shadows" as an example of authentic poetry "full of the spirit of the open air." Lighthall urged Pauline to visit England so she could make the acquaintance of Mr. Watts-Dunton. Pauline valued Lighthall's counsel: "For years [I] have regarded you as my Literary Father," she replied. She told him that she hoped to visit England one day. Right now, however, she had a more immediate preoccupation: "I am going to make a feature of costuming for recitals."

But she had a problem: "For my Indian poems I am trying to get an Indian dress to recite in, and it is the most difficult thing in the world." No such thing as "an Indian dress" existed on her own Six Nations

Reserve. By now, almost all the women there preferred full-skirted European skirts and gowns. Only a handful of female elders still clung to traditional outfits, which consisted (like the clothing of women in most Indian bands) of tunics, leggings and blankets. Traditional Indian female clothing was similar to the clothing worn by older men. Pauline had in mind something more flattering, an outfit based on an American illustration of Minnehaha, wife of Hiawatha, in the copy of Longfellow's epic poem she had enjoyed as a child at Chiefswood: "Minnehaha, Laughing Water. / Loveliest of Dacotah women."

"Now I know *you know* what is feminine," Pauline wrote to Lighthall. "So can you tell me if the 'Indian Stores' in Montreal are *real* Indian stores, or is their stuff manufactured? I want a pair of moccasins, worked either in coloured moose hair, porcupine quills, or very heavily with *fine coloured beads*, have you ever seen any such there? . . . If you see anything in Montreal that would assist me in getting up a costume, be it beads, quills, sashes, shoes, brooches or indeed anything at all, I will be more than obliged to know of it."

Pauline sent the same request to the Hudson's Bay Company in Winnipeg. A company clerk replied that they could supply her with an entire outfit, including moccasins and a buckskin top and skirt, plus cuffs, collar and belt decorated with beads, moose hair and porcupine quillwork. Pauline immediately sent off a money order. As soon as the parcel from Winnipeg arrived at Napoleon Street, Pauline retreated upstairs to her bedroom. The two-piece buckskin outfit was fringed at mid-calf to show a red lining. The neck was round and, by 1892 standards, cut daringly low. When Pauline tried the outfit on, she was disappointed with what she saw in the mirror; it was both drab and lacking in style. Hearing her sister on the stairs, she called to Eva to come and see. Eva took one look at Pauline's bare arms, visible through sleeves of buckskin strips, and agreed that the costume would not do. "After contemplating the dress for a few minutes I said to Pauline: 'Why not leave one sleeve the way it is and make the other of the wild beast skins you have?'" Eva recorded in her memoirs. "Pauline thought a moment, then said, 'That is exactly what I shall do.'" She cut off the left sleeve, then attached some rabbit pelts to the left shoulder of the bodice; the pelts hung demurely past her elbow.

She decorated the front of the costume with the silver trade brooches she had inherited from her grandmother, and tied to the waistband her father's hunting knife and a Huron scalp that had belonged to her grandfather. Finally, she threw over her shoulder the scarlet blanket on which the young Duke of Connaught had stood in 1869 next to George Johnson for his induction as a chief into the Six Nations.

Once again she gazed at her reflection in the mirror. This time she was satisfied. The costume, with its asymmetrical sleeves and glittering silver decorations, combined shapely femininity with exotic appeal. The skirt was daringly short and the bodice audaciously low, but buckskin leggings and the appropriate necklace would deflect charges of immodesty. And the costume's loose fit had an additional advantage: Pauline would not have to lace her corset too tight while she wore her new outfit. This would allow her to take deeper breaths and to project a stronger voice.

A few days after this dress-up session, Pauline received a note from William Lighthall suggesting she mention her costume requests to the poet Charles Mair. Mair lived far out west, in Prince Albert, where he was employed by Ottawa as an immigration officer for the Department of the Interior. Pauline already knew of Mair, who in 1886 had published a long verse play about the War of 1812 entitled *Tecumseh: A Drama*. Mair's view of Indians was entirely sentimental: he romanticized the dead Indian leader Tecumseh, but showed little sympathy for the living Indian and Métis people around Winnipeg and on the plains. Most moderates in Central Canada regarded him as a hothead. His contempt for the Métis had helped provoke the first Métis uprising in 1869, during which he was briefly imprisoned by Louis Riel. In 1885, he was part of the force sent west to suppress the North-West Rebellion. But Pauline had a naïve reverence for anybody who took aboriginal history seriously. All she knew of Mair was his verse play, which she admired for its portrayal of the Indian chief as "A tameless soul—the sunburnt savage free—Free, and untainted by the greed of gain." For his part, Mair was flattered by Pauline's admiration and found her combination of native blood and European manners charming. He was more than happy to contribute to her "Indian poetess" stage persona. He agreed to keep an eye out for the kind of savage

*By late 1892, Pauline was bewitching audiences
with wampum belts, trade brooches, a bear-claw
necklace and fiery oratory.*

accessory she was looking for: eagle feathers, bear's teeth and claws, arrows.

Pauline's theatrical instinct proved infallible. She wore her "Indian" outfit, which was an entirely synthetic creation, to recite her Indian poems in almost all her subsequent stage performances. From then on, the first part of her programme consisted of Pauline in her Indian costume, electrifying her audience with melodramatic poems such as "A Cry from an Indian Wife," "Ojistoh" and "As Red Men Die." During a

brief interval she would hurriedly strip off the buckskin and moccasins, tighten the laces on her corset, slip on an elegant evening gown,
silk stockings and pumps (and often a picture hat), then step back onto
the stage and woo her listeners with verse about birdsong, landscapes,
mountains and trains. The evening gown was as much a theatrical costume as the native outfit. Pauline's audiences were bewitched by the
idea that one woman could embody two such different identities.
"Miss Johnson on the platform," wrote an anonymous *Saturday Night*
reviewer in December 1892, "is very different from the accomplished
lady so well known in social circles; when reciting one of her own fiery
compositions on the wrongs suffered or heroism displayed by her
Indian race, she becomes the high-spirited daughter of her warrior sires
and thrills the reader through and through."

Spirited performances in buckskin were not Pauline's only attempt
to destroy the stereotype of the passive Indian maiden that too many
non-native writers employed. In May 1892, she gave vent to her exasperation with the way Indian girls were treated in modern fiction in
an article called "A Strong Race Opinion," published in the *Sunday
Globe*: "The story writer who can create a new kind of Indian girl or
better still portray a 'real live' Indian girl will do something in Canadian literature that has never been done but once. . . . Half of our
authors who write up Indian stuff have never been on an Indian
reserve, have never met a 'real live Redman,' . . . [no] wonder that
their conception of a people they are ignorant of, save by hearsay, is
dwarfed, erroneous and delusive."

At the same time, Pauline wrote a short piece of fiction in which
the main character was just the "new kind of Indian girl" she was
talking about. She submitted "A Red Girl's Reasoning" to *The
Dominion Illustrated*'s 1892 short story competition. "It does not
stand a ghost of a chance," she told Archie. She was wrong. The story
won the contest and was published in February 1893—Pauline's first
piece of fiction to appear in print. The story describes a love match
between Christie Robinson, a beautiful young half-Indian woman,
and Charlie McDonald, a handsome blond Englishman. Christie, the
heroine who is "the offspring of red and white parentage," looks
remarkably like Pauline herself: "olive-complexioned, grey-eyed,

black-haired, with figure slight and delicate." And Christie is no dog-like Wanda. Her husband is horrified when she innocently reveals to a society hostess in a provincial capital that because there was no missionary at the isolated Hudson's Bay post where she was raised, her own parents were married in a traditional native ceremony rather than a Christian ritual. Charlie accuses his wife of publicly humiliating him with this revelation. Cut to the quick by his hypocrisy in valuing his heritage over hers, Christie doesn't hesitate for a minute. She walks out on him and refuses to be reconciled. "Why should I recognise the rites of your nation when you do not acknowledge the rites of mine?" she asks. By the end of the story, in a reversal of *The Algonquin Maiden*'s stereotype, it seems that Charlie, rather than Christie, will expire from unrequited love.

Pauline Johnson had taken the first steps towards standing "by my blood and my race," as she had told Archie she intended to do. However, her adoption of "Indian dress" and her celebration of the native point of view were geared as much to promoting her own career as to confronting wrong-headed theories. In fact, her stage act inadvertently implied that Indians might eventually be assimilated into the dominant society. If she could switch smoothly from Indian to European dress, couldn't the rest of Canada's native peoples?

Pauline was still writing from limited personal experience. She came from the wealthiest, most Europeanized Indian reserve in Canada and knew only a province where non-natives vastly outnumbered the handful of Indian peoples. She was playing with her Indian heritage; her own identity was firmly rooted in the British traditions passed on by her mother. She would have to travel into Western Canada, where the majority of Indians lived and where they faced much harsher government policies and attitudes, before she would realize the full impact of "the Indian Extermination and Non-education Theory"—and truly start to identify with Canada's native peoples.

Pauline was now in demand everywhere, thanks to her Toronto successes and Frank Yeigh's adroit management. She had become a regular contributor to *Saturday Night*, where the assistant editor, Hector

Charlesworth, bought anything she offered him. (Pay, however, was absurdly low: $3 for "The Song My Paddle Sings.") Charlesworth was an unabashed admirer of Pauline, whom he had first encountered when he was in his late teens. "I never met any native-born Canadian who gave a more complete sense of aristocracy than Pauline Johnson," he declared in his memoirs, "though when I first met her she was very poor." The critic, Pauline's junior by eleven years, was one of the first of a string of young men who became ardent fans of the Indian poet. Apart from enjoying Charlesworth's company, Pauline also realized he was a useful contact: *Saturday Night*'s notices of her performances were always positive. Pauline batted her eyelashes at young Hector and allowed him to squire her to lunches with actors such as Rosina Voke and the Belgian artiste Hortense Rhea. For his part, Charlesworth made sure that her recitals were described in *Saturday Night* in such fulsome terms as "a particular event of the season." Pauline was given as much space as rivals with far larger reputations, such as the opera singer Matilda Sissieretta Jones, "the Black Patti," and Miss Jessie Alexander, "who stands at the head of the elocutionary profession in Canada."

Hector Charlesworth, editor of Saturday Night *and subsequently chair of the Canadian Radio Broadcasting Commission. As a young man, he revered Miss Johnson.*

The summer after her Toronto debut, Pauline managed to take a few weeks off for a trip to Lake Rosseau, but by the fall her diary was full of engagements. Between October 1892 and May 1893 alone, she gave 125 recitals in 50 different towns and cities in Ontario— Paris, Fergus, Berlin, Strathroy, Watford, Renfrew, Smiths Falls, Rockland, Kingston, Lindsay. . . . The poet sometimes felt that wherever steel rails went, she was bound to follow. Yet she enjoyed the constant motion as the steam locomotives puffed from one small town to the next on the network of branch lines and private railroads that criss-crossed the province. The landscape through which she travelled was a monotonous sequence of log barns, pasture fields fenced with clumsy stumps or rail fences, swamps, woodlots and lumber towns. Like most late-nineteenth-century poets, Pauline ignored the muddy, rutted roads and mean-looking farms and saw only the purple clover, scudding clouds and church steeples. She could not read on these bone-rattling journeys, so she always took a piece of needlework with her. She was on the move. Between carefully counting her cross-stitches and gazing out of the window, she was seldom bored.

A week in advance of Pauline's appearances, Frank Yeigh would send out notices, with a picture of Pauline, to each town, announcing a run of five or six "concerts." The local bill-poster would plaster the notices on every available surface, then collect a fee when Pauline finally arrived. There would be a small advertisement in the local paper notifying readers of the Indian poetess's imminent arrival. The venues were usually modest: the local schoolroom or church hall, occasionally someone's drawing room. The performances were often sponsored by a local organization such as the Odd Fellows, the Freemasons, the Knights of Pythias or the Young Britons. Sometimes Pauline found herself on the same bill as a local fire brigade band or school choir. Unpretentious as such performances sound today, they attracted good audiences in the pre-cinema, pre-television era. Compared to alternative forms of public entertainment (usually Sunday sermons, minstrel shows and perhaps a travelling circus), Pauline was a huge novelty. In November 1893, for example, she performed for the Young Women's Guild and the Women's Chapter of St. James Anglican Church, Stratford, Ontario. She collected a fee of $25 plus expenses for her appearance—considerably more than she earned for any poems published. On the other hand, the total take for the evening was $137, so her hosts made a handsome profit.

Around this time, a young man named Orlando John Stevenson heard her for the first time. "I was fresh from college then, with the echoes of Shelley's 'East Wind' and Wordsworth's immortal 'Ode' in my ears," Stevenson wrote later in a 1927 book about Canada's finest writers. "But I can still call up the picture of the dingy lamp-lit parlor of an old manse in Eastern Ontario, where I met and talked with [Pauline Johnson]. I recall the fascination with which I listened to her recital of 'As Red Men Die' and 'The Song My Paddle Sings' in the equally dingy and almost funereal atmosphere of the village church near by. It was a new kind of poetry, which jarred and jangled strangely. . . . To this day as I recall her recital I cannot think of the march of the Iroquois chieftain over [the] bed of burning coals without an indescribable thrill."

Not all Pauline's appearances were in small towns. "I am to go to Ottawa," she wrote gleefully to William Lighthall, "and am looking forward to seeing our friends and fellow-singers there. I say 'our' in a Canadian use of the word, not personally for it sounds rather saucy." Pauline was too modest to claim membership in "the ranks where you and Lampman, Campbell and Scott . . . stood so long before I breathed poetic air. . . . My work would be little without the 'booming' or if it had been written by one without romance of ancestry." However, she proved a big hit in the nation's capital, where she performed in front of the Governor General and his wife, Lord and Lady Stanley, and several members of the Conservative Cabinet. The weather was terrible and the streets had turned into rivers of mud, but the hall was overflowing. According to the *Globe*, "It is very rarely that the vice-regal party sit out an entire programme, and that they did on this occasion was a tribute to the artiste."

Pauline acquired many new friends on her travels—often strategically placed friends who, she hoped, might help her professionally. The Indian poetess entranced an eager young Ottawa lawyer named William Scott. When she returned to Brantford after her Ottawa run, she received a short, stilted note from Scott, asking for a copy of "In Days to Come." Pauline already knew the identity of her new admirer who was so eager to reread a poem in which the poet recalls "drifting through the sunlit June" with a lover. She knew that he came, in Sandra Gwyn's words in *The Private Capital*, from a "rollicking noisy clan of sisters and brothers and cousins and aunts and uncles, who all but overflowed onto the sidewalk from the big square redbrick house" in the Sandy Hill neighbourhood. She knew that his father was Sir

Ottawa in the 1890s: Elgin Street from Parliament Hill.
The Russell House hotel, where Pauline always stayed,
is in the centre on the left of the street.

Richard Scott, a prominent Liberal politician. Stagefolk were always welcome in the Scott home: Lady Scott, William's mother, came from a family of Irish actors. The Irish-Catholic Scotts were not rich, but they were respectable—and popular, thanks to their lively parties, which often included charades and singsongs round the parlour piano. And William's cousin Agnes was a neophyte writer.

In time, Agnes Scott would emerge as the capital's most gifted social columnist, with regular columns in *Saturday Night* (under the pseudonym Amaryllis) and the Ottawa *Free Press* (where she wrote as "The Marchioness"). In 1892, Agnes was contributing anonymous reviews to the Ottawa *Citizen*. Pauline recognized that William and his cousin were useful allies in the capital. She sent William a handwritten copy of her poem, with a charming note. She also commented to him on a "very pretty" review in the *Citizen* of her performance: "I have an idea that some of your party wrote it up. That pretty cousin of yours, so apt with her pen, perhaps is at the root of the matter. At all events, whoever the writer may be, they have pleased me, and you may thank them for me for a very dainty compliment daintily expressed." And Pauline carefully noted the Scotts' Daly Avenue address in her address book so she could call on them when she was next in the capital. One just never knew when friends with contacts in the theatrical and political worlds might be helpful. . . .

Pauline also honed her ability to confuse observers with the ambiguity of her background. She was delighted when invitations began to arrive from Indian and historical societies in New York, New Jersey, Connecticut and Massachusetts—finally, she was getting international exposure. In Newark, New Jersey, members of the local canoe club escorted her from her hotel to her recital, like the praetorian guard around a Roman emperor. She bewitched a reporter from the *Boston Herald*, whose gushing article about her appearance in Boston began, "As she threw aside her Indian mink-trimmed garment . . . and stretched out a welcoming hand yesterday, one would never suspect her as being the granddaughter of 'Disappearing of the Indian Summer Mist.'" Pauline milked this encounter for all it was worth. The dazzled reporter described her as "in conversation . . . brilliant, in appearance handsome and attractive. . . . Already she has been lionized by the Hub's bright literary set."

Despite the frenetic travel and pace of performance, Pauline continued to think of herself primarily as a poet. Yet verse was only a small part of her output, and the least lucrative. In 1892 she published articles on subjects as varied as a canoe trip down the Grand River, Indian medicine men, skating and the game of lacrosse. The following year, she wrote a long account of the August meet of the American Canoe Association in the Thousand Islands region of the St. Lawrence River for the *Illustrated Buffalo Express*. But gradually she realized that stage performances were her most satisfying outlet, and the easiest way to earn money. This was particularly true after Frank Yeigh started pairing her up for recitals with a witty young Englishman named Owen Alexander Smily, a veteran of the British music halls. Smily was a versatile performer who could imitate any accent, from Cockney to Yankee, and play anything at the piano. Blond, good-looking and eight years younger than Pauline, he was the kind of young man whose company Pauline usually enjoyed. The relationship appears to have remained on a strictly professional level; Owen never married and seems to have displayed little interest in women.

For the next six years, the Johnson–Smily partnership worked well: the two managed to travel together, perform together, share the same dressing room and eat their meals together without irritating each other too much. Only when business sagged did relations deteriorate. "This place is deadly dull, we have played to poor business. . . . There is absolutely nothing going on," a tetchy Pauline wrote to a friend from Montreal at one point. "Mr. Smily and I are forced to drive about the mountain daily, at the immense threat of everlasting poverty in consequence of such extravagance, but if we did not do something, we would grow heartily tired of one another and probably quarrel." By 1893, Pauline and Owen had their act down pat. Owen always introduced the programme, which started with some sketches by him. His forte was monologues, such as "How Billy Atkins Won the Battle of Waterloo," and ventriloquist sketches with titles like "The Slum'rous Citizen and the Midsummer Fly." Owen used a lot of music hall business in his act: he would crack little jokes about local personalities, throw in some doggerel about a recent event, imitate the local accent. Then Pauline would step onto the stage in her Indian outfit and recite a few of her best-known poems, including "The Song My Paddle Sings" and "A Cry from an Indian Wife." The evening would culminate with a joint presentation: a version of "A Red Girl's Reasoning" that Pauline had rewritten as a playlet. Owen, in tie and tails, looked dash'd handsome as Charlie McDonald, while Pauline, in exquisite satin, played the fiery Christie.

Pauline's part of the programme was not always well received. Some rural Ontario communities found no charm in Pauline's beguiling looks or in her verses about warrior wives. Rowdy schoolboys liked to unnerve performers with ear-splitting imitations of cocks, dogs and cats or a steady barrage onto the stage of nuts and hard candies. Pauline was mortified in July 1893 when Archie Kains came to see her perform in Vankleek Hill, a hamlet fifty miles (eighty kilometres) east of Ottawa. In front of a meagre audience of flinty Eastern

Ontario farmers, her performance fell flat. "Gods! I wish I could forget that night," she wrote to him in New York City a few days later. "It rises like a nightmare, and blots out for the time every triumph I had last season. I wanted to do so well, to please you, to do justice to myself, and I can frankly say I never had such a failure. . . . How could one be artistic, emotional, fervent with such rows and rows of unencouraging humanity before them?"

In time, however, Pauline mastered the art of keeping spectators' attention. She acquired several professional tricks from Owen, particularly his knack for witty little asides. She recalled Rosina Voke's techniques for establishing a personal rapport with each audience. Her stage persona became less inhibited, more inviting. Although Pauline would not dream of describing herself as an "actress," with its undertones of vulgarity and impropriety, she was now comfortable and animated when she was in front of the footlights. She threw herself into her blood-and-guts narrative poems. A shiver ran through each audience when Pauline let loose an eerie, off-stage war whoop, then glided softly to centre stage to recite "The Avenger."

Theatre reviewers liked the change. "Miss Johnson," announced the *Globe*, "has improved her elocution." She received "a pretty and flattering" notice in the Toronto *Empire*, for which she wrote a charming note of thanks to the author, Faith Fenton. (Faith Fenton was the pen name of a Toronto schoolteacher, Alice Freeman, to whom Pauline sent "love, to a fellow craftsman, or rather woman.") When Pauline appeared at the Toronto Cricket Club's annual concert, she was given a standing ovation. The Toronto *Daily Tribune* reported that "as a reader of her own poems, [Miss E. Pauline Johnson] is a great success, possessing as she does a clear, musical voice and an unusual gift of expression." At a performance at Brantford's Grace Church—her own church—the "enraptured assemblage became wild with enthusiasm," according to the local paper.

But some friends who had known the "old" Pauline were not so sure. Harry O'Brien was a Toronto lawyer Pauline had met in 1892 in Muskoka, where he was Commodore of the Muskoka Lakes Canoe Association. A jovial fellow who always wore a battered yachting cap, he loved the Pauline he had first met—a dignified young woman who wrote lyrical verse about maple-mantled hills, or stirring monologues about long-forgotten braves. After he saw her in performance early in 1894, he found himself unable to say anything to her about her act. He had hated the way she now catered to appreciative crowds and fed on their laughter and applause. He reproached her for debasing her talent.

Harry's disapproval stung Pauline to the quick. She knew that respectable people, including her mother, felt this way about actresses. Suddenly the "heights of Literature" to which she had always aspired seemed to slip into the distance. Archibald Lampman and Duncan Campbell Scott would never spend their lives touring one-horse towns, imitating the local landowner and making grocers and blacksmiths laugh. On the other hand, Scott and Lampman didn't have to—they both had government jobs. "More than all things," she wrote to Harry, "I hate and despise brain debasement, literary 'pot-boiling.' . . . The reason for my actions in this matter? Well—the reason is that the public will not listen to lyrics, will not appreciate poetry, will in fact not have me as an entertainer if I give them nothing but rhythm, cadence, beauty, thought." Pauline's earnings helped support her family and her ambition. Although she knew that Harry was right—that she was fast becoming an entertainer rather than a poet—she could not afford to step off the stage if she was going to follow William Lighthall's advice and go to England.

Pauline had nursed an ambition to go to England for as long as she could remember. It is not clear why London was a greater magnet for her than New York City, a rival (and more easily accessible) publishing mecca to which writers like Bliss Carman had gravitated. Perhaps it was her upbringing, steeped in loyalty to all things British, and the traditional Iroquois assumption of a "special relationship" with the Imperial Crown. Perhaps it was Michael Mackenzie's accounts of life in the Old Country. Perhaps it was Watts-Dunton's gratifying review of "In the Shadows." Whatever the reason, Pauline wanted to be accepted within the heart of the society from which English-speaking Canada took its cue. She wanted recognition and status in the country from which her mother's family had come. As early as 1888, Pauline had told William Lighthall that "my intention is to publish [my work in] a book sometime in the future." By 1894, she had decided she wanted such a book published in London. And she had finally scraped together enough money to pay for the trip.

"The committee, who had charge of the entertainment to be given for Pauline a few days before her departure, asked whether she would rather have money or a piece of jewelry as a gift," Evelyn Johnson wrote in her memoirs, as she recalled the send-off that Brantford gave her sister in April 1894. "Pauline said that she would rather have the money to help her on her undertaking. The day before she left on her trip the citizens of Brantford presented her with a purse of gold. We all drove down to the Kerby House where the entertainment was to take place. Just as we stepped out of the cab, the Reverend Mr. Mackenzie came forward to assist Pauline and the rest of us. He said, 'This is the very thing that should have happened: your clergyman to meet you and escort you up the stairs.'"

Pauline, resplendent in a white cashmere gown trimmed with heliotrope-purple velvet, spent the evening receiving the burghers of Brantford in the salon where the Prince of Wales had been entertained in 1860. After shaking dozens of hands, she gave a graceful little speech of thanks and recited one of her poems. In the audience, Emily Johnson must have felt her heart swell with pride. She followed Pauline's career with intense interest; when Pauline performed in Toronto or in any town close to Brantford, Emily was always there. She admired Pauline's creative achievements and her ambition, despite her own instinctive distaste for the theatre. She believed that once Pauline had found a London publisher for her poems, her younger daughter would leave the stage. Now Pauline was going to return to the land from which she herself had sailed sixty-two years earlier. What mother would not be suffused with both happiness and anxiety on behalf of her daughter? Especially one as obsessed with respectability as Emily.

The following day, Friday, April 27, Pauline climbed aboard the train at Brantford's Grand Trunk Railway depot. Her brother Allen and sister, Eva, travelled with her as far as Harrisburg, Pennsylvania, then Pauline went on alone to New York. There she boarded the Cunard steamship *Etruria* for passage to Liverpool. The *Etruria*, which operated a weekly service between Liverpool and New York,

Emily Johnson wished that her talented daughter
would settle down and stay close to home.

was a prestigious vessel on which to travel. It had won the Blue Ribbon six years earlier for the fastest crossing of the Atlantic, and both Lord Curzon and the British music hall star Marie Lloyd crossed the Atlantic on it the same year as Pauline. Once Pauline had set foot on British soil, she would take the train south from Liverpool to London. The flinty farmers of Vankleek Hill were behind her; the elegant salons of Mayfair lay ahead. Surely now, she must have felt, she was on the right path to Parnassus.

11

SMOG AND
SNOBBERY IN THE
IMPERIAL CAPITAL

1894

I N 1894, London throbbed with its own wealth and success. It was
the biggest city on the globe and the centre of the largest empire
the world had ever seen. But Pauline's first glimpse of the Imperial capital left a great deal to be desired. Travelling alone into Euston
Station on the Great Northern Railway from Liverpool, all she could
see in the watery May sunlight were the cramped backyards of terrace
houses, their brickwork blackened with soot, in the dreary suburbs of
East Hampstead and Cricklewood. Beyond them was an immense sea
of little chimneys rising from slated roofs, while in the distance tall
industrial chimneys belted out black clouds. Smoke from coal fires,
factories, steam trains and freighters was a constant feature of London's
atmosphere. The smog routinely dimmed the light, created mon-
strous fogs, or "pea-soupers," and speckled faces, cuffs and collars
with dirty smuts or "blacks." Late-nineteenth-century Toronto, with
a population of 200,000, was dirty enough, but London, ten times
larger, was filthy.

Pauline had been dreadfully seasick on her transatlantic crossing.
When the *Etruria* finally docked, she wrote to Harry O'Brien, it took
her a long time to recover her "land gait." She was still feeling
unsteady when she disembarked from the train. Her first glimpse of
Euston Station's vast glass-covered terminus took her breath away. So
did the noise that echoed across all the platforms: the yells of porters,

the clatter of horse-drawn carriages, the squeal of train brakes, the *whoosh* of steam. Clutching her valise, she asked a porter to help her hire a hansom cab and learned to her dismay that half of London's 11,000 cabdrivers were on strike against the cab owners. They were demanding a fare hike because (in the words of their petition of grievances) "omnibuses, telephones, messenger boys and other appliances of civilization have cut down their business enormously." The Euston cab rank was empty. She would have to store her steamer trunk at the station to collect later, and take an omnibus. Because of the cab strike, the vehicles of the London General Omnibus Company were jam-packed with disgruntled travellers. Pauline eventually discovered one going in her direction and struggled up the staircase to the open-air "garden seats" on the roof. At least, she consoled herself, the weather was fine and she would get a good view of London and its citizens.

She had barely sat down before the driver flicked his whip across the rumps of his two horses and the omnibus trundled off. Its route, with frequent stops, took it along Euston Road, through the maze of streets in Marylebone and onto leafy Bayswater Road. Pauline gazed out at an ever-changing vista. The streets around Euston reminded her of Toronto's Cabbagetown; they were lined with homely shops, food stalls and crowded housing. Most of the people she passed were poorly dressed; the women's aprons were dirty, and the men, in flat caps and grubby vests, were obviously labourers. But as the bus creaked around Marble Arch and set off down the Bayswater Road towards Holland Park, Pauline saw the leafy expanse of Hyde Park on her left and on her right, creamy-white terraces of four-, five- or even six-storey houses with pillared porticos and elaborate plasterwork. Elegant women, wearing the latest leg-of-mutton sleeves and beribboned bonnets, leaned on the arms of top-hatted, frock-coated gentlemen as they strolled down the pavement. Delivery carts, private carriages, cyclists and some strikebreaking hansom cabs narrowly avoided each other as they rolled down the street. There was a continuous rumble of wooden wheels on cobbled streets and a pungent smell of horse manure, human sweat, gas fires and rotten fruit.

Pauline's destination was 25 Portland Road, Holland Park West. Portland Road was situated at the northern limits of one of London's most respectable districts, the Royal Borough of Kensington. The smart end of Kensington lay to the south, between Kensington High Street and the Old Brompton Road. Every summer afternoon, the open-air tea rooms in Kensington Gardens hosted throngs of wealthy area residents, who took tea under the elms and listened to military music from the regimental band playing in the bandstand. Nurse-maids pushed well-sprung baby carriages around the Serpentine and supervised small boys in sailor suits as they launched their toy boats on the Round Pond.

The Royal Borough's north end, where Pauline was headed, was a great deal less sophisticated. Portland Road was a pleasant enough street of four-storey Georgian terraced houses, with iron railings around their basement areas and big casement windows. However, most of the houses had been subdivided into dwellings for two or three families. The end of the street closest to Holland Park Avenue was still a professional preserve. Architects, successful merchants and clerks lived there, and most employed servants. But as the road headed north, the number of people in each house increased and their occupations became humbler: dressmaker, ironmonger's assistant, plasterer, tailor's apprentice. The far end of Portland Street was close to one of the poorest areas of West London, Notting Dale. Here, pigs snuffled along crowded lanes, and each ramshackle cottage housed two or three families. Notting Dale men laboured in the local brickworks. Their womenfolk spent their days up to their elbows in soapsuds, doing laundry for the gentry who lived in Mayfair and Knightsbridge. Notting Dale pubs did a roaring trade every night. The death rate in this district was more than double that for Kensington as a whole, and nearly half the babies born in the cheap lodging houses, furnished rooms and brothels died before they were a year old. For more than a century, the area had been a major stopping-off place for brightly coloured gypsy vans in the late spring. Pauline would have seen wild-haired gypsy women telling fortunes on Holland Park Avenue and swarthy rag-and-bone men driving their barrows around Notting Hill.

Pauline dismounted from the bus on Holland Park Road, turned right into Portland Road and looked for Number 25. She found it on the west side of the street, comfortably close to Holland Park Avenue.

The house belonged to a retired schoolmaster from Suffolk named Thomas Sheffield, who usually had two boarders in the house in addition to his wife and daughter, a music teacher. It is likely that Sir Richard Scott, the prominent Liberal politician Pauline had met in Ottawa in 1892, had suggested Pauline stay in Holland Park. A branch of the Scott family headed by a Mr. James Scott and his wife, Emma, lived at Number 23, next door to Mr. Sheffield, and probably arranged her lodgings. It must have been reassuring for the young poet to hear familiar Canadian voices amongst the medley of London, Suffolk and Scottish accents of the street's residents. Pauline had taken a brave and unconventional step when she had purchased her ticket to England. Although she was now thirty-three and accustomed to travelling around Ontario on her own, it was a very different matter for a respectable young woman to reside unchaperoned in London. Back home, her reputation preceded her, and she was usually able to enlist the patronage of the local mayor or church minister in the friendly small towns she visited. In London, she was alone, unknown and vulnerable. The city teemed with prostitutes; between 80,000 and 120,000 "ladies of the night" plied their trade within its population of 2.25 million. Some were like the miserable women, victims of vice, who stumble through the novels of Charles Dickens, but many were fashionable courtesans who openly competed with their "respectable" rivals. The plethora of prostitutes at every social level meant that any unaccompanied female might be regarded as "fair prey" as she walked along the street or mingled in a crowd.

Pauline had brought mementos of home with her, which were soon artfully displayed in the studio apartment at the top of Number 25. On the mantelpiece, she placed a fierce medicine man mask from the Six Nations Reserve. On a screen, she draped her stage costume: her buckskin tunic, ermine tails, scalp and beaded wampum belt. She had also brought several photographic portraits of herself, taken by Mr. Cochran in his Brantford studio. Most important, in the bottom of her valise, she had the poems for which she intended to find a publisher, and the letters of introduction from prominent Canadians with which she hoped to secure some public engagements. She knew that the key to publication would be to establish a reputation as an artistic performer. As a penny-pinching, unknown colonial, she could not afford to rent a hall for a recital or hope to attract an audience off the street. Instead, she planned to make a name for herself as a drawing-room performer, entertaining Mayfair society in its own opulent homes.

During her early days in London, Pauline methodically learned the city's geography as she walked around Knightsbridge, Mayfair and Chelsea delivering her letters. She called on two former Governors General, both of whom had visited the Johnson family in its glory days at Chiefswood. The first was the elderly Marquess of Dufferin and Ava, who had come in 1874; the second was the Marquess of Lorne, with his wife, Princess Louise, whom she had met in 1879. She left her card at the mansion of Mr. Edward Piggott, Deputy Lord Chamberlain of London, along with a letter from the Reverend Professor William Clark, the amiable Professor of Mental and Moral Philosophy at Trinity College in Toronto. As she trudged around, she became progressively more discouraged. "The boy in buttons at the stairway perceptibly elevated his nose as he enquired what and who we wanted," she later wrote. "The footman, resplendent in the glory of gold braid and pompous consciousness of his own importance gave us a stony British stare." Too many of her evenings during her first week or two in London were spent by herself in her attic room, missing family and friends. A letter from Harry O'Brien arrived, advising her that "what is gained without a struggle is not so much worth the having." She shed a tear at the sight of his writing, but she took the advice to heart. "The words did me good," she acknowledged in her reply.

Two individuals proved to be the most useful allies in Pauline's cam-

Sir Charles Tupper, the former Premier of Nova Scotia and future Prime Minister of Canada, welcomed Pauline to London.

paign to conquer London. The first was Sir Charles Tupper, the ebullient Maritimer and former Premier of Nova Scotia who was currently serving as Canada's representative in London. (In 1896, he would be summoned home to become Prime Minister of Canada, then would lead the federal Conservatives to defeat in the 1896 election.) Sir Charles could never resist a pretty face; he was a well-known womanizer whose nickname back home in Nova Scotia was "the Ram of Northumberland." He invited Pauline to the annual Dominion Day celebration at the Westminster Palace Hotel. There, Pauline was welcomed into the small but lively colony of Canadians in London. After several days' exposure to buttoned-down Brits, Pauline revelled in the company of her fellow countrymen. "We Canadians laugh so much more than the people here," she wrote to Harry. The second ally was the Earl of Aberdeen, Britain's representative in Canada, who had admired Pauline's performance in Ottawa the previous year. Through him, Pauline secured an invitation to tea with Lady Ripon, wife of Britain's Colonial Secretary and one of London's most intelligent and celebrated hostesses. Over six feet tall, Lady Ripon entertained, according to her contemporary E. F. Benson, "with a touch of that apotheosized Bohemianism of which nobody else ever quite had the secret." The encounter between the tall and overwhelmingly grand Lady Ripon, sparkling with diamonds and *bons mots*, and the small, slender Canadian in her slightly outdated Brantford tea gown, makes a beguiling picture. But Pauline was obviously at her most charming and ladylike in Lady Ripon's Bruton Street drawing room. A few days later, the summons for which Pauline longed arrived at 25 Portland Street. Lady Ripon would like Pauline to attend her next dinner party and recite some of her poetry afterwards. London Society would at last have the opportunity to inspect "the Mohawk poet."

By now, Pauline had realized that upper-crust Londoners were intrigued by her Indian ancestry. Buffalo Bill Cody had already toured England, putting on spectacular open-air shows with his troupe of hundreds of cowboys and Indians, and sparking British interest in "Redskins" in buckskin and feathers. But Pauline offered a new angle on North American natives. She was the first female "Redskin" to appear; Buffalo Bill included no Indian women in his troupe. She was

In London, Pauline acquired the mannerisms appropriate for aristocratic drawing rooms.

the first native North American who claimed both a pedigree and a poetic gift that made her acceptable in the drawing room. She decided to play up to the interest in her Iroquois pedigree. Still, this did not mean dressing in her beads and buckskin for a Society dinner. Although she could never compete with the trappings and tiaras of Society's *grandes dames*, her evening gowns passed muster. And a couple of evenings' exposure to the British aristocracy were all that a mimic like Pauline needed to absorb the la-di-da mannerisms of a duchess.

However, Pauline did not forget her Mohawk heritage as she strove for acceptance in Mayfair. At the Ripons' dinner, she found herself seated at the immense mahogany dining table between Lord Ripon and the Deputy Speaker of the House of Commons. She gently let rip in the candlelight. "I talked politics and constitution," she boasted to Harry O'Brien, "and told them there was *no* government existing save the confederated government of the Iroquois, that Hiawatha was the only statesman who ever solved the problem of perfect government and economy." The two middle-aged parliamentarians were captivated by this beautiful young woman. She conformed comfortably to their idea of how such a "fine-lookin' gel" should behave; her manners were as good as those of any young debutante from the Court of St. James. Yet she spoke so thrillingly about people they had assumed were savages. Lord Ripon and his guest rarely met anybody at a dinner party whose grandparents, let along parents, hadn't known each other since childhood. In their circle, families of almost identical backgrounds had intermarried for generations. A woman who was not only the product of such divergent backgrounds but who also juggled with such finesse her two identities—Mohawk and English Canadian—was fascinating. Her subversive political commentary was downright delightful.

Pauline was secretly amused at the aristocrats' obvious excitement that "they had got hold of something new to them." She also managed to tuck into a "disgracefully large dinner" before the party moved into the drawing room for her recital. Lady Ripon was sufficiently pleased with her guests' reaction to Pauline that she invited the young Canadian to return for a whole evening of readings. "So it seems," Pauline gloated to Harry, "that notwithstanding my dissertation on statesmanship and my unusually large appetite, that I scored a success."

Lady Ripon's drawing room led to more invitations. Pauline formed a lasting friendship with Lady Blake, the Irish-born wife of Sir Henry Austin Blake, who was currently serving as Governor of Ceylon. However, Pauline could see that the route to publication was not through the Ripons and the Blakes. London Society loved novelty because boredom was an occupational hazard for the British aristocracy of this period. Edward, Prince of Wales, set the tone of London's *bon ton*, and it was a tone that valued appearance over intellect, entertainment over philanthropy. Each spring, a new sensation emerged to amuse the wellborn. One year it was Mrs. Shaw, the American society whistler, who pursed her lips so prettily. Next came Lillie Langtry, who parlayed her classical features and naughty wit into an affair with the Prince himself. Mrs. Langtry, in turn, was supplanted by the French actress Sarah Bernhardt, who was rumoured to travel with a circus of pet cheetahs and to sleep in a coffin lined with pink silk. A home-grown favourite (until he stepped over the line) was Oscar Wilde, who strutted about in silk knee breeches, a green carnation and lilac gloves (carried, never worn) declaiming the new doctrine of aesthetics. In 1894, Pauline found herself in competition with two American poets as the "latest thing." The first was a fixture of London salons: the flamboyant Californian Joaquin Miller, who strode into ducal houses in boots, spurs and flowing hair. Miller liked to fling a buffalo robe on the Aubusson carpets and declaim his poetry from the horizontal position. The second drawing-room sensation of the season was Paul Lawrence Dunbar, who, according to the *Illustrated American*, was lionized "not because he is a poet but because he is a negro who writes poetry. A freak is apt to interest London Society." In Canada, *Saturday Night* magazine made the sour suggestion that Pauline Johnson was similarly celebrated in the Imperial capital not because she was "a poet of authentic gift," but because, "being an Indian, she could write at all. . . . Let a man be a poet if he will, but the great thing is that he should be a curiosity. Then, for a day and a night, he may have London at his feet."

Most of these sensational entertainments soon faded from view. In 1878, the fashionable London magazine *Vanity Fair* summed up the privileged ennui that afflicted the British aristocracy: "London Society has a high and holy mission. That mission is to amuse itself; and the only amusement it has yet discovered, or ever seems likely to discover, is that of meeting itself. . . . At noon, when the day of Society may be said to begin, . . . comes the morning walk or ride, followed by luncheon, a drive, dinner, and the evening parties. In none of these is anything like conversation to be found. It would be considered impertinent and presuming for anybody to make a remark exceeding twenty words in length, or including more than one idea." Pauline might briefly amuse a few members of this selfish little world, but they felt no obligation to help her achieve her ambition.

The Canadian poet recognized this. "They invite me to their houses as 'a great American Indian author,'" she admitted to O'Brien, "an astoundingly clever poet, a marvellous new interpreter of verse etc., and I go, and am looked up to, and dined, and wined, and I amount to a little tin god, for the titled people pretend not to literature." Their philistine gullibility shocked her: "They are good enough to be blinded by my posings, and mistake my fads, my love of race, my Indian politics for exceeding brightness, and the outcome of extreme originality and talent. Bah! And I without enough education to pad my intellect, let alone form the substance. . . . They cannot be clever to be deceived so easily."

Pauline needed an entrée into what she called "*thinking* London" to get her poems published. But all the soigné self-assurance she displayed amongst aristocrats deserted her when she was amongst writers and artists. "The great minds make me feel uncomfortable, illiterate, woefully lacking, terribly ignorant and insufficiently read," she confided to Harry. "They do not mean to, but they do." As the days ticked on and she was no closer to getting into print, her spirits drooped and her confidence seeped away: "I feel a worm, a veritable *nothing* in the critic's den or the author's library." She decided to get her manuscript typed, in the hope that when she eventually met a potential publisher, the poems would have more credibility. But the typist did a terrible job, and Pauline subsequently discovered that no poet worth her or his salt bothered with such irrelevancies.

It has never been easy for outsiders to penetrate London's fast-paced cultural life. Moreover, Pauline had arrived in London at a point when the arts were in flux. Crowds still flocked to the old standbys of Victorian theatre—Henry Irving in Shakespearean classics at the Lyceum Theatre, Marie Lloyd in the music halls. Every summer, the Royal Academy was filled with conventional landscapes and portraits. The Romantic poets for whom Pauline had always professed admiration— the early works of Swinburne, Tennyson's *Idylls*—remained in print. However, the mid-Victorian taste for melodrama and romance in drama, fiction and poetry was being challenged by the new fin-de-siècle taste for decadence. Queen Victoria remained firmly on the throne, but a younger generation of artists was already caricaturing the moral earnestness of the Victorian era. Writers like Oscar Wilde and Richard Le Galienne suggested that art and morality were separate realms; with behaviour that ranged from perverse through paradoxical to shocking, they insisted on the aesthetic doctrine of "art for art's sake." On stage, playwrights like Henrik Ibsen and Sir Arthur Pinero skewered the hypocrisy of nineteenth-century life. George Bernard Shaw was teaching theatregoers, in the words of E. F. Benson, "that plays were not meant to amuse them but to make them think." An artist like James McNeill Whistler, the American who painted so many of London's Society beauties, unsettled the establishment with his arrogant combination of genius and disrespect for his patrons.

The shifting values of cultural life in London were most obvious in get-togethers that took place in artists' studios. These gatherings were Bohemia's equivalent of Society's dinner parties and drawing-room entertainments. Unlike the monosyllabic banalities of drawing rooms, conversation in artists' studios crackled with conflicting opinions, theatrical monologues, passionate debate and the cross-fertilization of ideas. "Thinking London is so very clever, so far beyond me, so great, so penetrating," wailed Pauline to Harry O'Brien. Yet this was the milieu she longed to join. She wanted to be accepted as a poet by her peers, rather than as a novelty by "all the lordlings and ladylings in London" who rarely opened a book. "I *like* my Lord's presence, though I *seek* the great thinkers."

Through dogged effort, Pauline managed to elbow her way into "*thinking* London." A Toronto friend had given her a letter of introduction to Charles Hamilton Aidé, one of Victorian London's more intriguing personalities. Born in Paris and educated in Bonn, Aidé had served in the British army before publishing his first novel in the 1860s. From then on, according to *The Times*, he was "one of the people you 'met everywhere'—at worldly or literary dinner tables, at great receptions and at 'first nights.'" Multilingual and immensely talented, he published poetry and fiction, wrote successful plays and was an accomplished watercolourist. When Pauline arrived in London, Mr. Aidé—or "Cynicus," as he styled himself—was adapting a French farce entitled *Dr. Bill* for a production at the Court Theatre; its risqué subject matter and dialogue caused a furor when it was eventually staged. Aidé lived in an elaborately decorated apartment in Hanover Square, between Bond Street and Regent Street. This allowed him to keep one foot in the swanky Society of Mayfair and the other in the theatrical demi-monde of Soho.

Perhaps it was Hamilton Aidé's cosmopolitan background that made him far more open to new voices, and outsiders, than most Londoners. Hospitable and charming, he was best known for the afternoon salons he organized, at which invited guests performed in front of the cultural elite. In early June, Pauline appeared in his Hanover Square drawing room. With Old World courtesy, Aidé ensured an impressive turnout for his New World ingenue. Among those present for Pauline were several artists (including George Frederick Watts, Sir Frederick Leighton, Lawrence Alma-Tadema and Edward Burne-Jones), the novelist Jerome K. Jerome, George Alexander (actor-manager of St. James Theatre) and the literary critic Percy White. None of these men could be said to be particularly avante-garde; most were close to their host in age, and their work fed the mainstream tastes of mid-Victorian life. However, Aidé's guests were well-known and well-established, and Pauline knew that their good opinion could be valuable. She recited for them all the poems, both nature and Indian, that had won the most applause in the small towns of Ontario. She also performed a dramatization of her story "A Red Girl's Reasoning," in which she played the parts of both Christie Robinson, the beautiful young half-Indian woman, and handsome Charlie, the English husband whom she abandons when he refuses to recognize her parents' marriage.

Aidé's friends loved her. Pauline's poetry, like her conversation at the Ripons' dinner table, had challenged many of the unthinking assumptions of British imperialism—the superiority of British culture, the intellectual inferiority of natives, the impossibility of bridging a racial gulf. George Alexander (who was sufficiently daring to stage the plays of Oscar Wilde) was so taken with "A Red Girl's Reasoning" that he considered making a full-length drama out of it. Along with his fellow guests, he decided to promote this young visitor from the colonies. He sent her complimentary tickets to his show at the St. James Theatre. He introduced her to two members of the theatre's royal family: Herbert Beerbohm Tree, actor-manager of the Haymarket Theatre, and his wife, the actress Helen Maude Holt. Soon there were no more lonely evenings on Portland Street. Pauline received complimentary seats for theatres all over London—for Daly's Theatre to see Eleanora Duse in *La Signora dalle Camelie*; for the Lyceum Theatre to see Henry Irving and Ellen Terry in *Faust*; for the Opéra Comique to see Lillie Langtry in *Society Butterfly*.

Just as Pauline had picked up clues on how to perform for Toronto audiences from watching Rosina Voke glide across the stage of the Grand Opera House, so she now educated herself in how to appeal to London audiences. Inspired by Duse's and Langtry's sense of style, Pauline went shopping. On Kensington High Street, there were three big department stores that catered to the desire of the emerging middle class to dress as well (if not as expensively) as London's grandees. Pauline fingered the silks and satins of the evening gowns in the ladies' departments of Barker's, Derry & Tom's and Ponting's, eventually settling on a creamy brocade dinner dress from Barker's, with a

Barker's department store on Kensington High Street
provided Pauline with a glamorous new wardrobe.

bustle and a low-cut bodice. She also ordered four ballgowns from a well-regarded (but moderately priced) seamstress on Westbourne Grove. These became the costumes for the second half of her stage performances.

Thanks to Hamilton Aidé, Pauline gained access to some of the most exotic artists' salons of the 1890s. Sir Frederick Leighton, the sixty-four-year-old artist who had become President of the Royal Academy in 1878, invited her to walk over to the incredible house he had commissioned for himself on Holland Park Avenue. Leighton House boasted black and gold lacquered woodwork, ornate furnishings and elaborate Corinthian pillars. Its pièce de résistance was the Arab Hall, completely covered in gold and turquoise Turkish tiles, creating the atmosphere of a harem. Pauline was so overcome by the richness of the decor that, on impulse, she presented the bearded patriarch with one of her precious wampum belts. Leighton dashed off a note of thanks to her in which he acknowledged, "My compunction lies in the fact that to you it represents a valuable personal relic, and have therefore some scruple in robbing you of it." However, the wealthy old man did not return the belt to his impecunious guest, or even send her one of his own sketches in return.

Pauline was equally overwhelmed when Alma-Tadema invited her up to what she described as his "paradise home" in St. John's Wood to see some of his much-admired genre paintings of ancient Greek and Roman subjects. Alma-Tadema had just spent 70,000 pounds (over $3.5 million in today's currency) remodelling a large, secluded house he had purchased in 1884 from the portraitist and caricaturist Jacques Joseph Tissot. The result was a sixty-six-room Pompeiian extravaganza that included a billiard room, three large studios (Alma-Tadema's wife, Laura Epps, was also an accomplished painter), antique Dutch woodwork, Byzantine leaded windows and a wealth of works by contemporary artists. The vaulted ceiling of Alma-Tadema's vast studio, which was modelled on an early Christian church, was coated in aluminum to maximize the northern light. Alma-Tadema himself, a squeaky little man dwarfed by his own ambitions, held regular afternoon gatherings, cloyingly described as "Twosday At Homes." Visitors drifted through the studio, muttering "very par'ful" or "perfectly sweet" as they gazed at canvasses depicting Greek youths and maidens reclining on marble benches, with an azure sea visible through pink flowering almond trees. Pauline could barely suppress a smile as she watched her host "trotting about his studio in a very inartistic tweed suit, serving tea to his guests." In an article she wrote four years later, she described his "effervescent manner that would seem schoolboyish in anyone else."

Alma-Tadema made a fuss over his Canadian guest. He led her to the grand piano and showed her the underside of its cover, which had been covered in parchment and bore the autographs of most of the great pianists and vocalists of the day. He was thrilled because the Polish pianist Ignace Paderewski had added his signature that morning. Pauline immediately felt that she too must make an offering on the Alma-Tadema altar; Alma-Tadema promptly suggested that she should write a poem for him. Ever mindful of the importance of Alma-Tadema's patronage, Pauline composed a verse that would flatter the fifty-eight-year-old painter. The result, "The Art of Alma Tadema," celebrates "the Master's touch" which makes "the marbles leap to life":

> There is no song his colours cannot sing,
> For all his art breathes melody and tunes
> The fine, keen beauty that his brushes bring
> To murmuring marbles and to golden Junes.

Through all this coming and going, Pauline never lost sight of her first priority: to get her poetry published. She knew that this required her to build a public profile, and also to knock on publishers' doors. Soon after she arrived in London, her exotic origins successfully snagged the attention of the press. On June 13, *The Sketch*, a chatty London weekly, carried an article entitled "Tekahionwake," which began, "Do not be alarmed, gentle reader. This is no word puzzle. It is the name of a charming young Mohawk Indian lady who has come to England to sing the songs of the Iroquois in the English tongue, and to awaken us to a truer sense of the mental power and high qualities of the people who have the best claim to the title deeds of the vast continent of North America." Tekahionwake (pronounced "dageh-eeonwageh") was Pauline's grandfather's name, and she had no legal claim to it. There is no evidence that she had ever used it before she crossed the Atlantic. But in London its use paid off: it gave her added cachet and underscored her novelty. From then on, she incorporated it into her public image.

The writer from *The Sketch* went all out in his description of Pauline. Ignoring her true colouring and her gentle grace, the anonymous journalist extolled her "brilliant black eyes, high cheekbones and olive complexion. . . . My eye chanced to fall upon the picture in which a Cherokee Indian, brandishing a scalping knife in a most murderous attitude, stands with foot upon the throat of a writhing Mohawk. 'But you can't say you like that sort of thing, Miss Johnson?' [the writer asked]. 'I love everything Indian,'" a defiant Pauline replied. Pauline knew instinctively how to play her hand; she both embraced and confronted the stereotype of Indians held by her listener. "I am a Red Indian," she told the writer, who was thrilled by the young woman's panache, "and feel very proud. . . . You English, who owe so much to the Indian—where would your British America have been had he helped the French as he helped you long years ago? I daresay you, like the rest, think and write of [the Indian] as a poor degraded savage, walking around with a scalping knife in one hand and a tomahawk in the other, seeking whom he may devour. . . . [But] put a pure-blooded Indian in a drawing-room, and he will shine with the rest of you." Pauline then recited part of her bloodthirsty poem "The Avenger," about a young Mohawk warrior who stabs to death his brother's murderer.

The *Sketch* writer was hooked: "Yes, I thought to myself, such a picture of Indian life, delivered in costume, with all the fire of an Indian's nature, would form a striking contrast to the skirt-dance and *tableaux-vivants* of the London drawing-room." *The Sketch* illustrated the article with two of Mr. Cochran's photos of Pauline in her "Indian outfit." In one, Pauline's expression is as ferocious as a warrior's, in the other, as heavy-lidded and passionate as a royal courtesan. Pauline, now an expert in manipulating her image, could not have paid for better advertising.

A few days later, a writer from another London publication, *The*

Gazette, interviewed Pauline. This time, the journalist was less impressed by the Indian paraphernalia draped around Pauline's room and more interested in the status of native people in the Great Dominion of the North. Pauline met the challenge with a graceful, but firm, description of history from the Indian point of view. She spoke of the political sophistication of the 400-year-old Iroquois Confederacy, and quoted Henry David Thoreau, Francis Parkman and the anthropologist Horatio Hale. She described the welcome given by Canada's natives to European settlers, and the arrogant assumption of successive British governments that they could take possession of the continent. She explained the art and science of wampum belts, and when asked if she had ever "eaten the Canadian national dish," replied with a straight face, "No, you have killed off nearly all our beavers."

The writer from *The Gazette* was taken aback by this forthright young woman. He respectfully suggested to Pauline that "You yourself would hardly be leading your present life of culture had it not been for the white man's invasion."

Pauline's response hints that underneath her bold public face, she was finding it increasingly difficult to retain her self-possession. Here in the heart of the British Empire, the tension between her identities was starting to tell. "Perhaps not the same kind of life," she replied. "But there are two of me. Sometimes I feel I must get away to the Highlands among a people who seem somehow akin to mine."

By the end of June, Pauline's perseverance had borne fruit. The same Professor Clark in Toronto who had given her a letter of introduction to the Deputy Lord Chamberlain of London had also supplied one to Clement Scott, a respected reviewer whose flowing fur coat and well-filled white waistcoat were watched for with dread at every opening night in London. He had established a reputation for astringent criticism in the 1880s at *Punch*. Now he was the dean of the metropolis's critics and wrote for the *Daily Telegraph*. Scott cultivated the image of an unfriendly curmudgeon, but he had a soft heart as far as husky-voiced young women were concerned. Lillie Langtry, for example, had completely seduced him through a combination of flattery and deference. While other reviewers dismissed her performances as wooden and vulgar, Scott wrote and translated plays for her and gave her warm reviews. Perhaps Pauline knew this, as she employed the same transparently manipulative tactics as Langtry when she bearded the old lion in his den. "He glanced up through an awful scowl," she later recorded, "growling out, 'Well?' There is only one way to deal with a man—that is through his vanity—so I turned to the door again saying, 'I'm afraid to come in!' " It is hard to imagine that the young woman who had travelled alone across the Atlantic and braved London Society on her own was really scared, but her girl-ish tactic worked. Scott summoned her back and was flattered when she explained that she was afraid of a man "who can make one or ruin one with a stroke of his pen." Pauline showed him her poetry and said she was looking for a publisher. After glancing at her work, he scrib-bled a line of recommendation for the London publisher John Lane.

Scott's decision to send Pauline to John Lane at Bodley Head was astute. Lane was a self-educated farmer's son from Devon who had persuaded an antiquarian bookseller in Exeter, Charles Elkin Mathews, to go into partnership with him on a publishing venture. In 1887, the two men had set up a bookstore and publishing company just off Bond Street, in the heart of London's West End. Lane recognized that as lit-eracy levels rose in industrial Britain, the market for attractive and provocative books was expanding fast. His partner, Mathews, was a cautious bibliophile whose main interest was producing poetry and essays for the literary elite. But Lane, a clever hustler with a genuine interest in new ideas, pushed their firm in more daring directions. He attracted a diverse group of new writers to Bodley Head: exponents of naturalist fiction, women's rights and erotic decadence. He bought subsidiary rights to remaindered books; in 1892, Bodley Head issued a collection of poems by Oscar Wilde originally published in 1881. Bodley Head subsequently published other works by Wilde himself and by members of his circle: the comic author Ada Leverson, the poet John Gray, the illustrator Aubrey Beardsley. By the early 1890s, Bodley Head was acknowledged to be a leading publishing house, with an interesting list of writers and the ability to produce beautifully designed limited editions.

Lane was particularly interested in new talent—hungry young writ-ers who challenged convention and accepted low fees. One of his

greatest coups was the 1893 publication of *Keynotes*, a collection of
short stories by Mary Chevalier Dunne, whose nom de plume was
George Egerton. Dunne's stories appealed to "New Woman," who
resented the limited roles available to her and the Victorian dismissal
of her creative and erotic impulses. The phenomenal sales of
Keynotes convinced Lane that women writers and women readers
were untapped goldmines. Soon he had a stable of writers who looked
at marriage with a jaundiced eye. One of his most provocative acquisi-
tions was a manuscript with the racy title *The Woman Who Did*,
about a Cambridge-educated heroine who did what no self-respecting
Victorian woman would consider doing: she lived in sin and bore a
child out of wedlock. (The author, Grant Allen, came from Kingston,
Ontario.) "It is just possible, to say very likely," gloated its Bodley
Head editor, "that it might produce a wholesome and much-needed
. . . controversy." Scott had assumed, quite rightly, that a Canadian
Indian who wrote erotic nature poems and stirring verses about murderous women would intrigue John Lane.

John Lane's racy tastes caused tension in the Lane–Mathews partnership and would lead to its breakup within a few months. But the
tension did not dampen Lane's appetite for new writers. He sent
Pauline's poems to a couple of readers to assess. One of them, Pauline
later told *Saturday Night*'s Hector Charlesworth, was John Davidson,
a clever and depressive Scotsman who wrote unproducible verse
plays. Davidson advised Lane the poems should be published; Lane
assigned to Davidson the task of editing them. At first, Pauline found
her new editor terrifying; she described to Charlesworth how he
would "damn emphatically" some of her lines in his rasping Scots
accent. But he also praised others warmly. Steeped in the history and
nationalism of his own native land, Davidson must have admired
Pauline's commitment to stand by her own "blood and race." The
Canadian Indian writer and the Scots editor had much in common—
love of wild, open landscapes, respect for the complicated clan systems of their own peoples, resentment of the English takeover of their
lands. Davidson would have been deeply familiar with the novels of
Sir Walter Scott, who had captured Scots' imaginations with his "twi-
light of the nobility" prose that struck many of the same nostalgic

notes as did Pauline's poems about long-dead Indian warriors. It may have been Pauline's conversations with Davidson that inspired her wistful comment to *The Gazette* that she wished to go to the Highlands and be amongst a people "somehow akin to mine."

As a Bodley Head author, Pauline was welcomed at John Lane's tea parties in his bachelor flat behind the Bodley Head premises. She met critics, authors and editors there, as well as the illustrator E. H. New, who had been commissioned to design her volume. Although only eight of the thirty-six poems selected by Davidson had Indian themes, John Lane mirrored Pauline's own tactics as he shaped the promotion campaign for her book. Both "E. Pauline Johnson" and "Tekahionwake" were to appear as her bylines on the title page. The first section would consist entirely of the Indian ballads. E. H. New designed a tomahawk and wampum belt to adorn the fine leather cover. Finally, Lane encouraged Pauline to call her slim volume *The White Wampum*. Pauline's dedication similarly played up to her image:

> As wampum to the Redman, so to the Poet are his songs; chiselled alike from that which is the purest of his possessions, woven alike with meaning into belt and book, fraught alike with the corresponding message of peace, the breathing of tradition, the value of more than coin, and the seal of fellowship with all men. So do I offer this belt of verse-wampum to those two who have taught me most of its spirit—my Mother, whose encouragement has been my mainstay in its weaving; my Father, whose feet have long since wandered to the Happy Hunting Grounds.

By now, Pauline's money was running out. Although she always made friends easily and she had the satisfaction of achieving her goal of publication, she was increasingly lonely. Nobody is more homesick than a Canadian accustomed to gloriously long, lazy summer days spent by lakes and rivers who finds him- or herself stuck in a crowded, stuffy, smoggy city. Pauline's discomfort was aggravated by the fact that she spent her time crouched over her proofs, reading her own lush descriptions of amorous canoe expeditions, achingly beautiful

Muskoka sunsets and the haunting cries of loons and owls. A hunger for Rosseau swept through her as her pencil lingered over her own words from the poem "Under Canvas, in Muskoka":

> Across the lake the rugged islands lie,
> Fir-crowned and grim; and further in the view
> Some shadows seeming swung 'twixt cloud and sky,
> Are countless shores, a symphony of blue.
>
> The scent of burning leaves, the camp-fire's blaze,
> The great logs cracking in the brilliant flame,
> The groups grotesque, on which the firelight plays,
> Are pictures which Muskoka twilights frame.

One day Sir Charles Tupper, the Canadian High Commissioner who had developed a very soft spot for the attractive young poet, escorted Pauline through Whiteley's, the department store off Bayswater Road. As Pauline admired the echoing marble-floored atrium with its twinkling glass dome four floors above, Sir Charles explained to her that the founder, William Whiteley, claimed to be "the universal provider." "Why," Sir Charles laughed, "they will secure you guests for your dinner, if others fail. They will marry you here, sell you cradles for your babies, and finally make arrangements for your funeral." He challenged her to ask an assistant for the item she thought the least likely to be in stock. It took Pauline only a few seconds to think of an item for which she yearned, and that she was confident Whiteley's would not have: a Peterborough canoe.

It turned out that Whiteley's did stock canoes, on the fourth floor. Pauline was impressed. But the sight of her favourite vessel beached in a London store reminded her that it was now July, and at home the canoe meets had begun. When she heard that the American Canoe Association was competing in sailing-canoe races in England, she decided to go and cheer for the leading North American contender. "I hope he will win," she wrote to Harry O'Brien, her fellow canoe enthusiast. "It would be horrible for a Britisher to beat us on our national sport. The course is a regular mud pond, so cramped and small."

Pauline had been in London nearly two months. She had achieved an astonishing amount within a remarkably short space of time: features about herself in national newspapers, publication of her verse, acclaim within both aristocratic and intellectual circles, important new patrons. She had been vindicated as both a performer and a poet, and she had proven she could pursue her career on her own. Her London success would add immeasurably to her reputation back home.

And it was time to go home. She had had enough of London's smogs, strikes and snobbery. She would not wait for *The White Wampum* to appear in print, although John Lane assured her publication was imminent. She took the train to Liverpool, and on July 9 she stepped aboard a steamship for the return voyage to New York. In a few weeks' time she would think back nostalgically to England's "warm hearts, its applause, its possible laurel wreaths." She confided to Harry O'Brien "the real heartache I had at leaving it just when I had made dear friendships there." Right now, however, she was glad to be going home—but not as glad as was a large, talkative American woman next to her at dinner one night. Pauline's neighbour was busy grumbling about the discourtesy of British waiters. "When I asked for ice water," she complained, "they looked at me as if I were a North American savage." Pauline stared at the woman through hooded eyes, then replied, "Do you know, that's just the way they looked at me." The American, remembering Pauline's history, enquired, "Was your father a real wild red Indian?" When Pauline said "Yes," her neighbour continued with a blithe lack of concern: "Excuse me! You don't look a bit like that!" "Oh?" replied Pauline. "Was your father a real white man?" "Why, sure," replied the puzzled American lady. "Excuse me, but I'm equally surprised," snapped Pauline, who rose from the table and stalked off to her cabin. Tekahionwake was more determined than ever to combat thoughtless stereotypes.

12

ACROSS CANADA
BY TRAIN
1894

ACK in Brantford, Emily Johnson ached to see her daughter.
Pauline had written from London, reassuring her mother that
she was mixing with the "right" people and making her reputation as a poet. When the Reverend Mackenzie called at Napoleon
Street, Emily proudly mentioned that Pauline had dined several times
at the London home of Lady Ripon and had attended the theatre with
Lady Blake, wife of the Governor of Jamaica.

Emily longed to question her daughter about things she herself
remembered—the kind of everyday details that lodge in a child's
memory and years later come unbidden to the surface. Emily may
never have visited the Imperial capital, but she had spent her first
eight years in Bristol, another English port. Did barrow boys still
hawk steamed winkles, cockles and eels on street corners? Were
London's Bath buns as big, sugary and shiny as the ones baked in Bristol? Were there flower girls selling bunches of lily-of-the-valley to
passersby? Had Pauline seen houses with roofs made of straw, or carriages with ducal coronets painted on the doors?

Pauline's sister Evelyn watched their mother's mounting anticipation with exasperation. Emily had been hysterical with worry when
Pauline left on the long transatlantic voyage the previous April. Each
evening she had made Evelyn join her to sing the hymn "For Those in
Peril on the Sea." Eva knew they would go through the same agitated
ritual during Pauline's return voyage. She would be the one obliged to
calm her mother's nerves until Pauline eventually swept in triumph

into the Johnson home, indifferent (in Eva's opinion) to her mother's anxiety. So Evelyn sent a wire to Pauline's Portland Street studio asking her not to tell them when she expected to get home—"Mother would then not have the anxiety I knew she would again experience during Pauline's homeward voyage."

When Pauline finally arrived at Brantford Station on Thursday, July 26, 1894, Eva had managed to keep her sister's travel plans so secret that no one met the returning heroine. The complex dynamics of the Johnson household, in which the two women competed for their mother's approval, were further strained by Pauline's next move. She was scarcely through the door when she announced that she was leaving three days later on a new tour with Owen Smily. She wanted to build on her London success, and replenish her empty purse. Pauline's determination to stay in the public spotlight appalled her mother. Emily Johnson had always disliked the idea of her daughter appearing on the stage; in her opinion, performing in public was simply vulgar. She saw no glamour in Sarah Bernhardt and Ellen Terry. She had always assumed that once Pauline had achieved her ambition of finding a London publisher for her poems, she would settle back into her Brantford home. Meanwhile, a spurt of jealous rage surged through Evelyn. Once again, Pauline was going to flit off for new adventures while Eva remained to cope with the cramped day-to-day existence of Napoleon Street.

Much of Pauline's brief Brantford visit was spent in press interviews and in courtesy calls on the prominent citizens who had given her such a generous send-off. *Brantford Expositor* readers learned that their local celebrity had reached new heights of poise: "She is the picture of good health and spirits," the reporter noted, "and in that

As soon as she reached home, Pauline arranged a photographic portrait session to show off her London finery.

charming manner, peculiarly her own, chatted most pleasantly of her experiences in the great city of London."

A series of photographs taken at this time capture how breathtakingly attractive Pauline appeared when things were going right for her. The portrait session was probably prompted by Pauline's desire to be photographed in her new London finery. One photograph depicts her as the complete debutante in her creamy brocade silk dress from Barker's, a diadem perched in her thick, curly hair. A second portrait shows a laughing young woman in an audaciously feathered hat, with a nosegay of sweet peas pinned to a velvet jacket. In each photo, Pauline looks younger than thirty-three. Almost iridescent with *joie de vivre*, she is voluptuous and sensual. Pearly teeth, lustrous eyes, a tiny waist and velvet-smooth skin—an observer might easily assume that Pauline owed both her looks and her self-possession to membership in Canada's British-born elite.

The irony is that while Pauline (who always loved dressing up) had acquired some of the glamorous wardrobe of an upper-class Englishwoman, her resistance to being identified exclusively with that elite had been strengthened in London. Much of her success there had been due to her identity as "Tekahionwake." But when Pauline loosened her corsets and stuck an eagle's feather in her hair, she wasn't simply play-acting in a bid for attention. She was juggling two identities so that she could pay homage to her father's heritage and politely challenge thoughtless stereotypes. Soon after her return from England, she met the naturalist Ernest Thompson Seton, who was just starting to make a name for himself as an artist and author. In her first conversation with Seton, she was even fiercer in her championship of native peoples than she had been in her letter to Archie Kains a few years earlier. "Never let anyone call me a white woman!" she told Seton. "There are those who think they pay me a compliment in saying that I am just like a white woman. My aim, my joy, my pride is to sing the glories of my own people."

Like many men before and after him, Seton was swept off his feet by this glowing young woman. He shared the poet's love of nature; when he was growing up in Toronto, he had camped out in the city's ravines and (in his own words) "played Indian." Now he was enthralled by the romantic image Pauline presented in her speech and her person. He gave her a necklace of bear's claws. Twenty years after their first encounter, he set down his memory of the "shy Indian girl . . . developed by white-man training [into] the alert, resourceful world-woman." She explained to him, he recalled, that "Ours was the race that gave the world its measure of heroism, its standard of physical prowess. Ours was the race that taught the world that avarice veiled by any name is a crime. Ours were the people of the blue air and the green woods, and ours the faith that taught men to live without greed and to die without fear."

North American natives fascinated Ernest Thompson Seton, who as a child had "gone native" and camped in a Toronto ravine for days at a time.

When it came to extolling native nobility, no one could beat Pauline Johnson for hyperbole. She had now firmly incorporated her Mohawk heritage into her off-stage persona. Yet she was on shaky ground when she rhapsodized about her people or her race. She knew that there were as many different Indian bands in North America as there were nations in Europe. In her 1892 article "A Strong Race Opinion," she had reproached non-native writers for bland generalizations about generic "Indian maidens." But she herself was completely unfamiliar with the culture, politics and way of life of native peoples beyond Ontario's borders.

However, her forthcoming tour would change that. She was going to travel 3,000 miles (4,800 kilometres) and enjoy one of the most exciting experiences of the era: a journey across the width of a vast continent on the curving steel rails that the Canadian Pacific Railway had completed for passenger trains only eight years earlier. The transcontinental railway was reshaping Canada both physically and psychically. The West had always existed in the national imagination as a vast, unexplored wilderness of immeasurable potential wealth. But now it was accessible—to promoters, to settlers, to tourists. It was developing a voice of its own in national debates. It held out endless possibilities of new beginnings for the rejected, dispossessed or frustrated. For Pauline, the opportunity to go west was especially intriguing. The trip would take her through the vast open spaces over which native peoples had roamed for centuries—Ojibwa and Plains Indians very different from her own Iroquois forebears.

After a strained weekend with her mother and sister, Pauline packed her valise and steamer trunk and took the train to Toronto. Her new manager, Ernest Shipman, had arranged a rendezvous for Pauline and her partner the following day. The Johnson–Smily act now had a professional manager because Pauline's old friend Frank Yeigh was too busy with his boss at Queen's Park, Arthur Hardy, MPP, to study train timetables and correspond with theatre managers out west. Shipman had scheduled an ambitious tour for his stars. It began with a performance in Orillia on August 1 and ended two gruelling months later with a show in Victoria, British Columbia. Pauline and her partner were to perform four or five nights each week, in a different venue almost every time, as they travelled west.

The CPR's transcontinental train began its westbound journey at Montreal. Toronto passengers could join the train at one of three points. The most direct route was to take a train north to North Bay, on Lake Nipissing, and meet the CPR train there. The cheapest and most complicated route was to travel by steamer across Lake Huron from Owen Sound to Sault Ste. Marie, double back on the slow-moving eastbound train to Sudbury and then connect there with the westbound transcontinental train. The third, most luxurious alternative was to take the steamer all the way to Port Arthur (now Thunder Bay), near the northernmost point of Lake Superior, and pick up the train there. Shipman, who put cost above comfort, had booked his duo on the second route. So after their Orillia performance, Smily and Pauline took a train west to Owen Sound and boarded a steamer that would thread its way through Georgian Bay, past Manitoulin Island to port, up to Sault Ste. Marie. As Pauline leaned against the rail and

Massive C P R locomotives thundered across the continent,
equipped with bells to warn of their advance, cow-catchers
to clear stray animals and spotlights to pierce the dark.

watched the pink granite islands of Georgian Bay slip by, she felt a
pang of nostalgia for her beloved Lake Rosseau. She knew her Brantford Canoe Club pals were enjoying their annual vacation.

Sault Ste. Marie, which straddles the rapids on the St. Mary River
below the southern tip of Lake Superior, offered welcome distrac-
tions. Founded in 1668 as a Jesuit mission, the town had subsequently
become a North West Company trading post. But Pauline and her
partner were less interested in the historic fort than in the modern
technology on view. Smily stared in amazement at the complicated
engineering of the four American locks that allowed shipping to pass
between Lake Superior and Lake Huron. He disembarked from the
steamer so he could watch vessels of every shape and size, many of
them loaded with ore from northern mines, manoeuvre through
them. A weather-beaten captain informed him that more tonnage
passed through these locks than through any other locks in the world,
including those on the Suez Canal.

Pauline was far more interested in the rapids alongside the locks.

The roar of the surging, white-capped water as it thundered round rocks and through narrow channels was intoxicating. She persuaded a local Algonquin guide to run the rapids with her in his birchbark canoe and enlisted a photographer to record the event. As the canoe careered through the water, the guide yelled an eerie, blood-curdling shriek of "Hi! yi! hi! yi!" which echoed along the shore and terrified onlookers. In an account of the adventure that she and Smily wrote for the *Globe* under the coy byline "Miss Poetry and Mr. Prose," she admitted that her "reckless taste for this sort of water-tobogganing" meant that she nearly missed the train to Sudbury. She arrived at the dock "out of breath, just in time to swing gracefully (perhaps) on the last car as it moved out." It was worth it, she insisted: she had caught "some music from the rapids as well as a fine large cold in the head." Determined to make this tour as lucrative as possible, she quickly got out her pen and composed "The Leap of the Ste. Marie":

> Lend me your happy laughter,
> Ste. Marie as you leap;
> Your peace that follows after
> Where through the isles you creep.
> Give to me your splendid dashing,
> Give your sparkles and your splashing.
> Your uphurling waves down crashing,
> Then, your aftermath of sleep.

The train to Sudbury crept along the rails; passengers joked that it would be faster to walk. When the track cut through the granite of the Canadian Shield, ochre and russet stains on the rocks gave some hint of the mineral wealth—nickel, copper, iron—that lay beneath the bush. Everywhere Pauline looked in the August sunshine, she could see either smouldering bushfires or blackened areas of burnt forest. Once again, she reached for her pen, to celebrate the fireweed: the "sweet wild flower [that] lifts its purple head" and hides the scars of forest fires. By the end of the journey, she intended to have enough verses to form the core of a second published volume. She also planned to write some articles for the CPR to use in its promotional material.

At Sudbury, the platform was thronged with bearded, booted, slouch-hatted miners. Hungry for investors who might put money into their mining claims, they clustered around the debonair Owen Smily, with his English accent. But the grizzled hustlers realized he was penniless as fast as he recognized their "seams of gold" as glittering but worthless iron pyrite. The good-natured banter continued until, to their great relief, Pauline and Smily heard the long, low wail of an approaching locomotive.

When the two travellers clambered aboard the CPR Pullman car, they gasped at the space and luxury inside. Until now Pauline's experience of rail travel had been based on Ontario's smaller railways and England's Liverpool–London route. The design of carriages on most of these railways was based on the design of the stagecoaches they had replaced. There was usually no communicating corridor between carriages, and passengers sat facing each other on benches that were at right angles to the tracks. Local Ontario trains, which offered quicker and cheaper transport than travel by road, were usually hot and crowded. The great transcontinental trains, in contrast, were designed on the same principles as the luxury steamers that coddled wealthy passengers during ocean crossings. William Cornelius Van Horne, the CPR's General Manager, had personally designed the sleeping cars and parlour cars to ensure maximum comfort and aesthetic appeal. Van Horne, a powerfully built man who had recently received a knighthood, considered no detail too small for his attention. He instructed his draughtsmen to make all doors, berths, windows and furniture large— or, as he put it, "fat and bulgy like myself." As Clark Blaise, biographer of the CPR's Chief Engineer, Sandford Fleming, has written, "The size and power" of the great steam locomotives "encouraged a swagger, a certain Gilded Age social and economic flamboyance, a cigars-and-brandy, god-like, frontier-pushing presumption of entitlement."

The Pullman saloon car, Pauline discovered, was lined with beautifully carved mahogany, upholstered with green plush and liberally fitted with bevelled mirrors and brass fixtures. The floor was richly carpeted and the ceiling high; the seats were upholstered in red velvet and the plate-glass windows were large. At one end of the saloon car there was a retiring room for ladies and a tiny bathroom with a washbasin and mahogany-seated lavatory. At the other end was a smoking room, which a few brave women had dared to invade despite ostentatious disapproval from some of the gentlemen. At night, the sofas turned into lower berths, and upper berths were unhooked from the ceiling. The porter then made up with clean linen as many of the twenty-four berths as were required. Every saloon car had its own porter; Pauline noticed that all the porters were, in the parlance of the day, "coloured." Each porter's job was to ensure that his passengers had all the towels and water (for drinking and washing) they needed. When a passenger was ready to disembark, the porter would energetically brush the dust off the passenger's coat until his battered victim proffered a decent tip.

When Pauline had got herself settled and her baggage stowed, and the locomotive had uttered a long, low exhalation as it left Sudbury's station, she set out to explore her temporary home. From the platform, she had admired the huge iron locomotive and she had seen the coal car, the mail car and the baggage cars. Now she found, beyond the saloon car, "the colonists' car," which was filled with large, noisy families and piles of shabby baggage. Here, newly arrived immigrants made up wooden berths with their own bedding and cooked their own food on a little iron stove. The smell in this car was indescribable, thanks to the crowding, the glowing stove and the steamy weather outside. "There is such a variety of nationalities to be found in the colonial cars," Pauline noted. "'Arry's from England, Murphy's from Ireland, Sandie's from Scotland . . . but Chinamen seem to be in the majority most of the time." The CPR itself had been responsible for the surge of immigrants from China in the 1880s; without an army of more than 10,000 Chinese labourers, the company could never have fulfilled its contract to build a coast-to-coast railway within four years.

Pauline also discovered the dining car, where passengers could enjoy breakfast, luncheon or dinner for 75 cents a meal. This was even more like luxury steamship travel. Stewards in blue uniforms with brass buttons served locally caught fish (trout and whitefish near Lake Superior, salmon around the Rockies and on the west coast), lamb cutlets, fried chicken, veal cutlets, buckwheat cakes and eggs in every style. Van Horne, whose own appetite was legendary, kept an eye on the menus, insisting on fresh produce and good desserts—"Deep apple, peach and etc. pie should be the standard in the pastry line." CPR dining cars never stayed with a train for the entire two-week Montreal-to-Vancouver journey. After a white-coated chef had pre-pared a day's meals, his car was uncoupled at the next convenient sta-tion, to be cleaned, restocked and coupled to the next train coming the other way. In theory, the outward-bound locomotive would pick up a fresh dining car in time for the following day's breakfast. But Pauline heard plenty of horror stories about trains delayed by snow-drifts and landslides, which meant no dining car at breakfast time and passengers going hungry for hours. She got into the habit of taking hard-boiled eggs with her on transcontinental journeys.

The train steamed across Northern Ontario, pausing at thirty-six small stations before the next major stop, Port Arthur. Some of these tiny clearings in the forest, such as Biscotasing and Missanabic, had originally been Ojibwa fishing or hunting camps. Others were merely wood and water depots, with a couple of shanties for labourers work-ing on the line. From Port Coldwell, the track ran alongside Lake Superior. Everything about the endless expanse of water was on a far grander scale than the Canadian rivers and lakes further south that Pauline knew. Superior's mighty headlands were covered in giant cedars; immense boulders lay along the shoreline. Boat traffic was minimal, and signs of human habitation rare. But soon the grain ele-vators, warehouses and wharves of Port Arthur came into view. Smily and Pauline walked up the hill above the town while the train refu-elled. The air was still and the streets were empty. "It was only after we commented on the hush that seemed over everything," Pauline noted, "and in the search for some expression that would fittingly describe it, had hit upon the phrase 'Sabbath calm' that we realised it was the seventh day." The majestic silence prompted Pauline to write a poem that would appear in the *Globe* under the title "Benedictus":

Something so restful lies on lake and shore,
The world seems anchored, and life's petty war
Of haste and labor gone forevermore.

From Port Arthur to Rat Portage (happily renamed Kenora in 1905), Pauline sat by the window, mesmerized by the view. The miles of track between Lake Superior and the Manitoba border had been some of the most expensive to lay. The muskeg swamps had turned out to be quagmires of gelatinous peat, capable of swallowing tons of sand and gravel and anything else the engineers dumped on it. Nine thousand men had worked on this section; in one area, seven layers of rail lay buried, one on top of the other. Laying track across 300 miles (480 kilometres) of Ontario muskeg, Sandford Fleming had recorded, cost the same as laying track across 2,000 miles (3,200 kilometres) of prairie. Alongside the track was the old "tote road," along which men, machinery and stores had been hauled while the rail line was constructed. Its value now gone, it was already reverting to bush.

Endless miles of tangled forest, gaunt dead pine trees, swamps and muskeg stretched before Pauline under a wide, clear azure sky. But the late summer vista was far from dreary. Sumac bushes were turning deep red as the evenings cooled; the blackened skeletons of burnt timber were covered by the ubiquitous purple fireweed; there were occasional glimpses of glassy blue lakes and foaming rivers, edged with dark green shores. When anything of particular interest was sighted (a moose, perhaps, or a bear), Smily and some of the other men crowded onto the open-air platform at the back of the train.

Pauline had always found natural beauty inspiring, be it the Grand River or Lake Rosseau. But now the sheer size of Canada and its extraordinary natural wealth filled her with almost unbearable joy. She felt no nostalgia for her stuffy little room in Holland Park or the cosmopolitan delights of England. "The little island has dropped many thousand miles behind me," she wrote to Harry O'Brien from Rat Portage, where she and Smily left the train and installed themselves at a small hotel called Hilliard House. "This 'great, lone, land' of ours is so absorbing, so lovely, so magnificent, that my eyes forget the beauties of the older land. Ah! There are no such airs as these in England, no such skies, no such forest scents and wild sweet perfumes. These August days are gorgeous. The atmosphere is rife with amethyst, amber and opal tints, parented by the far-off bush fires, and the thin north air. The sun lays like a ball of blood, and oh! The stillness, the silence, the magnitude of this country impresses me as it never has before."

Dramatic scenery was not the only aspect of Canada firing Pauline's imagination. "We are getting into Indian country now," she told O'Brien. "Every town is full of splendid complexioned Ojibwas, whose copper colouring makes me ashamed of my washed out Mohawk skin, thinned with European blood. I look yellow and 'Chinesey' beside these Indians." An Ojibwa camp bordered the tracks east of Rat Portage. Men in black hats smoked pipes while women hung fish out to dry and barefoot children ran between the teepees. Most wore traditional dress; their dark hair was long, and they had blankets from the Hudson's Bay Company wrapped around them. Pauline found everything about them intriguing.

Shipman had secured eleven bookings for the Johnson–Smily act between August 27 and September 11. Four were in Winnipeg, but the rest were in a circle of little communities such as Morden, Boissevain, Brandon, Manitou, Selkirk and Carman. Some of the towns were accessible by branch lines; others required Pauline and Smily to hire a four-wheel cart, in which they bumped along the rough roads. They must have cursed their manager for not looking at a map as he made the bookings—they often had to double back for an engagement before proceeding west. They also had to deal with third-rate hotels, bad meals and dirty water. At Boissevain, a "villainous smelling compound" was produced in answer to a request for a pitcher of water. Smily said they didn't need fancy drinks; simple water was sufficient. "Wal, that's what ye've got," replied the waiter.

Pauline refused to be daunted. She was particularly struck by Winnipeg, capital of the province of Manitoba, where she and Smily spent over a week in early September. Since 1881, when the CPR had decided to route the railway through Winnipeg, the city's population had exploded from 5,000 to 35,000. Steamboats plied the two rivers on which the city sat, the Red and the Assiniboine. The huge railyards, which included two roundhouses and miles of track, were well on their way to becoming the most extensive in the British Empire. When the Winnipeg Grain Exchange opened in 1887, the city became the undisputed centre of Canada's grain trade. By the time Pauline arrived, seven private and eight chartered banks were already doing a roaring business. Winnipeggers had big dreams for their city, which they festooned with such grandiloquent titles as "Gateway to the Golden West," "Bull's Eye of the Dominion" and "the Chicago of the North."

Pauline walked along a Main Street that was 140 feet (42 metres) wide, lined with sturdy wooden sidewalks, and that claimed to stretch for 2 miles (over 3 kilometres). She admired the new stone post office, the horse-drawn street railway and the magnificent 1,250-seat Princess Opera House, which had opened in 1883. She and Smily played in far more modest venues; a portion of the admission fee from each performance went to the sponsoring organization. Their first show was at the Winnipeg Grace Church. Subsequent evenings were spent at the Rover Bicycle Club, the Winnipeg Church of Zion and the North Presbyterian Congregation.

Winnipeg audiences gave standing ovations to the Johnson–Smily double act. Many of the city's new immigrants were young Englishmen, lured by CPR promises that there was a fortune to be made in the newly opened Prairies. They roared with laughter at the music hall patter of Smily, a fellow Englishman. Pauline, billed as "fresh from a triumphant London season," enthralled them with her combination of aristocratic grace and native spirit. It was months, if not years, since most of the spectators had seen a woman in a fashionable silk gown from Kensington High Street. Admirers sent gifts round to her hotel: flowers, bags of apples, sugared biscuits, photographs of the city. The warmth of the reception suggests that for all their boosterism about the "Gateway to the West," many of the new Winnipeggers felt a long way from home. "The Peg" was a boom town engulfed by untamed prairie. A quarter of a century earlier, when it was still known as "The Forks" and was part of the Red River Colony, it had resounded with the sounds of marching soldiers, yelling officers and gunfire in the first Métis uprising led by Louis Riel. In 1885, the citizens of Winnipeg had waved at the trains that carried government troops further west to put down the splutterings of the North-West Rebellion in Batoche and Fish Creek, and capture Riel. Winnipeggers had hung Louis Riel in effigy on Main Street in July 1885. Pauline was well aware of the tension between natives and settlers within Winnipeg; her ballad "A Cry from an Indian Wife," which championed the Indian point of view, was a staple of her stage programme wherever she performed. But the two Métis rebellions against the Dominion government in Ottawa, and the subsequent surrender to Ottawa's authority of the great Plains Indian leaders—Poundmaker, Little Poplar, Lucky Man and, finally, Big Bear himself—now seemed like ancient history. All Pauline saw was energy; all she heard was enthusiastic applause. She determined to return.

By the second week in September, Pauline and Smily were back on the transcontinental train. Shipman had failed to secure any bookings between Brandon, 134 miles (216 kilometres) west of Winnipeg, and Medicine Hat, 142 miles (228 kilometres) east of Calgary. For the intervening 600 miles (965 kilometres), Pauline divided her time between talking to her fellow passengers, doing needlework and gazing out of the window. Within the past decade, the railway had spawned one-street communities at regular intervals along the track; eventually, the CPR would foster the growth of more than 800 villages, towns and cities in the three Prairie provinces. Pauline stared with curiosity at the red-painted grain elevators, the plaid-shirted farmers driving teams of horses, the chickens scratching in dusty backyards, the wooden frontages of stores and saloons. Although the constant travelling was hard, she loved the "great brown prairies," she wrote to Harry O'Brien. "This trip is a revelation to me," she added. She and Smily then spent five days in the Calgary area, performing at Medicine Hat, Pincher Creek, Lethbridge and Fort Macleod, as well as Calgary itself.

There were plenty of novelties to spark Pauline's muse. She watched a pack of wolves snarl over the bones of a luckless stray steer: "Those fellows had as distinctive dispositions as seven men. In the brief moments we had to watch them, we could distinguish the fighting wolf, the gluttonous wolf, the mean wolf, the amiable wolf, the timid wolf—why, there was even a *lazy* wolf who, famished as he was, would put himself to no undue exertion to secure bones." She serenaded a gopher: "A merry little rascal, with a saucy little way / Who dresses like a hypocrite, in soft, religious grey." She marvelled at the glimmering peaks of mountains on the horizon. She and Smily sweltered through

*In the 1880s the Sarcee people were confined to reserves
by the Dominion government, but still clung
to their traditional way of life.*

"the steam-pipe breath of the Chinook wind," which left them dehy-drated and covered in grey dust. Her euphoria grew with every mile she travelled: "I cannot tell you how I love my Canada, or how infinitely dearer my native soil is to me since I started on this long trip."

They were now in real Indian country. For the first time, Pauline was seeing native peoples who were only one generation away from their ancestors' traditional lifestyle, untouched by European influ-ences. Plains Indians such as the Cree nations, the Blackfoot Confeder-acy (which included the Blood, Crowfoot and Sarcee peoples), the Stoney nation and the Sioux peoples still spoke their own languages, wore traditional dress and lived in teepees. However, the buffalo on which they once depended were gone, and each band had now been restricted to a reserve. In theory, the Dominion government was teach-ing native people to farm. In practice, the experimental farms were not going well. This was hardly surprising, given the contemptuous offi-cial attitude towards Indians. "It is policy of the Government," accord-ing to the 1892 edition of the *Statistical Year Book of Canada*, "to endeavour as much as possible to persuade Indians to give up their wandering habits and stay on their reserves. . . . Only those brought into personal contact with the Indians can understand the ignorance, superstition and laziness that have to be overcome before the Indians

By the late-nineteenth century, there was
a thriving market in Central Canada for pictures
of the Blackfoot and Cree peoples of the Prairies.

SIUPAKIO AND SIKUNNACIO
SARCEE INDIAN GIRLS
TIME AND PLACE History -- Geography VISUAL TEACHING

can be persuaded to take genuine interest and perseverance in the simplest farming operations."

After the first few years, Ottawa never allocated adequate rations, adequate supplies or competent teachers to the native farmers. Labour-saving machinery was deliberately withheld from them, on the grounds that they would never learn how to service complicated implements. Moreover, many of the farms, like the reserves, were on poor land, miles from the railway. The majority of European settlers who acquired similar tracts simply gave up and either returned east or moved to areas with richer soil, higher rainfall and better access to markets. But native peoples were trapped: legislation made it illegal for them to leave their reserves. No wonder that several bands, particularly those within a day's ride of the CPR tracks, had discovered an easier way to make a living: playing "Red Injuns" for the benefit of tourists who were arriving in increasing numbers on the trains.

Tourists were transfixed by "braves, squaws and papooses," as they liked to call such Plains Indians as they saw. An affable fellow named Edward Roper, whose account of transcontinental travel was published in 1891 under the title *By Track and Trail*, was most impressed by the Crowfoot people. He described them as "really very good-looking. . . . Comparing a crowd of Kentish hop-pickers with a band of uncivilized Indians, decidedly the latter would bear away the prize for cleanliness and decency." He enjoyed throwing oranges and small coins from the back of the train and watching the children scramble for them in the dust. Roper was fascinated by Canadian attitudes to Indians. They seemed to regard natives, he reported, "as a race of animals which were neither benefit nor harm to anyone, mentioning that they were surely dying out."

Other travellers were less sympathetic. Douglas Sladen, a dyspeptic English academic who crossed Canada the same year as Pauline, photographed a Stoney Indian family and was furious when "as soon as the operation was completed, he would advance toward you and intimate with blood-curdling signs that the person who was photographed ought to be paid." In his memoir, *On The Cars and Off*, Sladen also recorded some Cree Indians, "very much painted and in very gaudy blankets, who were trying to sell cow horns as the real buffalo."

When Pauline and Smily arrived at Fort Macleod, they discovered that the Blackfoot Indians there had organized "a sort of miniature Buffalo Bill's Wild West." They were just in time to watch "an Indian race on Indian ponies that alone was worth five dollars to see." In their description of the race published in the *Globe*, there is no hint that one of the two authors was an Indian herself. They and their fellow passengers all found the spectacle satisfyingly "savage":

The race usually ends in a fight between the various competitors but it is exciting enough without the fracas. The riders dispense with saddle and ride barebacked (both horse and jockey). An article resembling an apron is the only habit of the latter. When the word is given to go, they go! They do not temporise, neither do they dally. They are not trained jockeys and so understand nothing about pulling or any of those eastern wiles, but they get there, yea, verily, they get there! It is the very opposite of an eastern race. There the onlookers do all the yelling, but the uproar of the spectators at Macleod was as the snap of a toy pistol to the bang of a rifle compared with the sustained war-whoop of that mob of naked Indians as they whirled past.

Yet Pauline was also aware that the Indian peoples she saw were impoverished, demoralized shadows of their once proud selves. Disease and alcohol had decimated their numbers. Away from Smily and the other backslapping English tourists, more sombre sentiments prevailed. At the train's frequent stops on its journey west, she bought photographs of some of the famous scenes and leaders of the "dying race." Her collection included a photograph of a "Sun Dance Teepee," postcards of Stoney Indians and their camp, and portraits of three important chiefs: Big Bear, Poundmaker and Piapot. Piapot, a Cree chief who had not participated in the 1885 North-West Rebellion, spoke for many of his fellow chiefs when he described the Dominion government's treatment of Indians out west: "In order to become sole masters of our land they relegated us to small reservations as big as my hand and made us long promises, as long as my arm. But the next year the promises were shorter, and get shorter every year until now they are about the length of my finger, and they keep about half of that."

Pauline had neither the time nor the opportunity to make personal contact with the Blackfoot horse-racers or with any of the silent Indians who stared impassively at the train as it steamed across their ancestral lands. They were as foreign to her as Sicilians or Castilians would be to a Welsh person. To them, she was simply another white woman from the east. Nevertheless, she was stirred by their plight, particularly when she focussed on individuals. She wrote a poignant poem called "Silhouette," about a Sioux chief glimpsed from the train window. The glimpse must have triggered memories of her own long-dead father and his struggle to protect Iroquois lands from encroachments:

> Etched where the lands and cloud-lands touch and die,
> A solitary Indian tepee stands,
> The only habitation of these lands,
> That roll their magnitude from sky to sky.
>
> The scraggy tent poles lift in dark relief,
> The upward floating smoke ascends between,
> And near the open doorway, still and lean
> And shadow-like, there stands an Indian chief.
>
> With eyes that lost their fire long ago,
> With vision fixed and stern as fate's decree,
> He looks toward the empty west to see
> The never-coming herd of buffalo.
>
> Only the bones that bleach upon the plains,
> Only the fleshless skeletons that lie
> In ghastly nakedness and silence, cry
> Out mutely that naught else to him remains.

The predicament of native peoples who, within the space of a few years, had seen the buffalo disappear and their way of life destroyed by strangers, haunted Pauline for the rest of her life. Proud and fearless nomads had become pathetic "fleshless skeletons."

Pauline's first trip west was thus a revelation to her. The majestic landscape had held her spellbound. The Prairie "Redmen" had fascinated her. Most important, her imagination was gripped by the raw frontier spirit—the sense that everybody was welcome, and that newcomers could reinvent themselves in this wide-open land.

But her excitement came to a crashing end when she reached Calgary on September 19. A telegram from Eva was waiting. Pauline hoped that it would be the news for which she had been waiting since she had left England: *The White Wampum* had finally been published. She ripped open the envelope—but her face froze when she read the contents. Five days earlier, her older brother had been found dead on the street in Columbia, Pennsylvania. Beverly Johnson, who had been promoted to Superintendent of the Columbia office of the Anglo-American Savings and Loan Association of New York, was said to have died of heart failure, aged forty. By the time Pauline received the telegram, his body had been returned to Brantford. Recognizing that it was impossible for Pauline to get back in time for his funeral, Evelyn Johnson and her mother had gone ahead and buried him at the old Mohawk Cemetery.

Despite her grief, Pauline knew the Smily–Johnson show must go on: she was under contract. She played the two Calgary shows, then travelled on to Banff, where they were scheduled to spend a

Beverly Johnson gave this photo to Pauline in 1890, and wrote on the back, "Your big brother Bev." Four years later, aged only forty, he was dead.

night at the Banff Springs Hotel. But her delight in the new sights and sounds of the West had evaporated. Banff's walls of towering stone and its hot springs were wasted on her. She had a dreadful cold, a snowstorm had blotted out any view of the mountains and she grieved for Beverly. "No-one knew he was ill," she wrote to Harry O'Brien a couple of days after she heard the news. "It was so sudden, and the shock to me was awful. . . . It was worst while he lay dead, and I in gay gowns, and with laughter on my face and tears in my heart, went on and on—the mere doll of the people and slave to money."

Pauline dutifully fulfilled her obligations in Golden, Vancouver, New Westminster, Nanaimo and Victoria, but her euphoria had evaporated. The glistening mountains on each side of the railway track, the elaborate trestle bridges crossing deep gorges through which water thundered, the Illecillewaet glacier (300 feet—91 metres—deep, and 15 miles—24 kilometres—wide)—Pauline was almost blind to the splendours opened up to travellers by one of the world's greatest engineering triumphs. The effects of grief were most noticeable in the poetry she wrote during the final leg of the tour. Alliteration and doggerel rhythms predominated. A verse about Kicking Horse River included the unfortunate couplet, "It flips its little fingers / In the very face of fate." Possible the worst piece of poetry that Pauline ever wrote was entitled "Little Vancouver." It began, "Little Vancouver was born in the west, / The healthiest baby on Canada's breast," and went on to describe how

> Motherly Canada nursed the wee youth,
> And brought it a railroad to cut its first tooth.
> And soon it grew out of its swaddling bands,
> To slip from the lap and the old nurse's hands.

Smily and Pauline gave the final performance of this tour in Victoria on September 29. The following day, they took the early ferry to Vancouver, where they boarded the eastbound CPR train. Owen Smily tried to keep his partner's spirits up during the two-week return journey. He knew Pauline played chess, so he acquired a travelling chess set in a folding wooden box. He suggested to her that whoever won the most games before they reached Toronto could keep the set. But try as he might, he couldn't lose: Pauline's heart was not in the game. By mid-October, Pauline was back in Brantford, where she accompanied her sister and mother to the Mohawk Cemetery to visit Beverly's grave.

Once again, Emily was delighted to have her younger daughter home. But tension between the two sisters quickly erupted. Not unreasonably, Evelyn wanted her sister to take over some of the household duties, while she spent her days at the office job that paid most of her bills. But Pauline had no intention of being sucked into the domestic routine. She wanted to rest, unpack her steamer trunk, sort out her wardrobe and visit friends. Washing windows at Napoleon Street was an abrupt comedown after the action and excitement of the western tour.

There is no evidence that while she was in Brantford, Pauline made any effort to reacquaint herself with her Indian heritage by going back to the Six Nations Reserve. Her Indian ballads were about the mythology she had learned as a child, rather than the reality of her relatives' lives. She saw herself as a poet who recited her own work rather than an anthropologist recording native culture. Audiences had already demonstrated that they liked her act as it was—indeed, they were clamouring for more. In notes from Toronto, both Shipman and Smily urged her to build on her successes so far. Within a week, she had packed her trunk and embarked on a two-month tour of Ontario towns.

13

WHERE DO YOU
GO FROM HERE?
THE WHITE WAMPUM
1895—1896

P AULINE's life was now dominated by her tour schedules. After
a series of appearances in Ontario in late 1894, she and Owen
Smily did a second western tour in early 1895. They took a brief
break around Toronto, then they were off again—this time to Quebec,
Vermont and the Maritime provinces. The following year they made a
wide sweep across the northern United States, drawing audiences in
Michigan, Indiana, Ohio and Iowa. There were return engagements
"by popular request" in the heartland of Ontario, and further trips out
west. One day, Owen Smily sat down at a piano and improvised a
musical answer to the question they were asked most frequently:

> Where do you go from here?
> Say! Where do you go from here?
> We hear the same old question
> Wherever we may appear.

> The barber as he shaves us
> Remarks with an accent queer,
> "Fifteen cents, t'ank 'e sah!
> Where do you go from here?"

And sometimes we go to a hotel
In trembling and in fear,
Perhaps they don't like "show people",
And want us to "go from here".

And when we go to heaven
St Peter looks out with a leer:
"Oh yes! I know you're show people.
Say, where do you go from here?"

They appeared in theatres, hotel dining lounges, "Opera Houses" (as dusty little halls were grandly titled), church basements, schoolrooms, drill sheds and drawing rooms. In cities they treated themselves well, enjoying the comfortable mattresses and substantial dinners provided by Montreal's Windsor Hotel, Grand Rapids's Morton House and Ottawa's Russell House. But in places like Chapleau in Northern Ontario or Carman out west, there was little choice. They lugged their heavy trunks into ramshackle frame hotels with wide verandahs, and often shared their bedrooms with cockroaches, bedbugs and rats. Meals were 25 cents, beds 25 cents and drinks 5 cents each or six for a quarter. In 1895, Pauline wrote to Harry O'Brien from the Windsor Hotel in Montreal: "The hotel is as usual, big, dull, ponderous. The waiters proud in their majesty and refusing to run even for a 'quarter.' Tuesday, however, we leave for the small towns, where we shall probably long for the Windsor again. . . . Horrors! What a life."

The pattern of their one-night stands was always the same. They would walk over to the hall where they were booked, to check that the organizers had done their job with promotion and ticket sales. They would ensure that the stage was secure and the lights were adequate. They would shake out their costumes and hang them in whatever oversized closets were euphemistically described as their "dressing rooms." (At Schreiber, Ontario, they changed in the barbershop next to the hall. In Rossland, BC, they changed behind a screen of Hudson's Bay blankets in a corner of the hall.) Then they would return to the hotel for dinner. In Toronto or Vancouver, oysters, venison, "supreme

Like many of the venues in which Pauline performed,
the Opera House at Grand Forks, British Columbia,
was less opulent than its name implied.

de volaille" and ice cream were offered on the engraved menu. But the choice in more rough-and-ready hostelries, rattled off by ill-trained waitresses, never varied: "Termater soup, roas' mutton, roas' pork, dressed heart, tin' salmon, pie, tea blacker green, coffee, glass'a'milk' a'water." After dinner, they would stroll back to the venue. Pauline would change into her buckskin outfit for the first half of the evening, while the excited buzz of conversation and the scraping of seats in the auditorium filtered backstage.

By and large, the content of the Johnson–Smily show remained the same throughout their partnership. Owen would open so he could warm up the audience with a couple of comic monologues and ensure that even the most fidgety, inattentive spectators were settled in their seats. Then Pauline, the acknowledged star of the partnership, would glide onto centre stage and recite a couple of stirring Indian ballads, such as "As Red Men Die" or "Ojistoh," in her low, melodious voice. She usually followed up with a canoe poem or one of her popular verses about nature. There would sometimes be a musical interlude, provided by locally hired (and unreliable) talent. In the second half of the programme, Pauline, now in corset and satin, might recite a few more nature verses and Owen sing some popular music hall songs. The evening would end with a jointly written, jointly performed skit, such as "Mrs. Stewart's Five O'Clock Tea," about the wife of an MP from a small town who tries to make a splash in Ottawa social circles by giving a tea that will be the envy of every Ottawa hostess.

As Pauline's confidence as a performer grew, so did her gift for barbed comedy. Her sense of humour and her ear for accents were given full rein. One of her favourite anecdotes concerned a Scots clergyman in a town near Winnipeg who told her that he could not possibly attend her recital because he had to take in cabbages and turnips that night to escape the frost. Deadpan, she went on to relate to her audience how she said to him, " 'Then you must be a vegetarian.' 'I'm nae vegetarian, I'm a Presbyterian,' he replied."

Smily and Pauline usually left town before any reviews appeared in local papers. Comment was consistently admiring through the 1890s. "The two artistes more than sustained their well known reputations in all of their selections," according to the *Orillia Times*. Vancouver's *Daily World* gushed that the Johnson–Smily evening "could hardly have been more interesting. Miss Johnson possesses a strong personality and her wonderful elocutionary and dramatic powers combined to give a perfect rendering of her graphic descriptions of Indian life. . . . Even if Mr. Smily were not an effective mimic and had not a fine stage presence, a well-trained voice and marked musical ability, his selections would be funny in themselves . . . his efforts were greeted with continuous rounds of applause." In Indiana, the *Terre Haute Express* reported that the programme provided by the Johnson–Smily combination was "a delightful one from beginning to end." Vancouver's *Daily News-Advertiser* declared that "the talented poetess . . . charmed her audience by her wonderful facial expression, beautiful voice and perfect elocution, receiving loud applause and encores for every selection she gave."

There were plenty of other "show people" on the same circuit; the CPR transcontinental train had opened the West to all manner of entertainers as well as to homesteaders and tourists. The talent ranged from blackface troupes to illusionists, from full-throated bird impersonators to full-chested operatic contraltos. Violinists, cartoonists, comedians, lecturers—in the pre-movie period, travelling shows filled the halls. Agnes Knox of St. Mary's, Ontario, declaimed Browning throughout America. Norah Clench played the violin and Jessie Alexander cracked jokes across the breadth of the continent. Harold Jarvis performed sailors' jigs and the Fax brothers (Jim, Sim, George and Rube) sang wink-and-nudge vaudeville songs. One of the most popular attractions in North America was the Marks Brothers of Christie Lake, Ontario, who called themselves the "Canadian Kings of Repertoire." From 1870 onwards, the five brothers (two more had left the show after only a couple of years) promised their audiences "mellerdramas and stage villainy . . . many startling novelties, one hundred new sensations, time-tried favourites . . . and a record of promises fulfilled." With their Prince Albert coats and handlebar moustaches, these five farmer's sons claimed to have entertained more than six and a half million North Americans before they hung up their top hats in 1920.

Yet Pauline Johnson was special. She was the only poet reciting her own verse, and she was the only recitalist who had learned how to control her audience through sheer skill and force of personality. When performing before dignitaries such as the Governor General's entourage in Ottawa, she stunned spectators with her aristocratic hauteur and (to use a Victorian term of approval) exquisite "daintiness." In Montreal, the great railway magnate William Van Horne himself invited Pauline to lunch with him in his Westmount mansion. (Pauline adored his combination of down-home charm and elevated taste. "'They put up something very good' as the out-west senator said," she wrote to Harry O'Brien. "His pictures are glorious. Rousseau, Corot, Doré, Reynolds—all the great names.") In small towns with a surfeit of saloons, she employed different tactics. Rowdy young thugs at the back of the hall would frequently interrupt shows with their own chorus of wolf whistles, jeers and shrieks. "When I see a crowd of boys having a good time in the gallery I am always sorry . . . ," Pauline began stiffly on one such occasion, before giving a wicked grin and continuing. "Yes, I always wish I were among them."

She had become a charismatic artiste who had learned how to intrigue and thrill. It was not just that she straddled two worlds, appearing first as an Indian maiden and then as a Mayfair lady. It was also that she combined elements of two different fantasies—earthy and passionate in buckskin for the first half of her programme, ethereal and unobtainable in silk brocade for the second half. She appealed to instincts both gallant and erotic. Which was the real Pauline? Was she a savage free spirit or a fragile maiden? Did she want animal passion or gentlemanly protection? Or, her many admirers must have wondered with an illicit thrill, both? The more sophisticated audiences of Toronto and Vancouver could handle the clash of images. Elsewhere, however, spectators were less comfortable. "Isn't she savage?" she heard one man say, after a performance in Medicine Hat. "I wouldn't like her for a wife."

But who *was* the real Pauline? She herself never believed that any of the characters she portrayed on stage really caught her essential self; she knew she was more complex, and less public, than the captivating caricatures she presented. "I never felt it was I," she wrote to the poet and literary critic John Daniel Logan at the end of her life, "but rather the characters I assumed that the eyes were upon, and under these conditions [my] shyness was non-existent." She was both Indian maiden and English lady, yet she knew she was on the margins of both the Iroquois community of her birth and the class-ridden society of British settlers.

As her acting and control improved, Pauline enjoyed performing more. The benefits of this were considerable: her reputation spread, and receipts from the show increased. By now, she and Smily were asking $75 a performance (although the price dropped to $50 if the house was poor). In a two-month tour, she might give thirty performances. This would yield at least $1,000 for each of them (and Pauline, as the bigger star, might have taken more than half the proceeds). After travel, hotel and costume expenses were subtracted, with careful management Pauline might save as much as $500 per tour. In theory, this would cover her living expenses when she was not working, to allow her to rest and write more. Three such tours per year (and most years she spent more than six months on the road) should have permitted her to set aside money for the future. At a period when a schoolteacher earned $50 a month during the school year, Pauline was doing well. But Pauline, as her sister Evelyn constantly complained, was extravagant. She was generous to friends and casual acquaintances, an easy touch for anyone with a hard luck story. When she returned to Brantford, she would shower her family with gifts and fresh flowers. She never saved for a rainy day. "Do you know what I would do," she once asked a friend, "if I had only two dollars in the world and knew it would be my last? I'd spend half on my body and half on my soul. With one I would buy a wacking good meal and with the other a dozen cut carnations. Then I could die happy looking at my lovely flowers."

Pauline's increased renown also gave her a good excuse to keep her Brantford visits brief: twenty-four hours with her mother and sister was enough to make her chafe with impatience. Emily continued to feel uncomfortable that her daughter appeared on the stage, even if Pauline called herself a "recitalist" rather than an actress. However, Pauline explained that recitals, rather than poetry, paid her bills. And she also pointed out that she was finally making the professional contacts for which she yearned. In May 1895, for example, she joined Duncan Campbell Scott, Archibald Lampman and Frederick George Scott, leading poets all, for an evening of poetry reading at Ottawa's Normal School.

But Pauline's love of the melodramatic was starting to taint her artistic reputation. She often let her desire to captivate her audience override her sense of social nuance. In Ottawa, when she was invited to join her fellow poets for dinner at the Campbell Scotts' house on staid Lisgar Street, she asked if she could wear her Indian costume. Mrs. Scott, who was a towering Boston snob, decreed that it was inappropriate. Pauline's fellow guest Frederick Scott, a genial Anglican clergyman, was disappointed: "I should have loved to have been able to boast to my grandchildren in my old age that I had once taken a lady to dinner in her buckskins."

Moreover, the incessant touring came with a price. Pauline had less time to write poetry, and when she did take pen in hand, the product was suited more to performance than to print. Smily's style infiltrated hers: she started to compose what her critics regarded as lowbrow entertainment rather than highbrow art. For a woman who insisted she was a poet first and a performer second, this was hurtful.

The first critical slap in Pauline's face was prompted by a flippant little ditty entitled "His Majesty, the West Wind" that she and Smily included in the article "There and Back" published by the *Globe*, about their first cross-Canada tour. Referring to her now-famous poem, "The Song My Paddle Sings," Pauline had written:

Once in a fit of mental aberration
I wrote some stanzas to the western wind,
A very stupid, maudlin invocation,
That into ears of audiences I've dinned.

I never thought, when grinding out those stanzas,
I'd live to swallow pecks of prairie dust,
That I'd deny my old extravaganzas,
And wish his Majesty distinctly cussed.

The ditty sparked outrage from "Malcolm," a columnist for the St. Thomas *Evening Journal*, who considered that it proved that Pauline Johnson was only "masquerading . . . as a poetess." Malcolm went on to sneer that "As long as Miss Johnson was content to shine in her own immediate circle of friends it was nobody's business but her own; but when she lays distinct claims to poetic ability, and is heralded on her English visit as a leading Canadian poetess, her work at least becomes public property."

Literary spats are always good newspaper fodder, and Pauline had broken a cardinal rule of the Canadian literary community: she didn't take herself sufficiently seriously. The waspish *Evening Journal* paragraph was reprinted in *The Week*. *The Week*, which had used several poems by Pauline between 1885 and 1889, was the self-styled "Canadian Journal of Politics, Society and Literature" founded by Goldwin Smith in 1883. A heated correspondence ensued. Frank Yeigh rushed to his friend Pauline's defence, suggesting that Malcolm's column was "unfair, uncalled for, and undeserved." He listed the prestigious publications in which Pauline's work had appeared and the eminent people who had endorsed her poetry. But Malcolm was not the only Canadian critic who found Pauline's music hall humour déclassé. Another contributor objected to her use of slang ("What a hubbub it would have created had Tennyson foisted these stanzas upon us"). A more tolerant reader urged his fellow correspondents to "admire her for her many good works and forgive her her occasional lapses from the path of literary rectitude."

It was a relief for Pauline when, in the summer of 1895, *The White Wampum* finally appeared. Now she had a handsome volume of verse to present as her poetic credentials, rather than simply a collection of dog-eared clippings from the *Globe, The Week* and *Saturday Night*.

The London reviews of *The White Wampum* were mixed. The *National Observer* considered the volume "pleasant and wholesome, singularly fresh and vigorous, and at once thoughtful and free from all taint of pessimism." *The Sketch* acknowledged Miss Johnson as "a pretty poet." But other comments from the Imperial capital were characterized by a cavalier, often careless reading of the book. *The Scotsman* declared the narrative poems "gracefully written," but got Pauline's gender wrong. The verses, it stated, "do credit to their writer in marking him [*sic*] out as a Canadian poet in so far as he [*sic*] is true to the proper history and character of the Dominion." The *Manchester Guardian* went further—it got her ancestry wrong: "The idea of posing as an Indian bard cannot be counted among her happiest inspirations . . . we much prefer the poems in which Miss Johnson, who is, it appears, a Canadian, condescends to touch the humbler lyre of the palefaces." A third critic (in an anonymous clipping) wearied of all the mentions of "An ancient dying race, strange customs and costumes, fierce passions, barbaric heroisms, long unpronounceable names, tomahawks, Happy Hunting Grounds, canoes, 'redmen,' cattle thieves, melodrama and rhetoric."

Back home, the reception was much warmer. The *Canadian Gazette* called the book "a charming, if unpretentious collection, [which] suggests that the writer has greater work before her." *The*

Week's reviewer wrote that "We have read them all—some more than once—and we have found not a bad or indifferent poem in the collection! No one can fail to be struck with the musical rhythm of her lines, and she has great power of rhyming—no slight accomplishment, and one which we venture to think constitutes a very considerable ornament to English poetry." In direct rebuke to the cantankerous Malcolm, the reviewer singled out "The Song My Paddle Sings" as "a good example of charming word painting."

Pauline's old friend Hector Charlesworth reviewed *The White Wampum* for the large-circulation *Canadian Magazine*. Charlesworth was still star-struck by "the charm and power and music" of the "red-skinned muse." He declared Pauline "the most popular figure in Canadian literature, and in many respects the most prominent one." He predicted that the "luxurious bibliophile will have something to delight his senses," thanks to the quality of binding, type and design of *The White Wampum*. He praised the lyrical poems as striking a "universal note; they have music in them that lingers in one's ear, and sentiment that grows tuneful in one's heart." He wrote that the Indian ballads were "fresh and stimulating to healthy people with dramatic intelligence."

But even Pauline's enthusiastic fan had developed reservations about the Indian ballads, which smacked, he said, of "a fine Mohawk barbarity." Charlesworth was uncomfortable with Pauline's bias. Like many critics, he objected to the use of art for propaganda purposes. "She is a partisan of the red man," he explained. "His wrongs burn within her, but in reality one cannot put partisan emotions into poetic bottles with success." Charlesworth echoed Malcolm's criticisms about Pauline's work when he suggested that her work veered towards "melodrama": "she has marred works that are in essence poetic and strong with mere polemics."

Like any writer, Pauline brooded over her reviews. She was exasperated that *The Sketch* had declared that "Longfellow and Whittier have done more for the red-man she loves and champions." She was affronted by an anonymous comment from London that her poems were made "as the degenerate Redskin has learnt to make his moccasins and snowshoes and even his gods for the European bric-a-brac market." But she treasured the review in the *Manchester Guardian* because it suggested her poetry was good enough to be compared to that of Charles G. D. Roberts, the Confederation Poet best known and most admired outside Canada. In 1892, Roberts had described Pauline in the *Globe* as "the aboriginal voice of Canada by blood as well as by taste and the special trend of her gifts." Roberts's praise after her triumphant Toronto debut had reassured Pauline that there was a place for her in the literary establishment. The *Manchester Guardian* critic reinforced Roberts's assessment: "Now that Canada has added Miss Johnson to Mr. Roberts, British North America may safely challenge non-British [America] to play it doubles in poetical tennis."

A few weeks later, Pauline met Charles G. D. Roberts on his home turf, the Maritimes. Pauline and Smily were booked for a series of shows in the east. Their journey to New Brunswick, on the Intercolonial Railroad, took them past mile after mile of the great, grass-covered Tantramar salt marsh, on the upper Bay of Fundy. Roberts himself had immortalized the marsh's "gossiping grass" and wide red flats "pale with scurf of salt, seamed and baked in the sun" in his poem "Tantramar Revisited." Like the English poet Thomas Hardy, Roberts wrote unpretentious, beautifully crafted lyrical verses about the day-to-day scenes around him. Pauline was inspired both by his nature poetry and by his insistence that "Beauty clings in common forms!" As the train steamed towards Fredericton, she gazed out at a landscape that, as she wrote in *Massey's Magazine*, "is not grand scenery, to some it may not even be distinctive, but it is more than that, it is *Roberts*. The marshlands are himself, the sea voices, the tides, the sands, the wet salt breath of the margin winds—all are Roberts, and all are his atmosphere."

This was the first time that Pauline had met Canada's most famous poet in person, and as the train squealed to a stop, she was overcome with shyness. Roberts had already spent ten years as a full professor of English literature at King's College, Nova Scotia, and had the kind of literary standing she could only dream of. What would he think of "show people," especially Owen Smily with his vaudeville humour? But as she and her partner staggered onto the platform, loaded with bags, they heard a cheerful shout of "Welcome" from an untidy man with a thick, tobacco-stained moustache. "We knew him at once," Pauline recalled, "that eager, tenderly-strong face, that firmly-knit athletic figure, that easy Bohemian manner of dress, that happy trick of absolute good fellowship, it was undoubtedly he, of Tantramar, Roberts himself, with as warm a handclasp for us both as though we had all known each other for years."

Roberts was as struck by Pauline as she was by him—but his admiration was probably more physical in nature. Pauline was the kind of dark-haired beauty that he loved: a notorious philanderer throughout his long career (he died in 1943 aged eighty-three), Roberts would spend most of his life swanning round the world while his wife, May, raised their four children in poverty in Fredericton. At the time of Pauline's visit, he was involved in several amorous entanglements, including one in his own home, Kingscroft, with his children's governess, behind May's back. Perhaps these sordid complications in Kingscroft lay behind Roberts's insistence that Owen Smily and Pauline must stay at the home of his parents. His father, the Reverend George Goodridge Roberts, was rector of St. Anne's Church, Fredericton, and a canon at Fredericton Cathedral.

The rector's family made the two performers completely at home in the sunny, red-brick rectory. Charles's sister Elizabeth, nicknamed Nain, also wrote poetry and so was thrilled to meet another female poet. In no time at all, Pauline noted, Charles Roberts and "my philistine fellow-artist were addressing each other *sans ceremonie*, as 'Old fellow' and 'Say, old man,' which shows that of all things, Roberts is first a man, among men." Roberts, Pauline realized with pleasure, was far too much a Bohemian to sneer at lighthearted verse. He had little time for Toronto pretensions and he was fun. He once penned a snappy little verse about the humdrum need to make a living under the title "The Poet is Bidden to Manhattan Island." It began,

Dear Poet, quit your shady lanes
And come where more than lanes are shady.
Leave Phyllis to the rustic swains
And sing some Knickerbocker lady.

And it ended,

> You've piped at home, where none could pay.
> Till now, I trust, your wits are riper.
> Make no delay, but come this way,
> And pipe for them that pay the piper!

Within a couple of years, Roberts had followed his own doggerel advice and had left New Brunswick's salt marshes and shady lanes for the salons and shady ladies of Manhattan. There he enlarged his reputation as a poet (and a lady-killer). To augment his income, he wrote animal stories which were based on the careful observation of animal behaviour he had made as a youngster. Before he said good-bye to Pauline in 1895, he gave her two presents that she always treasured: the manuscript copy of his 1893 sonnet sequence, *Songs of the Common Day*, and the pen with which he had written it. Pauline always felt that she owed Roberts a debt of gratitude because as literary editor of *The Week* in the 1880s he had included several of her verses in the magazine. She was also flattered that he had sent a letter of introduction on her behalf to the influential New York critic Clarence Edward Stedman. Had she seen the letter, she might have been less impressed. Roberts was more interested in describing her looks, and her respect for him, than her literary achievements: "Our Canadian Mohawk Princess, Pauline Johnson, is going to New York soon, and to see you. She is a devout admirer. I gave her a card to you. Beware, beware, beware! She is charming and a poet!" Pauline never described herself as a princess; the phrase "Indian princess" had already become as much of a bloodless stereotype as the phrase "Indian maiden" against which she had railed in 1892.

Pauline loved Atlantic Canada, with its gentle landscape and historic associations. She was fascinated by the lore and legends of the Miqmaq people. The gentle beauty of the Annapolis Valley bewitched her. Since childhood, she had known by heart Longfellow's poem *Evangeline*, about the expulsion of the Acadians, the French who had settled in the Annapolis Valley in the seventeenth century and who were deported by the British in 1755. Now she described the area as teeming "with olden romance as well as luxuriant orchards. . . . The monstrosity of cities has never touched even its margin; it is primitive, melancholy, indescribably placid, faultlessly beautiful and strangely aloof from every other portion of Canada." On one of her visits east, she met "a typical Blue Nose" (as Maritimers were nicknamed) sauntering along a lane next to an ox cart loaded with apples. He allowed her to climb onto his cartload of apples to be photographed, then urged her (since she liked the valley so much) to remain there. "What have you got here to keep me?" she enquired, and laughed heartily when he replied, "Poetry and pippins."

But Pauline did not belong in Nova Scotia. Moreover, she was beginning to wonder whether she still belonged in Ontario. She found it easier to stay in touch with her mother by letter than in person. On the long waits at railway stations, or during hot afternoons in some remote, dusty town, she would pull out her navy leather writing case, unclip its brass clasp, remove a piece of paper from one of its pockets and place it on the blotting-paper flap. Then she would dip her nib in a portable inkstand and write an account of her travels. Unhappily, none of Pauline's letters home have survived, and only a couple of Emily's wistful replies remain. "My dearest Pauline," Emily wrote, in a shaky scrawl, to her daughter during these years. "Only a wee note dear this time to thank you for your dear, long, kind letter. . . . I think of you every Sunday in church and often wish you were with me, but I hope the time will come some day. Please give my love to Owen. . . ."

Family politics were not the only frustration for Pauline in Ontario. As the province prospered, its society became more stratified. After 1890, groups of southern Italians, Jews from the Russian Pale, Poles, Slavs, Hungarians and Greeks started to arrive. Most of the immigrants spent their summers working in Northern Ontario's mines and at railroad sites. Laid off when the snow came, they gravitated to Toronto in the winter, congregating in cheaper neighbourhoods like St. John's Ward. This rectangular area, squeezed within the grid of College Street and Queen Street, University Avenue and Yonge Street, was soon known simply as "the Ward." Four out of five of the jerry-built shacks in the Ward were rented from greedy absentee landlords. In the laneways, Italian and Jewish ragpickers stacked their junk. Barefoot, dirty children splashed through open cesspools. Lacking adequate sewage or water facilities, its boarding houses crammed with Eastern and Southern Europeans, the Ward became a byword for urban squalor. Typhoid, cholera and scarlet fever flourished.

Since the Ward was on the doorstep of some of Toronto's more affluent neighbourhoods, it was impossible for older, wealthier residents to ignore their city's changing face. Professors hurrying towards Trinity College dodged peddlers and hurdy-gurdies on the sidewalks. Debutantes strolling under the flowering chestnuts of University Avenue were assailed by the pungent odours of unfamiliar cuisines and bad drains. The same clash between English-speaking families who had settled in Canada at least three generations earlier and these newer, "foreign" immigrants was enacted on a more modest scale in the province's smaller manufacturing or industrialized towns, like Hamilton and London. But standards of social behaviour for the province were set in Toronto. It didn't take long for Toronto's fine old families to close ranks against newcomers, who usually had darker skins, little English, less money and no roots in the British Empire.

By the mid-1890s, Toronto's upper strata had congealed into an exclusive WASP clique determined, by and large, to defend its position and privileges. It was almost impossible for outsiders to penetrate its inner circles or understand its etiquette. "Mrs. Kirkpatrick's Wednesdays lose none of their *chic* and charm," began *Saturday Night's* Social and Personal Column on November 21, 1896, in a description of an At Home given by the wife of the Lieutenant-Governor. "On Wednesday, *petite* Miss Nordheimer, in a charming little gown of madder red *velour*, received many welcoming words. The Misses FitzGerald, Mrs. Melfort Boulton, Mrs. McCarthy and Mrs. FitzGibbon, Mrs. and Miss Cattanach, Mrs. Macdonald, Mrs. Duncan Coulson, Miss Skeaff and ever so many more were at Government House." The grandes dames of this *beau monde* dictated the conventions to be followed at the top of the social pyramid. Their husbands spent their days building up the Dominion's economy. Their sons followed their fathers into business or the professions; their daughters were groomed to become the wives and mothers of the next generation. They all shared the credo that monetary success and British ancestry were synonymous with moral superiority.

Most well-bred young women spent an inordinate amount of time on their appearances, which were catalogued in excruciating detail by fawning social columnists. "Miss Kathleen Murphy was very pretty in pink silk, and Miss Belle in black, relieved with pale blue velvet," ran one such column about the 1899 Argonaut Rowing Club dance. "Miss Evelyn Cox wore white satin with violets, and her cousin Miss Beatrice Myles wore pale blue satin. Miss Florrie Patterson wore black net *paillette*; Miss Heaven wore buttercup *mousseline*; Miss Bessie Thompson, primrose organdie with *entredeux* of black lace." The main events of the social season, such as the St. Andrew's Day Ball each December, were elaborate mating rituals for the elite. "Toronto is growing a big place," reported *Saturday Night*'s Social and Personal Column in December 1896, "for though everyone appeared to be at the ball, I have been surprised since to remember how many were not there." It is unlikely that the social columnist had in mind residents of the Ward in her sweeping generalization about "everyone."

Where did Pauline belong in a world increasingly preoccupied with pedigree and black net *paillette*? At Lord Ripon's dining table in London, she had shown that when necessary, she could give the appearance of sliding effortlessly into this world. She had recited her poems to many members of this elite; the more intellectual and literary types within it were her audience. And there were a few others with ancestry similar to hers who had proven acceptable to the social arbiters. Dr. Oronhyatekha, the Mohawk from the Tyendena'ga Reserve who was now the Supreme Chief Ranger of the Foresters, cropped up on society pages, smiling "with calm, classic countenance."

But Pauline was an outsider; she could never compete with Miss Heaven in her costly buttercup *mousseline*. She was too poor to afford the latest fashion in primrose organdie: a decade later she was still wearing the gowns she had bought in London in 1894. She was obliged to live on her wits. Worse yet, she was on the stage. She might have convinced her mother that she was a recitalist not an actress, but the snobbish Mrs. Kirkpatrick and the haughty Miss Nordheimer were unlikely to appreciate such a subtle difference. And as Toronto's population swelled with impoverished people from different ethnic backgrounds, an ugly racism gathered force amongst the Kirkpatricks, the Boultons and their ilk. Proud as Pauline was of her lineage, it was perceived as a little too exotic by families now clinging to Anglo-Saxon bloodlines. As an Indian and as a female performer, she was doubly disadvantaged. The menfolk of the fine old families might find her thrilling, but the womenfolk would never accept her.

Moreover, Pauline didn't particularly want to fit in. She was determined to maintain her dual identities: she was Tekahionwake as well as Miss Johnson. When fashionable Toronto artists offered to paint her portrait, she was more than happy to wear her buckskin costume for the sittings. J. W. L. Forster, a Paris-trained painter whose usual subjects were such civic dignitaries as Timothy Eaton and Sir Oliver Mowat, waived his $500 fee in order to capture the Mohawk poet in oil. Forster adored what he called "her full possession of the valkyrie-like wild passion of the traditional Red Indian." His portrait shows a stunning young woman, an eagle feather in her curly, dark hair and a bear's claw necklace round her long neck, against a background of sun-dappled leaves.

Audiences loved what a Grand Rapids newspaper called in 1896 "a wondrous beautiful young Indian maiden, possessed of all the romantic charms read in story books descriptive of her vanishing race. As lovely as Minnehaha and as eloquent as the noted chiefs of her tribe, . . . she is proud of her blood and says her father was great and good. She alludes to him as an Indian Napoleon." Tekahionwake continued to be a stronger draw than Owen Smily at recitals. "His style was perhaps as good as Miss Johnson's, but lacking in the novelty that she possessed," commented the Grand Rapids reporter.

But as Pauline embarked on yet another tour of the Midwest in 1897, her uncertainty about who she was and where she belonged began to show. A reporter from the *Chicago Tribune* found her attractive, but touchy: "Miss Johnson wears Frenchy looking gowns and neatly fitting shoes and gloves. She doesn't powder her face nor rouge her lips, but she curls her front hair and manicures her nails. In fact, she does pretty well everything that a real Indian would not be expected to do. . . . And she talks like a Vassar graduate." But when the reporter seemed more interested in whether "real Indians" manicured their nails than in Iroquois legends and customs, Pauline snapped at him: "If you don't want to hear about the history of my people, what did you come to see me for?"

Pauline's insecurity was compounded by money worries. Her extravagance was getting out of hand. Despite her successes, she was always scrambling for ready cash to pay her travel, hotel and clothing bills. In 1896, she tried to sell some Indian masks to Washington's Smithsonian Institute. She wrote to the anthropologist Horatio Hale, who had often visited the Johnson family at Chiefswood, and asked him to authenticate the masks. "My dear Miss Pauline," he wrote back. "It is too bad that after doing so much and so well in your profession, you should be left . . . in pecuniary troubles. But these, I presume, are only temporary." Hale was wrong: financial worries ate away at Pauline all her life. Her profligacy shocked her frugal sister, Evelyn, who never bought a dozen cut carnations and always counted her change as she carefully slipped it into a little black purse.

As Pauline criss-crossed the continent day after day, trying to keep her costumes clean and her creditors at bay, she began to feel her age. When she checked her appearance in the mirror before she glided onto the stage each evening, she could no longer ignore the wrinkles at the corners of her eyes or the deepening grooves between her nose and mouth. The beautiful young Indian maiden was not so young anymore. She shrewdly refused to tell reporters the date of her birth. "You see," she wrote to the literary critic J. E. Wetherell in 1895, when she was thirty-four, "When a woman depends upon the public for her bread and butter, she must not get old. I lose money every time people undertake to establish when I was born." In late-Victorian Canada, women were old at forty and few lived beyond their fifties. Pauline asked herself for how long North Americans would pay to see a middle-aged woman recite her own verse.

In the final weeks of 1897, Pauline seems to have taken stock of her circumstances and decided that she needed a change. She acknowledged to herself that she no longer felt at home in Ontario. She could see that after five years, her partnership with Owen Smily was coming to an end. Smily was tired of endlessly playing second fiddle to an aging Pauline, who had learned so much of her stagecraft from him but always assumed he would carry her bags. She recognized that she needed to go where she could pull in the best audiences, earn some money and perhaps make new friends.

So she decided to make a fresh start for herself in Winnipeg. She was comfortable in the West, she told a Winnipeg newspaper, with its "go-ahead institutions, its kindly people, and appreciative, though discriminating, audiences." She loved the fluid, accessible society of Winnipeg, and its surfeit of young swains who paid court to her after her recitals. The Indian peoples she had seen on the Prairies and in the foothills, who still rode bareback with scalps tied to their belts, intrigued her. Plenty of respectable citizens in Western towns had both British and Indian blood, and there was little stigma attached. So she booked herself into the Hotel Manitoba and announced that she had come to stay.

And at Winnipeg's Grand Opera House on December 29, 1897, she had a capacity audience rolling in the aisles with laughter. She performed a new sketch entitled "The Success of the Season," in which she skewered a Toronto grande dame and her social-climbing ambitions. "She afforded much amusement by her pictures of the follies and insincerities of fashionable, or would-be-fashionable, society," noted the *Winnipeg Free Press*. Pauline had left social pretensions behind in the East. She wanted a new life in "the Chicago of the North." Within a few weeks, it seemed that she might have found it.

14

"A HALF-BREED BUT SUCH A NICE ONE": CHARLES DRAYTON

1897—1899

THE sound of wild applause was still echoing around the Grand Opera House on December 29, 1897, when Pauline Johnson gave a final curtsey and retired to her dressing room. She had scarcely sat down and kicked off her shoes before there was a loud knock on the door. Checking her reflection in the mirror, she rose and answered the summons. In the dim light of the backstage corridor, she saw a square-jawed, bull-necked young man who immediately thrust a bouquet of flowers at her. Flowers, in the middle of a Winnipeg winter, were a more than extravagant gesture.

Pauline had lots of admirers in Winnipeg, but this particular beau was more persistent than most—and had received more encouragement. His name was Charles Robert Lumley Drayton, and he was twenty-five years old. His story was typical of many of the young men working in Winnipeg in the 1880s and 1890s. He was the younger son of a well-to-do Toronto family who had been sent out to make his way in the West and "help put the 'Win' in Winnipeg," as the locals liked to say. And he was just the type of man to whom Pauline was always drawn: a youthful athlete more than ten years younger than herself, with impeccable English manners.

Charles Drayton's parents had not been in Canada long. His father, Philip, originally arrived in Ontario as an officer in the British army. He had then been posted to Barbados and, after resigning his commission in

1874, returned to Toronto to settle there with his wife, Margaret Covernton. There was already a Drayton living in Ontario, east of Toronto—Philip's cousin Reginald Drayton, a British remittance man. Reggie could not have been more different than Philip, the ultra-respectable former army officer. Reggie, a rascal since boyhood, had been sent to the colonies by his clergyman father in Gloucestershire to keep him out of trouble in the Mother Country. His father paid for him to live in the Rice Lake area north of Cobourg with Clinton Atwood (son-in-law of the writer Catharine Parr Traill), who was supposed to teach the irrepressible Reggie how to farm. Unfortunately, Charlie Drayton's Uncle Reggie had absolutely no time for agriculture but all the time in the world for drinking and hunting.

Perhaps stuffy Philip followed scruffy Reggie to Canada to keep an eye on him; perhaps, as a former army officer with limited means, when he returned to Britain after years in the colonies he felt out of place in a country where engineers and entrepreneurs were the new heroes. By the time the Philip Draytons settled in Toronto, they had two sons: Henry, born in Canada in 1869, and Charles, born in Barbados in 1872. A daughter, named Margaret after her mother, was born in Toronto. At first, the boys' father remained relentlessly British in loyalty; while he studied and then taught law at Osgoode Hall, he sent his sons to the English public school Harrow. As Philip Drayton's income steadily increased, the Draytons' allegiances slowly shifted and the family merged into Toronto's WASP elite. Philip served on City Council as an alderman, and both boys eventually graduated from Upper Canada College.

Henry was a model son: he studied law and, when only twenty-four, was appointed Assistant Solicitor for the City of Toronto. Henry always took himself very seriously; he was careful, restrained and, wrote a contemporary, "never made a statement that was good for a headline, or coined an epigram, or lost his temper." His thick brown hair was slicked back with brilliantine, his bushy moustache was trimmed within an inch of its life and his stiff collars gleamed with starch. Ambitious socially and professionally, he was said to be at his best when "sitting in a club lounge with a prosperous cigar, explaining his opinions to men not quite as important as himself."

His younger brother, however, was a different character. Charles was high-spirited, energetic and a bit of a rake. Like his brother, he had a posh English accent and posh English clothes, but unlike Henry, he had a devil-may-care approach to life. Philip Drayton must have feared he had sired another Reggie. Had he still lived in England, he would probably have purchased a commission for Charlie in his old regiment, the Queen's Own 16th Rifles, and sent him off to one of Britain's distant little wars—Sudan, perhaps, or northern India. But since the Draytons now lived in the colonies, Philip did the next best thing. He persuaded the head of the Western Canada Savings and Loan Company to employ his younger son as an office boy in its Toronto headquarters, with a view to sending him out West once he had proved his reliability. Charlie rose to expectations: in 1891, the nineteen-year-old was dispatched to the company's Winnipeg office. For the stocky, muscular young Charles, with his unruly dark hair and ready laugh, it was the perfect destination, a city that consisted of rounds of drinks, rolls of money and the ever-present clatter of hammers and saws.

"Society in Winnipeg is noticeably young, with the high-spiritedness of youth and something of its impatience of control," a correspondent wrote in the *Montreal Daily Star* in October 1888. The correspondent was Sara Jeannette Duncan, Pauline's Brantford-born school friend who wrote under the pseudonym Garth Grafton. In 1888, Sara crossed Canada by train on a round-the-world trip with a friend, and later published her account in *A Social Departure: How Orthodocia and I Went Round the World by Ourselves*. (This convoluted title was a "New Woman" pun, since an orthodox woman would never travel by herself.) Sara found Winnipeg a lively, attractive place in which well-bred young women were given an enthusiastic welcome. Her description reflected all the characteristics of this wide-open pioneer city that would persuade Pauline to settle there a few years later: "Its friendliness, without restraint or reserve, is delightful. . . . There appears to be a great abundance of young men in the place. . . . The number to be met at a five o'clock tea, usually contemned of masculinity, is surprising. Something in the air of the country makes everybody vivacious."

Sara devoted several inches of her column to an institution of which Charles Drayton would inevitably become a member. This was "the Shanty": a boarding house in which various well-off bachelors lived together and "give dinners and drive in the most charming and individual fashion and who form an important element in all that is 'going on' in a social way in Winnipeg." The institution of the Shanty began in the early 1880s when, following the advance of the CPR tracks, the city's population exploded with railway managers, land speculators, merchants and white-collar clerks for banks and insurance companies. Since then the Shantymen had changed their quarters occasionally, and their membership regularly, but never their "fraternal spirit," according to Sara: "Those of its members removed by matrimony or other providential causes, [the Shanty] considers not lost but gone before."

The Shanty was one aspect of Winnipeg's surfeit of eligible bachelors that appealed to independent-minded young ladies like Sara and Pauline. But there was a seamier side to Winnipeg's male-dominated demographics to which neither Pauline nor Sara would have dreamt of alluding. Men outnumbered women by two to one in the city, and most of them were not well-dressed young bucks from Eastern Canada like Charlie Drayton and his friends. Thanks to the railway, Winnipeg, like Toronto, was facing a rising tide of immigration from Eastern and Southern Europe. At the same time, an economic depression in Quebec and Ontario was behind an influx of unemployed men (including a fair number of gamblers, drifters and ne'er-do-wells) from Eastern Canada, who had left sweethearts, wives and families back home until they could get established. As an old Ontario folk song put it,

> One by one they all clear out,
> Thinking to better themselves no doubt,
> Caring little how far they go
> From the poor little girls of Ontario.

The rooming houses and hotels in the vicinity of Winnipeg's CPR station were crammed with single men. They worked sixteen-hour days in the rapidly expanding boom town, doing all the heavy work that today is done by machine. They excavated the city ditches, dug the sewers, laid the water mains, mixed the concrete, graded and gravelled the streets. In construction jobs, they manhandled foundation stone, bricks, mortar and steel into place. Lonely and poorly housed, in their off-hours these men congregated in the only recreational centres available to them—bars, brothels and pool halls. By 1900, there would be three times as many brothels in Winnipeg as there were churches. The largest, busiest bordellos were just north of Portage Avenue on Thomas Street ("John Thomas Street" to regulars, later elevated to Minto Street, after the Governor General). Winnipeg was as well known for its prostitutes as for its pioneers.

It was the prospect of a quick fortune that brought all the punters, rich and poor, to "the Chicago of the North." And by 1897, when Charles Drayton began paying court to Pauline Johnson, he was well on his way to prosperity. He had been appointed an Assistant Inspector for the Western Canada Savings and Loan Company, later renamed the Canadian Permanent Loan Company. There was barely a community in the Prairies or British Columbia that Charlie hadn't visited in order to assess its land potential. He had bounced in a horse-drawn buggy along primitive tracks and through mountain passes, and stayed in the same ratty hotels that Pauline stayed in. He was rapidly emerging as one of the leading authorities on property values in the West. In short, he was turning into the kind of respectable banker that his father had hardly dared hope he would become.

Charlie Drayton's success had allowed him to graduate from his convivial boarding house to the elegant Clarendon Hotel. He still loved the thigh-slapping informality of life in the West, compared to Toronto's buttoned-down society. But the charms of the bachelor life had begun to pall. He had lived through six bone-chilling Winnipeg winters and six blistering, bug-ridden Prairie summers. Many of his fellow Shantymen had either married or returned east. He wanted to settle down and make a home. However, the shortage of eligible brides in Winnipeg was a problem. Then Pauline Johnson came to town. And from the moment Charles Drayton first laid eyes on her, declaiming her verses on stage or perhaps slipping into the Hotel Manitoba, which was next door to the Clarendon, he was smitten.

Once Pauline was living in Winnipeg, events moved quickly. After a brief tour of southern Manitoba in early January, she returned to Winnipeg and boasted about her dazzlingly ambitious plans for the coming year to a reporter from the *Manitoba Morning Free Press*. She was going to travel west to perform in Prince Albert and Regina, she announced, then travel east for an Ottawa engagement, then south to New York City to publish a book of short stories. She would then make a tour of the United States before leaving for Australia in the fall. In other words, she would be on the move for the next twelve months—unless a better offer came along.

These plans were not just ambitious, they were also unrealistic. There is no evidence that Pauline had written any short stories since "A Red Girl's Reasoning" had appeared in 1892. She did not have the money or a partner for a demanding tour of the United States or Australia. In her 1981 biography of Pauline Johnson, author Betty Keller describes the plans as a ruse to force Charlie Drayton's hand. "For nearly twenty years," suggests Keller, Pauline "had been hearing wedding bells every time a new man entered her life. . . . Charles Drayton fitted Pauline's dream of the perfect husband and she was determined to marry him." Charlie didn't need much of a nudge. On January 25, the Toronto *Globe* announced the engagement in Winnipeg of Miss E. Pauline Johnson and Mr. Charles R. L. Drayton: "Each of the principals is receiving the congratulations of their numerous friends in the city and in the east." The wedding would take place the following September.

The engagement took their respective friends and relatives by surprise. Amongst Pauline Johnson's personal papers, no letters between Pauline and Charlie, or their families, have survived. If Pauline kept such letters, they would certainly have been amongst those that her sister Evelyn burnt after her death in an effort to protect Pauline's reputation. So it is impossible to know exactly how the Draytons or the Johnsons reacted to Pauline and Charlie's engagement. Emily Johnson almost certainly regarded Charles Drayton as a "catch" for her strong-willed daughter as Pauline's fortieth birthday approached. Pauline's mother must have hoped that a husband would persuade Pauline to stop appearing on stage and settle down to a more respectable life as a wife. She must also have thought wistfully of grandchildren. By now, both Evelyn and Allen were living at home—Allen had abandoned his job in insurance and appears to have become a chronic depressive. Neither of Pauline's siblings showed any inclination to marry, so Emily's hopes were pinned on her youngest child.

Charlie's Toronto family and friends, on the other hand, would most likely have been horrified by the difference in age (Charlie was eleven years younger than his intended) and background. Mixed marriages were increasingly frowned on within Canadian urban society. The opinion of Henry Drayton, Charlie's elder brother, would carry particular weight within his family, and inevitably it would be hostile. Henry would not have been the success he was in stuffy Toronto if he welcomed his brother's unorthodox choice. By now, Henry Drayton had secured his own "catch": Edith Cawthra, whose forebears had been part of the Family Compact autocracy that had controlled Upper Canada in the early nineteenth century. Edith's father was a banker, and her family was so much grander than Henry's that when their engagement was first whispered, Henry's sister, Margaret, commented, "Harry will have to carve out his fortune first before he can dream of asking her hand in matrimony." By 1892, however, Henry had successfully scaled the Establishment heights and married Edith ("a sweet, unaffected girl," Margaret reported to Reggie Drayton's wife, Agnes). The wedding took place at the Cawthras' Rosedale residence, and Edith was promptly swallowed up by the Society cycle of At Homes, garden parties and charity work. A half-Mohawk sister-in-law who appeared in buckskin in opera houses and church halls may not have appealed to Mr. and Mrs. Henry Drayton.

Yet affairs were more complicated than this. Not everybody in 1898 took the view that the proposed marriage was inevitably a triumph for Pauline and a disaster for the Draytons. Pauline was a celebrity whose fans, for example, liked her the way she was. Would marriage diminish her mystique and smother the dangerous eroticism of her half-English, half-Indian theatrics? "That her rare accomplishments and pleasing personality should win many bids in the matrimonial market was to be expected," commented the *Brantford Courier*. "But Miss Johnson was enthroned by her genius far above the commonplace of life and getting married is such an ordinary thing to do that it was the last thing expected of her."

And the Drayton family was not as rigid as it might appear. Charlie's sister, Margaret Drayton, wrote to her aunt, Agnes Drayton, "I suppose you have heard that Charlie is engaged to Miss Pauline Johnson, the Indian poetess. . . . Her mother belonged to a very good English family and was related to Howell the American writer. Her father was a very clever man and every one says he was so nice. He was head chief of the Mohawk tribe and interpreter for the six nations. Pauline an Indian Princess herself is a half breed but then such a nice one. When she was over in England she was received everywhere and she recited for the Princess of Wales." Maybe Margaret was a little too insistent that the Johnson family was "nice," but Pauline's achievements counted for something. Charles's mother and sister were not unhappy with the engagement.

Meanwhile, Pauline herself was less certain about the match than she appeared. Charlie was doubtless a dear boy. But unlike her suitor Michael Mackenzie, a decade earlier, apparently he did not inspire a single love poem. No "wave-rocked and passion-tossed" verses survive from 1897; no young Apollo throws the poet into a painful emotional maelstrom. The few poems that can be dated to this period are mainly about Indians and Indian legends. "The Corn Husker," dating from 1896, describes an old Indian woman, bent with age and hunger, scavenging for forgotten cobs after the corn harvest. Pauline's growing commitment to her Indian heritage, despite developments in her personal life, is unmistakeable:

> And all her thoughts are with the days gone by,
> 'Ere might's injustice banished from their lands
> Her people, that today unheeded lie,
> Like the dead husks that rustle through her hands.

Deliberately defying convention, Pauline insisted that she would continue stage recitals after her wedding. "It is a matter for congratulation," reported the Brantford paper, "that Miss Johnson does not intend to abandon her professional life." She was still busy embellishing her image as "the Indian poetess." A few months earlier, on a second visit to Fort Macleod, she had seen a Blood Indian chief ride into town at the head of fifty warriors in war paint and buckskin. The chief had seventeen Sioux scalps hanging on his belt. "The desire of my life had been to possess an Indian scalp," Pauline confessed to an officer of the North-West Mounted Police. The latter persuaded the chief to present to the Mohawk maiden one of his trophies, decorated with rows of turquoise-blue Hudson's Bay Company beads. Pauline immediately attached this treasure to the waist of her own Indian costume. It is hard to imagine that marriage to young Charlie was going to extinguish her resolve "to stand by my blood and my race." A life of five-o'clock At Homes in Rosedale would never be enough for a woman whose idea of a corsage was sometimes a Sioux scalp.

A few days after her engagement was announced, Pauline demonstrated her determination to continue her career by setting off for the promised tour of Western towns. Despite –30 degree Celsius temperatures and mountainous snowdrifts, she boarded the CPR train westbound. But when she arrived in Regina on February 20, she found a telegram with dreadful news from Brantford. Her mother was very ill. Pauline cancelled her bookings, turned around and clambered aboard the next train going in the opposite direction. The weather was so bad that the eastbound train could only crawl along the thousands of miles of track or steam to a standstill when snow blocked the rails. For seven wretched, long days, Pauline stared out at blizzards or tried to concentrate on the piece of velvet she was embroidering. She changed trains in North Bay and then in Toronto. At Union Station, she was touched to find Charles's mother, Margaret Drayton, waiting on the platform, ready to accompany her on the last leg of the journey to Brantford. The train journey was an opportunity for Mrs. Drayton to get to know her future daughter-in-law, but it was also a kind gesture of support for an exhausted and grief-struck woman. By the time the two women stumbled through the front door of 7 Napoleon Street, Emily Johnson was unconscious. Less than an hour later, she passed away.

All the old friends congregated for Emily's funeral. The Reverend Mackenzie conducted a short service in the house, then a longer one at

Emily Howells Johnson always insisted to her children that it was possible to honour both their Mohawk and their British heritage.

the Mohawk Chapel. There were three Indian and three non-native pallbearers, just as there had been fourteen years earlier for George Johnson. The Indians were Allen Johnson, Chief William Wedge and Chief John Hill. The non-natives were Colonel J. T. Gilkison, the former Superintendent of the Reserve, Mr. Dingman, Inspector of Indian Affairs, and Hugh Hartshorne, Pauline's former paddling partner, who was now an up-and-coming Toronto lawyer. "Mother had requested that Old Hundred be sung at her funeral," Evelyn recalled sadly, "and this was done." As the hymn "All People That on Earth Do Dwell" filled the chapel, Pauline stifled her tears and stared at the mounds of flowers covering the coffin. Among the wreaths were several from Johnson relatives, such as Mansel Rogers in Kingston, the Washingtons from Hamilton and Miss Howells from Toronto. Charlie's mother brought violets, and he himself wired an order from Winnipeg for cut flowers from a Brantford florist.

Evelyn, Allen and Pauline Johnson stood together in the front pew, stiff with self-control. Emily Johnson's death was a painful wrench for each of them. She had helped her children define who they were and had bequeathed to them an intimidatingly stern example of how to behave. It wasn't just her insistence on well-pressed collars and perfect table manners. It was also the commitment she had instilled to both their Mohawk and their English blood. After the funeral, Pauline read and reread the newspaper obituaries. The *Brantford Expositor* spoke of Emily's deep religious faith: "The deceased was sincerely beloved by all who knew her, and her true Christian life and many estimable qualities endeared her to all with whom she came into contact." The Toronto *Globe* delved further back into history: "Elderly people . . . will remember well the astonishment with which society received the news of the engagement and subsequent marriage of the popular and much-admired Miss Emily Howells to a full-blooded Indian, Chief Johnson by name. That this unusual marriage should have turned out most happily is only another proof of the fact that what everybody says is not necessarily true."

Pauline must have compared her parents' perfect marriage to her proposed union with Charlie Drayton. Would he respect her Indian blood as Emily had respected George Johnson's? Or would her fiancé Charlie behave as the character Charlie McDonald had behaved in her story "A Red Girl's Reasoning" and regard his British heritage as superior to the native heritage of his Indian bride? As she had sat with Charlie's mother on the train journey from Toronto to Brantford, Pauline had been charming but uncompromising about her pride in her Mohawk heritage. She was not prepared to try to "pass as white." "She told mother," Margaret reported to Agnes Drayton, "that she had always said she never would marry a white man but you see she is going to after all. . . . Mother and in fact all of us are quite contented about the match as she is devoted to Charlie and he to her."

A string of crises put the relationship under severe stress in the next few months. First, Pauline developed a throat infection, probably triggered by staphylococcus bacteria related to the erysipelas that had killed her father. The throat infection led to a bout of the rheumatic fever that would dog Pauline for the rest of her life and that would weaken her heart. She tried to fulfill recital commitments in Toronto, Ottawa, Sudbury and the northern United States, but was repeatedly forced to retreat to Brantford to rest. Next, Charles Drayton's own mother, who was only fifty-one, died suddenly and unexpectedly in early July; the cause of her death is not recorded. And at the end of July, Pauline and Evelyn had to go through the emotionally taxing process of dismantling the Napoleon Street household. Allen had already found lodgings elsewhere, Evelyn could not afford to live there alone and Pauline made it clear that she would never return permanently.

Evelyn insisted on dividing up their family possessions item by item. She negotiated with her sister as to who would have the red tablecloth and the photo of the Grand River Canoe Club (Pauline), and who would take the paper rack, two large milk bowls and their mother's linen blouse (Evelyn). Pauline's careless attitude to possessions exasperated Evelyn, who scraped by on her meagre salary and treasured every reminder of past happiness. "Where is the pleat for the front of the linen blouse?" she later complained to Pauline. "I saw you with it, you said you did not want it, but I can't find it. It was embroidered with pink lining."

Poor Evelyn. Neither sister now had a home of her own, but Pauline's prospects appeared so much more glamorous and secure than those of her elder sister. While Pauline was about to marry into a well-off family and had her own income from her poetry, Evelyn must now make her way in the world as an impoverished, ill-educated, forty-four-year-old spinster. The Brantford newspapers rubbed salt in Evelyn's wound by its constant attention to her younger sister. When their mother passed away, the *Brantford Expositor* headlined its story, "Mother of Pauline Johnson Died Last Night After Lengthy Illness." When they finished packing up the house, the *Brantford Courier* announced Pauline's departure: "Countless friends and admirers of Brantford's talented authoress, Miss E. Pauline Johnson will be sorry to learn that she is about to sever the ties which have hitherto bound her to this community. Tomorrow she leaves on an eastern tour then followed by a trip through the North-West. After this her marriage takes place in Winnipeg." There was no mention of the sister who had nursed Emily through her lengthy illness, who now remained in humble lodgings in Brantford, working as a typist for the Waterous Engine Works.

But Pauline already knew that her supposedly rosy future was less settled than Evelyn imagined. Her engagement was unravelling. She had barely seen Charles for the previous five months, and doubts on both sides eroded their confidence in a shared future. There is no evidence of exactly what went wrong. Was Charles irritated by Pauline's insistence that she should continue to perform as "the Indian poetess"? Did Pauline find Charlie a little too conventional, his expectations too constricting? When Charlie's mother died, did Pauline lose her strongest Drayton supporter and Charlie find his elder brother Henry's snobbish disapproval too much to resist? Whatever the cause, the engaged couple made less and less effort to see each other. They kept up the pretense of an impending wedding. Pauline's friends continued to assume that the marriage would go ahead. "I . . . congratulate you heartily on your approaching entry into double bliss," Ernest Thompson Seton wrote from Manitoba, where he had already heard Charles Drayton described, he reported, as "a fine fellow." Pauline's future, though, appeared increasingly uncertain.

Pauline's response to uncertainty was to throw herself into a demanding schedule of recitals, under the direction of a new manager, Thomas E. Cornyn. She had the usual reason for a new tour: she needed the money. But more complicated motives were involved, too. She was determined to continue with her professional life. And she was damned if she was going to let Charlie think she was a wilting violet or that age or grief was slowing her down. So she put herself back on the treadmill of small towns, bad hotels and uncomfortable travel. In the early fall, she completed another Western tour on the main CPR line. "September is a good month for entertainment," she wrote to a member of the Department of Education in the North-West Territories (now Saskatchewan). "The harvest money is in, the schools are open etc. This is all business detail, but we must all take small things into consideration in these matters." In late November, she took a trip up the branch line from Portage la Prairie to Yorkton, performing in the tiny settlements of Minnedosa, Rapid City, Birtle, Binscarth, Russell and Saltcoats. She followed this with another branch-line tour, from Regina to Clouston, calling in at Saskatoon and Duck Lake, the community in which seventeen people had been killed during the 1885 North-West Rebellion.

It is hard to imagine a sadder or more gruelling period in Pauline's life. Her health was still poor (there were regular attacks of rheumatic fever), and she was now travelling by herself in the depths of a harsh Prairie winter. She had to entertain her audience solo for over two hours, with only a few minutes' break as she changed from buckskin to satin. It also meant long journeys sitting alone in the railway carriage, alternately freezing and boiling according to the whims of unreliable heating systems, watching the flat white expanse of snow-shrouded prairie, its few trees glistening with ice, slip past the window.

When massive snowstorms brought the locomotive grinding to a halt, there was only Pauline to telegraph ahead and reschedule. When she finally arrived at a destination, huddled in a threadbare wool cloak against the bitter wind, there was no Owen Smily to help carry the bags and arrange overnight lodging. In the hotel dining room, she could expect only her own company. When she felt tears flood her eyes because the audience was poor, the train was delayed or the memory of her mother's death stabbed her, there was no one to raise her morale.

Perhaps she and Charlie were still exchanging fond letters at this stage. But even the occasional *billets doux* would not blot out the hardships and indignities of a theatrical tour through the boondocks in the depths of winter. "Now, friends," the master of ceremonies at a shabby little hall in Medicine Hat said, by way of introduction, "before Miss Johnson's exercises begin, I want you to remember that Injuns, like us, is folks!" An expression of weariness and disillusion begins to creep into photographs of the poet from this period. Her skin was still velvet-soft; when she smiled, warmth flooded her face and her eyes sparkled. But in repose, her lips formed a thin, grim line, and the grooves etched from nose to mouth had deepened. The loneliness must have been almost unbearable. She had no stage partner, little real prospect of marriage to Charles, the vaguest of plans for the future and no home of her own. While she was on tour in February 1899, she heard that the Manitoba Hotel had burnt to the ground. Even her tenuous connection with Winnipeg had gone up in flames.

Two weeks after Emily's funeral in 1898, Pauline had received a letter that Emily had written and mailed to her daughter as her death approached. Pauline could not bring herself to open the letter straight away. She kept the sealed envelope in her jewellery case, occasionally pulling it out on chilly nights in Portage la Prairie, Russell or Saltcoats, and staring at the familiar handwriting. Weeks turned into months, and still the envelope remained sealed. Why couldn't Pauline open it? What did she fear her mother had written? Did she suspect that Emily had poured out her hopes for a happy union between her daughter and Charlie, and for Pauline's exit from the stage? Did Pauline feel that she had betrayed her mother's hopes and could not bear Emily's disappointment, even from beyond the grave? Or was it simply that while the letter was unopened, Pauline took comfort from an unfinished conversation with the mother she missed so much? She was losing Charlie; she couldn't bear to accept that she had lost her mother too. The sealed envelope remained tucked amongst her rings and brooches, a talisman of Emily's continued presence in her daughter's life. "I shall go to my grave," she confided to a friend in later years, "with the seal of my mother's last letter unbroken."

Pauline had a variety of well-developed survival strategies. One was to immerse herself in her career as an artiste and as a champion of Indian nobility. Another was to find for herself powerful protectors who would both respect and help her. In the newly opened West, the most powerful person in many of the raw clapboard towns was the commander of the local detachment of the North-West Mounted Police. In the twenty-five years since 300 young recruits marched west to stamp out the illegal whiskey trade, this red-coated police

In isolated detachments across Western Canada, the North-West Mounted Police were the symbol of order and the authority of the Dominion government.

force had acquired its own mythology. Its men revelled in their reputation as heroes who had pacified the Indians, busted the bootleggers, stared down the Americans and brought law to the frontier.

The realities of Mountie behaviour were often less splendid than the mythology suggests. The force had more than its share of thugs and bullies within its ranks, who were repeatedly (but ineffectively) disciplined for brawls, drunkenness and harassment of Indians. But by the end of the century, the N W M P (which had been formed originally as a short-term measure) was a significant presence throughout the Prairies and the Rockies. Over a thousand Mounties were spread out in nearly seventy detachments. Some detachments, like those at Crow's Nest and Dunmore, consisted of a sole constable; at the Regina headquarters, there were close to 200. Their duties included border patrols, provision of escorts for visiting bigwigs, military drills, erection of barracks and stables, distribution of food and seed to both Indians and settlers, and putting out prairie fires. By all accounts, they were an impressive bunch. "We have very few men," one commissioner boasted in the annual report, "who cannot ride day in and day out their fifty miles. In physique we are second to no force in existence."

In January 1899, Pauline arrived in the tiny community of Duck Lake in the middle of a blizzard. There was no possibility of continuing her journey in such foul weather, but the town's hotel was overflowing. Pauline threw herself on the mercy of Mrs. Hooper, wife of Reverend Lewis Hooper, who was in charge of the local N W M P barracks. This was not the first time she had stayed in the home of a Mountie officer, and it would not be the last. Her reputation both as a top-drawer performer and as a woman of irreproachable character preceded her, so she was a welcome guest. Women like Mrs. Hooper usually yearned to talk to a female visitor from the East, and Pauline always made herself extremely agreeable. "My dear Mrs. Higginbotham," she wrote to another of her hostesses. "I do not know of any home that I have ever entered as a stranger that I have left with the regret I have twice felt as I drove away from your hospitable doors. You are always so good to me, and I am so much at home with you all it is like leaving old, old friends when I come away each time."

Pauline did more than avail herself of Mountie hospitality. From now on, she contributed to the force's heroic mythology. In poems and stories, she highlighted the courage and even-handedness of its members. In Saltcoats, she had seen a young trooper fling open the door of the hotel saloon, "his bridle across his arm, cheeks that peculiar white of frozen flesh, his eyelashes frost fringed and gummy with ice." He was in determined pursuit of evil cattle thieves; ignoring his frostbite, he had stopped only because he needed a new mount on which to gallop off into the bitter cold. The hotel-keeper, in Pauline's stirring account, shook her head sadly: "That boy will kill himself. . . . He thinks of nothing but his horse and his duty."

One of the most popular of Pauline's performance pieces from 1899 was her paean to Mountie magnificence, "The Riders of the Plains." She always introduced this piece of Kiplingesque bravado by telling the story of its origin. At a dinner party in Boston she had been asked, "Who are the North-West Mounted Police?" When she replied that they were the pride of Canada's fighting men, the arrogant Bostonian quipped: "Ah! Then they are only some of your British Lion's whelps. We are not afraid of them." When Pauline told this anecdote to her Canadian audiences, they registered the same outraged patriotism that she had felt at the time. They nodded approvingly at Pauline's poetic rejoinder, loving every word of its chest-thumping indignation, its cheap alliteration, its imperialist bluster:

> These are the fearless fighters, whose life in the open lies,
> Who never fail on the prairie trail 'neath the Territorial
> skies,
> Who have laughed in the face of the bullets and the edge of
> the rebels' steel,
> Who have set their ban on the lawless man with his crime
> beneath their heel;
> These are the men who battle the blizzards, the suns, the
> rains,
> These are the famed that the North has named the "Riders
> of the Plains",

And theirs is the might and the meaning and the strength of
the bulldog's jaw,
While they keep the peace of the people and the honour of
British law.

These are the men of action, who need not the world's
renown,
For their valour is known to England's throne as a gem in
the British crown;
These are the men who face the front, whose courage the
world may scan,
The men who are feared by the felon, but are loved by the
honest man;
These are the marrow, the pith, the cream, the best that the
blood contains,
Who have cast their days in the valiant ways of the Riders of
the Plains;
And theirs is the kind whose muscle makes the power of old
England's jaw,
And they keep the peace of her people and the honour of
British law.

In her recitals in each small Prairie town, Pauline would include a
few digs at the force in the repartee that spiced up her programme. She
would speak about the courage of young troopers who confiscated
whiskey from outlaws and cattle thieves, then speculate aloud on
where the confiscated hooch ended up. But the Mounties in the audience always chuckled as loudly as everyone else. After all, the chorus
of their unofficial theme song made the same point:

Then pass the tea, and let us drink,
We guardians of the land,
You bet your life it's not our fault,
That whiskey's contraband.

Pauline's unabashed admiration for both Mounties and Indians seems an ironic contradiction of current attitudes to Western Canadian history. From today's perspective, the North-West Mounted Police was the force that ensured native submission to non-native rule, enforcing laws that robbed Indians of their traditional way of life and kept them corralled within their reserves. Yet to Pauline, steeped in her father's Loyalist history and her mother's British education, the Mounties were upholders of Imperial rule and manly virtues. Increasingly anti-American, she celebrated the Mounties because they defended the weak against the strong, and Canadians against the Yankees. Besides, in a young nation like Canada, there was a hunger for unifying myths that, onstage, she was happy to feed. Western audiences enjoyed "The Riders of the Plains" as much as, ten years later, they would relish Robert Service's "The Shooting of Dan McGrew."

By late 1899, Pauline had been touring almost non-stop for over a year. In Prairie settlements and mining camps, she was treated for the most part with awed respect, and her show was always well-attended. The Cranbrook *Weekly Herald* reviewer gushed about her graceful movements and charming appearance during her British Columbia stops: "Her compositions are in nature's own language and she displays the true poetic instinct in the grouping of ideas and her rhythmical combination of words." At Manitou, a little town in Manitoba, she filled the Methodist Church on two consecutive nights.

Sitting at the front of the admiring Manitou audience was the young wife of the local drugstore owner, who in a few years would herself be as well known as Pauline. Nellie McClung, the future advocate of women's rights and temperance, was swept away. "Pauline was at the zenith of her power and beauty," recalled McClung in her memoirs. "[Her] advertising had shown only the Indian girl in her beaded chamois costume and feather headdress, so when a beautiful young woman in white satin evening dress came out of the vestry door and walked to the platform, there was a gasp of surprise from the audience." Pauline began her show with "The Song My Paddle Sings" ("Pure music," thought McClung) and then changed into buckskin for her Indian ballads. "I think Pauline must have been an actress of great

Raised on a Manitoba homestead,
Nellie McClung (1873–1951) would
become a fierce advocate for
temperance and women's rights,
as well as a bestselling novelist.

power," wrote McClung, who never forgot the blood-curdling moment in the programme when an Indian maiden stabbed a treacherous non-native man. The following day, McClung and her sister-in-law called on Pauline at her hotel, the Cassin House: "She was the first great personage we had met, and we knew it was a time for white gloves and polished shoes." The two young women invited her to Sunday dinner, and Pauline graciously accepted. That afternoon, as a bitter winter wind whistled down Manitou's Front Street, the McClung family sat entranced by Pauline's stories of Iroquois history, of the Mohawk Chapel, of her own struggles to get published. "The shutters creaked in the blast," McClung recalled. "But we were living in another world, touching the hem of our own romantic past."

But in larger towns, Pauline now competed with trained singers and actresses, and reviews were more critical. The *Vancouver Province* critic complained that she shouted too much: "Miss Johnson showed a fault which she seems to have slipped into . . . that of relying on gesture and forceful delivery for effects of vehemence rather than by more intimate study, obtaining the result through intellectual means and aiding her own cause by the suggestion of reserve."

All this time, the private Pauline had been coming to terms with the end of her engagement to Charles Drayton. After his mother's death, Charlie had spent some time back in the bosom of Toronto Society, and his engagement to a Mohawk poet—however "nice" she might be—was beginning to look like a ghastly faux pas. His brother Henry's disapproval had got to him. According to Betty Keller, he returned to Winnipeg and met Pauline one last time around Christmas 1899. He asked her to release him so that he could marry someone else. Pauline consented with quiet dignity.

On June 18, 1900, at the Church of the Messiah on Avenue Road, Charles Drayton married a young woman of whom his older brother (who was best man) must have heartily approved. Lydia Howland was the daughter of H. S. Howland, a former Mayor of Toronto who was President of the Imperial Bank of Canada, and the granddaughter of Sir William Howland, who had been Lieutenant-Governor of Ontario. Within a few years, the Charles Draytons had moved to Vancouver along with their two young sons, and Charlie had established himself as a pillar of the financial community, a bulwark of the Anglican Church and an upstanding member of the Vancouver Club. "There are no esoteric chapters in his life history," noted a city directory approvingly. "Diligence, determination and sound judgement have been the salient factors in his career." Despite his family's early fears, Charlie Drayton had followed in the footsteps of his respectable father rather than those of his reprehensible Uncle Reggie.

For Pauline, who read a brief notice of the wedding in the *Manitoba Morning Free Press*, it was not the loss of Charlie's love and companionship that made the broken engagement so painful. They had spent so little time together that her day-to-day life was barely affected.

Instead, their parting spelled the end of her romantic dreams—the death of the sweet optimism of her youth, when young men flocked to her side and offered her their hearts. Charlie had shattered her unconscious assumption that she could marry anyone she liked, that her mixed parentage was no barrier. One poem from this period reflects some of the heartbreak that she suffered. She always insisted that the inspiration for this poem came from the sight of a beautiful young black-robed nun in the churchyard of Winnipeg's St. Boniface Cathedral laying flowers on the grave of a young unwed mother. The idea of the girl who had been betrayed by a man, and the sight of the nun who had turned her back on worldly pleasures and dedicated herself to celibacy, resonated powerfully with Pauline's feelings about her own life. Her heart was heavy, and her pen produced one of the most poignant poems she ever published:

> My heart forgot its God for love of you,
> And you forgot me, other loves to learn;
> Now through a wilderness of thorn and rue
> Back to my God I turn.
>
> And just because my God forgets the past,
> And in forgetting does not ask to know
> Why I once left His arms for yours, at last
> Back to my God I go.

Would Pauline have enjoyed marriage to someone who turned out to be as conventional as Charles? Hard to know. Yet there survives one final glimpse of Pauline's own attitude to the affair. After her death, Charles Mair mentioned the broken engagement in an article he wrote for *Canadian Magazine*. Evelyn Johnson was most offended; "It would have been better to have ignored the incident and left it to the family to explain," she wrote to an acquaintance. But she admitted that as far as she could see, Pauline bore no scars. "My sister," she wrote, with obvious distaste for such flippancy, "never hesitated about speaking about the matter to anyone, and constantly joked about it when she met her one-time fiancé in this city where he lives." Pauline always used her humour to mask the deeper hurts in her life. But perhaps in later years she also recognized, with the benefit of hindsight, that she could never have squeezed herself into the role of Mrs. Charles Drayton.

15

A NETWORK
OF TRAGEDY
1899—1901

We first saw light in Canada, the land beloved of God;
We are the pulse of Canada, its marrow and its blood:
And we, the men of Canada, can face the world and brag
That we were born in Canada beneath the British flag.

Few of us have the blood of kings, few are of courtly birth,
But few are vagabonds or rogues of doubtful name and
  worth;
And all have one credential that entitles us to brag—
That we were born in Canada beneath the British flag.

We've yet to make our money, we've yet to make our fame,
But we have gold and glory in our clean colonial name;
And every man's a millionaire if only he can brag
That he was born in Canada beneath the British flag.

The Dutch may have their Holland, the Spaniard have his
  Spain,
The Yankee to the south of us must south of us remain;
For not a man dare lift his hand against the men who brag
That they were born in Canada beneath the British flag.

PAULINE'S 1897 poem "Canadian Born" summed up the muscular optimism that pervaded the young Dominion of Canada as it hurtled into the twentieth century. British North America had begun the previous century as a handful of small cities clustered on the eastern side of the continent, behind which stretched a vast wilderness that only its indigenous peoples and a few intrepid employees of the Hudson's Bay Company knew. By 1900, it was a thriving and united federation of seven provinces plus the vast North-West Territories. Its population had risen from fewer than 350,000 to 5.4 million. The CPR transcontinental train, a novelty in 1894 when Pauline took her first trip, was now old news. Urban Canadians were embracing streetcars, telephones, kerosene, electric lights, central heating and indoor toilets. In rural Canada, steam-powered Massey-Harris threshers and barbed wire were making life easier for farmers and homesteaders. Across the Prairies, settlers had abandoned their sod cabins in favour of frame farmhouses and brick-built towns. Prairie housewives were ordering kitchen pots, carpet sweepers, woollen underwear and children's clothing from the Eaton's catalogue. Members of the emerging business dynasties (the Eatons and Masseys in Toronto, the Dunsmuirs in British Columbia, the Cunards in Halifax, the Molsons in Montreal) lived in vast mansions and travelled by private railway car. The *Toronto Daily Star* of May 30, 1900, trumpeted the good news that the average lifespan of a resident of Ontario had jumped by nearly a third since Confederation, from twenty-eight to thirty-six years. (It is not clear where the newspaper got its figures; a more accurate figure would have been above fifty years.)

But there was a dark side to this breakneck rate of progress. Children as young as ten worked 12-hour days in Toronto's tobacco factories and Nova Scotia's coal pits. Women in the Montreal garment industry scrambled to make a living from underpaid piecework. The citizens of Western towns like Regina regularly succumbed to typhoid epidemics, thanks to undrained cesspools. Respectable critics such as Goldwin Smith, who lived in splendour at the Grange in Toronto, promulgated virulently racist views; Jews, he charged, were "parasites" and "enemies of civilization." On the west coast, Chinese immigrants were required to pay a punitive head tax of $100 and received wages that were half those paid to people of European origin. But Canada continued to be the infinitely desirable Golden Mountain for impoverished peasants from South China and the Promised Land for refugees from Europe's ghettoes and slums.

The surge of immigration, industrialization and wealth was reflected in a new-found national confidence. The Liberal Prime Minister, Wilfrid Laurier, who had defeated Pauline's friend Charles Tupper in the 1896 election, personified this confidence. With charismatic assurance, he would predict in 1904 that if the United States had dominated the nineteenth century, "the twentieth century shall be filled by Canada." A master of the great Canadian art of compromise, Laurier nimbly balanced dual loyalties. He spoke for both English Canada and French Canada; he juggled fidelity to the British connection against commitment to Canada's autonomy. His balancing act secured national unity, kept him in power for fifteen years and embodied the promise of a new kind of nationality based on common allegiance rather than common identity.

"Canadian Born," Pauline's patriotic recital piece, reflected the same inclusive spirit. Birth in Canada under the British flag, rather than race or blood, was the glue for the new nation, in which people of different languages and blood could flourish. She revealed her own dual loyalties when she introduced "Canadian Born" from the stage. If there were "unpatriotic citizens in Canada," she told her listeners, "they are certainly not the Iroquois Indians." From Halifax to Vancouver, audiences rose to their feet and roared their approval as the beautiful and passionate poet, her dark curls cascading around her shoulders and the silver brooches on her buckskin tunic glinting in the stage lights, repeated the jingoistic refrain: "And we, the men of Canada, can face the world and brag / That we were born in Canada beneath the British flag."

At one level, Pauline's ability to balance her English and her Mohawk loyalties appeared to have both enriched her view of the world and brought her professional success. By now she was a poet with a national reputation, popular amongst Ottawa politicians and Prairie farmers alike. When a writer named Henry Morgan put together an album of well-known Canadian women entitled *Types of Canadian Women,* he wrote to Pauline requesting a photograph for inclusion. (She did not send him one because, as she explained to Harry O'Brien, Morgan "demanded that I pay ten dollars for the 'privilege' of being included in this book. I have become horribly wary, for twice I have been caught with this ten dollar scheming.")

Her support was sought for the great causes of the era. In January 1900, she left Winnipeg to travel to Toronto to give a concert in aid of the Canadian troops who were fighting the Boers in South Africa. English-speaking Canada was gung-ho to fight alongside the British on the dusty veldt, but Quebec was not enthusiastic about contributing to one of Britain's Imperial adventures. With typical dexterity, Sir Wilfrid Laurier navigated safely through competing currents of opinion. Canada would recruit and send a contingent of 1,000 troops, but Britain would foot the bill for transportation, equipment, supplies and pay. In order to channel Ontario's pro-British pugnacity into constructive activity, Laurier decreed that the costs of medical services, family and widows' benefits, and personal comforts for the Canadian boys would be covered by volunteer efforts within Canada.

When Pauline stepped off the train at Toronto's Union Station, she plunged into war fever. Newsboys selling copies of the *Star,* the *Globe* and the *Mail and Empire* yelled out the latest news of the Siege of Ladysmith, where Imperial troops were defending the British military depot. "Boers Repulsed at All Points After Many Hours of Fighting," read the headline in the *Globe.* Travellers whistled popular airs such as "Who Would Not Die for England?" and "Goodbye Dolly Gray." As she sat in the cab on the way to Rossin House, she saw Union Jacks in all the store windows and heard trumpet players on the street corners belting out martial music.

Le tout Toronto was gathered at Massey Hall on the evening of Wednesday, January 10, for the Red Cross fundraiser organized by Mrs. G. Allan Arthurs and Mrs. Grayson Smith. All the old Family Compact dynasties were represented, including the Denisons, the Cawthras and the Ridouts, plus plenty of members of the city's new industrial class, such as the Gzowskis and the Gooderhams. The two front rows were occupied by the contingent of volunteers due to leave three days later for South Africa. "How very young most of the men look, mere boys many of them," commented the *Globe*'s reviewer, adding that, nevertheless, they were "such men as any country would be proud to own." The evening began with a series of patriotic *tableaux vivants* in which Toronto's *jeunesse d'orée* (including Miss Heaven and Miss Evelyn Cox) depicted scenes from the Siege of Ladysmith and a tableau of Queen Victoria. Next, a popular local baritone sang "Take the Muzzle off the Lion" and "We Won't Stand It Any Longer." But the star attraction of the evening was Pauline Johnson, who appeared in the second half of the programme. Her renditions of "Canadian Born" and "Riders of the Plains" brought the audience to their feet.

There were several rival fundraisers for Canadian boys in the Transvaal during the winter of 1900. In Ottawa, a similar *tableau vivant* starred the Governor General's niece, and later in January, Owen Smily gave a recital in Toronto. However, the Massey Hall fundraiser was the highlight of the season. By popular request it was repeated on both Thursday and Saturday nights. Pauline's jingoistic verses hit just the note of Imperial fervour that the audience wanted to hear. At the same time, her Indian costume reassured her audience that while French Canadians might not support the war, anti-Boer feeling was not confined to Anglo-Saxons.

Lady Ishbel Aberdeen (1857–1939), wife of the Governor General, founded the National Council of Women and the Victorian Order of Nurses.

Pauline's stature was further enhanced when she was asked to contribute to a booklet about Canadian women to be distributed at the Paris International Exhibition of 1900. The handbook was the brainchild of Lady Ishbel Aberdeen, the formidable wife of the Marquess of Aberdeen, Governor General from 1893 to 1898. It included sections on various aspects of women's lives and achievements, including their legal and political status, educational and career opportunities, achievements in the arts and sciences, and volunteer activities. By the time Lady Aberdeen started lobbying for the handbook, she had already established the National Council of Women and the Victorian Order of Nurses. Not surprisingly, the handbook's tone was staunchly feminist and its prose drenched in her well-meaning but relentlessly bossy personality. Lady Aberdeen believed that Canadian women had the capacity, as yet untapped, to be a wholesome influence in an untamed country. She herself tapped the potential of some of Canada's most important hostesses for her handbook, including the wives of Thomas Ahearn (a prominent Ottawa businessman) and R. L. Borden (the Halifax MP who would later become Prime Minister), and the widows of the late Sir James Edgar, Speaker of the House of Commons, and Dean Boomer, of the Diocese of Hurontario. The contributors also included Marie Gérin-Lajoie, who taught at the Université de Montréal; writer Mary Agnes FitzGibbon, granddaughter of Susanna Moodie; Adelaide Hoodless, founder of the Women's Institutes; and Clara Brett Martin, Canada's first woman lawyer. All in all, it was a prestigious list that Pauline had been invited to join.

The final section of the handbook was entitled "Indian Women." The first three essays were smug accounts of how the lives of Indian women had improved since the white man arrived. "Twenty-five years ago . . . their lot was indeed hard," wrote Madame Henriette Forget, Honorary President of the Daughters of the Empire and wife of the Lieutenant-Governor of the North-West Territories. "Polygamy was the general practice. . . . The marriage ceremony was as meagre as the bride's dress—among some tribes nothing but a cedar-bark petticoat." Now a visitor to the Canadian West "sees bright-eyed, chubby, happy-looking damsels." Although most of these damsels "are not brilliant successes as cooks," at least the cedar-bark petticoats had been replaced by "the neat dress of modern make."

The fourth essay, however, struck a different note. "The Iroquois Women of Canada" was proudly identified as being "by One of Them—Miss E. Pauline Johnson, Brantford." In her opening paragraph, Pauline launched her well-polished broadside at European stereotypes:

To the majority of English speaking people, an Indian is an Indian, an inadequate sort of person possessing a red brown skin, nomadic habits, and an inability for public affairs. That the various tribes and nations of the great Red population of America, differ as much one from another as do the white races of Europe, is a thought that seldom occurs to those disinterested in the native of the western continent. Now, the average Englishman would take some offence if any one were unable to discriminate between him and a Turk—though both are "white"; and yet the ordinary individual seems surprised that a Sioux would turn up his nose if mistaken for a Sarcee, or an Iroquois be eternally offended if you confounded him with a Micmac [*sic*].

Pauline went on to write specifically about the Iroquois: "This people stand undemolished and undemoralized today, right in the heart of Canada, where the lands granted a century ago in recognition of their loyal services to the Imperial Government, are still known as the 'Six Nations' Indian reserve of the Grand River." An Iroquois woman, she argued, "is behind her white sister in nothing pertaining to the larder, the dairy or the linen press." Onlookers were mistaken when they presumed that an Iroquois woman's "placid, brown face" suggested she was "quite unintelligent." In Pauline's view, the Iroquois people were the aristocracy of North American natives, and "Miss Iroquois" was treated with far more respect by Iroquois men than the women of many so-called civilized races were treated by their menfolk.

Yet Pauline was less in control of her world than her firm opinions and popular success would suggest. For all her spirited defence of the Iroquois, her connection to them grew more tenuous each year. There is no evidence that she visited the Six Nations Reserve during these years. The only cousin with whom she kept in close touch was her mother's niece Katie Howells. Katie had married Stephen Frederick Washington, and the Washingtons' house in Hamilton, Ontario, became a regular refuge for Pauline. Her visits became even more frequent in 1901, when her sister Evelyn left Brantford to study domestic science at Toronto's Technical School. Evelyn then moved to New York State, where she took a series of low-paid but genteel posts, including matron of a girls' hostel and companion to a wealthy widow. Pauline's older sister remained close to Iroquois friends and relatives on both sides of the border, mixing more easily in Indian than non-native society. But Pauline's own circle was dominated by middle-class Canadians of European origin—the kind of people to whom she gave her recitals. She was a sturdy defender of Indian interests, proud to be labelled "One of Them" by the likes of Lady Aberdeen, but her contact with the day-to-day lives of Indians dwindled.

At the same time, Pauline could see that the gap between Canada's indigenous peoples and Anglo-Canadian society was widening rapidly. In poems like "Canadian Born" and "Riders of the Plains," she played along with the myth that allegiance to Britain and its laws was what defined and united Canadians of every colour and creed. This was the story her audiences wanted to hear. But she also told a reporter from a Western paper that "she deplored the condition of her noble race in the great lone land. Of the reserves she visited she always spoke in tones of regret." And a powerful short story she wrote around this time painted a darker picture. "As It Was in the Beginning," which appeared in the 1899 Christmas issue of *Saturday Night* with illustrations by the Canadian academician Carl Ahrens, reflects an angry assessment of what was really going on.

The story begins dramatically: "They account for it by the fact that I am a Redskin, but I am something else too—I am a woman." Esther, the narrator, is a spirited and beautiful young woman of part-Cree, part-European heritage. When she is a little girl, a black-robed missionary, Father Paul, persuades her father to send her to a residential school so she can be raised as a Christian and forget the "evil pagan influences" of her people. Esther is stripped of her buckskin dress, forced to wear a stiff calico uniform and leather shoes, and forbidden to speak in the Cree tongue. However, she is befriended by Father Paul's young nephew, Laurence. As Esther matures, she hungers for her old way of life, but she is always called back to the mission by Laurence. By now Laurence has changed from a cheerful young boy into the classic Johnson hero: "a tall slender young man . . . with laughing blue eyes, and always those yellow curls about his temple." Laurence and Esther declare their love to each other, although Esther recognizes that if she marries Laurence, she will have to surrender her own culture: "No more the wild stretch of prairie, the intoxicating fragrance of the smoke-tanned buckskin; no more the bed of buffalo hide, the soft, silent moccasin; no more the dark faces of my people, the dulcet cadence of the sweet Cree tongue."

Laurence tells Father Paul about their love. The black-robed old man, whom Esther has loved and trusted, is appalled by Laurence's news. Within earshot of Esther, the priest tells Laurence he cannot marry Esther because she comes of "uncertain blood," and "you can never tell what lurks in a *caged animal that has once been wild. . . . You can never trust her. . . . She reminds me sometimes of a strange— snake.*" Esther, devastated by such venomous words, must then suffer a second betrayal: she watches Laurence accept his uncle's reasoning. Esther immediately gathers up her belongings and creeps out of the mission building—but not before she has leaned over Laurence's sleeping form: "His curving mouth that almost laughed even in his sleep, his fair, tossed hair, his smooth, strong-pulsing throat. God! How I loved him!" But Esther cannot forgive the treachery of either the priest or his "weak, miserable kinsman." Without waking Laurence, she scratches his arm with a flint covered in deadly snake venom. The final line of this story of vengeance and murder echoes the opening line: "They account for it by the fact that I am a Redskin. They seem to have forgotten I am a woman."

Pauline's raw hurt about her broken engagement to Charles Drayton underscores "As It Was in the Beginning"; there are obvious similarities between the weak-willed Laurence and Charlie. The story also echoes "A Red Girl's Reasoning," the tale Pauline published in 1893 in which another heroine of mixed race, Christie, punishes her lover for bowing to British prejudice. But the tone of "As It Was in the Beginning" is much angrier, and the climax more brutal. It reflects Pauline's disillusion with Anglo-Canadian attitudes and her deepening concern with the predicament of Canada's native peoples. Since 1893, she had travelled across Canada several more times, and she had seen what was happening on the Prairies and farther west. As the nineteenth century drew to a close, the Dominion government in Ottawa had grown increasingly impatient with the slow pace of its assimilation policy amongst Indians. So it had toughened up measures to reshape Indian behaviour into "civilized" patterns. Polygamy was banned. Indians were prohibited from being on reserves other than their own without official approval. Important cultural practices such as the prairie Indians' Sun Dance and the coastal Indians' potlatch ceremonies were prohibited.

The most significant, and coercive, initiative taken to Europeanize natives was the extension of the system of residential schools, run on the same lines as the Six Nations Reserve's Mohawk Institute, which Pauline's two brothers had attended. Father Paul, the priest in "As It Was in the Beginning," is only describing official policy when he says to Esther's father, "Give me this little girl, chief. Let me take her to the mission school; let me keep her, and teach her of the great God and His eternal heaven. She will grow to be a noble woman." As the 1889 annual report of the department of Indian Affairs put it, "The boarding school disassociates the Indian child from the deleterious home influences to which he would otherwise be subjected. It reclaims him from the uncivilized state in which he has been brought up. It brings him into contact from day to day with all that tends to effect a change in his views and habits of life. By precept and example he is taught to endeavour to excel in what will be most useful to him."

Pauline herself believed strongly in the importance of literacy. She made a point of visiting residential schools. According to a reporter who accompanied her to the Lebret Industrial School in Saskatchewan's Qu'Appelle Valley, "her greatest interest when visiting the industrial school was in the musical attainment of the children." But the portrait of a mission school in "As It Was in the Beginning" is blisteringly critical. Esther's nostalgia for "the intoxicating fragrance of the smoke-tanned buckskin; . . . the dulcet cadence of the sweet Cree tongue" is an elegy for a lost culture: Pauline recognized that uprooting children from their families and traditions was harmful. And the portrayal of Father Paul illuminates the hypocrisy of the religious authorities who ran most residential schools.

*At the Dunbow Residential School, built in 1884, Indian
children were schooled in English and the catechism, and
forbidden to speak their own languages.*

Pauline had almost certainly heard complaints about harsh discipline, corporal punishment and poor food. Clearly she also recognized the more subversive damage that the schools were perpetrating. One of the most powerful poems that appeared on her recital programme in this period was entitled "His Sister's Son," and it dealt specifically with the plight of residential school students. The poem was never published, perhaps because it made audiences so uncomfortable. An assiduous reporter preserved one bitter, tragic verse:

> For they [killed] the best that there was in me
> When they said I must not return
> To my father's lodge, to my mother's arms;
> When my heart would burn—and burn!
> For when dead is a daughter's womanhood
> There is nothing left that is grand and good.

If Pauline was troubled by the deliberate campaign to eliminate native traditions, she must have been dismayed by the complacent assumption, now spreading with accelerating speed, that Indians themselves were headed for extinction. "A Dwindling People," read a headline in the *Globe* of July 5, 1895, in an account of a confrontation on the Blackfoot Reserve, near Gleichen in what is now Alberta, between a native man and a missionary. The confrontation, suggested the reporter, "may be taken to be the last flicker of an expiring lamp, for the Indians of those reserves appear to be a doomed people. The change of life appears to be fatal, and the evil effects are still felt of the carnival of drunkenness and disease which succeeded the signing of the treaty [establishing the reserve] a dozen years ago, just before the C.P.R. was built through the country. There is something rather pathetic in this dwindling away of a famous race."

The population decline was real. Between 1881 and 1915, while the non-native population was booming, the native population dropped from about 108,500 to 103,750. The residential schools were a significant element in the decline. Around one-quarter of the pre-1914 students succumbed to disease, predominantly tuberculosis, during or shortly after their stay at the schools, and the death rates in the schools were becoming a public scandal. At the same time, homesteaders were encroaching upon reserve lands, while Ottawa's support for native farms had almost dried up. If the "famous race" was dying out, the government in Ottawa reasoned, there was no point in investing too much money in it. It was a policy that turned out to be both wrongheaded and ultimately counterproductive: in the 1920s, the Indian population decline was reversed. But during Pauline's lifetime, the policy left most native peoples impoverished and demoralized.

In poetry and prose, Pauline tried to make her audiences see events from a native point of view. "Why do they always call an Indian victory a 'terrible and bloody massacre,'" she asked in an 1897 article, "and a white victory a glorious defeat of the rebels?" But hers was a balancing act as personally tricky as anything Prime Minister Laurier faced. She would become an instant outcast—"One of Them" for ever—if she overstepped the limits of what non-natives would regard as "good taste" in her protests. She relied on polished manners and good looks to cushion a message that most of her listeners did not want to hear. "My aim, my joy, my pride is to sing the glories of my own people," she had told Ernest Seton. But by 1900, Indians had been pushed to the margins of public life and the popular image of an Indian had shifted from that of noble Redman to that of a doomed savage. Pauline was one of the few natives who could capture non-native attention. Yet she knew her audiences paid to see a thrilling performance rather than to hear polemics about mistreatment of Canada's native peoples.

And Pauline needed those audiences. The constant gnaw of money worries kept her incessantly on the road. She frequently had to turn to friends and patrons for loans or help in finding engagements. "I managed to tide over the momentary difficulty," she admitted to the Montreal literary critic William Lighthall after he organized some performance dates for her, "but am yet on uneven ground." When Kate Simpson-Hayes, a Saskatchewan journalist and writer, invited Pauline to stay with her in Regina, Pauline admitted to her lively new friend that a mountain of bills "has made us stare poverty in the face, and now I have to *work.*" On this occasion, Pauline was lighthearted: "Now you know how alluring your invitation is like—sin, tempting, insinuating, insistent, and I in virtuous chase after dollars, stoically turn my back on it, prayerfully resist it and with bated breath, locked teeth and averted eyes—dash past, resisting the fascination of it and thus gaining a crown of glory—composed of many bank notes and jingling crown of the realm." But a later letter was suffused with quiet despair: "My debts are a continual source of worry to me. . . . People calling for money daily at the hotel when I have none. . . . My jewelry is not yet out of pawn. I have not a ring to my name. I owe six printers & I don't know when I can pay them."

Perhaps it was uncertainty about her feelings, her future and her finances that drove Pauline into an ill-advised venture in 1900. A century later, only the bare outlines of what happened during this *annus horribilis* are visible. The first suggestion of an abrupt change in pace came in a letter she wrote to the Honourable Clifford Sifton, federal Minister of the Interior and Superintendent General of Indian Affairs, a few weeks after her Toronto fundraiser for Canadians in South Africa: "Will you grant me one . . . favour, one that is urgent, and will most greatly assist me at this time when I am financially embarrassed and seeking backing for my proposed Australian tour." She wanted to borrow $500 against future rents due on Chiefswood. Since the property was on an Indian reserve and she herself was a status Indian, the loan could only come from the Department of the Interior. Sifton duly arranged the loan, which represented Pauline's share of the rental income for the next three and a half years. It was a significant amount: at least $10,000 in today's values.

At the same time, Pauline also sent a handwritten note to the Prime Minister: "My dear Sir Wilfrid, I am taking this liberty of recalling myself to your memory. You will perhaps remember that about three or four years ago I gave some recitations in the drawing room here at one of Lady Laurier's receptions—I am the Indian girl who writes and recites her own poems. I am arranging a trip to Australia and would beg that you would accord me a brief business interview at some hour tomorrow if the stress of your many duties will permit it." Laurier took time out of his schedule to see the poet and give her letters of introduction to the governors of various Australian states.

Where did Pauline's renewed energy, and talk of an Australian tour, come from? The trigger for this burst of ambition was a new manager. Charles H. Wuerz was a German-born impresario from New York who dropped into Pauline's harassed existence like the answer to a prayer. "My new manager is gradually pulling me out of the worst of [my debts]," a relieved Pauline told William Lighthall on May 5, 1900. "On the 15th I go to Montreal and in the meantime my manager will go ahead and hunt up a nice place for me to live." Lighthall had suggested that Pauline join him and his wife for a trip up the Saguenay River. "I cannot say yet about that long trip to the Saguenay," she replied. "I *hope* I will be working too hard to take it, much as I desire to go." Instead, she and Wuerz took a trip to the pretty Quebec resort of Ste-Agathe-des-Monts in the Laurentian Mountains at the end of the month. Wuerz then organized an extensive tour in which Pauline was booked into every fishing village and one-horse town in the Maritimes. He printed lavish posters advertising "Miss E. Pauline Johnson (Tekahionwake) in Her Unique and Refined Recitals of Her own Works. Canada's Foremost Comedienne and Poetess. Pathetic. Dramatic. Patriotic. Endorse and Applaud Her." He designed new letterhead for Pauline, which announced Miss E. Pauline Johnson's "Tour of the World" under the "Direction of Mr. Chas. H. Wuerz." Lastly, he spent a considerable amount of Pauline's money advertising her forthcoming appearances in the *Halifax Herald*.

Pauline dutifully filled most of her bookings, although in June she fell ill with exhaustion and remained confined to a Halifax hotel room for twelve days. By mid-August she was in Charlottetown. In early September she was in Shediac, New Brunswick, and by the end of the month she had reached St. John's, Newfoundland. Newspaper reviews of her recitals were good, but Pauline's heart sank as summer drew to a close, the temperature dropped and the days shortened. Her schedule required her to criss-cross the Maritimes in increasingly brutal weather, on every branch line and ferry in service. In one Newfoundland fishing village, there was no audience because goats had eaten the playbills off the noticeboards. In New Brunswick, en route from St. Stephen to Fredericton, she found herself snowed in for an entire day at McAdam Junction, where there was nowhere to buy food. She busied herself with crocheting purple pansies that she intended to give as Christmas gifts and chatting to a fellow passenger who generously shared her lunch with the stranded celebrity. The conversation took Pauline's mind off the fact that her Fredericton concert would be cancelled but she would still have to pay for the hall. A few weeks later, the ferry from Prince Edward Island to Cape Tormentine was frozen into the Northumberland Strait for six days. Once again, she was unable to fulfill her bookings but forced to swallow the costs of the cancelled recitals.

Laura Wood, the wife of a prominent New Brunswick businessman, befriended the poet and invited her to drop in to the comfortable Wood home in Sackville whenever she passed through the little town. "I shall always have a picture," she wrote years later in a memoir, "of a lithe figure, stalking with true Indian grace and freedom on the gray sea sand of the Sydney Bay shore. The wind blowing furiously carried out far behind her a long skein of brown kelp which waved serpent-like and shiny in the gale. Perhaps the thing which impressed it upon my mind was that I knew her heart was heavy with the loneliness of life. Not long before, her mother had died and besides she had other griefs which were more poignant because they could not be talked of."

Pauline came in from her windswept walk and smiled bleakly at her hostess. "I have come to a place today," she confided to Mrs. Wood, "where I feel that no one is worrying about where I am, and there is no necessity for my writing anyone of my whereabouts, and it is the most desolate feeling in the world." She told Mrs. Wood that she was thinking of going into vaudeville in New York. Vaudeville represented a hideous drop in status, but at least her income might rise. Mrs. Wood was horrified by Pauline's predicament: "Improvident as all Indians are, she was in difficulty. I have always heard that she supported an idle and dissipated brother, whom she adored with all her heart." Pauline may have been sending money back to Allen, although there is no evidence of this. However, Mrs. Wood's reaction to the idea of vaudeville registered with her: "She saw the shock it was to my feelings to hear this news." Nevertheless, Pauline replied, "My clergyman urges me not to do this, but what shall I do? I must live."

Grim humour kept Pauline going until Christmas. On December 6, she appeared at the Saint John Mechanics' Institute in aid of the New Baptist Tabernacle on Haymarket Square. "The audience expected to find Miss Johnson an impressive reader of her own poetry," according to the *Saint John Daily Sun*. "But her remarkable varied dramatic gifts, her power to personate all the characters in humourous stories came as a surprise. Her best known poems have something tragic in them, and there is a great power in her rendering of the Mohawk's wife who stabbed her Huron abductor while she whispered words of love in his ear. But for much of the evening Miss Johnson kept her audience laughing by her accounts of her own experiences, her description of life and people in various parts of the world, and her representations of some phases of society life."

All the unkind reviews, the offhand remarks about "squaws," the snobbery of Toronto hostesses, the chilly hours on snowed-in trains, were transformed into witty anecdotes for Pauline's performances. She surmounted the snubs and hardships by using them to her own advantage and getting audiences to share her reactions. She had developed a series of verse playlets, for example, in which she played all the characters. One sketch included an aggressive American matron who deplored the primitive standards of British hotels. Another sketch,

"Mrs. Stewart's Five O'Clock Tea," was the playlet which she and Owen Smily had worked up about the socially ambitious wife of a Member of Parliament, and which she had rewritten so she could play all the roles. When the guests arrived, Pauline played Mrs. Stewart welcoming each one, then moved into the character of each guest—a pompous railway director from Vancouver, a rough Ontario mining man, a shabby curate and an infant prodigy. She had met the prototype of each character on her travels.

Despite her exhaustion, Pauline continued to exert her magic—the magic of a performer who was both the smouldering stranger with a feather in her hair and a knife in her hand and the well-bred, soignée lady giving her provincial audience a delicious glimpse of the self-importance of the rich and powerful.

But grim humour and protean talent were not enough to keep Pauline going indefinitely. Her professional relationship with Charles Wuerz was clearly ill-judged. He had blown the $500 earmarked for an Australian tour on extravagant advertising and an over-programmed tour schedule that neither Pauline's health nor the climate would allow. By Christmas 1900 she was back in debt and completely exhausted. Moreover, there was a personal side to the relationship with Wuerz that was equally disastrous.

Once again, there are only the briefest hints of what happened; most of the evidence must have gone up in smoke in Evelyn Johnson's bonfire of Pauline's papers. But Charles Wuerz ignited a passion in the poet that Charlie Drayton had never lit. In the Johnson papers in the McMaster University archives, there is a poem in Pauline's handwriting on letterhead from the Queen Hotel, Fredericton, NB, with the date, 190–, incomplete. The two verses, entitled "To C. H. W.," are a startling and poignant echo of the passionate love poetry that, over a decade earlier, Pauline had written to her blond lover in her canoe:

> In Heidelberg, where you were born
> The sunshine must be fine and rare
> To leave such warmth within your heart
> Such warmth of yellow in your hair,

To touch your thought and soul with that
Which neither suns nor stars impart,
That strange exquisite gift of God,
That fine and fairy thing called art.
Did Fate decree your art and mine
Should weave into a future skein
When you were born in Heidelberg
And I was born in Vain?

In Heidelberg where you were born
The day dawn must wear strange disguise
Now it has left its wealth of grey
And melting shadows in your eyes
From whose deep sombre beauty all
Your soul God-given speaks the clear
Unblemished strength of all your art
And writes that soul, a soul sincere,
Did Fate decree your promise hour
Meet mine of storm and stress and rain
When you were born in Heidelberg
And I was born in Vain?

Perhaps Charles Wuerz was already married, as Betty Keller suggests in her biography of the poet. Perhaps he was a swindler who took advantage of Pauline's financial gullibility. Perhaps Pauline, as she approached her fortieth birthday and with the Drayton debacle behind her, was so emotionally vulnerable that she recklessly and thankfully sank into the arms of an attractive blond German who promised to look after her. The Heidelberg verses imply a passion that was consummated, despite the reputation for moral probity that Pauline so carefully nurtured. She recognized that the relationship was bound to be short-lived; in a poem written at Easter 1900, called "Morrow Land," she anticipates grief tomorrow even as she enjoys passion today:

In Morrow Land there lies a day,
In shadows clad, in garments grey,
When sunless hours will come, My Dear,
And skies will lose their lustre clear,
Because I shall be leagues away.

Has Fate no other kindlier way,
No gentler hands on me to lay,
Than I to go, than you to stay
In Morrow Land?

And O! These days will be so dear,
Throughout the cold and coming year,
This Passion Week of gold and grey
Will haunt my heart and bless my way
In Morrow Land.

Her instincts were correct. Charles Wuerz disappears from the record at the end of 1900. And for three months, so does Pauline.

The missing three months in Pauline Johnson's life have sparked endless speculation. She was clearly distraught and exhausted, and she may have had some kind of physical or psychological breakdown. A rumour circulated around the Six Nations Reserve that she had a baby in this period. Certainly, the nine months that elapsed between Easter 1900, when she wrote about "this Passion Week" in "Morrow Land," and her disappearance at the end of the year are ominous. Yet given her age and the fragile state of her health, a pregnancy seems improbable. More likely, the vivacious and determined Pauline Johnson had simply reached the end of her tether. She had never given herself time to come to terms with the end of her engagement to Charles Drayton. The loss of her mother still haunted her: the sealed envelope remained unopened in her jewellery case. Now Pauline's unresolved tensions boiled over. She stared down the years ahead and realized she was on her own.

Consciously or unconsciously, Pauline Johnson had chosen the lonely and uncertain life of a travelling poet rather than marriage. Such a life was hard enough for any middle-class woman in the early twentieth century, when most of her sisters were tiptoeing around in hobble skirts, leaning heavily on the arms of gentlemen. It was doubly hard for Pauline. Notwithstanding the chirpy optimism of her poem "Canadian Born," she could see that racism was on the increase in Canada and that Indians were amongst its first targets. She had to acknowledge the corrosive prejudices developing against women of mixed parentage like herself and her fictional heroine Esther. She wanted to celebrate the double legacy of Indian and British culture, but she constantly risked being stranded between races. It was a recipe for psychic conflict, and sure enough, at this point in her life she tumbled into a black pit of "sunless hours." Where she spent the first three months of 1901 remains a mystery. But Charles Wuerz left a wound that did not heal. Pauline never published either of the poems he inspired.

Homeless and penniless, Pauline had few material resources to fall back on in 1901. But she did have talent and loyal friends. And she had a gritty resilience that allowed her to turn the page and begin a new chapter in her life.

"My dear fond friend," she wrote to Frank Yeigh on April 1, 1901, from a modest hotel in the Eastern Ontario railway town of Havelock,

> Now—when I wrote you—or rather wired you not to bother about that loan I was begging of you, I felt like an escaped convict—independent, free—everything that is glorious, albeit that I am in a network of tragedy—too sad for human tongue to tell—Now, could you *without* great inconvenience lend me the half of that amount I was so frantic about last week. That is—fifteen dollars to be repaid in a month's time—you could never quite imagine just "where I am at" or you would forgive me writing and asking this.
>
> Here I am, in Holy Week in Havelock, an economical town to pray in—also to eat in, and I *shall* be here all week. . . . Someday, when I see you again, I shall tell you all of it, and

grasp your good warm hands and congratulate you from my true Indian heart. . . . Will you write me here—*do*—if you can spare that little fifteen dollars, you will do more than churches, nor yet priests can do for me and yourself in the great Hereafter.

Thine, E. Pauline Johnson.

Somehow, the strong-willed Pauline had extricated herself from her "network of tragedy too sad for human tongue to tell." With the help of Frank Yeigh's loan, she pulled herself together and resumed her career as a poet and performer.

Her first step was to put herself back under the management of Thomas Cornyn. With Cornyn's wife, Clara, a concert pianist, she travelled east yet again. The two women gave a series of concerts in Newfoundland and New Brunswick, although they played to half-full halls and made no money. This time, Pauline decided to cut her losses. On October 9, Pauline once again appealed to Clifford Sifton, the federal Minister of the Interior and Superintendent General of Indian Affairs, who had given her $500 the previous year. Now she sent him a telegram from Campbellton, New Brunswick: "Can you arrange for three tickets from here to Montreal via Intercolonial want to leave at four tomorrow morning will be in Ottawa Saturday and remit payment want tickets in advance please reply immediately here." Sifton sent the tickets. By late October, Pauline was safely back in Ottawa, where she was always sure of a good audience and good receipts.

Pauline then terminated the relationship with Thomas and Clara Cornyn, and recruited another partner for her stage appearances, a young actor called Walter McRaye. Her relationship with this capricious, sycophantic but ultimately well-intentioned young man would dominate the rest of her life.

16

ON TOUR
WITH WALTER
1901—1905

ALTER McRaye was the kind of young man Emily Johnson had taught her four children to scorn. Evelyn Johnson, who inherited all her mother's attitudes, never warmed to Walter, whom she regarded as pushy and vulgar. She was convinced that her younger sister's professional relationship with him demeaned Pauline. Allen Johnson also found him distasteful and preferred not to see Pauline at all rather than see her in Walter's company. But Pauline was a realist. She recognized that she and Walter made a good fit. Maybe he didn't know which fork to use at a dinner table or how to address the aristocracy. Maybe his clothes were too flashy (particularly his thick gold ring and the beaver collar on his winter coat) and he was too familiar with strangers. She needed a stage partner who would act as her assistant; Walter needed to hitch his wagon to her star.

For more than a decade, the relationship suited each of them very well. It lifted the burden of organization off Pauline's shoulders. Walter, a wiry little man with an inexhaustible supply of anecdotes and energy, found porters for Pauline's heavy steamer trunk and ensured there was a dining car on the train for "My Lady." He organized ticket sales, checked hotel arrangements and booked railroad journeys. He chatted up stage managers and greeted by name every hotel porter in the country, from the Crosbie Hotel in St. John's to Victoria's Empress Hotel. And despite Pauline's occasional spurts of exasperation with "Dink," as she called Walter, his support allowed her to regain her old joie de vivre. "His management has indeed proved a great thing for me," she told Harry O'Brien in 1903, "and my freedom from business cares and anxieties has rejuvenated me beyond words."

In particular, the relationship with Walter enabled Pauline to move on, both personally and professionally. She was no longer the slender, shy ingenue from the forest with whom the scions of Canada's leading families had fallen madly in love. At forty, she was still beautiful; her low, musical voice still sent thrilling shivers through her listeners. But her upper arms were fleshy now, and her face had filled out. The bodices of her Barker's gowns strained at the seams, and she had been obliged to sew extra fabric into the waistband of her buckskin skirt. The old dreams were gone—the literary vision of sufficient acclaim to allow her to write poetry full-time; the romantic fantasy of a blond Adonis who would take her to the altar. Instead, she was a celebrity in the prime of life who had published some widely admired poetry and who had audiences eating out of her hand. She had become a champion for and authority on native peoples (although she herself recognized the limits of her knowledge) and she had emerged from personal setbacks with her reputation and self-esteem intact. Like many women as they pass forty, Pauline finally accepted that what she was living was the rest of her life. The companionship of a loyal, energetic young fellow performer enabled her to enjoy it.

Walter McRaye always behaved as a courtier (and sometimes court jester) around Pauline. Fifteen years her junior, he had been stage-struck since his first visit to the theatre. His real name was Walter Jackson McCrea, and he had been born in 1876 in a tiny village called Merrickville, which was one of the twenty-four lock stations on the Rideau Canal between Ottawa and Kingston. Walter was always determined to go places; he attended high school in nearby Smiths Falls and then managed to get himself hired as an apprentice in the Merrickville telegraph office. The telegraphs, run by the railways in that era, were cutting-edge technology, and they attracted ambitious young men who wanted to travel and keep abreast of progress. The railways were the symbol of future wealth. "I remember how the citizens of my own village pictured the prosperity that would come" in the trail of the local branch line, recalled Walter in his memoirs. He spent three years preparing himself for a career as a railway telegraph

*Walter McRaye (1876–1946) loved stylish
clothes and cheap laughs, but his loyalty
to Pauline never flagged.*

operator by learning Morse code and tapping out messages on brass
keys. By the time he was seventeen, he had managed to leave Merrickville behind and join a telegraph office in Ottawa, the Dominion
capital. During lunch hours there, he would station himself on Sparks
Street, just below Parliament Hill, where he might catch sight of such
well-known politicians as Sir John Abbott, who had briefly succeeded
Sir John A. Macdonald as Prime Minister, Liberal leader Wilfrid Laurier, Regina's Nicholas Flood Davin, and handsome old Mackenzie
Bowell from Belleville, the current Prime Minister, who would be
knighted in 1895. "To my youthful eye," recalled Walter, who never
met a famous person he couldn't idolize, "they seemed something
more than human."

But then Walter made his first visit to the theatre, and the magic of

Mackenzie Bowell didn't stand a chance. At Ottawa's dingy old opera house, misleadingly called "The Grand," Walter watched one of the great romantic actors of nineteenth-century North America, Edward Vroom, playing in Victor Hugo's play *Ruy Blas*. The effect of this second-rate melodrama on an impressionable, bored young man was electric. "My youthful soul was smitten," wrote Walter in his auto-biography, *Town Hall Tonight*. "After that every cent I could get went into dramatic literature, plays, dramas and stories of the stage. . . . Very soon I had memorized great blocks of Shakespeare, Sheridan, Bulwer-Lytton, Hugo and translations of Molière and Racine. At every carnival I would swank around in the costume of Hamlet, Don Caesar, Charles the First or some gay cavalier." Walter used the word "gay" in its original meaning in his own account of his life. But it was likely appropriate in its more modern sense, too.

In the next two years, Walter paid a quarter to sit far up in the gods for every performance at the Grand. He saw all the great actors of his day: Margaret Anglin, James O'Neill, Henry Irving, Ellen Terry, Forbes Robertson, Thomas W. Keene and Mrs. John Drew, the matri-arch of the Barrymore dynasty. He caught a couple of performances by Pauline's great teacher, Rosina Voke: "a delight in all her sketches, and what a company!" He loved plays like *The Count of Monte Cristo* and Oscar Wilde's *A Woman of No Importance*. He laughed uproariously at the monologues of the English comic George Grossmith, and was spellbound by the "thought transmission" tricks of Anna Eva Fay, "The Mystic." He wept as Madame Albani, the great Canadian soprano, gave her final farewell concert, and he wept again the following year when she returned for another farewell. He travelled all the way to Montreal to catch the ailing, aging Sarah Bernhardt: "What a personality was boxed up in her frail body." He decided that he was meant for better things than a telegraph office. In 1895, he caught a train to New York City, determined to conquer the "Great White Way."

Walter knocked on doors up and down Broadway, but no theatre manager was prepared to take a chance on a Canadian with no experi-ence. His money ran out; he signed on as a clerk in a molasses factory to keep the wolf from the door. For a few months he clung on grimly, buying the cheapest seats at theatres and giving impromptu recitals of poems and playlets to the other residents in his 34th Street boarding house. But he was forced to admit he was going nowhere. However, Walter McRaye was never one to let circumstances defeat him. So he hopped on the train back to Canada and printed up a circular introducing himself as "Entertainer and Monologist—Special rates to Churches, Clubs and Societies." His reviews were terrible; the local paper in Vankleek Hill (where Pauline had been booed) declared that "the only stage Mr. McRaye was fitted for went about five miles an hour." When he wasn't exactly overwhelmed with bookings, he joined a travelling theatrical troupe that even he admitted was "rotten." He struggled on, until in 1897 he was sufficiently confident in his skills and reputation to embark on a cross-Canada tour.

Walter had honed a series of popular recitations for his one-man shows. Highbrow selections from Tennyson, Owen Meredith and Shakespeare were interspersed with vaudeville favourites such as "Spartacus to the Gladiators" and "Tradin' Jo." He was always eager to watch other performers on stage so he could keep abreast of (and steal) material with obvious audience appeal. In Ottawa he had seen an old theatrical lag called McKee Rankin launch into a poem called "Wreck of the Julie Plante," spoken in a singsong French-Canadian accent. The poem was by Dr. William Henry Drummond, an Irishman who had emigrated to Quebec and, like Walter, had trained as a telegraph operator. Working in the bush near Lake Megantic, Drummond had been captivated by the idiomatic English of the French-Canadian lumbermen, canoemen and farmers. He himself went on to study medicine at McGill University and then to practise in Montreal, but his Megantic memories never left him. "Wreck of the Julie Plante" was just one example of the reams of humorous, and extremely popular, poems he wrote in this idiom.

Many French Canadians resented Dr. Drummond's verses, which they felt were Anglo caricatures of their lives—the literary equivalent of Cornelius Krieghoff's folksy paintings. Others enjoyed their humour; in 1897, Louis-Honoré Fréchette (brother-in-law of Pauline's cousin Annie Howells) supplied an introduction to Drummond's first book, *The Habitant, and Other French Canadian Poems.* For his part,

Walter McRaye did not give a moment's thought to the question of whether these were patronizing stereotypes. He seized on the book as a goldmine for a recitalist like himself, who relished exaggerated accents and slapstick humour. As he travelled west on the CPR, he sat in the railway carriage committing to memory some of Drummond's funniest and most moving poems. Newly arrived families from the British Isles, Poland or the Ukraine must have stared in wonder at this jaunty young man with a big nose and a weak chin, muttering to himself:

> Dere's a beeg jam up de reever, w'ere rapide is runnin' fas',
> An' de log we cut las' winter is takin' it all de room;
> So boss of de gang is swearin', for not'ing at all can pass
> An' float away down de current till somebody break de
> boom.

By December 1897, Walter had reached Manitoba on his transcontinental tour and had several bookings for the New Year in North Dakota and points west. A couple of days before Christmas he clambered down from the railway carriage at Winnipeg station. He noticed posters advertising Pauline's upcoming concert at Winnipeg's Grand Opera House on December 29. The idea of meeting the acknowledged star of the Canadian stage, and of learning a few stage tricks from her, was irresistible. As soon as her Grand Opera House performance was over, he was at the door of her dressing room. On this occasion, he was elbowed out of the way by Charles Drayton with his bouquet of flowers. But Walter hung around long enough to persuade Pauline to let him appear on stage with her in some upcoming bookings.

In early January 1898, Pauline and Walter performed together in Boissevain, Deloraine, Hartney and Souris. Walter then travelled on to North Dakota, while Pauline returned to Winnipeg—and Charlie Drayton. The paths of the two performers did not cross again for four years.

The intervening years were as unkind to Walter as they had been to Pauline. There were too many cut-rate Mark Twains and George Grossmith imitators stumping across North America. His audiences remained small. One winter, he was reduced to living in a wooden shack in Northern California, stealing food from local gardens. He managed to work his way back to Central Canada, appearing as warm-up act in the ragtag shows put together to raise money for the soldiers in South Africa. But he could never make it on his own: he needed to ride someone else's coattails. When he found himself once again in the same city as Pauline in November 1901, he immediately got in touch with her at Ottawa's Russell Hotel to suggest they perform together. After the past few months with the Cornyns, Pauline knew she needed a new partner. She must have decided that Walter's enthusiasm might compensate for his lack of talent. She invited him to appear with her at Ottawa's Orme Hall on November 6.

The Orme Hall recital was important to Pauline, both as the relaunch of her own career and as the lift-off of the new partnership. Leading members of Ottawa's political elite were in the audience, including some of Pauline's most important supporters: Governor General Lord Minto and Lady Minto, Prime Minister Wilfrid Laurier and Lady Laurier, Mr. and Mrs. Clifford Sifton. Pauline had sent Sifton two tickets in gratitude for the money he had sent so she could limp back to the capital after her disappointing tour in Eastern Canada. The stress of the past couple of years was obvious in the performance, as the Ottawa *Citizen*'s critic was quick to point out. She had almost no new material, he wrote, and her acting was almost mechanical. Her style was "vigorous and energetic, although rather exaggerated from an artistic standpoint." McRaye's reviews weren't exactly glowing, either, although expectations for a newcomer were lower. He was judged to be adequate but amateurish, with his shrill, piping voice and peculiar habit of going up at the end of all his lines.

But the show was a success as far as Pauline was concerned. Enthusiasm amongst Ottawa's politicians for the Mohawk poet was undiminished: the audience gave her a warm welcome. And although Walter's elocutionary technique left a lot to be desired, he looked after her splendidly. Walter was always supremely self-confident. He needed to be, to protect himself—he knew his talent was slight and that he was far too fey for small-town Canada. So Walter always ignored reviews, and his jaunty self-confidence helped Pauline to pay less attention to them too. She agreed that they should team up for a limited tour.

First she had to raise money to cover costs until they began earning. She wrote around to all her usual supporters, including her cousin Annie Howells Fréchette in Ottawa. Annie's husband, Achille, sent some money but commented to his wife, "The poor thing has a hard time of it, I'm afraid, and this life does her no good." Achille had heard that Pauline had teamed up with Walter, of whom he had a low opinion. Thanks to his comfortable income as a House of Commons translator, Achille had never had to live off the slim returns of poetry. He dismissed Pauline and Walter's recital as "a third-rate show," adding haughtily that they were not doing "much for Art nor for themselves."

Pauline could not afford such artistic scruples. Instead, she insisted that Walter had to improve his act. As they hopscotched their way across Southern Ontario, she drilled him in some of the techniques and sketches she had acquired from Owen Smily. This went on for six weeks. It cannot have been easy for Pauline, spending her afternoons teaching new tricks to a young dog and then having to compensate for his shortcomings each night. She quickly realized she was never going to make Walter McRaye into Henry Irving. She must have wondered whether the effort was worth it. But the Johnson–McRaye partnership was cemented that winter when Pauline was felled by a potentially fatal illness and Walter showed unexpected reserves of loyalty and compassion as he cared for her.

The week before Christmas, Pauline and Walter arrived in Orillia, 100 miles (160 kilometres) north of Toronto on Lake Simcoe, where they were due to give two performances. Pauline had been suffering from headaches and nausea for a couple of days, and she collapsed onto the bed when she was shown into her hotel room. Her skin prickled and her face was flushed. She had told Walter that they must have a run-through on the stage, so she reluctantly struggled to her feet and staggered over to the washstand to splash her face with cold water. When she looked at the mirror, she gasped. There was a large raised red patch of skin on her cheek. She must have instantly recognized the symptom, because she had seen the same kind of glazed red patch on her father's face when he was sick. It was erysipelas, the virulent staphylococcus infection. In Orillia, the infection spread with terrifying ferocity. Within hours, Pauline's face was covered in scarlet, blistered patches and her temperature rocketed up. She lay on the bed, sweating and shivering, close to unconsciousness. Her joints ached and her throat was parched. Walter quickly cancelled all their bookings for the next few days, then sat anxiously at her bedside, giving her sips of water and willing her to recover fast.

By Christmas Day, Pauline was delirious. According to Betty Keller's 1981 biography, the erysipelas infection had now entered her bloodstream and caused cerebral thrombophlebitis, or, as the Orillia doctor called it, "brain fever." He prescribed morphine and told Walter there was nothing to do but wait and see if her natural resistance could conquer this devastating infection. She was likely to lose her hair, the doctor said, and he could not rule out a coma and then death.

Slowly the infection receded and, to Walter's immense relief, Pauline's temperature dropped and she regained consciousness. She looked dreadful: her beautiful thick brown hair was gone, and her face resembled a road map because the outlines of the erysipelas patches were still visible. Moreover, the Johnson–McRaye partnership was in serious financial difficulties: their six-week run had not yielded enough to cover the costs of a long convalescence. For the next few months, the two recitalists lay low. It is probable that Pauline was admitted to St. Joseph's Hospital in London, Ontario, run by a Roman Catholic order of nuns. A letter to Nurse Elizabeth King has survived, written by Pauline after she had been discharged from this hospital: "I am feeling very well and my face is all right so far. I do hope it will continue to improve," she scribbled in an uncharacteristically shaky, backward-sloping script. "I am sure the Reverend Mother will be pleased that I am better. So please tell her. And also remember me to Sister Sophia and Miss Ferguson. I want to thank you once more my dear girl for all your attention and kindness to me. With every wish for your happiness and success in which Mr. McRaye joins (he says he would like to hold your hand). I am, yours faithfully, E. Pauline Johnson."

By the time this letter was written, Pauline was already back on the road, desperately trying to cover her debts. She had acquired a wig to cover her bald scalp. From now on, she never appeared in public without makeup to camouflage the ravages to her face; jars of rouge, Na-Dru-Co Theatrical Cold Cream and Miner's Theatrical Blending Powder (No. 12, "Gypsy," or No. 7, "Flesh") were staples of her dressing case. On February 7, only six weeks after her collapse in Orillia, she performed in London, Ontario. From there she travelled to Blyth and then to Kingsville, on the shores of Lake Erie, where she wrote the letter to Nurse King. "We had a delightful audience at Blyth," she told Miss King. "They laughed at everything and I quite enjoyed working myself." She did not report on her partner's performance; as a critic wrote around this time, "Mr. McRaye can hardly be placed in the same class as his clever companion." But Walter had stuck with her when she was close to death, and he now fussed around her as she recovered her strength. He had earned a place at her side.

With a new partner in place, Pauline ached to return to the West. As Walter once observed, "Because of her lineage and love of the unconventional, [Pauline] seemed a very part of . . . the romance of the frontier [and] the old Western spirit of freedom and democracy." More practically, the West had always proved more lucrative for Pauline, and more inclined to welcome the Mohawk poet with Mayfair manners. By May 1902, she and Walter were in Northern Ontario, stopping off to give a show at each little railway town. At the remote mining settlement of Copper Cliff (rarely visited by entertainers), they stayed with "Kit" Coleman, a clever young writer for the Toronto *Mail and Empire* who had recently taken the rash step of marrying a physician employed by one of the big mining operations around Sudbury. Kit now spent her days breathing sulphur fumes on a landscape blasted by mines and smelters. Thrilled by these emissaries from sophisticated Southern Ontario, Kit gave them a glowing review. (She also tried to present them with a bouquet of red roses, but the roses wilted to dark brown in the sulphurous air.) She described Pauline as a "splendid Mohawk girl" and "a genius," and Walter as "par excellence, the best reader of dainty and clear poems I have ever heard. . . . He is a true artist." Pauline and Walter then travelled on to Winnipeg, where Pauline invited a few old friends, including a reporter, to visit her at the Leland Hotel. She spoke about her hair loss with wry candour. The reporter wrote, "Though traces of her recent severe illness are noticeable, she is fast regaining strength. A friend asked how she managed to dress for the stage with such shortly cropped tresses. 'Well, I'll tell you,' she replied, 'when reciting in Mohawk costume, I wear a wig, but it bothers me, seeming to irritate my head. When I don evening dress, I imitate the chorus girls and wear a large hat which people say is very becoming, and no one suspects the tragedy underneath.'"

But off stage, Pauline remained horribly self-conscious about her looks. She had received a formal invitation from the Lieutenant-Governor of the North-West Territories and his wife, Madame Henriette Forget. Like Pauline, Madame Forget had been a contributor

In late 1902, Pauline's hair was still short
after the bout of erysepalis, and her face
was often clouded with fatigue.

to Lady Aberdeen's publication *The Women of Canada*; like Pauline, Indian blood ran in her veins. Pauline appreciated Madame Forget's kindness but was filled with dread: "'They' are graciously offering their 'patronage' for our performance [in the city] and I am to be a guest at Government House while in Regina," Pauline wrote to a friend. "Imagine—poor me dining with my scarred face and cropped hair. Is it not awful?"

With each successive stop on the CPR line, however, Pauline's health and looks improved. Soon she felt well enough to write as well as perform. And on July 4, a brutal rainstorm provided her with the kind of material that made a great dispatch for the Toronto *Globe*. Two bridges across the Bow River were completely washed out, which brought one eastbound and two westbound transcontinental trains to a grinding halt. The CPR decided it should take drastic measures to entertain a crowd of over 600 passengers which included Japanese students, British aristocrats and a bunch of Doukhobor, Chinese, Galician, Swedish, Italian and British immigrants. So it ordered its locomotive drivers to move the trains to Gleichen, in the heart of the Blackfoot Indian reserve, where they would remain until the track was repaired. Pauline grabbed the chance to write up an account of a prairie Indian band, in which she could cast them in a positive light and herself as "One of Them":

> The Indians made a good thing out of the C.P.R. mishaps, for the tourists hired horses from them at "a dollar a ride" and even the tenderfoot would vault into the Mexican saddle and ride away across the plain. . . . Only one lamentable accident occurred, in the evening, when we had baseball and horse races. In the latter a fine grey pony, the property of a splendidly handsome blanket and buckskin-clad Blackfoot, plunged into a badger hole, fell, and instantly expired with a broken neck.
>
> And just here is time to relate an aspersion frequently laid upon our wilder Indian tribes of the great west. The prejudiced white man will tell you that the Indians will eat anything animal that dies of disease, unclean portions of meat,

etc. The detractors of the Redman, and there were plenty of them aboard, assured the crowd that "the Indians will have a great pow-wow, and the feast of the dead horse" over the unlucky animal that lay near the track. But the next morning and the next night, and yet another morning came and waned, and the horse lay where it had fallen, and the Blackfoot shook their heads when asked about a "feast." A goodly collection was taken up for the owner which reward he deserved, as his steed had expired in making "a white man's holiday."

This identical warrior exhibited great appreciation of class distinctions. A curious Chinaman came forth from his car, and a tourist asked the Blackfoot, "Is this your brother?" indicating the Mongolian. Such scorn and hauteur as the reply, "No" expressed, such a lifting of the red chin, and indignant glance. It amazed some, but I was proud of my colour cousin of the prairie, and of his fine old aristocratic red blood that has come down through the centuries to pulse in the conservative veins.

Within two days, the Bow River bridges were repaired and the trains steamed out of the reserve. The next stage of this particular Johnson–McRaye trip was a tour of the little mining towns of the Kootenay region in the southeastern corner of British Columbia, a region sandwiched between the main CPR line to the north and the states of Montana, Idaho and Washington to the south. The Kootenay region consists of four mountain ranges running north–south like giant snowcapped farmer's furrows, with long, fjord-like lakes between them. Only thirty years earlier, the sole occupants of this wilderness were about 500 Kootenay Indians, a few French-speaking fur traders and a handful of British remittance men. But between the years 1889 and 1892, five of the most productive mines that the world had ever seen were developed in the area. In 1887, the Silver King Mine was begun on Toad Mountain, outside Nelson. Two years later, rich deposits of silver, lead and zinc were found in what became the Ainsworth Mine, on Kootenay Lake. In 1891, the LeRoi goldmine at

Rossland and the Payne lead mine at Sandon, above Slocan Lake, were developed. The greatest of them all, the Sullivan silver and lead mine at Kimberley, was begun in the Purcell Mountains in 1892.

News of the gold and silver strikes touched off a mining boom. Burly hardrock miners, particularly from the United States, swarmed into the region to stake their claims in every creek and on every hillside in the area. The frenzy created instant shantytowns throughout the Kootenays: Rosebery, New Denver, Slocan City, Three Forks, Nashton, Argenta, Lardeau, Gerrard. Many of these settlements, such as Nakusp, on the Upper Arrow Lake, were accessible only by the steam-powered sternwheelers that plied the lakes and that needed only a foot of water beneath the keel and a wide enough channel to twist between the sandbars. Rudimentary muddy trails through primeval forest linked some of the other settlements. These trails hadn't improved since they were vividly described back in 1862 by the British engineer Lieutenant Henry Palmer: "Slippery precipitous ascents and descents, fallen logs, overhanging branches, roots, rocks, turbid pools, and miles of deep mud."

Miners laboriously bagged the ore from most of the mines, then packed it out of the mountains on horseback along these trails. Shipping expenses ate up the profits of even the richest mines. But as the extent of the mineral deposits became established, railway companies realized there was money to be made. A race quickly developed between two of the great railroad men of the era: William Cornelius Van Horne, the American-born President of the Canadian Pacific Railway, and his rival James Jerome Hill, the Canadian-born President of the American-owned Great Northern Railroad. Van Horne won the battle for control of water traffic when he took control of most of the sternwheelers on the rivers and lakes of the Kootenays. J. J. Hill, however, was determined to get a share of the branch lines linking the mines to the lake ports. And Van Horne was equally determined to keep out J. J. Hill's "hungry hounds."

Suddenly there was not just a mining boom—there was also a railway war as Canada's richest mining area became a battleground in the two companies' larger struggle for continental supremacy. It was vicious; at one point, a brand-new CPR station in Sandon was hooked

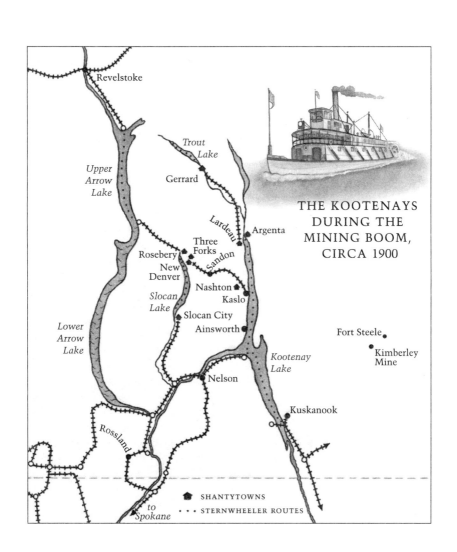

Revelstoke

Trout
Lake

Upper
Arrow
Lake

Gerrard

Lardeau

Argenta

Three
Forks

Rosebery
New
Denver

Sandon

Nashton

Slocan
Lake

Kaslo

Slocan City

Ainsworth

Lower
Arrow
Lake

Fort Steele

Kimberley
Mine

Kootenay
Lake

Nelson

Kuskanook

Rossland

to
Spokane

THE KOOTENAYS
DURING THE
MINING BOOM,
CIRCA 1900

⬠ SHANTYTOWNS
• • • STERNWHEELER ROUTES

up to a GNR locomotive and hauled to oblivion. The engineers faced formidable obstacles as they planned routes for narrow-gauge track through steep mountain passes and along the old Kootenay Indian trails. The narrow valleys with high summits and heavy snowfalls were so treacherous that no one would venture along them in spring after noon. An avalanche that came down Reco Mountain into the Slocan Valley in the early 1890s, for example, had covered the track to a depth of 170 feet (52 metres) and took six years to melt completely. Yet the railway companies persisted, and by the turn of the century there was a complete, if disjointed, system of sternwheelers on the Arrow, Slocan, Trout and Kootenay lakes, linked by short rail lines to the CPR main line to the north at Revelstoke and to the GNR main line to the south at Rossland.

The tangle of branch lines opened the Kootenays to every travelling singer, mesmerist, acting company, magician and recitalist who was busy criss-crossing the continent in this period. Pauline had heard from fellow artistes about the spectacular scenery, the demanding audiences and the perilous travel, and she looked forward to exploring the Kootenays for herself. In 1899, she had gotten as far as Fort Steele, at the junction of Wild Horse Creek and the Kootenay River. The Kootenays, though, were no place for a single woman to travel alone. But by 1902, she had Walter to ensure her safety, and to deal with the business side of the tour. According to Walter, Pauline's fame was such that all he had to do was "send out a batch of postal cards announcing her coming, and committees would form and arrange evenings, glad of the opportunity." So at Revelstoke they disembarked from the westbound CPR express and headed south.

One of their first stops was Rossland, a town of 7,000 people ringed by high-producing mines with the characteristically whimsical names that prospectors always favour—the original LeRoi mineshaft, Centre Star, War Eagle, the Black Bear, White Bear, California Josie, Annie, Nickel Plate, Spitzee, Nick of Time, Iron Mask, Enterprise, Columbia-Kootenay, Jumbo. The Johnson–McRaye performance faced tough competition in a town like Rossland, which was linked by a daily train to Spokane. Touring vaudeville shows, prizefights and classic opera were regular events at the International Music Hall and the Opera

*The famous LeRoi mine on Rossland's Toad Mountain,
British Columbia, was one of the most productive mines
during the Kootenays' mining boom.*

House. Nevertheless, Pauline and Walter found a full house waiting for them in the Methodist Church hall and enjoyed a warm reception.

The following day they climbed Toad Mountain to inspect the LeRoi Mine. The mine superintendent and his foreman greeted their celebrity guests enthusiastically, then guided them as they clambered down the narrow, dark shaft while loaded buckets clanged upwards on cables behind their backs. At the 300-foot level (just over 90 metres), they stopped to catch their breath, and two miners who had seen her show presented Pauline with pieces of gold ore from the rock face. She was much more excited by these nuggets than by the lengthy scientific lectures that Mr. Woodhouse, the superintendent, decided she needed. According to the *Rossland Miner*, he explained that "In amphorous minerals there is no trace of crystalline form or special characteristics of structure due to individual crystals, although intermittent deposits of the mass composing the mineral may give an occasional difference of hardness or texture." She nodded agreeably, so he went on to advise her that "The majority of the solid amphorous minerals are the result of the gradual change from a gelatinous state or the rapid cooling from the melted condition." Noticing an expression of some confusion on her face, he helpfully added that "The majority of them are the result of the alteration of pre-existing materials." Pauline smiled sweetly and replied, "I guess so."

From Rossland, the Johnson–McRaye partnership went on to Nelson, Ainsworth, Kaslo, Lardeau, Ferguson and Kuskanook. There was far less competition for audiences at the more remote towns, but there were no facilities for women either. Pauline was the sole female in the dining room of the hotel at Gerrard, at the south end of Trout Lake. "We ate in a small room at a long table with oilcloth on it, and 'Mobs,' the proprietor, in his undershirt, cooking at the end of the room," recalled Walter. "Pauline sat among the miners and prospectors, told them stories, listened to theirs, no one taking any notice of the unusual occurrence. The old-time miner had an innate chivalry that was particularly his own."

Any traveller would have revelled in the comforts of the CPR sternwheeler *Moyie* as it churned its way down Kootenay Lake,

*Pauline still projected the passion
and power of her Indian narratives
for her publicity photographs.*

announcing its imminent arrival at lakeshore settlements with its deep, resonant whistle. Up to 250 passengers could travel on the *Moyie*, the interior of which was designed with the same attention to detail as the CPR trains. In the spacious dining lounge, passengers ate clam chowder and stuffed wild goose from CPR-monographed china and silver plate while they gazed at a panorama of clear water and soaring mountains from the large windows. Pauline could retreat to the ladies' saloon, with its burgundy crushed-velvet settees, lace curtains and thick carpeting.

But Pauline even relished the more stressful moments. She was philosophical when mudslides or breakdowns threw Walter's travel plans. "Much disappointment was expressed last evening," reported *The Kootenaian* in July 1902, "when it was known that Miss Pauline Johnson and Walter MacRaye [*sic*] had missed connections and were unable to reach Kaslo in time for the performance, as arranged; however, the postponement was inevitable." Pauline never complained about the smuts and hard wooden seats of the narrow-gauge railways, which inched their way up steep mountain tracks and over rickety trellis bridges to isolated mining camps. In these bleak, sweaty communities, she and Walter usually found a ready audience, who were happy to buy tickets at $1 each to watch them. Working in inhuman conditions and risking their lives for only $3.50 for a ten-hour day, most miners were starved not only for entertainment other than drinking and gambling, but also for a glimpse of a lady. In those instant mining settlements, there were usually about ten men for every woman—and she was likely to be a prostitute.

Back in 1890, for example, Sandon Creek had been nothing more than a stream that gushed down a valley so narrow that the sun penetrated it for only about four hours on a summer's day. Then a rich vein of galena (lead, silver and zinc) was discovered. By the time Pauline arrived there, the town of Sandon had twenty-nine hotels, twenty-eight saloons, three sawmills, three butcher shops, two breweries, two newspapers (the *Paystreak* and the *Mining Review*), several pool halls, a covered hockey arena, a population of 6,000, and fifty buildings in its red-light district employing about 115 whores. There were so many card sharks and professional gamblers that this inaccessible, gimcrack town kilometres from any big city was known as the "Monte Carlo of Canada." Many a miner blew his grubstake on the infernal trio of "yellow liquor, green cloth and the women in red." Yet Pauline cast her usual magic in Sandon Creek's grimy little Miners' Union Hall. Bristle-faced miners suppressed their wracking coughs so they could hear her bloodthirsty Indian ballads, her sentimental love poems and her witty jabs at mine owners' arrogance. Afterwards, a shabby Englishman came up to the poet with tears in his eyes. He told her it was the first time in years he had seen a woman in evening dress.

Pauline was in her element. By now, she was such a skilled performer that she knew exactly how to play her audience. One of the most popular numbers in the Johnson–McRaye programme was "At the Ball," in which two guests at a ball given in Kensington Lunatic Asylum mistake each other for inmates. The sketch brought the house down. Pauline also knew that her Kootenay fans preferred humour and sentiment to high art; she usually followed "At the Ball" with a poem of pathos or patriotism that was guaranteed not to leave a dry eye in the house. In fact, she had become a bit of a ham. This approach suited wheezy miners and lumbermen, but her old admirers and the big city critics felt she had lost her finesse. When she and Walter finally emerged from the Kootenays in September to give a recital in Vancouver, the *Vancouver Province* critic remarked that she was struck by the "marked change which two or three years have brought about in her stage manner, her pose and even her delivery. Not that she has depreciated in any of these points but there is an air in all of them that is more professional and perhaps less charmingly ingenuous." An old friend from Brantford, T. S. H. Shearman, was harsher. He much preferred "the beautiful, timid Pauline Johnson of 1885" to the accomplished performer he now saw. With the blunt insensitivity of "an old friend," he told acquaintances that she had bartered her "divine gifts for a wretched mess of pottage." It was the same criticism that Harry O'Brien had made back in 1894.

A similar note of fastidious distaste emerged in the reviews of Pauline's second book of poetry. She had always planned to publish another book to solidify her credibility as a poet. Once she had paired up with Walter, she was able to prepare thirty-one poems for publication in 1903 by George Morang of Toronto in a volume entitled *Canadian Born*. The collection was difficult for critics to encompass since it includes both "highbrow" romantic verse and "lowbrow" stage recitations. Reflective poems like "Fire-flowers" and "Silhouette," which she had written while she was with Owen Smily, are interspersed with "Riders of the Plains" and the title poem that she had written later specifically for performance. Her London editor had rejected several of the poems when he was making his selection for *The White Wampum*. However, there are also some accomplished poems in the collection of which Pauline had every right to be proud—poems such as "The Corn Husker," which combine an eye for detail with the energy and sense of injustice of her earlier Indian narratives:

> Hard by the Indian lodges, where the bush
> Breaks in a clearing, through ill-fashioned fields,
> She comes to labour, when the first still hush
> Of autumn follows large and recent yields.
>
> Age in her fingers, hunger in her face,
> Her shoulders stooped with weight of work and years,
> But rich in tawny colouring of her race,
> She comes a-field to strip the purple ears.
>
> And all her thoughts are with the days gone by,
> Ere might's injustice banished from their lands
> Her people, that today unheeded lie,
> Like the dead husks that rustle through her hands.

Nevertheless, there is a slipshod quality to *Canadian Born*. It is best typified by Pauline's clumsy dedication to every potential reader she could capture: "Let him who is Canadian born regard these poems as written to himself whether he may be my paleface compatriot, who has given me his right hand of good fellowship in the years I have appealed to him by pen and platform, or whether he be that dear Red brother of whatsoever tribe or province, it matters not—White race and Red are one if they are but Canadian Born."

The review in the *Globe* was typical: "We had looked to see the level of her work sustained if not heightened by the passing years and I must confess to a feeling of disappointment. The collection at hand gives so little evidence of her finer imaginative vision and more culti-vated poetic diction."

The negative reviews stung. But Pauline had developed a tough skin, at least in public, and had learned from Walter to emphasize the positive. "Poor book!" she wrote flippantly to Harry O'Brien. "The Toronto *Globe* and *Saturday Night* gave it a most scathing roast. But the *News* and the Montreal *Star* gave me such splendid reviews. Lady Laurier wrote me such a kind letter. . . . Well, I must try a novel now, and get criticised." She had little time these days, though, to sit down and write anything. Her Kootenays trip had more than covered its costs, but she was still in debt. Rents for halls in Eastern Canada or cities like Winnipeg and Vancouver were high and competition for audiences fierce. So Pauline stayed on the small-town circuit, where she and Walter could keep expenses down and audiences up. In addi-tion, two of the handful of poems she wrote in these years were com-missioned pieces: "Canada for the Canadians" for the Summerland (BC) Development Company and "Made in Canada" for the Manufac-turers Association's annual banquet in Brantford. Both were designed to elicit bonhomie and patriotic cheers from businessmen after a good dinner.

The Johnson–McRaye schedule was relentless. In late 1902, they played the Prairie towns along the CPR route as they returned east. In 1903, they played various venues in Michigan and Illinois. (Pauline found the people of Michigan "*very* uncultured, very ignorant, very illiterate," she told Harry O'Brien. "Daily I grow to be more and more of a 'Cannuck' and Mr. McRaye is quite rabid as a Canadian patriot now.") In 1904, the partnership headed west again, ending up with a YWCA-sponsored concert in Vancouver's Pender Auditorium to raise money for a new ladies' hostel in the city. From there they travelled all over Vancouver Island and the Fraser Valley. In May, they were in Alberta; in June, they were back in BC's mining towns. In July, they made the 400-mile (nearly 650-kilometre) trip by horse and buggy up the Cariboo Trail to Barkerville, the site of the 1862 Gold Rush, giving concerts every time they stopped to change horses. The well-attended concerts were often followed by exuberant square dances. Pauline was thrilled by the adventure, and she was soon in rude health: "I slept like a baby, laughed like a child and ate like a lumber jack." They spent the fall of 1904 appearing throughout Manitoba and around Regina before returning to Ontario. In January 1905, Pauline and Walter launched a new tour which began in Ontario, moved into New York State and up into New Brunswick, then circled back into Northern Ontario. In September, they travelled west again to help the newly formed Prairie provinces of Alberta and Saskatchewan celebrate their births. They jogged backwards to Manitoba for November and December.

It was a breathless pace, and Pauline must have felt that her home was a railway coach. At one point, Harry O'Brien asked for the return of a book he had lent her. "Now Mr. McRaye and I have been in a stew over that booklet for months, we have misplaced it *some*where, but where? Some of our stuff, our books, pictures etc. are at Mr. McRaye's home, some with Allen and some with Mrs. Washington." The recitalists didn't always steam along in the comfort of a Pullman car; in order to get to the next town in time for the show, they often had to hitch rides in the cabooses of freight trains, construction trains and gasoline jiggers. There wasn't a branch line in Ontario that they didn't get to know intimately, whether it was the Brockville, Westport and Sault Ste. Marie line (known as the Brockville, Westport and Seldom See Money Railway) or the Kingston and Pembroke line (known as the Kick and Push). Most of these railways were unreliable and under-financed: the BW&SSM never reached Sault Ste. Marie, and the K&P never reached Pembroke.

"Throughout it all," recalled Walter in his memoirs, "Pauline Johnson kept her splendid spirit of optimism. Life with its many ups and downs, it successes and failures, never grew stale. . . . Our entertainments were given under all sorts of auspices and for all kinds of charities. In one Ontario village the funds were to purchase a wooden leg for the town constable." In Kuskanook, BC, the Johnson–McRaye partnership performed on top of a billiard table in one of the town's eighteen saloons to help raise money for the community's first church.

The rigours of constant travel were alleviated by the easy relationship that had developed between the two recitalists. As the train steamed west or the coach bounced north, Walter would read to Pauline from her treasured copy of Swinburne's poetry while she sewed or embroidered. Other times he would make her roar with laughter with the outrageous adventures of a whole host of imaginary companions: elves, a cat called "Dave Dougherty," an insect called "Felix the Bug" and "Baraboo Montelius" the mongoose. Pauline's siblings and friends resented Walter's baby talk, his endless bragging and the way he never let anyone else near to his "Lady." But to Pauline, he was always "the same unselfish, considerate boy."

Occasionally there were holidays with old friends. In August 1903, thanks to her Brantford canoeing partner Alick Mackenzie (younger brother of her beau Michael), Pauline was able to rediscover the pleasures of life under canvas next to a lake that the *Canadian Illustrated News* described as "possibly the prettiest locality in Canada." Alick Mackenzie was now an ordained minister, like his father, and the headmaster of the Grove, a small private boys' school in Lakefield, ten miles (sixteen kilometres) north of Peterborough on Lake Katchewanooka. Whenever Pauline was giving a concert in the Peterborough area, she would visit Alick and his wife in their comfortable stone home. Alick had always encouraged his students to spend their weekends paddling on the lake, or hiking and camping in the woods. Now he organized for Pauline an expedition into Stony Lake, two lakes north of Lake Katchewanooka in the Kawarthas.

Pauline's brother Allen and his new girlfriend, Floretta Maracle, a Mohawk schoolteacher from Ohsweken, joined Pauline, Walter and a large party of Mackenzies. So did a twenty-six-year-old woman and aspiring poet from Thorold, near St. Catharines, named Bertha Jean Thompson. Jean had met Pauline earlier in the year when Pauline and Walter gave a recital in Thorold, where Jean's father was the owner, editor and publisher of the local newspaper, the *Thorold Post*. "All the girls fell in love with Pauline," Jean later reminisced. In a typically spontaneous gesture of friendship, Pauline had invited her young admirer to join the camping party. The group spent long sunny days paddling among Stony Lake's 1,200 rocky islands or along the dramatic red granite rocks of its north shore. Pauline and Jean even called on Kate Traill on her three-acre island, called Minewawa. Kate was the daughter of Catharine Parr Traill, author of *The Backwoods of Canada*, who had been known as "the oldest living writer in the British Empire" before her death, aged ninety-seven, four years earlier. Pauline marked this occasion for Jean by presenting her with a copy of *Canadian Born*. For the rest of her life, Bertha Jean Thompson would treasure the volume, with Pauline's inscription: "Minewawa, August 1903." When Jean (under the pen name "Thornapple") later published a slim volume of her own verse, entitled *A Glimpse into My Garden*, she dedicated it to Pauline.

The two Johnsons, Allen and Pauline, thrilled their fellow campers with their canoeing skills, and Allen fed the party with a steady diet of freshly caught salmon trout, cooked on an open fire. Walter wore an eccentric succession of hats (a fez, a boater, an NWMP felt hat) and imitated everybody's accents. In the evenings, as the loons called and the stars twinkled, Alick led singsongs round the glowing embers. If Pauline closed her eyes, she could almost imagine she was back on Lake Rosseau with the Brantford Canoe Club. The only shadow on this idyllic interval in Pauline's hectic schedule was her brother Allen's mounting exasperation with Walter's constant chatter, familiarity and antics.

"Christmas on the road is a lonesome season for the touring entertainer," remarked Walter in "East and West with Pauline Johnson," an account of the Johnson–McRaye travels that he published in the *Canadian Magazine* in 1923. But one of the highlights of these busy years was the Christmas of 1905, which they spent in the lumbering and railroad town of Rainy River, on the Ontario–Minnesota border: "The spread set out here by the proprietor of the little hotel was a marvel. He had all kinds of meat—deer, bear, beaver, partridge, grouse, turkey and chicken." Most of the local citizenry appeared for this feast, then stayed on for a barn dance and a performance by the entertainers. It was the kind of occasion that Pauline had come to love: spontaneous, high-spirited and filled with good cheer. It matched her mood because these days, at age forty-four, she had a new-found optimism about the future.

The mature Pauline had taken two bold decisions. The first was to concentrate on literary activities that would yield a decent income. Primarily, this meant more recital tours. But it also meant a change of direction in her creative writing. In the past few months, Pauline had started writing in a genre that she was confident would be more lucrative than poetry. Her mentor Charles G. D. Roberts had already realized that although, in his words, he "lived *for* poetry," he had to "live *by* prose." Both he and Ernest Thompson Seton were quickly establishing reputations throughout the English-speaking world with nature and adventure stories for boys. Their success demonstrated that there was a market for short, lively, action-packed tales—a larger and better-paid market than for verse, although poetry was still regarded as the pre-eminent literary art. So Pauline followed suit. Earlier in the year, she had sent off to an Illinois-based magazine, *The Boys' World*, a story entitled "Maurice of His Majesty's Mail," about a brave boy who faced down bandits in the Canadian West and delivered wages to an isolated mining camp. In October, Elizabeth Ansley, the associate editor, had sent an enthusiastic letter back, describing the story as "beautiful" and asking for two more submissions of about 2,200 words each as soon as possible. In November, Miss Ansley had written again, approving of Pauline's suggestions for further stories. "What we are in need of are good Canadian stories," Miss Ansley explained. "We have experienced considerable difficulty in procuring Canadian stories with the real patriotic ring—stories where the loyalty does not seem forced." Miss Ansley assured Pauline that there would be little editorial interference in her prose, and asked her for a photograph to use in the magazine. *The Boys' World* paid $6 per thousand words. For the first time in her life, Pauline was writing on commission rather than on spec.

Pauline's second decision was that she would return to London the following year. Ever since her 1894 triumph in the Imperial capital, she had dreamed of another visit. In early 1904, she had asked the Prime Minister, Sir Wilfrid Laurier, for letters of introduction to various distinguished London residents, including the Canadian High Commissioner in London, Lord Strathcona. Laurier had obligingly supplied such letters, informing the recipients that Miss Johnson belonged to "the powerful Indian tribe of the Six Nations" and was "a very highly cultured lady . . . endowed with a remarkable poetic talent and with high dramatic powers." Now, nearly two years later and after four years of non-stop travelling, she had finally paid off most of her outstanding debts. She still did not have enough money to cover the costs of a transatlantic passage plus a flat in London, but she had some ideas on how to raise funds. And she had enough confidence in her stage skills that she felt ready to appear not in the confines of aristocratic drawing rooms, but in the more professional venue of a real theatre.

17

A PAGAN
IN ST. PAUL'S

1906

THE SS *Lake Champlain*, one of the CPR's fleet of ten passenger liners on the North Atlantic, drew out of Saint John, New Brunswick, with little fanfare on a damp and dreary Saturday in April 1906. It steamed down the Bay of Fundy, rounded the southern tip of Nova Scotia and set course east for the seven-day crossing to Liverpool. The ship's single stack belched out black smoke, and the CPR's famous red and white chequered house flag fluttered in the chilly breeze.

In the First Cabin, however, the mood was far from dreary. Most of the eleven passengers had already met on the CPR train journey across Maine from Montreal. It was a congenial group; besides Pauline and Walter, there were Ernest Ramsay Ricketts and the Henshaw family from Vancouver, Mr. and Mrs. Laird from Winnipeg and a Mrs. Sanford. There were also two young men who were thrilled to be travelling with the famous "Iroquois Indian Poet Reciter," as Pauline was billed on her new stationery. Archie Morton was a student from Halifax; Bert Cope was a talented seventeen-year-old violinist from Vancouver. Bert's mother, Margery Cope, had attended one of Pauline's recitals in 1904 and gone backstage to congratulate her; she had told her son to make himself known to the famous poet. By the end of the voyage, Archie and Bert had both formed friendships with Pauline Johnson that would last a lifetime.

Within a week of leaving Canada, Ernie Ricketts (who was manager of the Vancouver Opera House) had put together a shipboard concert in aid of the Liverpool Seamen's Orphanage. It included a violin solo by Bert Cope and a comic recitation by Walter McRaye. Pauline's name was not on the programme. Perhaps she had decided to take a well-earned rest or to stay out of the limelight to preserve her mystique. She had already discovered that she had some serious competition for the position of literary grande dame. Mrs. Julia Henshaw was a redoubtable Vancouver society hostess, novelist, journalist, botanist and Tory. Her wealthy husband, Charles, was a less impressive character: a gadfly who loved entertaining and was known as "Afternoon Tea Charlie." His reputation in British Columbia had never recovered from an occasion a few years earlier, when he had persuaded all his dinner guests to don specially imported Parisian bathing costumes for an impromptu swim in his magnificent pool. Within ten minutes, his guests were scrambling for cover because the swimsuits had dissolved, and Charlie was laughing himself silly. Charlie's frolics did not faze his wife. Julia had published a novel called *Why Not, Sweetheart?* and a book on Canadian wildflowers, and was a regular contributor to two of Vancouver's newspapers, the *Province* and the *News-Advertiser.* She was also a formidable organizer. Three days after the concert, Julia Henshaw sent out invitations to a musical At Home from 4:00 to 5:30 p.m. in the ship's first-class saloon.

Pauline undoubtedly behaved beautifully at the reception, although she never warmed to the large-bosomed Mrs. Henshaw. Still, Julia's imperious self-confidence and la-di-da manner made her irresistible material for a future sketch. Besides, Pauline had as her private audience Walter and her two young acolytes, Bert and Archie—or the "little divils," as she had already tagged them.

Despite Mrs. Henshaw's overbearing presence, the voyage to England was a tranquil interlude for Pauline. She had managed to scrape together the money for her and Walter's tickets by a variety of ingenious tactics. The previous August she had written to Ernest Thompson Seton—or "Wolf Man," as she always called him—for advice on how to sell the wampum belt that was part of her costume. She hoped Seton might purchase it himself, since he was besotted with his romanticized version of aboriginal culture. She told him the belt was "valued at $1600.00 as are all Hiawatha League belts . . . but of course

I would accept much less for it." Seton himself was now doing extremely well; after the runaway success of *Wild Animals I Have Known* (1898), his first general-appeal book, he had become a prolific writer. *Lives of the Hunted* (1901) and *Two Little Savages: Being the Adventures of Two Boys Who Lived as Indians and What They Learned* (1903) were both bestsellers, allowing him to buy an estate in Connecticut where he ran "Indian camp-outs" for local boys. Seton referred to participants at these bonfires as "braves," awarded feathers to those who demonstrated athletic prowess and threw himself into the role of "Black Wolf," the medicine man. Now he forwarded Pauline's request to a collector and sent Pauline a small loan. "You loyal Indian-man," Pauline wrote back with gratitude.

Pauline also travelled to Troy, New York, to ask her sister Evelyn for a loan. Evelyn was working as a matron in the YWCA hostel, but she still received her share of the rent from Chiefswood. (Pauline had already had her share; she had borrowed against future rents in 1900 to finance the proposed trip to Australia that Charles Wuerz was supposed to manage.) Eva was horrified to think that Walter would accompany Pauline on the trip. She told her younger sister that Walter's vulgarity would damage her image, and she certainly wouldn't help Pauline put a shadow on the Johnson name. Pauline was equally determined to take her court jester "Dink" with her to do the arduous legwork (carrying bags, finding taxis, delivering letters of introduction and promotional material). So the two sisters parted abruptly. Still, by one means or another, Pauline raised sufficient funds for her return to the Imperial capital. She remembered the triumphs of 1894—her success in the Ripons' drawing room, the laudatory newspaper articles, the important friendships, the publication of *The White Wampum*. She could hardly wait to "get me again to England," she told Seton, "where I know a large field in literature and art is open for me."

Once again, Pauline, this time with Walter in tow, landed at Liverpool's grimy docks. Once again, she took the cramped, creaky British train to London's Euston Station and made her way to Holland Park. She had found lodgings this time in St. James's Square (subsequently renamed St. James's Gardens), one block west of Portland Road, in an attractive four-storey Georgian townhouse. Number 53 St. James's

Square had been divided up into small apartments; she took one and Walter occupied a second studio apartment. Pauline's rooms overlooked the stolid mid-Victorian church that sat in the middle of the square's communal garden like a stern navy-uniformed nanny. An Anglican clergyman was also a boarder in the house.

Walter was thrilled to be in London for the first time in his life, and was soon exploring the neighbourhood and chatting up strangers in pubs. Pauline proceeded more slowly; she unpacked her battered steamer trunk, carefully arranging her remaining Indian artefacts around the room, and made a mental list of the friendships she would like to renew.

Within days of her arrival, she discovered that London had changed a great deal since her first visit. When Pauline had last seen the great metropolis, the elderly widow Queen Victoria was still on the throne and the city exuded a solemn self-importance. The louche behaviour of Bertie, Prince of Wales, had triggered the occasional scandal during the 1890s, but by and large the aristocracy had ostensibly conformed to rigid standards of conduct. The growing middle class had followed suit. Despite the ferment of fin-de-siècle iconoclasm that had galvanized "thinking London" on Pauline's last visit, conformity had stifled innovation in the arts. The London County Council kept a censorious eye on music hall lyrics. Oscar Wilde's outrageously unorthodox tastes had resulted in both a term in jail and social ostracism. (Novelist E. F. Benson, author of the gossipy *As We Were: A Victorian Peepshow*, dismissed Wilde as "an exceedingly witty trifler.")

But by 1906, the Edwardian Age had dawned. As soon as Pauline stepped out of her front door, she could see, smell and feel the difference. Progress was in the air, and speed defined the mood. The streets were busier and noisier than ever, but now few vehicles other than hansom cabs and omnibuses were drawn by horses. The army of small boys who used to sweep up the manure had almost vanished. Humber and Daimler automobiles careered up Holland Park Avenue with much tooting of horns and squealing of hard rubber tires. Electrified trams clanged down rails in the centre of the main roads. If Pauline wanted to visit Oxford Street, she could take the new "tube railway," which had opened in 1900 and ran all the way to Bank, in the heart of the City of London, from Notting Hill Gate station, for the flat fare of twopence. King Edward VII and his beautiful wife, Alexandra, had removed the shutters at Buckingham Palace, installed electric lighting and reintroduced the habit of state balls at which guests drank copious amounts of champagne and dined off gold plate. The look of the London crowds was different too. Women's waists had shrunk and their hats had grown—often to monumentally picturesque widths—while men, in imitation of the new monarch, had abandoned top hats in favour of soft Homburgs.

The theatre scene had caught the "anything goes" mood: tastes were changing and the appetite for popular entertainment was growing. There was a boom in concert hall and theatre construction. Just down the road from Pauline, the copper cupola of Notting Hill Gate's Coronet Theatre, which had opened in 1898, towered over neighbouring butchers' and stationers' shops. Fifteen more theatres would be built in London between 1900 and 1913. In 1905 the King and Queen broke several taboos when they visited the Palace Theatre in Cambridge Circus to see operetta. Music hall entertainers were now attracting professional and titled audiences in addition to their working-class regulars. King Edward himself was known to hum the tune of "Hulloah! Hulloah! Hulloah!"—a risqué number that was a staple of "the Great and Only" Marie Lloyd, the music hall favourite. (Marie Lloyd's songs, loaded with innuendo, included "She'd Never Had Her Ticket Punched Before" and "She Doesn't Know That I Know What I Know.")

With this cornucopia of public entertainment, wealthy Londoners had lost their taste for the kind of starchy drawing-room recitals with which Pauline had scored such success twelve years earlier. When Pauline started calling on old friends and delivering letters of introduction to new acquaintances, she didn't make much headway. Hamilton Aidé was now nearly eighty and seldom came to London; "Time flies with old people," his companion, Genevieve Ward, wrote apologetically. Sir Wilfrid Laurier's letter of introduction to Lord Brassey, a former Secretary to the Admiralty, didn't cut any ice. "Lord Brassey desires me to say," replied his private secretary to Pauline, "that he would feel greatly obliged to you if you would inform him as to the subject on which you desire to have an interview with him. At the present time he has many engagements and the difficulty in making appointments is considerable." Pauline's letter of introduction to the Duke of Argyll drew a similar blank; his secretary sent his lordship's regrets, with the information that the latter "would not be in London with the exception of two days from time to time." Even her Ottawa connections gave her the brush-off. Belle Scott, wife of the poet and civil servant Duncan Campbell Scott, had taken rooms close to Hyde Park for the London season. But when Pauline wrote Mrs. Scott a note to ask if she could call, she received this reply: "I am so sorry but I have an engagement for today, also am full up tomorrow and Wednesday."

A few old friends welcomed Pauline back. She was received enthusiastically by Lady Blake, the lively Irish wife of Sir Henry Austin Blake, who had spent several years as Governor of Jamaica before holding a similar position in Ceylon. The elegant Lady Ripon invited the Iroquois poet to dinner again. Pauline deliberately did not introduce Walter to her aristocratic friends, but this time she was bold enough to appear for the Ripons' formal dinner in her Indian costume. A young Guards officer, Lord Cecil Manners, who made up for in height what he lacked in intelligence, was stunned to be asked to take her into dinner. He gazed at the wampum belts, listened to her sophisticated conversation, then stuttered during dessert: "I say, Miss Johnson, you are the most absorbing woman." But Lord Manners's reaction was not enough to persuade Lady Ripon to invite Pauline to return for a recital in her drawing room.

Pauline was also less successful than she had hoped in placing stories and poems for publication. The editor of *Canada*, a newspaper published in London, turned down her account of travelling up the Cariboo Trail (which *Saturday Night* published the following October) and an article about Newfoundland. The editor of *Chums*, a boys' magazine with the postal address "La Belle Sauvage, E.C.," said he was "a little doubtful as to whether I can have the advantage of your assistance."

Lastly, there were few opportunities to perform. As soon as Pauline and Walter had arrived in England, they had registered with Keith Prowse, the theatrical booking agency, which included them in their newspaper advertisements under the heading "American and Colonial Artists." (Other entertainers in this category included "Cole and Johnson, the American Coloured Duettists," "Mr. Frank Lawton, Whistling Extraordinary," and "Dr. Byrd Page, prestidigitateur.") Pauline's striking stationery included a picture of the "Iroquois Indian Poet Reciter" in costume and announced that she and "Mr. Walter McRaye, Humorist" were "Now Touring England." But bookings were scarce, and the partnership never left London. Buffalo Bill and his Wild West Show had toured England repeatedly, and interest in "noble savages" had peaked. There was still a market amongst small boys for stories of braves in buckskin—boys such as Archie Belaney, in the seaside town of Hastings. Belaney was so fired up by Buffalo Bill's 1903 visit to Hastings and by Ernest Thompson Seton's story *Two Little Savages* that he was already fantasizing himself into a completely different life. In the 1930s he would become an international celebrity as Grey Owl, the "Indian" environmentalist. But as far as a London booking agency like Keith Prowse was concerned, professional Indians were passé. Pauline suggested to the agency that the Johnson–McRaye act would be good for garden parties. "I note what you say . . . [but] I have not yet received any enquiries," the manager wrote back.

In London, Pauline became a protegé of Canadian High Commissioner Lord Strathcona, whose own children were of mixed heritage.

Once again, however, the expatriate Canadian community rallied to Pauline's side. In 1894, the Canadian High Commissioner, Sir Charles Tupper, had been more than happy to take the young Mohawk poet under his wing. Sir Charles had been succeeded by the Scots-born financier Donald Smith. Before he returned to Britain and became the first Baron Strathcona and Mount Royal, Smith had been one of the most powerful men in the Dominion of Canada. He started life as a fur trader with the Hudson's Bay Company, rose through the ranks to become the Company's chief shareholder and Governor, and went on to become the President of the Bank of Montreal who gave crucial backing to the Canadian Pacific Railway. He had made and unmade John A. Macdonald's governments, and his stalwart support of the CPR had earned him the privilege of driving the ceremonial last spike into the track high in the Selkirk Mountains in November 1885.

By 1906, Lord Strathcona was a bearded patriarch of eighty-six, and had established himself at Canada House, in Trafalgar Square, as a ferocious champion of all things Canadian. He was delighted to become Pauline's patron. He had met her some years earlier when they were both crossing the Prairies on the CPR and he had invited her to join him for breakfast in the dining car. As a gesture of thanks for his hospitality, Pauline had presented him with two poems about CPR trains, entitled "Prairie Greyhounds," written on the back of the menu card. How could a self-made railway magnate who believed that the CPR would be the making of Canada resist a poet who serenaded the company's westbound express in such lines as

> I swing to the sunset land—
> The world of prairie, the world of plain,
> The world of promise and hope and gain,
> The world of gold, and the world of grain,
> And the world of the willing hand.
> . . . . .
> I swing to the "Land to Be,"
> I am the power that laid its floors,
> I am the guide to its western stores,
> I am the key to its golden doors,
> That open alone to me.

There was a further reason why Lord Strathcona made a particular fuss over Pauline. His own children, like Pauline, were of mixed

Pauline's elegance was undiminished, despite the advancing years.

heritage because his wife Bella, with whom he was deeply in love, was part Cree. He had frequently made speeches about the importance of religious and racial tolerance. During his successful election campaign in 1871 for a seat in both the Manitoba legislature and the Dominion Parliament, he had appealed to his audience to drop their prejudices against the Métis people. "Who are these Half-breeds?" he roared. "They are, let me say, men having in their veins blood of some of the best families in Scotland, England, France and Ireland."

In London, Lord and Lady Strathcona immediately put Pauline on the guest list for several forthcoming events. It was a good thing that Donald Smith had made an immense fortune, since the Strathconas never did things by half—the main challenge at their parties was crowd control. ("Old Strathcona is a dear old man," noted the fourth Earl of Minto, Governor General in Ottawa between 1898 and 1904, "but his hospitality was simply overpowering. Huge luncheons and dinners every day . . . one night there were around 1,000 present.") Pauline and her partner, along with Bert Cope and the famous Canadian soprano Madame Albani, were invited to perform at the Dominion Day celebrations that the High Commission was organizing (and for which Strathcona was footing the bill) at the Imperial Institute in Kensington. Walter was among the 400 men who received engraved invitations to the Dominion Day "Men Only" dinner to be held at the Hotel Cecil on the Strand. Guests dined on salmon trout, *ris de veau, mousse de jambon au champagne,* saddle of mutton and *"pêches albani glacées."* And both Pauline and Walter were among the 2,000 people invited to the Strathconas' garden party to be held on July 14 at Knebworth House, the country estate in Hertfordshire that Strathcona had rented for 2,000 pounds a year from the Bulwer-Lytton family. The band of the Royal Artillery *oompah*ed their way through Souza favourites while the likes of Sir Sandford Fleming and Miss Baden-Powell sipped strawberry cream soda, wandered through elaborate gardens and gazed in awe at Knebworth's crenellated towers and Gothic gargoyles.

"My dear Sir Wilfrid," Pauline wrote to the Canadian Prime Minister. "I feel that you will be interested and gratified to know that your gracious and flattering letter, introducing me to Lord Strathcona, has been the means of practically giving me a place in Society that I could never have attained without your introduction and his kindly aid."

The Strathconas gave Pauline a social entrée, but another well-known Canadian in London, novelist and parliamentarian Sir Gilbert Parker, gave Pauline the professional contacts she required. Born near Kingston, Ontario, the forty-six-year-old Parker was an intense and determined writer with a dazzling résumé. He had worked as a journalist in Australia, settled in England in 1890, published more than a dozen books plus assorted plays and volumes of poetry, married the American heiress Amy Van Tine, been elected to the Westminster Parliament as a Conservative-Unionist and received a knighthood in 1902. Several of his novels, including *The Seats of the Mighty* and *When Valmond Came to Pontiac*, were big bestsellers; he had adapted *The Seats of the Mighty* into an equally successful stage play starring Herbert Beerbohm Tree.

Canadian-born Gilbert Parker (1862–1932) was both a British MP and one of the most successful authors in the British Empire.

Parker had met Pauline briefly at Hamilton Aidé's salon in 1894. At the time, he had recently published *The Translation of a*

Savage, a novel about a beautiful Indian maiden who marries an upper-class Englishman. Parker's views on women were regressive even by the standards of the time ("When women in England get the vote," he snorted in 1906 when confronted by a suffragette, "I shall take the veil"). But he immediately took an almost proprietary interest in the Mohawk poet because his "Savage" heroine was as beautiful and demure—and as challenging to British views on race and class—as Tekahionwake. Since then, Parker's literary reputation had spread, helped along by gushing reviews from old friends like Bliss Carman and Duncan Campbell Scott. (Carman described Parker as "Canada's Kipling.")

Thanks to his own success and his wife's money, Parker managed to infiltrate London's xenophobic and haughty literary elite—no mean feat for a Canadian. He achieved this by a judicious mix of name-dropping and lavish hospitality. He often mentioned that both American industrialist Andrew Carnegie and Canadian Prime Minister Sir Wilfrid Laurier were close personal friends. Whenever he and his wife, Amy, visited his native land, he confided to British aristocrats, they stayed with the Mintos at Government House. He displayed prominently a photo of himself chatting with Edward VII at the Austrian spa Marienbad. He joined the best clubs, went to the leading tailor on Savile Row and frequented only the most fashionable resorts. Most important, he mixed powerful British politicians and leading writers at his parties in his large, elegant home just off Pall Mall and provided them with delicious dinners and original entertainments. The Parkers' soirees at 20 Carlton House Terrace were legendary: North American visitors such as William Van Horne, Charles G. D. Roberts and Mark Twain would rub shoulders with literary lions such as Arthur Conan Doyle and J. M. Barrie and political heavyweights such as Joseph Chamberlain and the young Winston Churchill.

Parker's raw ambition was not to everybody's taste; it particularly offended anybody who resented colonial arrivistes or who professed to scoff at British snobbery. The socialist essayist Sidney Webb once remarked that "In the dead silence of the night you hear a distant but monotonous sound—Sir Gilbert Parker, climbing, climbing, climbing." But Sir Gilbert used his contacts for the benefit of his fellow

Canadians. "He is constantly helping some struggling and ambitious youth to get a few rungs higher up on the ladder," the writer W. J. Thorold told *Massey's Magazine* in 1897. "There are not a few who owe much to the kindly influence of Gilbert Parker exerted for their advancement."

As soon as Pauline got in touch with the Parkers, Lady Parker invited her to give an after-dinner recital at Carlton House Terrace. The invitation was not unqualified: "I fear to be quite frank," wrote Lady Parker, "that I cannot offer you quite the full price you ask, but perhaps you would come for a little less." What Pauline sacrificed in income, however, she made up for in contacts. Before dinner, the attractive poet in her fringed and beaded buckskin made a strong impression on a well-mannered stranger who was fascinated by Pauline's descriptions of traditional North American native customs. He diffidently suggested she might be interested in contributing to his publications. His chief publication turned out to be the *Daily Express*—Pauline was talking to Sir Arthur Pearson, one of the most powerful media barons in Britain, who owned thirty newspapers. She was more than happy to agree to prepare some articles.

In addition, Sir Gilbert Parker wrote letters of introduction for Pauline to the editors of the *Daily Telegraph*, the *Morning Post*, the *Standard*, the *Pall Mall Gazette* and the *St. James's Gazette*. Last, thanks to the indefatigable Sir Gilbert, Pauline was invited to tea on the terrace of the House of Commons, overlooking the River Thames. Her host was Hamar Greenwood, another well-known Canadian in London, who had been the MP for York for several years. Greenwood put together an all-Canadian gathering for the visiting poet. It included Pauline's fellow poet Wilfred Campbell, the Attorney General of Manitoba and two Canadians who sat in the British House of Commons as Irish Nationalist MPs, Edward Blake and Charles Devlin.

Pauline approached all these social events with a purpose: to acquire wealthy patrons and to spread the word of her forthcoming public recital. She had booked Steinway Hall on Wigmore Street for the evening of July 16, and had flyers printed to advertise the event. Since she was virtually unknown in London, it was up to her and Walter to build an audience. "We are up to our ears in work," she told

Archie Morton in a scrawled note, "trying to plash [*sic*] sell or rob people for coin for tickets. Walter writes about forty letters daily and we are hoping for a house." Thanks to the Strathconas, the Parkers and other expatriate Canadians, by the day of the concert the majority of tickets were sold and leading reviewers had promised to attend. Bert Cope and Archie Morton would of course be in the audience. Sir Charles Tupper, now retired from Canadian politics and living in Bexley Heath, came in for the evening with his wife. Most of Pauline's part of the programme consisted of the Indian ballads she had written more than fifteen years earlier. These old favourites were greeted with gratifyingly enthusiastic applause.

The reviews in the papers the next day included complimentary comments that Pauline would use in all her subsequent publicity.

At Steinway Hall, London (seen here
in a photo taken c. 1920), Pauline appeared
to one reviewer as "an Indian Boadicea."

Most reviewers, however, either concentrated on her exoticism or damned her with faint praise. The *Pall Mall Gazette* described her as "an Indian Boadicea," and *The Times* suggested she was a powerful reminder of "a great moribund nation." The *Westminster Gazette* reviewer wrote that the "Iroquois Lady Entertainer" enunciated clearly and steered clear of affectations, "but otherwise her powers under this head can hardly be described as exceptional." The reviewer added that most people would never know about her "interesting ancestry" were it not for her "picturesque garb," since she looked like a young lady of "purest Canadian or American or, for that matter, English descent." Being a fourth-generation Canadian whose family had always lived on the American continent was not enough, in British eyes, to render Pauline of "purest Canadian descent."

Sir Gilbert Parker did one further service for Pauline that she never forgot. A few minutes after Pauline had left the stage of Steinway Hall, he ushered into her dressing room a large and boisterous man who greeted her like an old friend. This was Theodore Watts-Dunton, the critic who had singled out for special praise Pauline's verses in the 1889 Lighthall anthology, *Songs of the Great Dominion*. Pauline was overwhelmed by this august figure. Watts-Dunton never forgot how "with moist eyes she told her friends that she owed her literary success mainly to me." As he would later write in the introduction to a book of Pauline's verse, "Gratitude indeed was with her not a sentiment merely, as with most of us, but a veritable passion." It was also a most endearing form of flattery. Overcome by the passion of Pauline's thanks, Watts-Dunton invited her to dine with him at the Pines, his Putney home, the following night.

At the Pines, a further surprise greeted Pauline. In 1879, the avuncular Watts-Dunton had taken to live with himself and his wife Algernon Swinburne, the poet whom Pauline had admired since her teens. Swinburne had been living a wild, bohemian life, his financial and personal affairs totally out of control, until Watts-Dunton (a country lawyer by training) took him in hand. Now Swinburne was a wizened little old man, his flaming red hair faded to grey and his Dionysian habits long forgotten. Watts-Dunton's care had proved both wise and deadly: Swinburne's health had recovered, but his literary output had deteriorated. Pauline was appalled by Swinburne's appearance; she told Walter that he wandered around in a state of bewilderment and spoke incoherently. Nevertheless, she set out to charm the two aging patriarchs of British culture, and succeeded admirably. Two years later, when Charles G. D. Roberts dined at the Pines and the three men were discussing Canadian poets of merit, Watts-Dunton interjected, "Now, Algernon, don't forget our dear Pauline!" Swinburne replied, "I could never forget her!"

"We are in the heart of the London season, and doing well," Pauline wrote to a friend in faraway Saskatchewan. "England is lovely this year. We have been here two months and it has rained one day in all that time." Pauline's pleasure in their metropolitan sojourn was tempered by her concern about finances, but nothing could dampen Walter's high spirits. Edwardian London was a paradise for a thirty- year-old man with a taste for high living. He had joined the United Empire Club in Piccadilly, had ordered new dress suits from the J. R. Dale Company in Westbourne Grove and frequently met Bert Cope and Archie Morton for a pint in a pub in Leicester Square. In addition, he now had a glamorous young actress to squire around town.

Pauline had introduced her partner "Dink" to the Webling family, whom she herself had first met in Brantford in the early 1890s. The Weblings had spent a year in Brantford, and Josephine, one of the six Webling daughters, subsequently married a Brantford man. The rest of the family had returned to London, but three of the girls had developed a stage act with which they had toured North America. During the 1890s, they had occasionally run into Pauline and Owen Smily in the remoter regions of the Canadian and American West. In 1898, Rosalind Webling married a Vancouver photographer named George Edwards and settled in Canada. The Weblings were always glad to welcome Canadians to their home.

The Webling family star was the youngest girl, Lucy, who had spent nineteen of her twenty-six years on the stage (many of them playing Little Lord Fauntleroy in adorable curls and velvet knickerbockers). Lucy was talented and much tougher than her delicate appearance and sweet smile suggested; she kept stage-door johnnies at bay and was already writing poetry and short stories for publication. McRaye, aware of Pauline's sagging stamina, must have seen Lucy as a stage partner for the future as well as a sweetheart for the present.

Walter flirted with Lucy Webling, but he knew his first loyalty and financial security still lay with Pauline. He escorted his partner to several shows during their London stay. Their taste was relentlessly old-fashioned. Although provocative productions of plays by the likes of George Bernard Shaw and Henrik Ibsen were mounted that year, the two Canadians opted for conventional melodramas with titles like *The Case of the Rebellious Susan* and *Boy O'Carroll*.

Lucy Webling (1877–1952), the most talented of the six Webling sisters, spent part of her childhood in Brantford, Ontario.

They liked the London traditions of Elgar overtures before the curtain rose and trays of tea between acts. Walter revelled in what he described as "the old guard, the favourites of London for so many years"—George Alexander, Charles Hawtrey, Lewis Waller, Mrs. Patrick Campbell and, best of all, Beerbohm Tree, who had first trod the boards over thirty years earlier. But unlike Walter, Pauline was never able to completely immerse herself in Edwardian comedies.

One evening, she and Walter went to see Somerset Maugham's play *The Land of Promise* at the Haymarket Theatre. The play concerned homesteaders in Manitoba (which neither Maugham nor the set designer had ever visited) and reminded Pauline of her adventures out West. Walter turned to her and asked her in a whisper how she would like to be in British Columbia again, on the old Cariboo Trail. According to Walter, before the play's second act was over, Pauline had scribbled onto her programme "The Trail to Lillooet," a poem destined to become one of her most popular compositions. Its final two verses are filled with the same longing that assailed Pauline in the sticky English summer of 1894:

Trail that winds and trail that wanders, like a cobweb
  hanging high,
Just a hazy thread outlining mid-way of the stream and sky,
Where the Fraser River canyon yawns its pathway to the
  sea,
But half the world has shouldered up between its song and
  me.

Here, the placid English August, and the sea-encircled miles,
There—God's copper-coloured sunshine beating through the
  lonely aisles
Where the waterfalls and forest voice for ever their duet,
And call across the canyon on the trail to Lillooet.

"I remember," she told a friend some years later, "how terribly homesick I became for the Western woods and mountains. The great city
seemed to shut me in and smother me."

The most important contact that Pauline made during her 1906
London trip turned out to be from her homeland rather than from
within the heart of Imperial culture. In early August, a delegation
arrived in London from British Columbia asking for an audience with
King Edward VII at Buckingham Palace. It consisted of three native
leaders: Chief Joe Capilano of the Squamish people, Chief Charlie Sil-
paymilt of the Cowichan band and Chief Basil Bonaparte from Kamloops. All three spoke some English, and Joe Capilano, a kind and
dignified old man who had spent thirty years defending the interests
of his people, could easily make himself understood. (He was already
the *bête noire* of the Vancouver newspapers for his efforts to protect
an Indian burial site near Stanley Park against logging interests.) But
to ensure clear communication, the delegation included an interpreter, Simon Pierre of the Keatzie Reserve, Port Hammond.

 The British Columbian delegation came to London to protest new
game laws that had been introduced in their province. For years, BC's
native peoples had complained about encroachments on their lands by

*Chief Joe Capilano (in fox fur hat, centre left, carrying a blan-
ket) made a direct appeal to King Edward VII
for Indian fishing and hunting rights.*

miners, railroaders, fishermen and settlers. British Columbia was the
only province in Canada where Europeans had appropriated land from
the indigenous peoples without negotiating land treaties. Successive
governments had broken one promise after another regarding land settlements. Now they had unilaterally announced that Indians could
only hunt and fish in season. These days many Indians made a good
living in the fishing and lumber industries, but many still lived almost
exclusively off the land and the new laws would cause grave hardship.
Europeans (who regarded hunting as a sport rather than a food source)
respected neither the traditional division of game between bands nor
their informal agreements on how much game or fish might be taken
without depleting stocks. BC natives had protested vigorously, but
Canadian politicians were deaf to their arguments.

Joe Capilano resolved to appeal to the special relationship that supposedly existed between Canada's aboriginal peoples and the British

Crown. He had already learned the power of publicity, so (to the fury of local Indian agents) he decided to take the Indian case to London. "I go to see the king in England," he announced as he caught the eastbound CPR express at Vancouver Station. "I will speak to him of what his Indian subjects want. I will tell them when I come back what he says. I will shake his hand in loyalty for you. He is the king of the Indians and the white men. Under him they are all one big family. When I see the king I will tell him that his subjects are all faithful in British Columbia." As the train steamed out of the station, an Indian fife and drum band struck up "God Save the King."

The Indian delegation had no pre-arranged appointment with either King Edward VII or his ministers, and legally they had no direct right of appeal. Despite the fact they had no vote in Canadian elections and their bands had never signed land treaties with either Victoria or Ottawa, they were now the responsibility of the Canadian government. Chief Joe made headlines in London when he arrived at Euston Station in ceremonial dress: trousers and fringed buckskin shirt, a woven cedar-root blanket and an enormous fox fur hat with a tail that hung down his back. Lord Strathcona sent an official to meet the three chiefs and arranged for them to stay at the Chelsea Barracks. He showed them every courtesy, and rather surprisingly he notified the Secretary for the Colonies that they were the responsibility of the British government. The British minister quickly discovered that the chiefs had no intention of leaving until they had seen the King. However, the royal family was enjoying its annual holiday on the royal yacht *Osborne* during the Cowes sailing regatta and had no intention of returning to London for a few days.

Pauline and Walter were not in London on August 6 when the delegation arrived. They were taking a short holiday 80 miles (almost 130 kilometres) west of the capital in Inkpen, a beautiful Berkshire village with a thirteenth-century church and a seventeenth-century gibbet. (Walter was more interested in the pubs. He waxed lyrical in his memoirs: "The many country inns with their quaint names, 'The Olive Branch,' 'The Axe and Compass,' 'Ship at Anchor,' and 'The Four Tons of Hay' were a delight. What a lunch of rare beef, old cheese and homemade bread, washed down with good old ale, in a taproom hundreds of years old!") But one morning the village postmistress, Hortense Homer, arrived at the house where Pauline was staying with a letter from Sir Arthur Pearson. Would she come up to London to interview the chiefs?

With blithe British presumption, Sir Arthur appears to have thought one North American Indian would automatically speak the same language as all the others. In fact, not only could Pauline barely speak her own tongue, Mohawk, she was completely unfamiliar with any of the six different languages (let alone the numerous dialects) spoken by BC Indians. However, she did know a few words of Chinook, a hybrid language that west coast bands had developed in order to trade with Europeans. She and Walter quickly returned to London, and Walter bought a large supply of tobacco as a gift for the "three old boys with their blankets," as he referred to them. Lord Strathcona had organized a room for the encounter at Canada House, where the chiefs waited morosely. Lonely and isolated in the unfamiliar metropolis, treated like strange savages by its residents, the four men were already feeling a long way from home and no closer to attaining their purpose. With Sir Arthur's reporters close behind her, Pauline entered the room and greeted them: *"Klahowya tillicum skookum."* Their faces lit up. So did Pauline's at the sight of visitors from those dense forests, roaring rivers and copper sunsets for which she yearned. The occasion was the start of one of the most significant relationships in Pauline's life: her friendship with Joe Capilano, a full-blooded Indian who treated Pauline as a fellow Indian rather than as an emissary from the white world.

One week after the delegation arrived, the chiefs achieved their goal. Edward VII agreed to receive them at Buckingham Palace. On August 13, Sir Montagu Ommanney, permanent Under-Secretary for the Colonies, ushered them through a mirrored antechamber and into the Throne Room. The King and Queen were seated on a raised platform, but Edward immediately stepped off the platform, came forward and shook the hands of the chiefs. Next he led them over to Queen Alexandra and introduced them. Joe Capilano made a formal speech, describing how white people were crowding out his people and taking away their heritage. "We bring greetings to your Majesty from thousands of true and loyal hearts, which beat in unison beneath the red skins of our tribesmen," he read from a prepared text. "It is because of our love for your Majesty, coupled with the desire to live in harmony with the white people who are filling up our country, that we appeal to your majesty in person." He presented to the Queen four cedar baskets made by his twelve-year-old daughter, Emma.

When the delegation emerged from the palace half an hour later, a crowd of reporters was waiting for them. Chief Joe described the meeting. "The King he so pleased he laugh when he see the baskets," he told the reporter from *Lloyd's Weekly News*, "and he make me open them and show inside. Then I hand the great Queen a picture of myself and my little girl, and she laugh, and she thank me so pretty. When she go out she take up baskets in her very own arms and go away with them." "The Great White Father," as Chief Joe referred to the monarch, promised to look into the issue of fishing and hunting rights, although he cautioned that it might take as long as five years to sort out. Edward presented each man with a gold medallion on which he and the Queen were represented. The following day, the three chiefs and their interpreter took the train to Liverpool and returned to Canada on the CPR steamer SS *Lake Manitoba*.

Pauline's heart probably went with them. She had been cooling on London even before she met the BC chiefs. She had already written for Sir Arthur Pearson's *Daily Express* a series of articles under the byline "Tekahionwake (The Iroquois Poetess)" that drew heavily on her native heritage. The first of the four articles, "A Pagan in St. Paul's: Iroquois Poetess' Impressions in London's Cathedral," described a visit to St. Paul's Cathedral, "where the paleface worships the Great Spirit." The building's architecture and the boys' choir metamorphose into the "teepees of far Saskatchewan" and the "far-off cadences of the Sault Ste. Marie rapids, that rise and leap and throb . . . like the distant rising of an Indian war-song." A second article, "The Lodge of the Law-Makers," compared the Westminster Parliament, where male MPs argued vociferously across the floor, with the Iroquois system of government, in which chieftains chosen from certain families by tribal matriarchs quietly gnawed at an issue until consensus was reached. The final two articles, "The Silent News Carriers" and "Sons of Savages," were straightforward accounts of life on the Six Nations Reserve.

Pauline had developed for her *Daily Express* articles a new voice— the voice of a woman who had stepped straight from her Indian reserve (or from the world of Longfellow's *Hiawatha*) to the centre of the "paleface's" world. One article began, "Many moons before I set moccasined feet in these London highways. . . ." A second opened with the observation, "It is a far cry from a wigwam to Westminster." She called Buckingham Palace the "Tepee of the Great White Father" and the Houses of Parliament "this great council-house on the Thames river." No one who read these articles would know that the author's mother was born in Bristol and that Pauline herself could recite more English poetry than most English women. From a twenty-first-century perspective, Pauline's cliché-ridden, *faux naïf* voice is jarring—a Pocohontas act designed to fit comfortably into British stereotypes of Indian maidens, based on the cartoon characters the British had seen in Buffalo Bill Cody's shows and read about in the new genre of cowboys 'n' Injuns novels. At the time, though, the articles caused a sensation in London. Moreover, in their own way, they were subversive. "As with so much of Johnson's writing," point out critics Carole Gerson and Veronica Strong-Boag, "we soon discover another dimension." Pauline used her *Daily Express* articles to score some serious points. In "A Pagan in St. Paul's," she asserted the equality of Indian spirituality and Christianity. In "The Lodge of the Law-Makers," she pointed out that Iroquois women enjoyed a political power denied to British women. She regarded her *Daily Express* articles as amongst her best writing.

After four months in St. James's Square, Pauline's investment in a second trip to England appeared to have paid off. The *Daily Express* articles, the Steinway Hall show and the publicity surrounding her meeting with the Indian chiefs secured new bookings for the Johnson–McRaye partnership. "A Pagan in St. Paul's" attracted the interest of editors from a couple of other publications, who wrote to Pauline asking for contributions. "I am up to my ears in literature," she gloated to Archie Morton. "Lots of orders for stories and good money in view." Her friend Lady Blake suggested she do a tour in the British West Indies in January and February. Pauline quickly wrote to her most important patron: "My dear Sir Wilfrid. . . . Could you give me letters to any of the governors general of the British Islands. . . . I shall appear in Jamaica, the Barbados, the Bahamas, the Bermudas and Trinidad, also at Georgetown, British Guiana. . . . Once more my dear Sir Wilfrid, I beg to thank you for your unnumbered kindnesses to me." She also received what she described to Sir Wilfrid as "a splendid offer" from an American bureau to do a recital tour of several summer camps run by the Chautauqua movement in the American Midwest the following July.

But none of these small victories could curb Pauline's growing homesickness. She was increasingly exasperated by the sheer discomfort of living in London—the size of the city, the stark contrasts between rich and poor, British attitudes to colonials. As the chilly fogs of autumn mornings curled under the window sashes of her small rented apartment, Pauline felt the tug west. One particular incident confirmed her sense of alienation from the Mother Country, as most Canadians continued to call Britain.

Late one night, Pauline was sitting in her rooms in St. James's Square, writing at the table, when she heard someone walk down the hall and knock on the door of the Anglican clergyman. "He went out at all hours to visit the sick and dying, so I thought nothing of it when I heard two men pass," she recalled for a Canadian friend some years later. At two in the morning, there was a knock on Pauline's door. She gingerly opened it and was "horrified to see the clergyman standing there and shaking as though he had the palsy, while his face was the colour of ashes."

Pauline gave the poor man a glass of brandy and asked what had happened. The cleric explained that he had been summoned to baptise a dying child. He discovered that the address he had been given was a room in the worst slum imaginable, in which drunken men and women lay snoring on a bare and filthy floor. Leaning against a wall was a man who was stone-cold sober, with an infant in his arms. The man said to the clergyman, "This child will be dead in an hour and I want it baptised. But it's only fair to tell you that the young woman lying drunk at my feet is its mother, and I am both its father and its grandfather."

The clergyman grimaced as he told the tale to Pauline. Nineteenth-century Christian doctrine declared that a child of incest was damned, but he knew that a helpless soul was waiting: "In the presence of death there I had to decide." So he went ahead and baptised the baby, wondering all the while if he had perjured his own soul by this act.

Pauline listened sympathetically to this appalling story, which haunted her for years. She was shocked at the idea of such squalid depravity, the likes of which she had never seen on the Six Nations Reserve or in her subsequent travels. However, it was not the state of the clergyman's soul that troubled her but the hypocrisy of the British. As she put it to the friend in Canada, "With slums like this in the heart of London, they'll *dare* to send missionaries to our Indians in Canada!"

In November, Pauline finally booked passage home for herself and Walter on the CPR mail ship *The Empress of Ireland*, sailing on Friday, November 15, to Saint John, New Brunswick. Walter bid Lucy Webling a sad farewell, and Lucy promised to come to Canada in the near future. As Pauline watched the warehouses and hoists of the Liverpool docks recede into the horizon, she could mentally tick off an impressive catalogue of successes in the past few months: important new patrons, the Steinway Hall recital, the *Daily Express* articles, the prospect of tours in the West Indies and in the American Midwest. She had also had fun, both with Walter and with Bert Cope and Archie Morton, the "little divils" from the SS *Lake Champlain*. Bert Cope had booked passage on *The Empress of Ireland*, too, so he could remain close to his revered Iroquois poetess. Pauline had new London gowns in her trunk, plus souvenirs for her sister and coloured hatbands for her brother Allen ("If you see anything extra in black and red, bring one of that," he had requested on a postcard).

But once again, Pauline was coming home penniless. As she retreated to her cabin, she turned her mind to her usual, dreary preoccupation: how was she going to earn her living in the coming year?

18

THE CHAUTAUQUA
GRIND
1907–1908

PAULINE'S second visit to England raised her morale. After a slow start, she had achieved her goals: satisfactory reviews, commissions and opportunities for 1907. Moreover, while she was in England she had managed to complete more pieces for *The Boys' World*. When she submitted them to Elizabeth Ansley, the associate editor, Ansley accepted them enthusiastically. Most were run-of-the-mill adventure tales featuring plucky lads, loyal dogs and villainous bullies; all had happy endings. They were "red-blooded stories that will delight any real Canadian boy," in Walter's opinion. But a few were less conventional. Sometimes the hero was a wise Mohawk elder or a courageous Cree warrior. The most startling story appeared in the January 19, 1907 issue of *The Boys' World*. Entitled "We-eho's Sacrifice," it described in unflinching detail how a little boy's pet dog was strangled so it could become the burnt offering in the White Dog ceremony of the Onondaga Indians. "To endorse both the strangling of a pet and the practice of paganism in a magazine for children," suggest critics Veronica Strong-Boag and Carole Gerson, "was a remarkable gesture."

Pauline's success as a short story writer allowed her to dream of getting off the recital treadmill. But she had no permanent home in Canada where she could settle down to write. She had been on the road almost full-time for seven years, but she could not afford to slow her pace. Stage recitals were bread-and-butter for both her and Walter. Within a couple of weeks of their return from England, the Johnson–

McRaye partnership embarked on a tour of the Maritimes. They were scheduled to play Bridgewater, on the south shore of Nova Scotia, during the Christmas week, so Walter booked them into Clark's Hotel, a large frame building close to the station. As soon as they arrived, Walter went down to the bar to get a drink while Pauline began to unpack her trunk in her bedroom on the second floor.

It was a cold December night, and the windowpanes rattled in their frames as a sharp east wind gusted inland from the ocean. Pauline's sparsely furnished bedroom was lit by a single unshaded light bulb hanging from the middle of the ceiling. At about 7:30 p.m., the light went out. Pauline waited for a few minutes, expecting the bulb to flicker back on, but nothing happened. When she opened the door, she smelled smoke and heard an ominous crackling sound. The roof and the whole third floor of the hotel were in flames.

Pauline rushed to the banister and yelled down, "Fire! The hotel is on fire!" Since it was the holiday week, there were few people around. Walter took the stairs two at a time as he ran upstairs. He stared in horror at what was happening, then shouted at the reception clerk to call for help. When the firemen from the Bridgewater Hose Company arrived, they said the fire was so intense that they could not reach the third floor at all. With a sickening lurch, Pauline realized that she might lose everything—her Indian outfit with its silver trade brooches, ermine tails and wampum belts; her father's dagger; her London gowns; her writing case containing precious private letters (including the unopened envelope from her mother); her hairbrush with its Art Nouveau silver back on which her name was engraved; her half-completed stories and poems. She dashed back into her room, despite the heat and danger, and stuffed her possessions into her trunk. Then she did the same next door for Walter. Meanwhile Walter carried all their luggage to safety: three trunks, three valises and various travelling bags.

They were just in time. The water that the hoses spewed onto the roof poured down through the furnace pipes, soaking plaster and flooding halls, carpets, beds. Ceilings and stairways collapsed. Local residents stood across the street, staring as the flames leapt up into the dark sky. Many offered beds to the hotel guests since the sitting room and most of the bedrooms were ruined. "When I discovered the fire," Pauline wrote to her sister Evelyn, in a vivid description of the event, "I was the *only* person in each of the upper flats [floors] at the time. Had I been out undoubtedly the entire house would have gone. Luck and good fortune again. We would have lost *everything* we possessed. Think of the ruination to us. . . . I am so grateful."

Pauline and her sister had made up their quarrel. Pauline had sent Evelyn judicious quotations from the London reviews, plus copies of her *Daily Express* articles, to reassure Eva that Johnson family honour was intact in England despite Walter's presence. Eva didn't believe Pauline's protestations of success. In her own memoirs, she recorded how she and Allen had warned Pauline not to take Walter with her: "Just as we said, Pauline failed, and although people were nice to her on this trip, she never regained her former popularity." But family loyalties superseded private doubts. Eva sent Pauline a generous Christmas present: a bolt of fabric from which Pauline could fashion herself a blouse. "Thanks many times for the waist length," Pauline, who still enjoyed making her own gowns, wrote back in her letter from Bridgewater. "It is sure to be enough, for all waists have net yokes and elbow sleeves even yet in England and France, and the style is likely to remain for another year, the London houses predict." Notwithstanding the horrors of the hotel fire, Pauline's tone throughout her long letter to Eva was friendly and cheerful. She told her that the bitter cold had given way to "glorious, springlike" warmth, so she and Walter had gone for a walk in the woods—"Great pine woods, that border the town on all sides. I did wish you could have been with us. The bluebirds are chirping and I am enclosing the sprig of the green spruce we used to decorate the old Tuscarora Church with at Christmas."

Pauline's equanimity despite the Bridgewater conflagration was at least partly due to the thrilling prospect of her West Indies tour. She was looking forward to several lucrative weeks in the sunny Caribbean. But bad news reached Walter and her while they were still touring the Maritimes. In mid-afternoon on January 14, 1907, an earthquake destroyed the city of Kingston, Jamaica. Nearly 1,000 people died, including several delegates to the Colonial Agricultural Conference and the Imperial Cotton Conference, which the capital of Jamaica was hosting that week. Pauline had recently asked Sir Wilfrid Laurier for letters of introduction to the governors of islands in the British West Indies. Now she dropped him a sad little note from the Halifax Hotel: "In view of the present disaster in Jamaica, which I intended making my headquarters, I shall not attempt the trip this season."

Instead, Pauline took the train back to Ontario. She made an extended visit to her cousin Kate Washington in Hamilton while Walter—or "Dink" as she continued to call him—attached himself to an English company which was on a Western Canada tour. The Jamaican setback brought Pauline face to face with a fact she had hitherto tried to ignore: her ex-

Kate Washington always welcomed her cousin Pauline to her large, comfortable house in Hamilton, and allowed her to store her possessions in the basement.

haustion. In the December letter to Eva she had asked, "Did I tell you I was pretty thin? Lost pounds since I returned from England, but feel well outside eternal lassitude." In Hamilton, she tried to get her strength back. The Washingtons' home was a large red-brick house on a well-to-do street at the foot of the Niagara escarpment. Nursed by her sympathetic cousin and waited on by the Washingtons' housekeeper, Pauline recuperated in comfort. At the same time, she buckled down to story-writing.

Elizabeth Ansley had moved from *The Boys' World* to *The Mother's Magazine*, also published by the David C. Cook Publishing Company, a religious press in Elgin, Illinois. Ansley wrote to Pauline in Hamilton, asking her if she could produce a 3,000-word story ("for mothers, not women in general") within a month, to be published on Dominion Day. She also suggested topics for future issues of the magazine: "Outdoor Sports, Mother and Child out-of-doors, Health Exercises,

Picnics, Camping etc., all written especially for the mother and her family." Pauline sent along six story ideas, including "Mothers of the Iroquois Indian Race," anecdotes about "heroic but not dramatic motherhood," and descriptions of the traditional outdoor activities of a "Red Indian mother in her uncivilised but rare and beautiful life." Motherhood was not simply a biological activity in Pauline's mind; like almost all of her generation, she also saw it as an essential role for women. At the end of her list, she offered an additional idea—"A word for the foster mother"—and she frequently wrote about women who generously adopted children.

At $6 per thousand words, magazine commissions were relatively well paid. In April Pauline received $17.64 for "Her Dominion," the Dominion Day story for *The Mother's Magazine*, and $57.04 for three stories she had sent to *The Boys' World*. In the years 1907 and 1908, *The Mother's Magazine* published a total of ten pieces and *The Boys' World* used eleven stories by Pauline. Many of the stories had their origins in Pauline's experiences on the road. "A Night with North Eagle," which appeared in *The Boys' World* in January 1908, incorporated the occasion in 1901 when the CPR express on which she was travelling was parked on the Blackfoot Reserve near Gleichen. "Mother of the Motherless," which appeared in *The Mother's Magazine* the following November, described a farmer's wife Pauline met on a train crossing the Prairies who had just added her brother's four orphaned children to her own large family.

During these years, Pauline also had articles, stories and poems in publications such as the *Brantford Daily Expositor*, *Saturday Night* and *Canadian Magazine*. She dashed off most stories within a day or two, making prose a less demanding and more rewarding endeavour than poetry. She had already calculated that over the past two decades she had earned less than $500 from all her poetry, and by 1907 she had almost abandoned verse. But even with the higher rates paid for prose, she was still earning less than $300 a year from journalism and fiction. If she was going to rely exclusively on publication for income, she must either write more or find publications that paid more. Such publications did not exist in Canada. When the editor of Toronto's *Saturday Night* had accepted one of Pauline's articles the previous year he had bluntly informed her, "I suppose you know that we cannot pay anything like the rates that you will receive from London publishers."

As Pauline cast around for ways to increase her income, her thoughts returned to her London success. She recalled Sir Arthur Pearson's enthusiasm for her stories, for which he had paid 2 guineas each (about $12 in her day). She wondered whether, if she wanted to focus all her energies on magazine commissions, she should follow the examples of the male authors she knew and leave Canada. Charles G. D. Roberts was now in London, enjoying a steady stream of commissions for the kind of tales that could be told around a campfire. (He was also enjoying the life of a boulevardier, while back home in Fredericton, May Roberts struggled to raise their four children.) Sir Gilbert Parker was cutting a swath through London, writing historical fiction set in Canada. From his estate in Connecticut, Ernest Thompson Seton was churning out animal stories that drew on the extensive knowledge of natural history gleaned during his years living in the Carberry Hills of Manitoba.

Life with the Washingtons was comforting—but it was also boring. Pauline recalled the fun she had had in London the previous year. She knew that Bert Cope, the young Vancouver violinist she had met on the SS *Lake Champlain*, was back in England and would willingly squire her around the city.

In mid-April, Pauline sat down at the writing table in the bay window of the Washingtons' home and took out a sheet of her new stationery. Her 1907 letterhead announced that "The Iroquois Indian Poet Entertainer" was going to present "her own poems of Red Indian Life and Legend" in a new American and Canadian tour. Down the left margin of the paper ran quotations from the 1906 London reviews ("clever and effective verse," according to the London *Times*; "Miss Johnson has a dramatic manner," declared the London *Morning Post*). Pauline wrote in her firm, sloping hand Kate's address: 112 Aberdeen Avenue, Hamilton. Then she stared out at the well-trimmed garden, in which daffodils already bloomed, and pondered how to ask for a loan from someone she had not spoken to for many months.

"My dear Mr. Lighthall," she finally began. "How long is it since I have either seen you or written you." After a few brief pleasantries, she raised "a business matter." She wanted to spend a few weeks in England. She would return by July 1, "to open for a two month engagement for the Chautauqua Societies, the best occasions I ever signed for." In the short term, however, she was a little short of cash. She would forward to Mr. Lighthall some of the choicest articles in her Indian collection as surety for a loan of $100, which she promised to repay by August 1. She listed her treasures: moosehair and porcupine work, an Onondaga turtleshell rattle, the silver medal presented to her father by the Prince of Wales in 1860. "Of course, I would not part with one single article for any price. I would merely send them as a 'hostage' and when I meet my note, would expect these articles returned to me. . . . Could you arrange this for me?"

With her usual blithe optimism, Pauline had already purchased her ticket for the transatlantic crossing when she wrote this note. She was booked on SS *Lake Erie*, the CPR sister ship to SS *Lake Champlain*. Luckily, William Lighthall (now a prosperous local politician, former Mayor of Westmount and well-known writer in Montreal) came through. "Lent her $50 without security—really as a gift," he scribbled at the bottom of Pauline's letter. Pauline was on board ship in Saint John harbour when she received his letter telling her that the money would be waiting for her at the Bank of Montreal's London branch. "I thank you over and over and shall not forget your kindness," she wrote in a note of gratitude. "I would have liked you to have the Indian things, but it is also pleasant to have them with me on my trip. I shall work very hard for the six weeks I shall be in London, for I have had a great measure of success recently in literature of which I feel you will be most glad."

The prospect of another balmy London spring excited Pauline. But she was now forty-five, and unused to travelling by herself. The night before the SS *Lake Erie* sailed out of Saint John, she found herself uncharacteristically anxious. As usual, she turned to a friend to lift her spirits. Pauline sent a note to Archie Morton, who along with Bert Cope had kept her company on her previous voyage. "Dear 'Cute Little Divil,'" she wrote to the young law student. "Do come and say bon voyage to me. I am quite lonely without Dink who is in Winnipeg ahead of an English company. Our big engagements don't open until July and as I had nothing to do I thought I would holiday in - London. . . . Thine, E. Pauline Johnson." But Pauline remained alone. Archie was in Montreal and did not receive the note until weeks later.

How Pauline spent her time in London is not clear. Laura Wood, wife of the New Brunswick businessman who had met Pauline in 1900, reported that Pauline spent the summer of 1907 in "the English country[side] with four friends." Pauline certainly made contact with Lord Strathcona, who immediately invited her to give a recitation at his annual Dominion Day reception. His secretary enquired, "Will you let me know what I shall put down in the programme?" Pauline also had a brief brush with British aristocracy: among the scarce papers for this period is a souvenir programme for the visit of the King and Queen of Denmark to London. But there is no evidence of new professional achievements. If she tried to get work from London editors, she was largely unsuccessful. In June a short piece about a fellow Iroquois, long-distance runner Tom Longboat, appeared under the byline "E. Pauline Johnson, Tekahionwake" in the London-based magazine *Canada*. But there is no trace of Pauline's work in the columns of the *Daily Express* or any other large-circulation British publication. She did not secure a London publisher for the stories she had now completed. She did not re-register as a recitalist with the Keith Prowse Agency.

Perhaps Pauline simply enjoyed slowing down. Perhaps she spent most of the damp days of May and June back in the flat in St. James's Square, which she had rented once again, producing more material for Elizabeth Ansley's publications in the United States. Or perhaps she spent most of her time with Bert Cope and his musician friends.

Bert is another elusive figure in the story of Pauline Johnson. Despite an age difference of close to thirty years, Pauline and the talented young violinist from a wealthy Vancouver family became close friends. She later told a Vancouver newspaper that she and Bert " 'did' the theaters and concerts together, and had a right royal time." Pauline mentioned to Archie Morton that Bert's mother had also visited him and that she spent time with both of them. In later years, Fred and Margery Cope, Bert's parents, always welcomed Pauline into their family home in Vancouver, and often included her in Christmas and Thanksgiving dinners.

Yet the friendship was obviously more than a cordial alliance between two colonials in London. Pauline and Bert developed a very deep and special affection for each other. All her life, Pauline aroused and enjoyed the respectful love of men younger than herself. They loved her because she was charming and because she was fun. The age difference between Pauline and Bert was too wide to make a spring–autumn flirtation likely—an eighteen-year-old boy rarely finds a forty-six-year-old woman romantic. Pauline was now middle-aged and matronly. For Bert, Pauline exuded the mystique not of a wild Mohawk maiden but of a seasoned performer who could teach him how to hold an audience's attention. At Lord Strathcona's vast receptions, it must have been reassuring for the young man to swan around with one of the evening's stars on his arm. For Pauline, the admiration of a sensitive young artist was both flattering and a nostalgic reminder of all the heedless flirtations of her youth.

The exact nature of their friendship must remain conjecture. But there is one wisp of evidence about its importance to Pauline. In 1908, she published a sequence of love poems, "Autumn's Orchestra." These were the first such poems she had written since her disastrous liaison with Charles Wuerz in 1900, and the last she would ever write. There are clearly autobiographical elements in the sequence. "Autumn's Orchestra" is dedicated to "one beyond seas," and begins,

> Know by the thread of music woven through
> This fragile web of cadences I spin,
> That I have only caught these songs since you
> Voiced them upon your haunting violin.

The image of a distant violinist is woven into almost every stanza:

> There is a lonely minor chord that sings
> Faintly and far along the forest ways,
> When the firs finger faintly on the strings
> Of that rare violin the night wind plays,

Just as it whispered once to you and me
Beneath the English pines beyond the sea.

In the sequence's "Finale," the lonely ache for a distant soulmate is almost tangible:

But through the night time I shall hear within
The murmur of these trees,
The calling of your distant violin
Sobbing across the seas
And waking wind, and star reflected light
Shall voice my answering. Good-night, Good-night.

Pauline's third sojourn in London came to an abrupt end in mid-June. She received a cable requesting her immediate presence in the United States. "I had to come in by New York," she wrote to Archie Morton, "as our summer engagements began earlier than we expected." Between her arrival in New York and the opening of the Chautauqua season on July 1, she made a very quick trip north to Brantford. On June 25, her brother Allen Johnson finally married Floretta Katherine Maracle, the woman he had been seeing for at least four years.

Allen was the only one of the four Johnson siblings to marry, and his sisters must have wondered if it would ever happen. Already forty-nine, Allen had been jilted by another woman in the 1890s. Since then he had drifted around. Good-looking and lazy, he first lived with his mother and Eva in Brantford, spending his days moping in the back bedroom. After Emily's death, Allen moved to Toronto, held a series of inconsequential jobs and began courting Floretta Maracle. Floretta was a fine young woman who worked for the federal government's Department of Indian Affairs. One of six orphaned sisters from the Tyendena'ga Reserve near Belleville, she had been raised by relatives on the Six Nations Reserve and had attended the Mohawk Institute. She taught in the little Ohsweken schoolhouse before getting a job with the Department. Pauline was very fond of Flo, a petite and lively character who had been a member of the 1903 camping party on Stony

Lake. "Strong in her purity of power, / Fidelity her richest dower," runs a verse that Pauline penned to her new sister-in-law. Flo needed her fidelity—Allen took an age to propose to her. Flo and Allen settled in Toronto in what seems to have been a happy marriage. There were no children.

After the wedding, Pauline met up with Walter McRaye in New York for their tour of Chautauqua camps. Walter was in high spirits: Lucy Webling (who was still in England) had agreed to marry him. "Is not this news about Dink and Lucy?" Pauline wrote to Archie Morton. "Of course I am delighted, and when I am out of an engagement I tell them I shall come and camp on them for an indefinite time. I deserve it, as I introduced them."

Both Pauline and Walter were relying on their Chautauqua season to allow them to accumulate some capital. Pauline, as usual, had a pile of debts to pay, and Walter wanted to start married life with something in the bank. They would be paid $50 for each performance and had been booked for at least twenty Chautauquas. Even with Pauline taking a larger share of their earnings, both could hope to save several hundred dollars. Such a sum, they reasoned, would compensate for the hard work that fellow performers had told them Chautauquas demanded.

The Chautauqua movement had begun thirty-three years earlier, and took its name from a small resort in upper New York State close to Lake Erie. There, a Chicago minister named John Heyl Vincent founded a summer lecture series for Methodist Sunday school teachers in 1874. The lectures proved immensely popular, and by the late 1880s similar lecture series, known as "Chautauqua Assemblies," had been organized throughout the northern United States. In 1900, there were more than 400 local Chautauquas, most taking place in brown canvas tents pitched close to lakes, where soft breezes provided relief from summer heat. Families would rent a tent ($5.50 per session), eat at a communal cafeteria and enjoy up to sixty different entertainments over the course of ten days. The programmes had expanded from their original religious focus to include a potpourri of

Each summer, thousands of Americans
flocked to Chautauqua Assemblies
for entertainment and enlightenment.

education, culture and entertainment, with a stiff shot of temperance rhetoric. The fees offered to speakers were large enough to attract big names, such as Nathaniel Hawthorne and Ralph Waldo Emerson. Music helped raise the tone in these uplifting assemblies; brass bands, choral groups and string quartets provided anything from a choral mass to a spirited rendering of "Comin' Through the Rye."

By the time the Johnson–McRaye partnership got on the Chautauqua bandwagon, bookings for the various Chautauqua assemblies had been handed over to professional agents. The Clayton Lyceum Bureau in Chicago recruited Pauline and Walter to be part of the programme for Chautauquas in Indiana, Michigan, Nebraska, Colorado, Kansas, Missouri, Illinois and Oklahoma. The schedule was frenzied. They had to take the train over a huge distance to an unfamiliar destination, perform at the Chautauqua recital the next day and then catch the train to the next destination the following morning. Every night was spent under canvas; every audience (and they always seemed to include screaming babies and reluctant children) was a new challenge. The incessant travelling meant that Walter and Pauline did not even

*Pauline and Walter joined the Arkansas playwright
and novelist Opie Read on the Chautauqua circuit.*

have time to relax with their fellow performers and enjoy a good
grumble about the Clayton Lyceum Bureau's slave-driving attitude.

At Kewanee, Illinois, the Johnson–McRaye partnership took to the
stage after the Honourable William Jennings Bryan, who gave a three-
hour speech on "The Old World and Its Ways." At Paris, Illinois, the
Chautauqua programme included Miss Elma B. Smith, "the delightful
child impersonator and bird warbler," and lecturers who spoke on
everything from "Home Life in Greenland" and "The Bright Side of
Prison Life" to "How to Live Twice as Well and Twice as Long, or
How Funerals May Be Postponed." In Evansville, Indiana, Pauline and
Walter were up against Strickland Gillilan, "the funniest man on the
American platform who yet tinctures his humour with beautiful
thoughts."

For $50 a night, Pauline and Walter were prepared to grit their teeth
and get on with it. But it was not fun. Pauline and Walter were largely
unknown to their audiences. Pauline was advertised as "Tekahionwake, the Indian poetess" whose work had "a barbaric swing of pri-
mal emotion." Although "Civilization has touched her with its finer
qualities," the programme notes suggested she would be more like a

figure from a Wild West show than one from the literary salons of London. Most of the farmers and tradesmen who stared at the buckskin-clad woman on the stage waving her father's dagger at them had even less sympathy for native North Americans than did their Canadian counterparts farther north. They had been raised on the frontier legends of the genocidal campaigns by the US army during the 1870s Indian Wars; many might have agreed with the infamous remark of Union General Philip Sheridan that "the only good Indian is a dead Indian." Meanwhile, McRaye's strangled *habitant* accent, as he recited the poems of William Drummond, was incomprehensible to the rural folk of the Midwest.

As the season wore on, the pressure intensified. "In a big tent with noisy, crying babies, small boys with peanuts and people moving around," McRaye recalled in an uncharacteristically dour comment, "it is not always easy to get your talk over." One night, a train wreck ahead of them meant that they did not reach their destination until four o'clock in the morning. They then discovered that there were no beds available. They spent the night sitting in a park, waiting for breakfast. Walter stayed upbeat throughout, chatting away to all and sundry about his and Pauline's adventures. He told a reporter from the *Springfield Daily Leader* that "Miss Johnson has lately spent more than a year in England, where she was received with special favour by King Edward." (Pauline scribbled in the margins of this column, "McRaye twaddle.") But by late July, the gruelling pace had got to Pauline. Her health collapsed.

She described her plight to Ernest Thompson Seton, from whom she had borrowed money in 1906 that (along with several other debts including the 1907 loan from William Lighthall) she still had not repaid. "Such a disaster has befallen me," she wrote from Boulder, Colorado.

> A heathen Chautauqua manager, in that most heathen state Missouri, placed us in a huge circus tent to give the recital. A thunder storm blew up soaking the canvas, then the torrid sun teemed down. The tent steamed, filled with vapour, the [thermometer] at 98 degrees and—well! My throat went. For

nine days I did not speak aloud, and had every joint in my body swollen and scarlet with rheumatism. . . . Nine nights cancelled, at fifty dollars a night. Just a loss of $450.00 at one fell swoop. . . . And it was for this I came from England!

By the time she was writing to Seton, Pauline had recovered sufficiently to give two scheduled recitals in Boulder. She sent Seton a "miserable $10" to prove she was not a "Bad Injun," and promised to forward the rest of what she owed soon. "But I am afraid to part with it . . . in case my voice does not hold out."

Pauline managed to finish the season. She wrote to Archie Morton from her final appearance, in Bloomfield, Iowa, that she and Walter "have been working like nailers on our trip, matinees and evening performances almost daily." But her jarring experiences with Chautauqua left her fragile in health and temper. This was evident when a reporter from the *Boston Herald* interviewed her in September after a very successful recital at the Vendome for the Massachusetts Indian Association. As usual when confronted with a reporter, Pauline played up the sophisticated complexity of her heritage—her literary achievements, her Mayfair manners and her Iroquois pride. The reporter raised a sceptical eyebrow; like the Midwestern farmers, he couldn't quite believe that this well-dressed woman was a real Indian. Pauline's eyes flashed. "Ah, I understand that look," she snapped. "You're going to say I'm not like other Indians, that I'm not representative. That's not strange. Cultivate an Indian, let him show his aptness and you Americans say he is an exception. Let a bad quality crop out and you stamp him as an Indian immediately."

Pauline was tired. She was tired of performing, tired of being patronized, tired of scrambling to make a living. She was a trooper: as soon as her moccasin-clad foot stepped onto a platform, the adrenalin still flowed and her face lit up with energy. Her low, clear voice still echoed through hall, tent or theatre, rivetting her listeners with its haunting rhythms. But what had once been a deeply felt performance had become an act. She was tired of making the effort to please the public. She had lost the urge to "set people on fire" with her poetry.

At the end of the month, she and Walter gave a recital at the Roycroft Inn in East Aurora, outside Buffalo, New York. The inn was part of an extraordinary Arts and Crafts community founded twelve years earlier by an eccentric former soap salesman named Elbert Hubbard. Hubbard was the author of a series of biographical sketches of well-known artists and writers. The community had begun with a printing press on which Hubbard produced his books, then expanded to include furniture, leather, metalworking and bookbinding workshops. As visitors began to arrive to admire and purchase Roycroft artefacts, Hubbard designed and built an inn. The dining room of the Roycroft Inn was filled with original oil paintings (many by the Canadian artist Carl Ahrens) and the cool, quiet library was lined with beautifully bound books available to both residents and guests. Hubbard himself was a charismatic crank who had been inspired by William Morris, of England's Kelmscott Press. He saw himself as a prophet of aesthetic values, and he gave inspirational speeches all over the United States about the dangers of industrialization. By the time Pauline and Walter arrived in East Aurora, close to 500 people lived and worked within the Roycroft community.

Roycroft residents loudly applauded Pauline and her message of peaceful co-existence between races. For her part, over the next few days Pauline responded to the serenity of Roycroft. Hubbard himself was away at the time ("barnstorming the one night stands," as he scribbled in a note to them). Among the collection of postcards that Pauline kept in her navy leather writing case were several of Roycroft. Perhaps her favourite was a shot of the interior of the chapel, with its plain wooden benches. She spent many hours there, lost in reverie. A week after she had reluctantly left Roycroft and travelled to Manitoba, Pauline told a reporter from the *Winnipeg Tribune* that the Roycroft residents lived "ideal lives in many ways. Mr. Hubbard is not a slave-driver and they enjoy the greatest of freedom during working hours." Roycroft was far more uplifting than the grind of appearing at the "morally elevating" Chautauquas.

By mid-October, Walter and Pauline were back on tour. They made their way through Manitoba and Saskatchewan, giving performances at small towns they had last visited in 1905. In Edmonton on November 4,

Pauline had lunch with Ernest Thompson Seton, who had just spent six months in Northern Alberta. Then the McRaye–Johnson partnership travelled west as far as Kelowna, BC. Here Pauline insisted that she needed a few days off, so Walter left her at the Lake View Hotel and explored some of the local small towns. "Dink is away, looking for a ranch," Pauline wrote to Archie Morton. "We—ie. he, Lucy and I— hope to run a chicken ranch up here somewhere. . . . I am going to wear a blue check apron and feed corn to the 'chookies.' Better join the colony, my good friend." Archie was not the only person that Pauline hoped to recruit for her ranch fantasy. "Bert Cope comes into St. John via the *Empress of Ireland*," she added.

But the chicken ranch never materialized, and Pauline and Walter were soon on the road again. They turned east and went back to Battleford, Saskatchewan, spent Christmas on the Prairies, travelled as far east as the Maritimes for more performances in April and May of 1908, and finally returned to Ontario at the beginning of the summer. The Johnson–McRaye partnership had now been on the road, living out of steamer trunks and trying to keep both their skits and their outfits fresh, for nearly twelve uninterrupted months.

In early June, Pauline parted company with Walter and took the westbound express alone right to the end of the line in Vancouver. On June 29, she checked into the Hotel Vancouver for a month's rest. Her bones ached, her energy was low and she now slouched as she walked. There were other, more disturbing symptoms, too—flare-ups of fever, persistent lassitude. Most of all, she hated growing old. Her striking good looks had always been an important part of both her self-image and her carefully constructed appeal to others; like many beautiful women, she found a loss of looks was a blow to her self-esteem. She resented questions about her age. "Youth is the eternal heritage of the poet," she later wrote to a fellow poet, "and when the poet is a woman she is hurt and wounded and bruised, when the public clamours from curiosity to pry into her personal, sacred life and remark upon her age, when her whole being cries out for youth, and yet she knows it is lost for ever."

She could not afford to take things easy. "I say that I have come here for a rest and a holiday," she confided to a friend who worked at the *Vancouver World*, "but really I have a great deal of work to do." She wanted to write some more stories for Elizabeth Ansley at *The Mother's Magazine*, who had recently asked her for "some humour and bright, happy stories that will serve as a recreation for the mother when she picks up the magazine." By now, Pauline had learned how to make adroit use in her literary work of her own life—particularly its more dramatic aspects and episodes. She knew that her mother's history, especially Emily Howells's controversial marriage to a Mohawk chief, was excellent raw material for a story exploring prejudices within both the non-native and the Iroquois communities. She also intended to produce more articles for *The Boys' World*, which paid promptly and well for everything she wrote. As usual, she needed the money. The Hotel Vancouver's charges were very reasonable: $60 a month for a room and all meals. But Pauline would have to write several stories at $6 per thousand words to foot the bill.

Magazine pieces were Pauline's short-term objective. A larger issue she now faced was where she might settle if she decided to give up the stage and focus on prose. "Tekahionwake," according to her friend at the *Vancouver World*, "has called [Vancouver] 'The Smile of God,' and she says that she never will make her home anywhere except in Vancouver—or London, England." But London, England, had proved barren turf in her 1907 visit there. And Vancouver now had two significant new attractions for her. The first was Bert Cope, for whom (she told the *Vancouver World*) she predicted "great things in the future." The second was the welcome given to her by an unexpected delegation which arrived at the Hotel Vancouver soon after she had settled in there.

The delegation was led by Chief Joe Capilano—whom Pauline now learned to call by his Salish name, Su-á-pu-luck—and consisted of the men she had met in August 1906 in London. Clad once again in their ceremonial dress, they repeated to the poet the greeting she had given them the previous year in Canada House: "*Klahowya tillicum skookum.*" This time, it was Pauline's face that lit up as genial old Chief Joe bade her a hearty welcome to the West. She had journeyed far to get to Vancouver, he said with a warm smile, and they did not want the white people to be the only ones to greet her. By their words and their gestures, the chiefs made it clear that they considered the Iroquois poet to be one of them. Chief Joe invited her to visit the Capilano village across Burrard Inlet.

Pauline was deeply touched. No native peoples east of the Rockies had ever offered her this kind of welcome. She had lost any sense she may once have felt that she belonged on the Six Nations Reserve, and she was starting to lose confidence that Canada's native peoples would ever catch up with European immigrants in political and economic affairs. There was so much squabbling between bands, and so few leaders were emerging of the stature of Big Bear or Smoke Johnson. Was the noble independence of Indian peoples, which she had spent her life championing, a chimera? In January 1907, she had written to Prime Minister Laurier asking him to appoint a non-native man unfamiliar to the reserve as the new Superintendent of the Six Nations Reserve. "My people are a peculiar nation," she explained. "One odd thing is their indifference to persons they know too well. An absolute outsider, an utter stranger gains their allegiance and their confidence and their loyalty to a far greater degree than those they have about the Reservation and its environments. They are an exacting, difficult tribe to govern, often malcontents, often I fear apparently ungrateful, but never *really* so."

Now a chief who was not afraid to take political initiatives himself, and who would stare down any man who tried to bully him, wanted to help her feel at home in Vancouver. Nothing in her long public career, she told onlookers, had pleased her "more than this visit from her red brothers of the far west." She realized she could settle in Vancouver. Perhaps she might even recapture that sense of belonging that she had never felt since she waved goodbye to Chiefswood twenty-three years earlier.

19

A GREAT CHIEF DIES:
VANCOUVER
1908—1910

I N 1908, Vancouver was, as Walter put it in a letter to Archie Morton, "a great burg." Close to 100,000 people lived there, and the city boasted some fine civic landmarks, including the ever-so-British grey stone Christ Church Cathedral and the classic Greek temple façade of the Canadian Bank of Commerce. Streetcars trundled down the major streets and most houses were lit by electricity. Fantastic mansions, surrounded by smooth lawns and boxwood hedges, were springing up along Davie, Denman and Robson streets in the West End. Gabriola, the elaborate home built by sugar baron Benjamin Tingley Rogers, featured eighteen fireplaces and wood panelling imported from England. At Woodward's department store on Hastings Street, Vancouverites could purchase Cuban cigars and Paris fashions. There were three well-attended theatres, three lively newspapers and a well-stocked Carnegie library. The largest electrical store in the city was Cope & Sons Ltd. on Hastings Street, owned by Bert Cope's father, Fred.

The city's recent, raw beginnings still butted into its new-found sophistication. The sidewalks were wooden; monumental tree stumps disfigured building lots; huge lumber piles obstructed a clear view of the inlet and the mountains; primeval rain forest squeezed the city boundaries. Guests at older downtown hotels were still entitled to an "eye-opener" (a shot of whiskey before breakfast) as part of the price of their room. When Pauline had first seen Vancouver only fourteen years earlier, it had been little more than a remote logging town of 20,000 people huddled around Burrard Inlet. The promise of future development was

In 1904, Montreal photographer William McFarlane
Notman photographed Vancouver's urban sprawl.
Coal Harbour is in the distance, on the left.

already there, though, thanks to the arrival on May 23, 1887, of Engine
374, pulling the first transcontinental CPR express. "The Constantino-
ple of the West!" prophesied the British writer Douglas Sladen in 1895,
commenting on how "Nature and circumstance have been prodigal to
Vancouver." But back then, the place had been primitive by Eastern
Canadian standards. Its ramshackle buildings were dwarfed by ancient
cedars, spruce and Douglas firs. Owen Smily, who had accompanied
Pauline on that first 1894 visit, was kept awake half the night by the
crows outside the window of his Hotel Vancouver room.

Now, a few years later, Vancouver reminded Pauline of Winnipeg in
1897. It pulsated with the same attractive mix of comfortable wealth
and pioneer spirit. And there was something else about Vancouver that
fascinated her. Until the 1880s, the majority of people living on
Canada's west coast (which had become the province of British
Columbia in 1871) were members of the many Indian nations such as
the Shuswap in the interior, the Kaska and Sekani in the north and the

A group of Indians at Alexander Bay, at the foot
of Columbia Street: they formed a significant
proportion of Vancouver's population.

Haida, Nootka and Salish on the coast. And Indians were still a significant presence in the city in 1908. Although most Indians had adopted
the European style of dress, they maintained their old customs. On her
daily walks from the Hotel Vancouver, Pauline could see Indian tents
pitched on the shore of the Alexander Street warehouse district and
Indian fishermen setting salmon nets off English Bay. Across the inlet,
there was Joe Capilano's village, with its whitewashed houses and
Anglican church. The Musqueam band (like the Capilano band, part of
the Squamish people, a subgroup of the Coast Salish) had a settlement
on Point Grey. Moreover, Vancouver was too new for its elite to have
yet become sclerotic with imported class prejudices. There were
plenty of former North West Company and Hudson's Bay Company
employees among the better-established homeowners, and several had
some Indian blood (though they did not flaunt it). Well-to-do women
like Julia Henshaw in the West End, attending their At Homes every
weekday afternoon, were less obsessed with pure British pedigrees

than their counterparts in Toronto's Rosedale. Pauline did not feel the angry compulsion to "stand by my blood and my race" in the same way that she did when faced by Toronto's *crème de la crème.*

Layered over Vancouver's native peoples and original settlers was a mix of immigrants far more exotic than anywhere east of the Rockies. Most Vancouverites were born outside Canada, as the 1911 census would confirm. Most of those came from Europe or the United States, but many had crossed the Pacific Ocean. Between 1881 and 1884, more than 10,000 Chinese workers had been brought over to British Columbia to help build the Canadian Pacific Railway; large numbers subsequently gravitated to Vancouver. There were also Japanese immigrants who fished and worked in the canneries, and a small number of Sikhs employed in the lumber mills. Vancouver's free-and-easy atmosphere had not stopped the spread of rampant racism, with European residents pitted against both native peoples and the under-class of Asian newcomers. Non-whites were forbidden to own property, and Asian immigrants were herded into overcrowded ghettoes. By the turn of the century, Vancouver's Chinatown included several blocks of brick tenements; with a population of more than 3,500, it was almost as large as San Francisco's.

Racial animosity was overt within the working classes. The constant cutthroat competition for jobs in the city's boom-or-bust resources industries, such as lumber and fish, exacerbated ill-feeling between people who didn't look, dress or speak the same. In 1907, tension had exploded when the Asiatic Exclusion League accused the Chinese of causing an economic slump by working for less than standard wages. A mob of 15,000 people surged through Chinatown, smashing windows and beating up Chinese residents. The rabble then moved on to Japantown. Luckily, residents there had been forewarned and were able to defend themselves and their property with knives and broken bottles.

Meanwhile, the Coast Salish suffered and starved as a swelling tide of European settlers occupied their traditional fishing spots, logged their hunting grounds, despoiled their burial sites and banned potlatches, their ceremonial feasts. Chief Joe had had good grounds for his complaints to the "Great White Chief," King Edward VII, in 1906.

But his London adventure only confirmed his reputation amongst Vancouver's ambitious business and political leaders as a trouble-maker. When they heard that Capilano and the King had discussed the return of traditional hunting grounds to the natives, they accused the dignified and thoughtful chief of "inciting the Indians to revolt."

In June 1908, however, Chief Joe Capilano's attention was focussed not on Squamish grievances but on making the Iroquois poet from Ontario feel at home. The day after Pauline had received Chief Joe and his fellow chiefs, another visitor arrived at the Hotel Vancouver. Chief Joe's son Matthias had come to escort her to the band's village on the North Shore. They paddled over in his canoe, and Pauline met Chief Joe's wife, Mary Agnes (Líxwelut), and daughter Emma. Pauline loved being back in a canoe, and immediately warmed to the Capilano people. Chief Joe offered her the use of a light canoe during her stay.

Almost every day, Pauline would settle herself in the stern of the dugout and paddle along the shoreline of English Bay and Burrard Inlet. She had never canoed on salt water before, or explored a coast-line that changed according to the state of the tides. There were small bays to discover, with giant sun-bleached timbers washed up on the shingle. There was a constant bustle of vessels on the water. Little steamboats like the *Clayburn* ferried people to the North Shore. Elegant yachts belonging to the city's wealthy merchants creamed through the waves. At the wharves, the CPR's oceanliners unloaded cargoes of silk and tea from China and Hong Kong. Local passenger steamers *toot-toot*ed their departures for Victoria, Portland, Seattle, Nanaimo or Tacoma. And at the village on the North Shore, there were always Chief Joe, Mary Agnes, Matthias and Emma, happy to admire Pauline's paddling skills and teach her Chinook words and phrases.

One of Pauline's favourite destinations was a small basin of water tucked into the lee of Stanley Park. The cove was known to locals as Coal Harbour, since it was close to a CPR coalyard. "I always resented that jarring, unattractive name," Pauline later wrote, explaining that she preferred to call it Lost Lagoon. "This was just to please my own fancy, for as that perfect summer month drifted on, the ever-restless tides left the harbour devoid of water at my favourite canoeing hour, and my pet idling place was lost for many days." Pauline had almost abandoned poetry by now, but the timeless beauty of Lost Lagoon inspired verses reminiscent of the poetry she wrote in the 1880s, during her Muskoka trips:

> O! Lure of the Lost Lagoon,—
> I dream to-night that my paddle blurs
> The purple shade where the seaweed stirs,
> I hear the call of the singing firs
> In the hush of the golden moon.

The canoe expeditions were light relief: Pauline spent most of her time bent over the table in her hotel room, writing on lined legal-size pads in her flowing, forward-leaning script. The following year, 1909, *The Boys' World* would carry eleven stories by her, and eight more pieces would appear in *The Mother's Magazine*. Most of these were probably written during her summer sojourn in Vancouver during 1908. Most followed the successful and conventional formulas she had already developed for each outlet: plucky and truthful heroes for *The Boys' World*, women whose lives were centred on husbands and children for *The Mother's Magazine*.

There were two particularly significant pieces of writing that Pauline produced during this period. The first was her four-part series entitled "My Mother," which appeared between April and July 1909. It is a less than trustworthy memoir, but as critics Carole Gerson and Veronica Strong-Boag point out, it slotted easily into "the magazine's ideology of the sanctity of motherhood, the romance of the happy family, and the importance of good mothering to the future well-being of the nation." It was also Pauline's attempt, as she settled down and reviewed her own life, to make sense of the stresses she had faced as the product of a mixed marriage. In her account of her parents' relationship, she pretended that such a marriage was a metaphor for a larger ideal: that Canada might be strengthened by a union of European settlers and Indians in which the traditions of both peoples were respected. By the time she wrote "My Mother," it was obvious that the ideal had been shattered. One of the most popular poetry collections

*Hastings Street: the streetcars are on the "wrong"
side of the road because Vancouver used the British
system of driving on the left until 1922.*

published in 1908 was *The Empire Builders and Other Poems* by
Robert J. C. Stead. It included "The Mixer," a description of how the
country itself turned immigrants into Canadians. The poem had an
ominous last line:

In the city, on the prairie, in the forest, in the camp,
In the mountain-clouds of color, in the fog-white river-
   damp,
From Atlantic to Pacific, from the Great Lakes to the Pole,
I am mixing strange ingredients into a common whole;
Every hope shall build upon me, every heart shall be my
   own,
The ambitions of my people shall be mine, and mine alone;
Not a sacrifice so great but they will gladly lay it down
When I turn them out Canadians—all but the yellow and
   brown.

The second significant story that Pauline wrote during these weeks is "The Legend of the Two Sisters," which appeared in the January 1909 issue of *The Mother's Magazine*. This is the story of how the twin mountain peaks known to Europeans as the Lions of Vancouver received their Indian name, the Two Sisters. The legend is about two beautiful young sisters who persuade their father to end a brutal war with the Indian people farther up the BC coast. The legend, as Pauline recorded it for *The Mother's Magazine*, had been told to her by "a quaint old Indian mother"—almost certainly Mary Agnes, Chief Joe's wife. Pauline had quickly become fascinated by the west coast legends that she heard in the home of her Squamish friends. She loved listening to the sibilant accents and singsong rhythms of her new friends, experts in the art of storytelling, just as she had once loved listening to Iroquois elders. Pauline's growing determination to settle in Vancouver was fed by her discovery of this goldmine of Indian legend. Perhaps the ideal of harmonious co-existence between Europeans and Indians had been shattered, but that was no reason for Indian culture to vanish.

Chief Joe Capilano was not the only friend Pauline rediscovered on the west coast. Bertha Jean Thompson was the young woman who had joined Pauline and her friends for their 1903 camping holiday on Stony Lake. In 1906, Jean, who had graduated from teachers college, had moved to British Columbia and was living in a rooming house in New Westminster, where she gave piano lessons. She also wrote a column called "Up and Down the Pacific Coast" for her father's newspaper back in Thorold. Now thirty-two, Jean was an outgoing, impulsive young woman with thick, curly hair and clear brown eyes. She hovered between the self-assured independence of a "New

Bertha Jean Thompson, a young piano teacher from Thorold, Ontario, was a close friend of Pauline's in Vancouver.

Woman" and the insecure loneliness of a daughter far from home who missed friends, family and familiar surroundings. "Oh! The rain! It rains, and rains, and rains," she wrote in a 1906 column. "Yet when one beautiful day comes everyone forgets the rain and damp cold, and says, 'How is this for the coast? People in the east haven't got this weather to boast of, have they?'" When she read a newspaper announcement that Pauline was giving a recital in Fairview Hall, she immediately took the bus from New Westminster into Vancouver. After the performance, she called on the star at the Hotel Vancouver. It was an exuberant reunion: Pauline was as happy to see her young friend as Jean was to meet her heroine.

In a column published in August 1908, Jean described to her Thorold readers an incident in Pauline's life that suggests that the Hotel Vancouver—the CPR's flagship hotel on the Pacific coast—did not quite live up to its claims to being a "first class establishment." One evening, Pauline asked the head waiter to leave her supper on a tray in her room, because she would be out late. But when she returned to the hotel and lifted the napkin covering the tray, she found only three empty plates, plus a salad in a covered dish. "I was amazed," Pauline told Jean. "I concluded that, as I always left my door unlocked, some man, a little tipsy, had entered and eaten my supper, but had not cared for salads." The waiter, when summoned, was as flummoxed by this as she was. Pauline ordered a second dinner, and when she had eaten it, she went to bed. Then, she told Jean, "as soon as I quieted down I saw two enormous rats climb over the window-sill from the tin ledge outside. They scampered to the couch, and raced round and round, smelling where the tray had been, and the mystery of the empty plates was solved."

Despite the hotel rats, Pauline's six-week vacation did her good. She put on weight, and the bounce returned to her stride. According to a reporter from the *Vancouver World* who spoke to her in July, she radiated "the cheeriest optimism." She still tired easily, and when she was tired her sparkling grey eyes would sag and her lips, once full and smiling, would settle into a thin grim line. But she had regained the energy she needed to go on the road again. She wanted to do one last tour and earn enough money to set up a home in Vancouver.

On August 14, 1908, Pauline left Vancouver and joined Walter for more engagements through the fall in Ontario and Pennsylvania. After spending Christmas with Kate Washington and her husband in Hamilton, Pauline started the slow trek back to the Pacific. She and Walter stopped at the little Prairie towns strung out along the CPR rails, giving what had now become their "well-loved" (and rather threadbare) programme to audiences who had often seen her three or four times already. By May 6, 1909, Pauline was back in Vancouver, where she announced in the Pender Auditorium that she intended to settle in the city. The final Johnson–McRaye concert was given in Kamloops in July.

"Dink is fat, conceited and fur-lined," Pauline had written to Archie Morton, "and hoping to get wedded." As Walter McRaye's nine-year partnership with Pauline drew to its close, the young man adroitly fulfilled his hopes and at the same time recruited a new partner. In 1909, Lucy Webling had finished her last tour in Britain and crossed the ocean and the continent. She joined her sister Rosalind in Vancouver, where Ros's husband, George Edwards, was making a name for himself as a photographer. On August 24, the McRaye–Webling wedding took place in Vancouver's smartest church, Christ Church Cathedral at Georgia and Burrard. Walter waited at the altar with his best man, an actor named Jeremy Howard. Lucy looked like Lillie Langtry in her prime as she sashayed up the aisle. She wore an ivory silk gown with a huge hat swathed in chiffon and trailing long white ostrich plumes that she had brought from London. She was given away by her brother-in-law. After a three-day honeymoon in Victoria, the newlyweds immediately started a new tour. It was not

Lucy Webling and Walter McRaye on their wedding day, August 24, 1909.

a marriage made in heaven: Walter was more interested in Lucy as a stage partner than as a wife. Within a few years the couple would grow apart, and in 1924 Lucy made the definitive break and returned to England. But for now, the "McRaye Company" had got its show on the road.

With Walter's departure, an important chapter in Pauline's life had ended. After more than twenty years of recitals, she had finally fulfilled her mother's dearest wish: she had left the stage. The poet may have felt a spurt of nostalgia for all the adventures—the Cariboo Trail, Lady Ripon's drawing room, the energetic applause from British, Newfoundland and Canadian audiences. But Pauline's overwhelming sensation must have been relief. She no longer had the energy for constant travelling; she probably had suspicions that her declining health and stamina were due to something more threatening than the passage of time. She certainly recognized that the future for touring companies was precarious. Many of the mining towns in the Kootenays that had welcomed her so ecstatically were now bust. Greenwood, Sandon, Ferguson, Trout Lake, Moyie and Fairview were already ghost towns, their shafts abandoned. And there was new competition for audiences: moving pictures had arrived. Montreal already boasted seventy movie houses and Toronto had eighteen. More were opening in every town of any size across Canada. A Toronto city official, reported the *Toronto Star*, dismissed their spread as "a fad." Most people thought that the fad was unstoppable, and some even predicted that the new moving pictures sounded the death knell for live shows.

Pauline rented a two-bedroom apartment in a newly built, modest apartment block at 1117 Howe Street, two blocks from the Cathedral. The porter at the Hotel Vancouver loaded her steamer trunk and travelling valises into a cab for her. Kate Washington dispatched to Vancouver all the furniture and household articles that had been stored in her Hamilton basement ever since Emily Johnson's death. For the first time in her life, Pauline arranged a home for herself. The round oak table and chair from Chiefswood went into the sitting room and

1117 Howe Street, Vancouver:
Pauline's apartment on
the second floor was her
first permanent home
since she left Brantford.

became her work area. Emily's green china tea set, cut-glass sherry decanter and silver bonbon dishes were displayed in a glass-fronted cabinet. A smaller table, two chairs and all the household china and cutlery were arranged in the kitchen, where Pauline ate her meals. She hung her gowns and Indian costume in the larger bedroom behind a screen on which she had glued pictures of animals and Indian artefacts. She made up the second bedroom (which was so small that she endowed it with the splendid title "the steamer state room") for visitors.

Within days, Pauline knew the occupants of the other three apartments in the building. Buddy, the three-year-old son of her neighbours, was soon turning up at her door with bouquets of dandelions for "Johnson," as he called her. She took delight in the unfamiliar pleasures of housekeeping: she washed the curtains, polished her furniture, scrubbed the floor. She acquired a big black cat, which she named Tillicum (the Chinook word for "friend") and to which she fed a rarified diet of condensed cream, chops and sardines. And she began to entertain. "Bert usually dines with me on Sundays," she wrote to Archie Morton in November. "Did you even know that I am a crackerjack of a cook? Not a bad accomplishment when one lives in 'ranching' rooms as I do." Pauline's pride in her domestic skills amused her guests. "She was more genuinely pleased," noted one, "with a delighted remark over a grilled steak, a perfectly roasted chicken or a beautifully assembled salad than she was over a compliment paid to a new poem."

Now that she was no longer on the road, Pauline's gift for making friends blossomed. There was Rosalind Edwards, Walter's sister-in-law, who would call round for tea with her three children. Pauline often joined the Edwardses for dinner. There was Eileen Maguire, an Irish contralto who had given a performance at the Hotel Vancouver when Pauline had been a guest there the previous summer and who sometimes went on tour with Walter and Lucy. There was not only Bert Cope, turning up each week to sample Pauline's cooking, but also his mother, Margery. There were several women writers anxious to make the celebrated Mohawk poet welcome in their city. One of the most prominent was Isabel Ecclestone Mackay. Mackay was an Ontario-born poet whose work had appeared in major Canadian and American magazines and whose first book of verse, *Between the Lights*, had been published in 1904. Mackay, who settled in Vancouver in the same year as Pauline, was already a member of the Canadian Society of Authors and the Canadian Women's Press Club. Like Pauline, she revelled in the exuberant go-ahead style of Vancouver. Sights that would have shocked Toronto, such as women driving cars, women entering restaurants alone, women with bare heads, and female bylines in the newspapers, were commonplace here. Mackay was eager to start some sort of club for literary women.

One particular visitor to No. 1117 Howe Street had a special place in Pauline's heart. Jean Thompson loved her visits to Pauline's apartment, "where we enjoyed delectable dinners prepared by her in her little kitchenette." On warm days the two women would go off on canoe expeditions together in the light canoe that had been presented to Pauline by her Capilano friends. Pauline took to calling the young woman "Tommy," while Jean referred to Pauline as "Johnlums." The affection was mutual, and each woman gained a great deal from the friendship. For Jean, Pauline was "a woman of the world. She taught me in many ways, steering me clear of some things that could have been pitfalls to a girl alone in a big city—she would have been a glorious mother." For Pauline, Jean was a source of energy and laughter— particularly when she herself felt weary. "Sometimes I told her what I thought," Jean would recall in later years, "and she would listen with a funny look in her eyes, then 'Tommy' she would say . . . 'You're a source of continual amusement to me.'"

Jean took Walter's place in Pauline's life: she was an energetic comrade with whom Pauline could fool around. Where Pauline and Walter had had a menagerie of imaginary companions—elves, Felix the Bug, the cat called Dave Dougherty—Pauline and Jean could summon an invisible army of moods, to which they gave ridiculous names. Pauline's *alter ego* was "the Bug," a battle-scarred character who embodied Pauline's sense of independence. ("The Bug says, John, males is false, very false—don't you trust 'em, and the Bug knows," Pauline wrote to Jean.) Jean's contribution to Pauline's world of imaginary companions was "Belty," a character who had emerged in a dream. Belty was a young girl in a shirtwaist and cloth skirt with a leather belt and strong cowhide boots. The two women often used "the Bug" and "Belty" as mouthpieces for their own thoughts. It is unlikely that the friendship ever strayed beyond the conventions of a close female rapport, but Pauline was clearly the dominant partner, while Jean played up her own vulnerability. And there was an anti-male frisson to their delicious alliance.

One day when Jean was visiting Pauline, they were joined by another of Pauline's "regulars": Chief Joe Capilano. The bond between the genial old chief and the poet was stronger than ever. Pauline treated Joe with a deference quite unlike the gushing respect she accorded to powerful men whose help she had needed in the past—Clifford Sifton, Prime Minister Laurier or Lord Strathcona. With the Squamish chief, Pauline was quietly reverential. As a child, she had been taught to listen politely to the elders of the Six Nations, to respect their wisdom and their experience. For Pauline, an afternoon with Joe Capilano was like an afternoon with her grandfather, John "Smoke" Johnson.

Moreover, her relationship with Chief Joe gave Pauline a second chance. She had never forgiven herself for not listening to Smoke Johnson's tales of the past—the Iroquois legends handed down from one generation to the next, the tales of Mohawk bravery in battles against the American rebels. The Squamish people had a treasury of fables and stories at least as rich as that of the Mohawk people. And Joe Capilano was happy to share it. He would settle himself on Pauline's couch and sit silently for a while. Pauline would welcome him, offer him refreshment, then sit in silence with him. With a little prompting, he might begin a story in his halting mix of Chinook and English. He took his time, smiling to himself as he let a few sentences lie between them before embarking on the next part of the story. "She always let him tell the legends in his own way," Jean Thompson noted. "If she needed to make a note to assist her memory she went into the kitchen on the pretense of getting a drink of water and there jotted down the note. Never did she do this before her guest."

Pauline was fascinated by Chief Joe's stories. They included magic talismans, powerful medicine men, potent dreams and respect for the indwelling spirit of every waterfall, mountain, rock and tree. They invoked the divinity of Sagalie Tyee, who "moulded the mountains, and patterned the mighty rivers where the salmon run, because of His love for His Indian children, and His wisdom for their necessities." They spoke of the value attached to daughters, girls and women in Indian society. The spirituality, humour and beliefs embodied in the legends resonated with a woman who had spent her early years on a reserve, amongst people for whom magic and metaphors were important. Pauline the writer knew that Squamish folklore was a precious source of material for short stories. Pauline the woman embraced its deeper significance as a mythology that gave meaning to life. A premonition of her own mortality had begun to haunt her; she drew solace from the timeless spiritual wisdom offered by Squamish mythology.

The immediate challenge for Pauline, now that she had abandoned recitals, was to earn her living. All she had to rely on was her own pen; she had already taken all the rents due from Chiefswood, and neither Allen nor Evelyn could help her. She wrote to the Musson Book Company in Toronto offering them a complete collection of all her poetry, including the poems that had appeared in *The White Wampum* and *Canadian Born* (both of which were out of print) and all her fugitive work: "The demand for my complete works I find constantly growing, but the public does not appear to care for a 'selected' edition. They want one big volume of *all* I have ever written." She also offered Musson "a book of short stories for boys . . . the schools and Sunday Schools are crying loudly for boys' books." But she knew that reprints of her existing work would yield little income and that she had to keep writing. *The Boys' World* and *The Mother's Magazine*, the two magazines published in Elgin, Illinois, provided a steady market. Chief Joe Capilano's stories were an invaluable new source for her literary endeavours. But she needed additional outlets. So she made an appointment with Walter C. Nichol, owner of the *Daily Province*, the Vancouver newspaper with the most interesting weekend magazine. Nichol had attended one of her recitals and was more than happy to receive "Princess Tekahionwake," as he thought of her. He suggested that the magazine's editor, Lionel Makovski, join them.

Makovski was a young Englishman who had only recently immigrated to Canada and started work in Vancouver. At first, he was polite but distant with the shabbily dressed, middle-aged woman in his boss's office. Vancouver seemed to be full of lady authors who wanted to get their family histories, children's stories or nature poems into his columns. But his attitude changed as soon as he heard Pauline's name. Unlike Nichol, he thought not of the recitalist who had criss-crossed Canada but of the byline under an extraordinary piece he had read a couple of years earlier in the *Daily Express*. Several of his journalist friends in London had remarked on its originality. "Not 'A Pagan in St. Paul's'?" he exclaimed. Pauline's face shone with pleasure. "The same," she said. "The best piece of prose I ever wrote. How did you come across it?"

Nichol interrupted. "Miss Johnson has a story you might like to use for the weekly. I've got to go . . . excuse me, Miss Johnson."

Pauline proceeded to tell the astonished young editor her circumstances when she wrote her piece for the *Daily Express*: "I was giving recitals in London salons. In my Mohawk regalia . . . I must have been somewhat startling. But if I appealed to the audiences as a primitive from Canada, you can imagine how they impressed me amid their Victorian surroundings." With a charming smile, the poet moved quickly on to the purpose of her visit. Handing him a copy of "The Legend of the Two Sisters," the story that had recently appeared in *The Mother's Magazine*, she asked him if he could use it in his magazine. If he liked it, she could write more stories in a similar vein— "My friend Chief Joe Capilano is an untapped reservoir of such legends which should be preserved."

Lionel Makovski did like "The Legend of the Two Sisters," which appeared in the *Daily Province Magazine* in April 1910 under the title

"The True Legend of Vancouver's Lions." It was the first of twenty-one pieces by Pauline that appeared in the magazine that year, most of which were Squamish legends. Pauline had listened carefully to the tales told by both the old chief and his wife, tales characterized by the rhythms and repetitions of myths sustained within an oral tradition. She had reshaped them into the kind of linear narratives that would appeal to the *Daily Province Magazine*'s readers. Most were illustrated with photographs taken by George Edwards, Walter's brother-in-law.

"Amongst the red nations of America," Pauline wrote in "The Deep Waters: A Rare Squamish Legend," which appeared in September 1910, "I doubt if any two tribes have the same ideas regarding the Flood." She went on to describe how "my royal old tillicum" had arrived to see her one cold, wet winter day. "Woman-like, I protested with a thousand contradictions in my voice, that he should venture out to see me on such a day. It was, 'Oh! Chief, I am so glad to see you!' and it was, 'Oh! Chief, why didn't you stay at home on such a day—your poor throat will suffer.' But I soon had quantities of hot tea for him, and the huge cup my own father always used was his—as long as the Sagalie Tyee allowed his dear feet to wander my way."

Pauline's article continues with an account of how Chief Joe settled down, then hinted that he had a story to tell. "Immediately I foresaw the coming legend, so crept into the shell of monosyllables." The old man "plunged directly into the tradition, with no preface save a comprehensive sweep of his wonderful hands towards my wide window, against which the rains were beating. 'It was after a long, long time of this—this rain. The mountain-streams were swollen, the rivers choked, the sea began to rise—and yet it rained: for weeks and weeks it rained.' He ceased speaking, while the shadows of centuries gone crept into his eyes. Tales of the misty past always inspired him."

Chief Joe's version of the story of the Flood told how his people had climbed to the top of the tallest mountain as the rains fell. There the men had felled a huge tree, and "toiled over its construction into the most stupendous canoe the world has ever known. . . . Meanwhile, the women also worked at a cable—the largest, the longest, the strongest that Indian hands and teeth had ever made." As the rain fell and the waters continued to rise, the Indians lifted into the vast canoe every single child in the band; "not one single baby was overlooked." The bravest, most handsome man and the mother of the youngest baby in the camp were selected as guardians of the children. One end of the cable was secured to the canoe and the other end to a boulder, "a vast immovable rock as firm as the foundations of the world—for might not the canoe, with its priceless freight, drift out, far out, to sea, and when the water subsided might not this ship of safety be leagues and leagues beyond the sight of land on the storm-driven Pacific?"

Chief Joe described how the canoe was set afloat, how the doomed adults drowned, how for days and days there was "only a world of water." Finally, one morning at sunrise, "a speck floated on the breast of the waters." It was the summit of Mount Baker. The young man cut the cable and paddled to dry land. There the two guardians made a new camp and built new lodges, and "the little children grew and thrived, and lived and loved, and the earth was repeopled by them."

In Pauline's article, Chief Joe concludes with the words, "'The Squamish say that in a gigantic crevice half-way to the crest of Mount Baker may yet be seen the outlines of an enormous canoe; but I have never seen it myself.'"

Then Pauline herself left her readers with the image of the storyteller and his scribe, in quiet harmony: "He ceased speaking with that far-off cadence in his voice with which he always ended a legend, and for a long time we both sat in silence listening to the rains that were still beating against the window."

The same year, in addition to the twenty-one contributions she sent to Lionel Makovski at the *Daily Province Magazine*, Pauline produced fifteen pieces for *The Boys' World* and eight pieces for *The Mother's Magazine*. She had never worked so hard, or written so much, in her life. Such productivity required a strict routine. Pauline would rise at 7:15, eat breakfast and attend to domestic details until 9:00, then write all morning and (if necessary) into the afternoon. One week, she boasted to Jean, she managed to write a total of 12,500 words—"9,500 for the Elgin people at $6.00 for M [thousand] if it is all accepted and 3,000 for the Province, bringing me in about ten dollars. So, if everything is accepted, as I am pretty confident it will be, I shall net over sixty dollars for my week's work. . . . Today for a change I cut out a duck skirt for myself. . . . I am fair sick of a pen and the sight of ink."

Most weeks, however, she could not sustain that pace. She now admitted to herself that there was something seriously wrong. She was often overcome with fatigue. Shooting pains would paralyze her right arm and shoulder, preventing her from working. She was losing weight, and her face was drawn. Since the near-fatal bout of erysipelas in 1901, she had avoided doctors—life on the road had meant she had little time to find one, anyway. Sometime in 1910, she steeled herself to find a physician in Vancouver and consult him about something she had been trying to ignore for three or four years: a lump in her right breast. By the time she sought help, her breast was already swollen and uncomfortable.

Dr. Thomas Ransom Biggar Nelles was only twenty-six years old when Pauline found her way to his office. A graduate of McGill Medical School, he had done some post-graduate studies at the New York Skin and Cancer Hospital, then set up a practice in Vancouver as a general practitioner. For Pauline, his greatest appeal was that he came from Brantford, where his father had been a missionary amongst the Iroquois. "My doctor is a sincere boy," she wrote to Frank Yeigh. "His mother was a Miss Biggar of Brantford and I can remember her as a very beautiful young lady when I was a child. She was a great favourite with my parents. Dr. Nelles is . . . without doubt the most skillful medical man I ever had attend me." It helped that Dr. Nelles was the only physician in Vancouver with any training in the treatment of cancer—although that was not saying much. Treatment of any form of cancer was rudimentary at the start of the twentieth century, and breast cancer was particularly neglected because it involved a part of the body that was never discussed in "polite circles."

The only treatment for breast cancer in Pauline's day was surgical removal of the breast. Mastectomies had been performed on women with breast tumours since the late-eighteenth century. In 1812, the English novelist Fanny Burney, then aged fifty, underwent an agonizing operation to remove her right breast. The entry in her diary describing the seventeen-and-a-half-minute procedure is one of the very few memoirs of the brutal surgery that was the standard treatment for the next century. With a cambric handkerchief over her face and only a "wine cordial to drink," Fanny was fully conscious throughout the operation. As soon as her surgeon's "dreadful steel" was plunged into her flesh, "I began a scream that lasted unintermittingly during the whole time of the incision—and I almost marvel that it rings not in my ears still, so excruciating was the agony." Fanny's lump was probably not malignant: she survived for a further twenty-eight years after her mastectomy. Most women died within months of the surgical torture, often as a result of the surgery rather than of the cancer. Radical surgery rarely did anything more than delay death, since few surgeons understood that the cancer had likely spread to the lymph system.

By the time Pauline consulted Tom Nelles, her cancer had almost certainly metastasized. A century after Fanny Burney's excruciating agony, the only treatment choice available to Pauline Johnson was a similar operation, albeit with improved anaesthesia. Alternative medical therapies (caustic pastes and poultices) had proven ineffective, and radiation and chemotherapy still lay years in the future. Dr. Nelles told Pauline that a mastectomy was necessary but warned her that the outlook was not good.

"One day," recalled Jean Thompson in a memoir of Pauline that she wrote in 1931, "I was waiting for her to dress and she came out from behind her big screen with one bare shoulder. In a panic I saw that one breast was gone. Too ill to speak, I dropped back into the chair. We looked at each other and as she passed she touched ever so lightly the hair on my temple. 'Tommy's pretty hair,' she said softly. This was demonstrative for her but we both understood. She knew her days were numbered." But Pauline rarely wept in front of Jean, and she never complained of her pain to her friends. Her mother's training in stoic self-control and her father's example of relentless commitment to purpose sustained her.

Within a few weeks of hearing the bad news about her own health, Pauline suffered another blow. Chief Joe Capilano passed away in his sleep on March 10, 1910, a victim of tuberculosis, the "white man's disease" that had killed so many of his people. Chief Joe's funeral was held a week later, at the little white church in the Squamish village. A huge crowd of Indians and non-natives gathered to pay their respects to such a well-known and respected man. Matthias and Emma walked behind the coffin, carrying photographs of King Edward VII and Queen Alexandra. A Union Jack fluttered in the breeze outside the church.

Afterwards, the band elders took Chief Joe's ceremonial cloak, belt and medals from the coffin and adorned his twenty-five-year-old son Matthias with them to signify that he was the new chief. Slowly, Matthias picked up the tall fox fur hat himself and placed it on his head. Then Chief Joe's coffin was taken in a hearse from the church to the Indian cemetery on the hillside above Burrard Inlet. The Indian mission band led the funeral cortège, and two more Union Jacks, carried by two more chiefs, followed the hearse. After a lengthy oration by Chief Joseph of the Fraser River, the coffin was lowered into the ground. Pauline, who acted as mistress of ceremonies at the chief's house, helped Joe's widow, Mary Agnes, receive Indian delegations from all over the province. Each visitor was presented with a piece of the frozen fish that was piled up like cordwood against an outside wall. Pauline stood all day, drinking strong black tea to sustain herself.

Pauline's editor, Lionel Makovski, had stood close to Pauline at Chief Joe's graveside. Like so many young men before him, from Hector Charlesworth to Bert Cope, Lionel had become one of Pauline's devoted admirers. He was impressed with her prose and poetry, bewitched by the magic that she could still exert. He grinned like a small boy when Pauline referred to him as the "dearest of all men." He never forgot the words she murmured as the earth rattled onto the coffin lid: "I'm coming; I'm coming, I'm coming. . . ." Conscious of Makovski's gaze, she turned to him and said quietly, "It is one thing of which we are certain, isn't it?"

Not long after the funeral, Jean Thompson visited Pauline at Howe Street. Pauline was still locked in sadness as she described to her young friend the events of that cold, grey March day—the eerie chanting of the inconsolable women, the tearful faces of the members of the Indian Mission Band, the white lilies on the coffin as it was lowered into the ground. "When everything was over," Pauline told Jean, "the young chief turned and went away alone. At the edge of the hill I saw him drop to his knees and lift his hands to the sky. 'Oh, my father, my father!' he cried. Never have I seen anything so dramatic in my life."

Pauline shuddered at the memory, then spoke again. "It takes me back to my father's death—that was the last time the death cry was sent down the Grand River. It is sent only when a great chief dies."

Jean stared with distress at her grief-struck friend. "It was a cruel blow to her when he died," she said later, "It seemed now as though she were in a pit of Stygian blackness. For weeks gloom pressed her down."

20

SAILING INTO
THE CLOUD LAND
1910–1913

ROM then on, Pauline's state of health was unpredictable.
Sometimes callers at her Howe Street flat would find her inca-
pacitated by pain, or drowsy with the morphine that Dr. Nelles
gave her to control it. Other times she was almost her old self. "Her
vitality was astounding," reported Jean Thompson. "At times I feared
she would not last a month, and the next time I called she would be
out shopping." Throughout the ordeal, Pauline made it clear that she
did not want to discuss her condition, and she would not ask for help.
She made an effort to look her best, hiding the tendons that jutted
from her thin neck with starched white collars and a flamboyant
feather boa. She refused to be a victim, always trying to put the spotlight on others instead.

"Tommy my dear, your letter has just come," she wrote to Jean
Thompson, after the latter admitted in a sad little missive to feeling
wretchedly homesick.

> Now you are to put your toothbrush in your boot leg and
> come over to me on Monday for a nice two or three days
> visit and get rid of those double-barrelled glooms of yours.
> You need a change. We'll eat breakfast in the kitchen and
> have dinner in state at my round table. You can't come Sat-
> urday, you say, and Sunday I have an engagement. So you
> show up Monday any time. Tell your pupils to go to Jericho,
> that you are not well enough to teach, and come over to me.

The [McRayes] went two weeks ago so their steamer state-room is ready for you. I have an engagement for, I think, Tuesday night. The [Copes] are taking me to see David Warfield in "The Music Master." It is the best thing that has ever come out of New York, and you won't mind my trotting off to it with them, will you? The rooms are yours while you are here and you may write or read or do anything you like. Go out and come in—make tea—do anything and everything so long as you make yourself at home and feel happy. Bring an old gown as I go out rain or shine and get my skirts wet every day; and you'll come with me. It is the only way to chase the glooms away—go out, no matter what the weather. Let me know when to expect you and I'll be ready. Love ever and always.

Thine, "John."

For as long as possible, Pauline stuck to her own prescription. An expedition from her apartment to Stanley Park was part of her daily routine. The gaunt woman bundled up in an old-fashioned black cloth coat became a familiar figure as she walked through the West End towards the densely forested acres at the tip of the peninsula. The scent of cedar on the salty breeze as she stood by the shore or the rich, loamy smell of ferns and damp black earth when she strolled below the towering firs invigorated her. Most of all, in the summer she loved to look at Grouse Mountain and the towering peaks beyond, shrouded in the smoke of forest fires or the midsummer haze of pearly purple. Ethel Wilson, a young teacher who dreamed of being a novelist, recalled Pauline's "sad beauty" in those years: "she was ill, walking very slowly and lost in sombre thought." Jack Scott, a future *Maclean's* magazine writer, remembered her "leaning over the guard-rail near Siwash Rock [in Stanley Park] while the tide was out, always alone. Stoic and curiously dignified, watching the gulls."

On days when she felt her strength fail, Pauline would hire an open carriage to drive round Stanley Park. One evening, she recognized an old admirer from Brantford, Harry Weir, strolling through the park with his fourteen-year-old son, Harold. Father and son clambered into her carriage and sat on each side of her, holding her hands. As the shadows lengthened and the sun sank towards the horizon, Pauline lifted her eyes to the fading light and recited snatches of her poetry. Despite the lines of pain on her face, her magic remained undimmed. "As we parted from her," young Harold would always recall, "my father kissed her, whereupon I was overwhelmed with hobbledehoy embarrassment."

Faced with Pauline's determination to carry on as though nothing was wrong, her friends colluded in her denial. Mary Agnes, Joe Capilano's widow, would paddle across Burrard Inlet and meet Pauline at the north end of Howe Street for a canoe outing. Chief Matthias continued his father's habit of coming over and relating to her his people's legends. Pauline, now an acknowledged champion of the Squamish people, wrote a letter on his behalf to Sir Wilfrid Laurier in July 1910, asking the Prime Minister to receive Chief Matthias when he visited Vancouver later that month. She explained that the young chief wanted to "'shake hands with the government'—his own expression, and to assure you personally of his allegiance to His Majesty King George." When she was able to tell Chief Matthias that the Prime Minister had consented to see him, the young man's face underwent "a wonderful transformation from anxiety to delight."

Lionel Makovski, who was already a regular tea-time visitor, took to transcribing her stories as she dictated them, if she was in too much pain to write them herself. Another writer for the *Daily Province Magazine*, Isabel MacLean (who wrote under the pen name "Alexandra"), quietly activated support for Pauline within Vancouver's literary and social elite. Isabel had all the right connections; well-known as a journalist, she was also the daughter of Vancouver's first mayor. Before Pauline knew what was happening, she had been adopted by both the newly formed Vancouver branch of the Canadian Women's Press Club (of which both Isabel MacLean and Isabel Ecclestone Mackay were founding members) and by the Vancouver chapter of the Imperial Order of the Daughters of the Empire. Pauline was invited to speak at the first annual luncheon of the Women's Press Club, while the Vancouver IODE declared itself "the Pauline Johnson Chapter." Both these women's organizations, as well as the

Women's Canadian Club, would play a crucial role in supporting Pauline through the difficult times that lay ahead.

Fresh air and good friends could banish "the glooms" only so far: Pauline was still under constant pressure to earn her living. She gave a handful of recitals, usually with the Irish contralto Eileen Maguire since she was not strong enough to sustain an entire evening herself. By 1911, however, public performances were beyond her. She watched for poetry-writing competitions in the papers, but was rarely successful. ("I see a Sapperton man got *The World* contest prize, $250.00," she wrote to Jean Thompson. "I think I shall try the next one. I don't suppose he needed the money, do you?") With Lionel Makovski's help, she managed to produce a few more pieces for the *Daily Province Magazine*.

Jean Thompson continued to visit frequently, cheering Pauline up with anecdotes about her leaden-fingered piano pupils and her landlady's Chinese houseboy. She knew that Pauline's financial situation was dire but that the older woman was too proud to accept handouts. Pauline's apartment was often freezing since the kitchen range was "one of those diabolical quarter-in-the-slot contrivances" that regularly ran out of money. Jean found a surreptitious way to help Pauline. She would quietly leave a pile of shiny new quarters on a shelf by the kitchen door. They always disappeared. "Once, when I dropped into her apartment, Pauline was ill in bed and the gasman was reading the metre in the kitchen," Jean Thompson wrote in a later memoir. The gasman took $13.75 from the range, mainly in Jean's shiny new coins. One coin, however, was worn and black. Pauline suddenly asked Jean, "Have you a quarter?" When Jean produced the coin, Pauline asked her to give it to the gasman. Jean retrieved from him the black quarter, which was covered with a coat of shoe polish, and gave it back to Pauline. "It's the last money my mother ever gave me," Pauline explained, then turned her face into the pillow and heaved with terrible sobs.

Pauline's spirits rose whenever her finances received a boost. One day she told Jean with a chuckle, "Now Tommy, I've got some money in from the estate—Chiefswood, you know—and I'm going to pay my bills. Listen, and you'll have some fun. I'm going to phone each merchant [and tell him] that I want to settle my bill but am not well enough to go out. I'll thank them for their courtesy in waiting so long and ask them if they'll be kind enough to send their collector around this week. They'll all say that it doesn't matter at all, that any time will do—but every one will be here inside of an hour." Events unfolded as Pauline had predicted.

Such lighthearted occasions became increasingly rare. With a sinking heart, Jean watched Pauline decline. Tillicum, Pauline's cat, was killed in a fight with a dog, but Pauline continued to divert attention away from herself and onto her young friend. "Don't get homesick, Tommy dear," she wrote to Jean. "Eat good food and go out every day, rain or shine. Glooms are terrible to fight, as I know to my sorrow, but it can be done." Jean was at Howe Street one day when Dr. Nelles called. While he examined his patient, Jean waited in the kitchenette. Immediately after the physician's departure, Pauline refused to tell Jean what he had said. A few weeks later, she confided that Dr. Nelles had told her that her days were numbered, and that in addition to her cancer she also had a weak heart; "He said I might drop off any time— while I was shopping perhaps—Tommy dear, I do so want to die with my boots on!"

Pauline clung to life, despite the terrible bouts of pain. In March 1911, she celebrated her fiftieth birthday. A few days later, she showed Jean a small receptacle and told her, "I have something here to end it all, if ever I know that I shall linger on to be a burden to others." Yet she never resorted to the suicidal impulse—indeed, she regarded every month she survived as a personal victory. The last poem she wrote took its title, "And He Said, Fight On," from Alfred Lord Tennyson's stirring poem "The Revenge: A Ballad of the Fleet"; its first verse suggests that she saw death as the enemy:

> Time and its ally, Dark Disarmament,
> Have compassed me about,
> Have massed their armies, and on battle bent
> My forces put to rout;
> But though I fight alone, and fall, and die,
> Talk terms of Peace? Not I.

The most difficult moment for Jean Thompson came in late spring 1911, when she broke the news to Pauline that she was to be married. Jean had begun a correspondence the previous year with a young Methodist minister named Harry Stevinson, who was a friend of her younger brother Ted. Born in England, Harry had been a missionary in South Africa before emigrating to Saskatchewan, where he met Ted Thompson. A tall, serious and rather quiet man who loved to read, Harry was captivated by Jean's lively, amusing letters. When he travelled to Vancouver to meet her in person, he fell in love with her; within weeks he proposed. Jean knew that as the wife of a minister in Western Canada, she would live in draughty, badly furnished manses in dusty little towns for the rest of her life, moving every two or three years. But she was now thirty-four, tired of teaching music to tin-eared children and afraid of being dismissed as "an Old Maid." She accepted the proposal from her suitor, who was three years her junior.

"Don't do it, Tommy," Pauline exclaimed, when she heard her friend was to marry a man she termed "a devil-dodger." "You'll always have to play the church organ and you'll never get any thanks for it—and you'll be the target for all the natural meanness of the people every place you go." But Jean's mind was made up. On August 2, 1911, Bertha Jean Thompson married Harry Stevinson at Christ Church Cathedral, where Walter McRaye had married Lucy Webling two years earlier. With rouge and her feather boa to mask the physical effort involved, Pauline stood next to Jean at the altar as one of the witnesses. That evening, Pauline sat at her round writing table and gathered all her strength to write a farewell letter to "Dearest little Tommy." She knew that the friendship between "Tommy" and "Johnlums" was over: from now on, Jean's first loyalty would be to her husband. Drawing on her own experiences, Pauline offered some last advice on the give and take of an ideal partnership. Memories of past lovers—Charlie Drayton, Charles Wuerz, perhaps Michael Mackenzie—and of the sad end of each affair must have flooded in as she willed her emaciated hand to keep moving across the page:

> I want you to know that I am thinking of you very lovingly, that I am hoping for you all that is good, and happy, and

inspiring, and noble, and above all, humanizing. Love is hard to ensnare, hard to appropriate as one's own. I am so sure H. will make you happy if you will only leave yourself gently and sweetly in his hands. You looked so well today, so effectual. I was very proud of my pretty little campmate of years ago, and someway or other I had a certain pride in H., too. He is very real, Tommy dear, very manly and devoted. Try to make him happy as well as yourself. It is a poor rule that does not swing both ways. Good night, dear old girl, and may all the happiness go forth to you that your first girlish idealization longed or wished for—and for my part—this—

By the time the pen reached the bottom of the page, Pauline's arm ached and tears flowed down her face. Her signature was illegible through the blotches.

At the end of the year, the Stevinsons left Vancouver for Coal Creek, a tiny British Columbia community near Fernie, where Harry had been given a church. Within a few years, they had moved several times, they had two sons and Jean had discovered the truth of Pauline's warnings about the perils of being a devil-dodger's wife. Meanwhile, back in Vancouver, Pauline was left unbearably lonely—and desperately worried about money.

But Pauline was not alone. Her gift for friendship, and her national reputation, spurred her friends to action. In September 1911, Isabel MacLean arranged a meeting

After her marriage to Harry Stevinson (right) in 1911, Jean Thompson embarked on life in the isolated and rugged communities of rural British Columbia and Alberta.

between members of the Vancouver Women's Press Club, the Women's Canadian Club and Lionel Makovski and Bernard McEvoy, both of the *Vancouver Daily Province*. She also managed to rope in the Vancouver lawyer Sir Charles Hibbert Tupper, son of Pauline's great admirer, the former Prime Minister. Isabel explained to those present that the great Pauline Johnson was nearly destitute. The poet who had added such lustre to Vancouver's wafer-thin cultural community when she settled in the roughneck city needed their help. Isabel's audience was horrified: most assumed that a writer as well-known as Pauline had a comfortable income from publications. Isabel MacLean proposed that some of Pauline's Squamish legends should be published in book form, with the profits paid into a trust fund to provide an income for Pauline's remaining months. By the time the meeting broke up, a committee had been formed for this purpose, commitments made and a strategy developed to help Pauline without wounding her pride.

As Isabel anticipated, this proposal was welcomed by Pauline. She urged the committee to call the forthcoming book *Legends of the Capilanos*, as a tribute to Chief Joe, but accepted *Legends of Vancouver* as a title on the grounds that it would sell well. The Pauline Johnson Trust Fund sent out appeals to potential donors asking for help with the publishing costs. Sir Wilfrid Laurier contributed $10 after receiving a letter that read, "As we feel that the preservation of the legends she has gotten together is a work of national importance in which all will be interested, we take the liberty of enclosing you a copy of [the Trust Fund circular], as we feel you will be interested in this undertaking not only for its own sake but also on Miss Johnson's account." The first edition of 1,000 copies at $1 a copy, published by Vancouver's Sunset Publishing, appeared in early December. Thanks to the committee's enthusiasm, it promptly sold out. Another thousand copies were ordered.

News of Pauline's ill health spread across Canada. Her friends in Brantford rallied and held a collection for her. Evelyn Johnson scraped together $10 for her sister. "Dear old Ev," Pauline replied, in a warm letter that reflected the gush of relief triggered by financial security:

Your letter with the order for $10 came two days ago, and I want to thank you over and over for it. But *don't* send me any more money, the Brantford people made my testimonial $475.00 so you see that at last I am even with the world here and free from worry. I am so well, going out daily and so busy or I should have written before. . . . My book went out in the book stalls on Saturday at noon hour, and by Wednesday not a copy was left in the publishing house. Spencers (who is like Eatons in Toronto) sold 100 of them last Friday, there never has been such a rush on a holiday book here. Brantford telegraphed for 100 to be sent them, but Mr. Makovski could not let them have *one single copy*, the entire edition is sold out, is it not glorious? I am so tired with people coming here

Pauline, her face etched with pain, and Lucy McRaye on the steps of 1117 Howe Street. A few weeks later, Pauline moved to Bute Street Hospital for round-the-clock care.

with 4 or 5 books for me to autograph day in and day out. The books sell at one dollar and the reviews have been magnificent, all the papers seem to think I have done great things for the city by unearthing its surrounding romance.

Walter McRaye, who had just returned from a tour, presented Pauline with $5. ("I bought a swagger pair of boots with it," she told her sister, which probably exasperated the frugal Eva.) Walter also persuaded Pauline to autograph the next edition of *Legends*, then wrote letters to all Pauline's and his old friends across Canada, urging them to order the autographed copies at the outrageous price of $2 each. Orders flooded in. For the first time in her life, Pauline did not have to worry about money.

But a rush of cheques could not stave off cancer. In March 1912, Pauline's condition deteriorated rapidly and it seemed the end could be only weeks away. She had persistent bronchitis; deep, hoarse, tearing coughing fits left her drained and white. Dr. Nelles and the indefatigable Isabel MacLean decided that the Pauline Johnson Trust Fund should be used to move Pauline into a new private hospital on Bute Street, around the corner from the Howe Street apartment, where she could have round-the-clock nursing. As the days grew longer and the leaves unfurled, Isabel Ecclestone Mackay, Beatrice Nasmyth, Isabel MacLean, Lionel Makovski, Eileen Maguire, Lucy McRaye and Rosalind Edwards took turns sitting with their friend.

Sometimes they would chat with her, read the newspaper to her or support her back when a coughing fit took hold; other times they sat quietly as she slept, wondering whether her shallow breathing would cease as they watched. Her hands lay motionless on the bedspread, curled like claws, knucklebones white under the paper-thin skin. Pauline's room on the second floor was decorated with her most precious possessions—her father's dagger, her Onondaga turtleshell medicine rattle, her silver-backed hairbrush, her costume, including the scarlet blanket used when the Duke of Connaught was made an honorary chief of the Six Nations in 1869. Hyacinths, lilacs and tulips sent by well-wishers crowded the windowsill. But their heavy scent could not smother the sickroom smells of disinfectant, sweat, fear and mortal illness.

"Oh Tommy! All I ask," Pauline had said to Jean Thompson before her friend left Vancouver, "is one more summer to look off at my dream hills." To her friends' astonishment, it seemed her wish would be granted. After hovering close to death for weeks, she started to sit up, eat again and leave her room. Soon she was insisting on her daily walk. "My dear good Yeigh-Man," she wrote in triumph to Frank Yeigh in June, after he had sent her a generous cheque. "I am in hospital, but just now am very well. I go out walking daily and can take many little enjoyments when I am not suffering pain. My splendid young doctor . . . has pulled me up on my feet time and again, over and over, when the whole city has thought I should never be seen again walking its lovely thoroughfares. . . . I have just come through two months of being in bed, much of the time in extreme pain, but here I am, able to walk downtown and in Stanley Park and by English Bay, able to shop and sew and write and laugh and enjoy life for a little while." Her spirit was unquenchable. She signed her letter, "Always your old-time 'star,' E. Pauline Johnson."

By midsummer 1912, orders for *Legends of Vancouver* were pouring into the Pauline Johnson Trust Fund. Some of the subscribers had been contacted directly by McRaye or the trustees; others had read in the newspaper that she was terminally ill. "Pauline Johnson, song bird of the red men, will sing no more," read a brief item in the *Jarvis Record*, an Ontario paper. "Her physicians state that the renowned Indian poetess will never lift a pen again." The illness was not specified, since breast cancer was never mentioned in polite company. Pauline herself observed the taboo. "An organic trouble of my heart and an exceedingly painful complication of the glands have put me on the invalid's list for all the time I am to be here," she explained to Archibald Kains, who had sent a "more than generous cheque" when he heard the news. Pauline and Archie had been out of touch for years; now she was overwhelmed to receive word from him. She was finally able to tell him how grateful she felt for the way he had encouraged her to enjoy art: "You helped me to understand and love the art of

In September 1912, the Governor General, Prince Arthur,
Duke of Connaught, presented medals to Vancouver's
Boy Scouts, then took time to visit Pauline.

painting, in which I was so lacking. . . . I should never have been entertained in the studios of Sir Frederick Leighton, Byrne Jones [Burne-Jones], dear old Mr. Watts, Sir Lawrence Alma Tadema, had you not been the first to make me love pictures."

A sense that the clock was ticking for Pauline added urgency to every visit, every occasion. In September, a royal visitor took time out of his schedule to see the ailing poet. Prince Arthur, Duke of Connaught, had been appointed Governor General of Canada the previous year by his brother Edward VII just before the latter's death. One of the Duke's first official trips, which he undertook with the Duchess, was to Vancouver. En route, he inaugurated the new Connaught Tunnel, which carried the CPR through BC's Selkirk Mountains under the treacherous Rogers Pass. Once in the Pacific city, the vice-regal couple had a busy programme: in addition to a Canadian Club luncheon for

1,000 at the Arena skating rink and tea with the Daughters of the Empire, the Duchess opened the new Connaught Bridge and the Duke presented medals to local Boy Scouts in Hastings Park. But the Duke also spent thirty minutes at Bute Street Hospital with Pauline.

Her sense of occasion undimmed, Pauline insisted that the nurses help her struggle into a splendid new blue and gold kimono which the Women's Press Club had sent round for the occasion. Back in 1869, when she was eight years old, she had watched her father officiate at the ceremony in which the shy nineteen-year-old Prince Arthur was inducted as a chief into the Six Nations. Now an erect, military sixty-two-year-old with a gleaming handlebar moustache, the Duke admired a photo of George Johnson at Pauline's bedside and insisted that he remembered the dashing Mohawk chief from the 1869 ceremony. Pauline pointed out the red blanket draped over the chair on which he was sitting and told him it was the very same blanket on which he had stood on that momentous occasion. Her physical weakness had not diminished her professional savvy. By the time the Duke rejoined his aide-de-camp outside her room, she had secured his permission to dedicate to him her forthcoming volume of collected poems, to be published by Musson.

Two months later, another distinguished visitor arrived at Bute Street Hospital: Charles Mair, the poet whose 1886 drama about the Indian leader Tecumseh had been much admired by Pauline. Mair was shocked to see not the dusky Indian maiden he had always romanticized, but an old woman in pain: "Alas! The change! The worn face, with its sad but welcoming smile, the wasted form, the hand of ice! Never [could I] forget the shock as [my] thoughts ran back to the beautiful and happy girl of former days."

The irony was that now that Pauline was known to be dying, the kind of literary recognition for which she had always yearned suddenly seemed within reach. Demand erupted not only for the stirring poetry written for recitals, but for her whole oeuvre—adventure tales, personal memoirs, lyrical poetry, stories for mothers. By the end of 1912, *Legends of Vancouver* was into its fifth edition. In December, the Musson Book Company brought out a collection of Pauline's poems entitled *Flint and Feather*. It omitted many of

Pauline's verses, and the first edition contained many misprints ("a nightmare to me," Pauline fulminated to a friend). Nevertheless, it rapidly went into a second edition. Its splendid inscription did sales no harm: "To His Royal Highness The Duke of Connaught, Who is Head Chief of the Six Nations Indians, I inscribe this book by his own gracious permission."

Another Toronto publisher, William Briggs, started assembling some of Pauline's contributions to *The Boys' World*, to be published under the title *The Shagganappi* with an introduction by Ernest Thompson Seton. All this excitement galvanized the Ryerson Press into action: an editor there decided that twelve of Pauline's articles and stories (seven of which originally appeared in *The Mother's Magazine*) would make an attractive collection under the title *The Moccasin Maker*. Pauline's new-found literary celebrity was largely thanks to the Vancouver women's organizations that had publicized both her work and her plight. The cosy network of Canadian male writers—Roberts, Carman, Seton, Campbell, Scott—had rarely made any effort on her behalf, although they had constantly "boomed" each other's work. But the growing muscle of New Women lifted Pauline out of poverty.

Throughout the fall of 1912, there were days when Pauline was well enough to sit at a small table in her hospital room and acknowledge those who were working on her behalf. "My dear Mrs. Campbell," she wrote to a friend in Winnipeg in October.

> Three weeks ago last Tuesday you came to pay me a most delightful visit . . . and from all the Prairie towns there drifts in an almost daily evidence of the work you are doing for me. Orders for books and cheques also: I feel it is going to be difficult to find words to thank you for your interest and energy on my behalf. But my good friend I have the old Indian appreciation of a kindness just as strong within my being as if there was not a drop of "white" blood in my veins, and what you are doing sinks deeply within my heart, and some way or other I feel you know how grateful I am, even if my words cannot well express it.

However, Pauline's final months were not untroubled. Around this time, Evelyn Johnson heard that Pauline had taken a turn for the worse. Walter McRaye, in a misplaced respect for family ties, may have dropped Eva a line to tell her of her sister's decline. The sisters had not seen each other since their brother Allen's wedding in 1907, but had stayed in touch through the occasional warm but guarded letter. Now Evelyn felt an immediate obligation to be at her sister's side. She took the train to Vancouver and found a room for herself three blocks from the hospital. "I was living in Philadelphia at the time," she wrote in her memoirs, "but fitted myself out for a trip to Vancouver to be with Pauline. When I went there I found her entirely changed. She had turned against Allen and me. . . . I stood ready to help her, but she resented me."

Never had the starkly different personalities of the two sisters been more evident. Evelyn was appalled by the impact of chronic illness on Pauline's appearance, and refused to pretend that death wasn't imminent. She felt it her duty to insist that Pauline should conserve her strength and concentrate on putting her financial and spiritual affairs in order. She was horrified that such raffish characters as Walter McRaye and Lionel Makovski would sit around Pauline's bed, smoking and laughing. She discovered that Pauline still had debts in the city and had not paid Dr. Nelles's account in full ("I asked the doctor for his account, which I paid and made Pauline very angry"). She insisted on discussing Pauline's will with her because she wanted to ensure that any of their parents' treasures in her possession stayed in the family rather than being scattered amongst friends. Having failed to persuade Pauline that she should go east and die in Brantford, she argued that Pauline should leave instructions that she should be buried in Brantford. Her sister's body, she said, belonged in the cemetery of the little Mohawk Chapel alongside her parents and brother. In particular, as a devout Anglican, Evelyn probably urged Pauline to prepare herself for the end by seeing the Reverend Cecil Owen of Christ Church Cathedral every day.

Evelyn's company and constant nagging had always irritated Pauline. As an adult in a rapidly changing Canada, Evelyn had kept her bearings by clinging to the past—the religion and example of their parents, the happy memories of Chiefswood. These meant a lot to her younger sister, too, but Pauline had grown beyond them and had learned to rely far more on friends than on family. On her good days, she loved the lively company of both her Women's Press Club colleagues and gallant younger men like Walter and Lionel. She felt deeply grateful to them, and was determined to recognize their help with particular bequests in her will. She had already decided that her round oak table should go to Bert Cope, her cut-glass decanter and sherry glasses to his mother, her green china dessert set and Onondaga turtleshell rattle to Dr. Nelles and her mother's silver coffee spoons and porcupine quill mat to Eileen Maguire. She wanted her buckskin costume, including her grandmother's silver trade brooches, her father's knife and the red blanket she used as a cloak, to go to the museum of the city she regarded as home, Vancouver. She found Eva's scrupulousness about money infuriating—lots of people didn't pay their bills on time.

The subject of religion triggered an even deeper tension between the sisters. Pauline grudgingly agreed that the Reverend Owen should give her Communion. But she steadfastly refused to countenance the idea that her body should be buried back east. She believed she belonged in Vancouver. Moreover, she was ambivalent about the "white man's God" invoked to justify the existence of reserves, residential schools and land grabs. She had a spiritual hunger for a benevolent deity visible in the natural world that was unsatisfied by the Christianity of British Imperialists. She was far more drawn to Indian spirituality, embodied for her in the "Grand Tyee" of the Capilano people and the Great Spirit of the Onondagas. Before Jean Thompson left Vancouver, she had watched her friend drift towards traditional native beliefs as she faced death. Jean sympathized with it:

> Can anyone wonder that she, with her analytical mind, balanced the Pagan religion of the Indians against Christianity as she found it? She told me of the Onondagas, that tribe of the Six Nations which is still Pagan. "They will tell you," she said, "that Christianity costs too much coin. Their faith costs nothing but personal devotion. They object to Christianity

because of the incessant begging for favours from the white man's God. 'You are always asking the Great Spirit for endless things,' they will say. 'Let him alone. He knows what is good for you.'"

Evelyn Johnson, schooled in her mother's British faith, regarded Pauline's views as heathen.

The clash of wills between the two sisters was painful. By Christmas 1912, they could barely exchange a civil word. "I was an uncomfortable observer of a violent quarrel," recalled Beatrice Nasmyth, "about raincoats and whether people did or did not have to wear such garments in Vancouver. Pauline said they did *not* and Sister said 'They so *did*' and the air was blue for a time. . . . You never saw them together five minutes that they were not at it hammer and tongs over nothing. Two less compatible people it would be difficult to find."

It cannot have been a happy time for Evelyn, watching her sister die in a strange city, while Pauline's friends treated her with chilly condescension. Eighteen years after the event, Lionel Makovski reminded Walter McRaye in a flippant letter how they had "fought to keep the one who was of value to Canada alive and to keep the other from creating an atmosphere around her sick-bed." Pauline banished Eva from her sickroom, saying that only solitude would allow her to keep on with signing all the copies of both *Legends of Vancouver* and *Flint and Feather* that had been ordered. "I was merrily overworked before Christmas," she wrote to a friend in Montreal who had sent her a pretty hand-knitted bedjacket. "For five consecutive nights I worked inscribing books until 2 am and once until 4 am. I simply hate the sight of a pen . . . but I am also getting paid for it." On Christmas Day, Margery Cope sent her car to pick up Pauline for dinner. "I donned radiant robes, put a touch of rouge on my rather wearied face (I was tired out with work and excitement!) and away I was whisked to a jolly dinner with those I love and who love me."

Evelyn was not included in the Copes' party. But she sat with Pauline on New Year's Eve, and they listened together to the whistles and hullabaloo in the street below. It was a rare moment of family harmony, as the two sisters smiled together at memories of the New

Year's Eves of their childhood. Eva finally took her leave at 12:30 a.m. "As I passed the window, she leaned out to call good night and 'New Year' to me, and I called back to her, 'New Year! New Year!' I thought at the time how she must feel—knowing that it would be her last New Year."

Each time Pauline looked in the mirror, she could see death at her shoulder. "It hurts a woman's heart to grow old, particularly when the heart itself is in an everlasting April," she confided to a correspondent. After Evelyn had left, Pauline opened a biography by Elbert Hubbard of the artist Corot that she had bought at Roycroft five years earlier. On the title page she wrote a special inscription to her old "tillicum" Walter. She wrote as if she had already passed into the "Happy Hunting Grounds" of Indian legend: "Corot and I shall have both our pictures and poems ready to greet that royal soul of my old comrade Walter McRaye, when he too travels up the trail to the barbizon that we shall have created to welcome him."

She was now in constant pain and felt both physically and mentally weary. Dr. Nelles stepped up the morphine, and Evelyn planted herself firmly in the chair at her sister's bedside to ensure that visitors would not disturb the sickroom calm. But even Eva had to close her eyes sometimes. In the morning of March 7, 1913, she slipped out of Pauline's room and returned to her apartment, where she lay on her bed, fully clothed, and fell into a deep sleep. Her place at Pauline's bedside was taken by Mrs. Moran, the hospital matron. Pauline, now unconscious, gave a couple of low groans. Mrs. Moran leaned over her and gently lifted her shoulders. With a faint gasp, Pauline died in her arms.

Pauline had left instructions that nobody should see her body after death. While Mrs. Moran waited for Dr. Nelles to arrive and sign the death certificate, she wondered what to do. What about Pauline's sister? And all the friends who had sat with her? And Walter McRaye, who made her laugh and knew her perhaps better than anyone? And sculptor Charles Sergison Marega, who had already made discreet enquiries about the possibility of making a death mask?

A strange calm pervaded Pauline's room for a couple of hours after she had taken her last breath. Then Evelyn returned, discovered what had happened and asked indignantly why she had not been called. She telephoned her brother Allen and his wife, Floretta, in Toronto and her cousin Kate Washington in Hamilton. Meanwhile, Dr. Nelles alerted Isabel MacLean at the *Vancouver Daily Province*. The news of Pauline's death travelled in widening ripples, gathering force as it spread through Vancouver's literary community, along the streets of its West End mansions and its Squamish village, and across the Rockies into the nation's newsrooms, drawing rooms, reserves, small towns, government departments and publishing houses. Marega was allowed to make a plaster cast for the death mask. Newspapers rushed to prepare obituaries.

"By the death of Pauline Johnson, Canada loses a great daughter of the flag," declared the *Vancouver Daily Province* the following day, in an obituary probably written by Lionel Makovski. His lament for the departure of a national and well-loved celebrity was typical in tone of the obituaries in most Canadian newspapers:

> All she wrote betrayed her love of the country which had passed from the rule of her fathers into the hands of aliens. . . . Her *Legends of Vancouver* are a magnificent illustration of her understanding and her genius. Through them all runs that instinct for poetry which has found expression in "The Song My Paddle Sings" and many others of her poems. And on the fragmentary anecdotes of the Indians of the coast she built a saga that will live long after the generation that knew her has followed her across the Great Divide.
>
> The keynote of her whole disposition was a generous charity towards everything and everybody with whom she came in contact. . . . She loved life with a passionate devotion that was almost pathetic in its intensity. In spite of all her travelling, her experiences, which were by no means easy, Pauline Johnson never lost the capacity for getting the best out of life. . . . To all who knew her she was "the best beloved vagabond." It was always fine weather and good going on the trail when Pauline Johnson blazed the way.

The Vancouver branch of the Women's Canadian Club took charge of Pauline's funeral, which was scheduled to take place on March 10. The Club's president, Mrs. Elizabeth Rogers (daughter-in-law of the great sugar baron Benjamin Tingley Rogers), made sure Pauline was dressed in the garments and jewellery she had selected for the occasion: a grey cloth evening cloak, and round her neck the small gold locket containing the photograph of a young man. Pauline had shown her the photo inside, but Mrs. Rogers never asked the identity of the man. Pauline's secret went to the grave with her. Mrs. Rogers pressed into Pauline's hand the silver and ebony crucifix she had asked to hold as she was cremated. In the end, her Christian faith had prevailed.

The funeral cortège left Bute Street Hospital at 1:30 p.m., followed by a lengthy parade of the city's best-known men and women. Chief Matthias Capilano, in full ceremonial dress and the tall fox fur hat, was prominent amongst the official mourners. All along the three-block route to Christ Church Cathedral, the street was lined four or five deep with people, non-native and native. Throughout the city,

Georgia Street was lined with mourners, and flags were at half-mast, as Pauline Johnson's coffin was taken to the Mountain View Cemetery on March 10, 1913.

public offices were closed and flags flew at half-mast. This was the
largest funeral the young city had ever seen.

By the time the solemn procession arrived at the Cathedral, every
pew was jammed and a silent crowd filled the street outside. Evelyn
sat in the front, hiding her grief behind the impassive mask she had
assumed at the funerals of her father, her brother Beverly and her
mother. Although Pauline had requested that there should be no flowers, her coffin was piled high—a wreath from the Royal Society of
Canada, violets and ivy leaves from the IODE, violets and hyacinths
from the Vancouver Women's Press Club, a lyre of spring flowers
from the Canadian Women's Press Club, bouquets from friends and
relatives from all across Canada. Pauline had asked that Chopin's
"Dead March" should be played, but to Mrs. Rogers's frustration, the
organ was broken. The choir sang Pauline's favourite hymns unaccompanied, "Peace, Perfect Peace" and "Crossing the Bar." The Reverend Owen preached a sermon. The service over, the remains were
taken to the Mountain View crematorium. "A half glow seemed to
settle over the business and residential sections of the city. It was as if
the rush and noise of the city had been stayed in respect to this gifted
Indian woman," according to the following day's *Vancouver Sun*.

Three days after the funeral, Elizabeth Rogers and Lionel Makovski
went to the crematorium to pick up Pauline's ashes. "We were ushered into a room where a largish, squarish cement, very plain box
stood on a table," Mrs. Rogers later recalled. "The ashes were in a
small brown tin with white ribbon on the top and a label tied to it. . . .
The tin [was] about as large as a Dutch cleanser container." Lionel
placed a copy of *Legends of Vancouver* and a copy of *Flint and Feather*
in the cement container next to the tin. These were the only two
books by Pauline that were in print when she died. After the under-
taker sealed a lid onto the container, Lionel carried it out of the crematorium and placed it on the leather seat of Mrs. Rogers's car.

A few months earlier, some of Pauline's Press Club friends had
decided that the most appropriate place for Pauline's remains was
Stanley Park. There was a particular landmark of which she was very
fond: a column of grey granite called the Siwash Rock that jutted out
of the channel by Ferguson Point. Chief Joe Capilano had first shown

her the rock on an August evening while he was paddling her around the Stanley Park shoreline. She was fascinated by the way it "stood forth like a sentinel—erect, enduring, eternal." Chief Joe explained that according to Squamish legend, the rock was a monument to "clean fatherhood." As the old chief and the middle-aged poet sat in the canoe enjoying the glint of evening light on the water and the soft Pacific breeze, Chief Joe told her the legend of Siwash Rock. He described how emissaries of the Creator, the Grand Tyee, had turned a young father to stone because the man had refused to stop swimming and get out of the emissaries' way while his wife was giving birth in the nearby forest. Tribal law decreed that a father must swim, in a purification ritual, while his child was being born; the young chief had kept swimming because he wanted to set a spotless example to his newborn son. Pauline loved this story, and the noble notion of "clean fatherhood." While she was well enough, she often walked to Ferguson Point, from where she could gaze at the granite pillar rising monumentally from the water. She wrote up the legend for the *Vancouver Daily Province*. It was one of the fifteen pieces included in *Legends of Vancouver*.

The request that Pauline be buried in Stanley Park was highly unorthodox—it was a good thing that Pauline's Vancouver friends were well connected. The park, which was still a tangled and overgrown forest, was officially a federal military reserve that had been leased to the City of Vancouver for recreational purposes. There was no provision for burials there. But Elizabeth Rogers, whose millionaire husband was a member of the Parks Commission, had sent a breezy request to Ottawa requesting that the rules be bent for Pauline. In addition, when the Duke of Connaught had visited Vancouver the previous year, Mrs. Rogers and Lionel Makovski had extracted a promise from him that he would speed up formal approval. By March 13, when the casket of ashes was placed in Mrs. Rogers's car, permission had been granted. A small clearing on Ferguson Point overlooking Siwash Rock had been prepared for the burial, and a hole dug to receive the container of ashes.

Only Pauline's closest friends were told that her ashes were going to be laid to rest that day. Isabel Ecclestone Mackay, Isabel

*Special permission was given by the Dominion
government for Pauline's ashes to be buried in
Stanley Park, within sight of Siwash Rock.*

MacLean, Evelyn Johnson and the others pulled their winter coats tighter around themselves as they stood below an overcast sky on that damp and chilly March afternoon. When the Reverend Owen began to conduct a brief burial service, casual strollers through the Park joined the subdued crowd to see what was happening and stayed to show respect. Not a breath of wind stirred the giant oaks and firs as the cement container was lowered into the ground. Walter McRaye recited "The Happy Hunting Grounds," one of Pauline's early poems:

> Into the rose gold westland, its yellow prairies roll,
> World of the bison's freedom, home of the Indian's soul.

Roll out, O seas! In sunlight bathed,
Your plains wind-tossed, and grass enswathed.
. . . . .
Surely the great Hereafter cannot be more than this,
Surely we'll see that country after Time's farewell kiss.
Who would his lovely faith condole?
Who envies not the Red-skin's soul,

Sailing into the cloud land, sailing into the sun,
Into the crimson portals ajar when life is done?
O! dear dead race, my spirit too
Would fain sail westward unto you.

Then a granite boulder was rolled over the grave, fir branches were strewn over the ground and the crowd quietly dispersed. As the light faded from the evening sky, the faint sound of water rippling around the nearby Siwash Rock permeated the clearing. Had Pauline heard it, she might have closed her eyes and imagined herself back at Chiefswood, listening to the canoes of her Mohawk relatives skimming along the Grand River.

AFTERWORD

P AULINE'S journalist friends offered to collect up all the flowers
after the poet's funeral. There was a card appended to one particularly large and beautiful wreath: "To his dearest from her
dearest."

"Those who saw the card and the flowers," reads a note of events in
the archives of the Canadian Women's Press Club, "are still asking
themselves if it was a confirmation of an oft repeated story of
Pauline's great love for a suitor who had loved her as dearly, but was
steadfastly rejected since his family had once objected to the union
because of her mixed blood. It may well have been true, for she was
very proud of her Indian blood. We shall probably never know now."

Who was "her dearest" who sent the large and beautiful wreath?
Was it the same person as the young man whose photo was in the
locket that Pauline always wore? Who were the young men to whom
a youthful Pauline had addressed her passionate and erotic verses in
the 1880s? What was Pauline doing in those missing months in 1901?
Why did she return to London for her final trip in 1907? Were there
other love poems that never appeared in print?

We shall probably never know the answers to any of these questions, because neither Pauline nor her sister Evelyn wanted us to
know. Pauline never told anyone whose picture was in the locket.
After Pauline's death, Evelyn burnt as many of her sister's papers as
she could lay her hands on. Letters, unpublished verses, journals,
receipts, performance schedules—they all went up in smoke. Lionel
Makovski said, "Eva seemed to feel that Pauline's life as a 'trouper'

was something not to be mentioned." Emily Howells Johnson's last letter to her younger daughter, which Pauline never opened, must have gone up in that bonfire too. There were many secrets in Pauline's private life, and she left many mysteries behind. A biographer cannot hope to reveal all the truths.

Pauline's first biographer, Mrs. W. Garland Foster, was exasperated by Pauline's secrets. "Her sister Eva was most difficult about giving any information," she told Archie Kains in 1934, three years after her book *The Mohawk Princess* was published. "I am always hoping that she will relent and before she departs this life will leave the material she has for me to edit. There were things about Pauline's love affairs that I could not use, and others that I could not get because the men were still living and would object." But Evelyn Johnson never relented. She did not like *The Mohawk Princess*, and often repeated Pauline's remark to her: "Anyone can write anything they like about Indians, because they had no historian of their own." Before she died in 1937, aged eighty-one, in Ohsweken on the Six Nations Reserve, Evelyn studied Indian history and participated in debates about Indian rights. And she set down her own version of the truth about her sister and family in a memoir now in the Archives of Ontario.

"A biography is considered complete," remarked Virginia Woolf, "if it merely accounts for six or seven selves, whereas a person may well have a thousand." Like Mrs. Garland Foster and Pauline's four subsequent biographers, I can only draw reasonable conclusions from the evidence available—in Pauline's case, the letters that were not consumed in Evelyn's flames, the newspaper clippings that Pauline herself collected, the correspondence that has turned up in the papers of Pauline's contemporaries. There were tantalizing mentions on the Six Nations Reserve that a journal kept by Pauline Johnson existed as late as the 1950s; but if such a journal did exist, it has since vanished. From time to time, new collections of letters by Pauline Johnson emerge from attics and old boxes into the light of a new century. In 2000 the National Archives of Canada acquired eighteen letters to Archie Kains, and other letters were sent to me in the course of writing this book.

The narrative of Pauline's life is particularly hard to track because she herself is difficult to pin down. There were many selves, many identities. A woman who was both Mohawk and English; a native advocate who pleased non-native audiences; a lyric poet who performed comic skits; a New Woman who wrote for *The Mother's Magazine*—she blurred boundaries that her contemporaries saw as impermeable. Part of her appeal in her own lifetime was the way she blended literary genres and transcended social stereotypes. How many artists could attract audiences as diverse as the American Canoe Association, the Canadian Manufacturing Association, the Toronto Young Liberals, the Illinois Chautauqua, the National Council of Women, Lady Ripon's dinner guests, the Massachusetts Indian Association, Sir Frederick Leighton, and both Methodists and miners in the Canadian West? How many women in stuffy turn-of-the-century Canada could capture the hearts of so many young men and emerge without a stain on their character?

She has, however, left us one source which has proved a goldmine in the preparation of this biography: her own writing. Her poetry, journalism and stories follow the arc of her own life; her own experiences and emotions were her raw material. On them rests her reputation.

Yet her reputation as a writer has yo-yoed up and down and up again in Canadian literary circles. Assessments of her work have varied so wildly that it is hard to believe the critics are talking about the same pieces, the same writer. Pauline is best remembered for her poetry. Immediately after her death, the poet Charles Mair declared that "a star has fallen from the intellectual firmament of Canada" and commented that her poetry was distinguished by "its beauty, its strength, its originality." In 1920, the essayist and literary critic W. A. Deacon declared that Pauline was "in skill, sentiment and outlook, one of the most powerful" of the Confederation Poets. He suggested that she wrote "with a mastery equal at times to the best of them, and seldom much below it."

But only forty years later, Pauline's star appeared to have flamed out. Her work was omitted altogether from the 1960 edition of *The Oxford Book of Canadian Verse* because the editor found some of her poems "empty of content" and most "theatrical and crude." In 1961, the centenary of her birth, writer Robertson Davies dismissed her poetry as "elocutionist-fodder" and described Johnson herself as "not given to reflection." Professor Desmond Pacey, author of *Creative Writing in Canada*, said that Pauline's work was "cheap, vulgar and almost incredibly bad."

Pauline's mid-century downfall was largely due to changing literary tastes. The emergence of modernism (spare, fragmented and bloodless) as the preferred poetic mode relegated Pauline to a cultural backlot. Her image, promoted by Mrs. Garland Foster, as the "Mohawk princess" (a term she would have hated) trivialized her: it made her too Hollywood, too melodramatic. "There is a primitive beat of tribal tom-toms through her verse," quipped writer Jack Scott. Sometimes she was consigned to the pink ghetto of Victorian "parlour poets," along with Isabella Valancy Crawford and Marjorie Pickthall; other times she was herded into the "vaudeville poets" caravan, with other stage performers such as Robert W. Service and Wilson MacDonald. Her romantic poetry was buried, her nature poetry dismissed and her overtly political support for native rights ridiculed. Pauline's work continued to appear in school readers in some provinces until the late 1960s, but the elite ignored it. Canada as a vast, silent and threatening landscape, "empty as paper" in F. R. Scott's words, became the preferred vision in highbrow circles. There was no place for native peoples in either Group of Seven paintings or the poetry of A. J. M. Smith or Frank Scott.

However, as the twentieth century drew to a close, Pauline began to nudge her way back into the "intellectual firmament." In 1982, Margaret Atwood included two of Pauline's poems in *The New Oxford Book of Canadian Verse in English*, "one hair-raiser," she explains, "about rape and murder, and one nature poem that is by no means inferior to much work of the Confederation group." (The poems were "Ojistoh," about the Mohawk wife who kills her Huron captor, and "Marshlands," a lyric nature poem.) Atwood commented that Pauline Johnson, "usually known only for such familiars as 'The Song My Paddle Sings,' turns out to have been a poet of considerably more sophistication, despite her habit of dressing up in costumes and chanting in public."

More recently, Carole Gerson and Veronica Strong-Boag have argued in *Paddling Her Own Canoe* that Pauline's "often erotic love poems" were an entirely "original contribution to Canadian writing," and that Pauline's very complexity is the cause of "the general failure to recognise Johnson's contribution to the national imaginary." Literary critic Dennis Duffy says that "The Song My Paddle Sings" compares favourably with what was being written by her male competitors: "The verse of Roberts, Carman, Lampman: is it immortal for any reasons other than the nationalistic?"

There is no consensus on the quality of Pauline's work, and there is also no consensus on the issues that she engaged in poetry and prose. Instead, we have had a heated, century-long conversation in this country about the place of aboriginal people in Canadian society, the role of women and the need for a Canadian nationalism—all issues about which she wrote. But Pauline saw both sides of each argument. Before she ended "A Cry from an Indian Wife" on a note of native defiance, for example, she gave voice to both the Anglo-Canadian mother and the Indian wife, both of whose menfolk march off to the 1885 North-West Rebellion. As debate on Indian issues became increasingly polarized after Pauline's death, she was an uncomfortable symbol for either side to absorb.

When I sat down and read every poem I could find by Pauline, I was struck by two aspects of her work. The first was her incredible range of subjects and styles: she wrote love poems drenched in passion, hokey patriotic crowd-pleasers, lyrical nature verse, witty doggerel and the extraordinary Indian narrative ballads that can still make the hairs on the back of a reader's neck prickle. The second aspect of her poetry is the range of quality: I found a few poems that are heartstoppers, many that are enjoyable, some that are obviously derivative of others' work and a handful that are awful. Taken together, they reflect a writer of talent—uneven, perhaps, but talent nonetheless. More important, they also reflect a vibrant personality and a wonderful appetite for life.

Today, it is Pauline's personality rather than her poetry that speaks across the years. What other woman of her era crossed Canada nineteen times, visited England three times and chased the frontier because she was in love with "the last, best west"? In her day, only a handful of women managed to enter the teaching, law or medical professions and none voted; Pauline forged an independent literary and dramatic career and became an international celebrity. A performer with the commanding presence of a Jenny Lind or a Maria Callas, she held her audience in thrall from the moment she stepped onto the stage. "Though she had no training as an elocutionist," read the *Saturday Night* obituary, "her natural dramatic gifts, her striking presence, and her personal magnetism won instant success for her."

How beautiful she must have looked in her exotic buckskin costume, with the eagle feather in her hair and the silver trade brooches glinting on her blouse. She established an intimacy with her audience that could not be faked. Her vitality, her sensuality, her thrilling voice mesmerized Canadians. She gave them images of Indian bravery and nobility, delivered in ballads that far surpassed most of the doggerel served up in opera houses and town halls across the country. After the interval, she re-emerged as an elegant aristocrat, whispering enchanting verses about northern nights or imitating the pretentious hostesses she had met on her travels. If anyone in the crowd uttered a yawn or a catcall, she would reinvent herself again—with exuberant wit, she would skewer the hecklers. And she made her listeners love poetry. She was a magical storyteller. Her poetry was accessible and wildly popular, a distinction that few poets in later generations can claim. "The Song My Paddle Sings" is one of the few poems (alongside John McCrae's "In Flanders Fields") that many contemporary Canadians recognize.

Perhaps Pauline's act played to her audience's stereotypes. English-speaking Canadians wanted to see her metamorphose from native into non-native because the transformation implicitly confirmed the government's assumption that Indians were a disappearing race. They rarely understood, as she understood, that both the buckskin leggings and the Kensington ballgown were costumes. But they loved her—a century ago she was a star from coast to coast.

For Pauline's fellow Indians, she was an enduring success story who promoted the dignity and historical importance of her own people and won fans on two continents. It took decades for memories of her thrilling performances to flicker out. During the 1920s, the Cree recitalist Frances Nickawa followed in Pauline's footsteps, performing Pauline's poems on stages across Canada. With *Legends of Vancouver*, Pauline encouraged native peoples to record their own stories before the stories died with their elders. In 1989, the part-native poet Joan Crate published *Pale as Real Ladies: Poems for Pauline Johnson*. "Your voice / scrapes the bones of time," begins one poem in Crate's moving sequence of verses about a Mohawk with whom she feels a visceral connection.

Pauline Johnson was far more than her various disguises. She was one of those rare, remarkable women who rise above the conventions and assumptions of their day to carve their own paths. She had a vision of a society that drew on the strengths of its citizens regardless of race, colour or religion. Ahead of her time in many ways, she embodied the plural and protean identities that still challenge Canadians today.

SOURCES

PAULINE Johnson herself is the main source for this book, particularly her private correspondence. My first challenge as a biographer was to locate as many of her letters as I could find. The best collection of Pauline's correspondence is in the William Ready Division of Archives and Research Collections at McMaster University, Hamilton, Ontario. I found other materials in institutions all over Canada, including the National Archives of Canada (where the nineteen letters in the newly acquired Archibald Kains papers proved a goldmine), the Archives of Ontario, the Trent University Archives, the Queen's University Archives, the Thomas Fisher Rare Book Library at the University of Toronto, the University of British Columbia Archives, the Vancouver City Archives, the Brant County Museum and Archives, and the Chiefswood Collection at the Woodland Cultural Centre Museum. Some letters were sent to me by individuals when they heard I was writing Pauline's biography. Carole Gerson kindly gave me other letters that she and Veronica Strong-Boag had discovered while researching *Paddling Her Own Canoe: The Times and Texts of E. Pauline Johnson, Tekahionwake*. By the end of my trawl, I had collected in a ring binder 100 letters and cards in Pauline's flowing, forward-leaning handwriting, with its stylish loops and emphatic underlinings. The letters allowed me to hear Pauline's own voice, unfiltered by editors or reporters.

However, 100 letters do not constitute a major resource. (For a previous book, *Sisters in the Wilderness: The Lives of Susanna Moodie and Catharine Parr Traill*, I was able to draw on nearly 500 published

403

and unpublished letters.) I also relied on clippings of articles by and about Pauline, most of which I found in the National Archives of Canada and the William Ready Division of Archives and Research Collections at McMaster University. The unpublished memoir by Pauline's sister Evelyn, in the Archives of Ontario, both supplemented and balanced Pauline's account of her family and career. And I paid close attention to Pauline's own compositions, published within her lifetime or soon after her death. Five books bear Pauline's byline:

The White Wampum, London, 1895
Canadian Born, Toronto, 1903
Legends of Vancouver, Vancouver 1911, reprinted 1997
Flint and Feather, Toronto, 1912
The Moccasin Maker, Toronto, 1913, reprinted 1998

I did not do all the legwork alone: there are several previous books about E. Pauline Johnson on which I was able to draw. Four in particular proved to be extremely useful. Pauline's first biographer was Mrs. W. Garland Foster, author of *The Mohawk Princess: Being Some Account of the Life of Tekahion-wake (E. Pauline Johnson)*, published in 1931 (Vancouver: Lions' Gate). Mrs. Foster had the advantage of speaking to people who remembered Pauline; her anodyne account of Pauline's life is enlivened by their anecdotes. In 1981, Betty Keller published *Pauline: A Biography of Pauline Johnson* (Vancouver: Douglas & McIntyre), which first drew my attention to the fascinating story of this talented woman and which included much new research. Sheila Johnston's *Buckskin & Broadcloth: A Celebration of E. Pauline Johnson—Tekahionwake, 1861–1913*, a lively compilation of illustrations, photos, contemporary comment and verses, appeared in 1997 (Toronto: Natural Heritage Books). Johnston had located many previously unpublished photographs and poems, which she generously shared. A different approach to Pauline's life was taken in *Paddling Her Own Canoe: The Times and Texts of E. Pauline Johnson, Tekahionwake* (University of Toronto Press, 2000), by Veronica Strong-Boag and Carole Gerson. The insights I gained from this scholarly publication, and its bibliography and chronological list of all Pauline's works that have been traced so far, were invaluable.

Chapters 1 and 2

Pauline herself described both her idyllic Chiefswood childhood and her mother's early life in a series of sentimental articles for *The Mother's Magazine*, which were subsequently reprinted in *The Moccasin Maker*. A. LaVonne Brown Ruoff explored the background of Pauline's mother in her introduction to the 1998 edition of *The Moccasin Maker* (Norman: University of Oklahoma Press, 1998). The Howells family history is covered in "Thomas Howells of Hay and His Descendants in America" by Geoffrey L. Fairs in *The New England Historical and Genealogical Register*, volume 134, January 1980, pp. 27–47. Details about the literary life of early-nineteenth-century Bristol are taken from *A Passionate Sisterhood: The Sisters, Wives and Daughters of the Lake Poets* by Kathleen Jones (London: Constable, 1997).

Chapter 3

The authoritative biography of Sir William Johnson remains *Mohawk Baronet: A Biography of Sir William Johnson*, by James Thomas Flexner (Syracuse, NY: Syracuse University Press, 1979). Fred Anderson covers details of French–Indian conflicts in *Crucible of War: The Seven Years' War and the Fate of Empire in British North America, 1754–1766* (New York: Knopf, 2000). *Molly Brant: A Legacy of Her Own*, by Lois M. Huey and Bonnie Pulis (Youngstown, NY: Old Fort Niagara Association, 1997), is a brief introduction to one of the most interesting personalities of her time. I was also able to draw on the extensive knowledge of Bonnie Pulis herself, who is Interpretive Programs Assistant at Johnson Hall State Historic Site, Johnstown, New York. Pauline's articles about her mother and A. LaVonne Brown Ruoff's introduction to *The Moccasin Maker* covered the meeting between Emily Howells and George Johnson.

Chapter 4

Evelyn Johnson described her parents' marriage, the early years in Chiefswood and each of her siblings in her unpublished memoir. In *The Mohawk Princess*, Mrs. W. Garland Foster explores the tensions facing the young couple.

Chapter 5

Emily Howells Johnson's 1855 letter to her husband is in the Brant County Museum and Archives. Pauline's account of her mother's life in her articles for *The Mother's Magazine* is supplemented by two more articles for the same magazine, published in 1909, entitled "From the Child's Viewpoint." She also described some of the Iroquois spiritual beliefs in "Indian Medicine Men and Their Magic" in *Dominion Illustrated*, April 1892. Anecdotes about the distinguished visitors to Chiefswood appear in Mrs. W. Garland Foster's *The Mohawk Princess* and in Marcus Van Steen's *Pauline Johnson: Her Life and Work* (Toronto: Musson, 1965).

Chapter 6

Pauline's 1881 letters to Charlotte Jones are held in the D. B. Weldon Library at the University of Western Ontario. Peggy Webling recorded her impressions of the young Pauline in *Peggy: The Story of One Score Years and Ten* (London, 1924). Details about the early years of Brantford are drawn from Evelyn Johnson's memoir; from *Brant County: A History, 1784–1945*, by C. M. Johnston (Toronto: Oxford University Press, 1967); and from *The Way We Were: Glimpses of Brantford's Past* (Brant Historical Society and CKPC Radio Brantford, 1998). The Brant County Museum contains a reconstruction of a nineteenth-century street in the city.

Information about the changing legal status of Indians in this and subsequent chapters is drawn from *Skyscrapers Hide the Heavens: A History of Indian–White Relations in Canada*, by J. R. Miller (University of Toronto Press, 1989) and *Canada's First Nations: A History of*

Founding Peoples, by Olive Dickason (Toronto: McClelland & Stewart, 1992). For descriptions of Canada's different peoples, I looked at the 1932 federal government anthropological report *The Indians of Canada*, by Diamond Jenness (reprinted 1993 by University of Toronto Press in association with the National Museum of Man, National Museums of Canada, and the Publishing Centre, Department of Supply and Services, Ottawa).

Chapter 7

Besides the published books by Keller, Johnstone, and Strong-Boag and Gerson, and Evelyn Johnson's unpublished memoir, I was able to rely on two fascinating new archival sources for this chapter. The first was the Archibald Kains correspondence, donated to the National Archives of Canada by Kains's grandniece Joan Ritchie of New Jersey, through the good offices of Susan MacMillan Kains of Massachusetts. The second was the Mackenzie Family Memoirs, kindly lent to me by Senator Landon Pearson and Katharine Hooke.

The anecdotes about Emily gathering a last bunch of pansies in Chiefswood's grounds and the Reverend Mackenzie's affection for the song "When Polly and I Were Sweethearts" both come from cuttings held in the William Ready Division of Archives and Research Collections at McMaster University.

Marian Fowler described Brantford's "New Woman" in *Redney: A Life of Sara Jeannette Duncan* (Toronto: Anansi, 1983). More information about changing attitudes can be gleaned from *Aspiring Women: Short Stories by Canadian Women, 1880–1900*, edited by Lorraine McMullen and Sandra Campbell (University of Ottawa Press, 1993).

Chapter 8

A number of good books have recently appeared about canoes in Canada. They include *Bark, Skin and Cedar: Exploring the Canoe in Canadian Experience*, by James Raffan (Toronto: HarperCollins, 1999); *Idleness, Water, and a Canoe: Reflections on Paddling for Pleasure*, by Jamie Benidickson (University of Toronto Press, 1997); and

The Canoe in Canadian Cultures, edited by John Jennings, Bruce W. Hodgins and Doreen Small (Toronto: Natural Heritage Books, 1999). I found particularly useful a pamphlet written by Gerald F. Stephenson entitled *John Stephenson and the Famous "Peterborough" Canoes* (Peterborough Historical Society Occasional Paper, November 1987). I also found helpful information in *Gore's Landing and the Rice Lake Plains*, by Norma Martin, Catherine Milne and Donna S. McGillis (Heritage Gore's Landing, 1986).

For background on the Muskoka region I turned to the Rosseau Historical Society's 1999 publication *Rosseau: The Early Years*; Patricia Jasen's *Wild Things: Nature, Culture, and Tourism in Ontario, 1790–1914* (University of Toronto Press, 1995); John Denison's *Micklethwaite's Muskoka* (Toronto: Stoddart, 1993); and Geraldine Coombe's *Muskoka: Past and Present* (Toronto: McGraw-Hill Ryerson, 1976).

Pauline's articles about Muskoka are in the William Ready Division of Archives and Research Collections at McMaster University. The letter from the deputy editor of *Outing* magazine is in the Trent University Archives. The W. D. Lighthall letters are in the McGill University Library Rare Books and Special Collections.

Chapter 9

I enjoyed reading works by and about Canada's post-Confederation poets and the stirring of literary nationalism for this chapter. I began with Chapters 28 and 29 in one of my favourite books, Sandra Gwyn's *The Private Capital: Ambition and Love in the Age of Macdonald and Laurier* (Toronto: McClelland & Stewart, 1984), and then turned to the following sources: *Songs of the Great Dominion: Voices from the Forests and Waters, the Settlements and Cities of Canada*, edited by William Douw Lighthall (London, 1889); "The Singers of Canada," by Joseph Dana Miller in *Massey Magazine* (May 1895); *Poteen: A Pot-Pourri of Canadian Essays*, by William Arthur Deacon (Ottawa, 1926); E. K. Brown's *On Canadian Poetry* (Toronto: Ryerson, 1944); *The Oxford Companion to Canadian History and Literature*, by Norah Storey (Toronto: Oxford University Press, 1967); *The New*

Oxford Book of Canadian Verse in English, edited by Margaret Atwood (Toronto: Oxford University Press, 1982); and *Canadian Poetry from the Beginnings Through the First World War*, edited by Carole Gerson and Gwendolyn Davies (Toronto: McClelland & Stewart, 1994). For information on the Fréchettes, I read *Annie Howells and Achille Fréchette*, by James Doyle (University of Toronto Press, 1979).

Pauline's first Toronto recital was covered in the *Globe*, Monday, January 18, 1892, and in *Saturday Night*, January 23, 1892. Frank Yeigh recorded his own adulatory but inaccurate memories of the occasions in "Recollections of Pauline Johnson," *The Western Home Monthly*, October 1924, and "Memories of Pauline Johnson," *The Canadian Bookman*, October 1929.

Chapter 10

Reports of Pauline's recitals that appeared in newspapers including the *Globe*, *Saturday Night* and the *Boston Herald* are held in the William Ready Division of Archives and Research Collections at McMaster University. Enthusiastic descriptions by her contemporaries of Pauline in her early thirties appear in O. J. Stevenson's *A People's Best* (Toronto, 1927) and Hector Charlesworth's *Candid Chronicles: Leaves from the Notebook of a Canadian Journalist* (Toronto, 1925).

In *The Imaginary Indian: The Image of the Indian in Canadian Culture* (Vancouver: Arsenal Pulp, 1992), Daniel Francis discusses the stereotypes of Indians that Pauline tried to combat. Dr. Melanie Stevenson at McMaster University provided me with information about Buffalo Bill and the Wild West shows. Pauline's correspondence with William Scott is in the W. L. Scott Papers at the National Archives of Canada. Her correspondence with Harry O'Brien is in the Queen's University Archives.

Chapter 11

I was able to picture London through Pauline's eyes thanks to several books of old photographs, including Felix Barker's *London in Old Photographs, 1897–1914* (Boston: Little, Brown, 1995); John Coulter's *London of One Hundred Years Ago* (Stroud, UK: Sutton, 1999); *Kensington and Chelsea in Old Photographs*, by Barbara Denny and Carolyn Starren (London: Royal Borough of Kensington and Chelsea, 1995); and Shaaron Whetlor's *The Story of Notting Dale: From Potteries and Piggeries to Present Time* (London: Kensington & Chelsea Community History Group, 1998).

I drew information about the characters that Pauline encountered from *John Lane and the Nineties*, by J. Lewis May (London, 1936); Giles Walkley's wonderful volume, *Artists' Houses in London 1764–1914* (Aldershot, UK: Scolar Press, 1994); and *As We Were: A Victorian Peepshow*, by E. F. Benson (1930; Penguin Classics, 2001). Details of Hamilton Aidé's salon came from an unpublished letter from Pauline to L. W. Makovski, quoted by Betty Keller, from various dictionaries of biography and from his obituary in London's *The Times*. I learned much about the turn-of-the-century theatre scene from two engaging biographies: *Lillie Langtry: Manners, Masks and Morals*, by Laura Beatty (London: Chatto & Windus, 1999) and *Marie Lloyd: The One and Only*, by Midge Gillies (London: Gollancz, 1999). I found the *Gazette* and *Sketch* interviews with Pauline, and the Alma-Tadema anecdote (from a clipping dated 1899), in the William Ready Division of Archives and Research Collections at McMaster University.

My account of London's literary scene was coloured by Bernard Bergonzi's essay "Aspects of the *fin de siècle*," in *The Victorians*, edited by Arthur Pollard (London, 1969), and by *England in the 1890s: Literary Publishing at the Bodley Head*, by Margaret D. Stetz and Mark Samuels Lasner (Washington, DC: Georgetown University Press, 1990).

Chapter 12

Ernest Thompson Seton described his first encounter with Pauline in his introduction to *The Shagganappi*, the collection of Pauline's stories published in 1913 after her death. Pauline and her partner Owen Smily described their first transcontinental train journey in "There and Back by Miss Poetry and Mr. Prose," which appeared in the *Globe*, December 15, 1894.

The excitement of train travel in the 1890s is caught in two contemporary accounts: Edward Roper's *By Track and Trail: A Journey Through Canada* (London, 1891) and Douglas Sladen's *On the Cars and Off: Being a Journal of a Pilgrimage Along the Queen's Highway to the East, from Halifax in Nova Scotia to Victoria in Vancouver's Island* (London, 1895). Pierre Berton celebrated the CPR's singular achievement in completing the track in *The Last Spike: The Great Railway 1881–1885* (Toronto: McClelland & Stewart, 1971), while Clark Blaise explored the impact of the railway on society in *Time Lord: The Remarkable Canadian Who Missed His Train and Changed the World* (Toronto: Knopf, 2001).

Reliable, up-to-date sources on the Plains Indians in the late-nineteenth century are scarce. In addition to works cited by J. R. Miller, Olive Dickason and Daniel Francis, I looked at Sarah Carter's *Lost Harvests: Prairie Indian Reserve Farmers and Government Policy* (Montreal: McGill-Queen's University Press, 1990) and *The Face Pullers: Photographing Native Canadians 1871–1939*, by Brock V. Silversides (Saskatoon: Fifth House, 1994).

Chapter 13

Two lively accounts of the lives of travelling performers are Peggy Webling's *Peggy: The Story of One Score Years and Ten* (London, 1924) and Walter McRaye's *Pauline Johnson and Her Friends* (Toronto: Ryerson, 1947). I also benefitted from an exhibit at the Perth Museum in the summer of 2001 entitled "On Stage in Perth," featuring the Marks Brothers. Charles G. D. Roberts's comments on Pauline appear in *The Collected Letters of Charles G. D. Roberts*, edited by Laurel Boone (Fredericton: Goose Lane, 1989).

The changing face of Toronto is depicted in *Immigrants: A Portrait of the Urban Experience, 1890–1930*, by Robert Harney and Harold

Troper (Toronto: Van Nostrand Reinhold, 1975). Artist John W. L. Forster's comments on Pauline appear in *Under the Studio Light: Leaves from a Portrait Painter's Sketch Book* (Toronto, 1928). The anecdote about Pauline's views on money comes from an article that her friend Jean Stevinson wrote in the *Calgary Herald* in 1932. The Wetherell letter comes from the J. E. Wetherell Papers in the University of Toronto Thomas Fisher Rare Book Library. The figure quoted for a schoolteacher's salary appears on page 194 of *Canadian Women on the Move 1867–1920*, edited by Beth Light and Joy Parr (Toronto: New Hogtown Press/OISE, 1983).

Chapter 14

Much of the material on the Drayton romance comes from Betty Keller's biography. I found additional material in the Drayton Papers at the Archives of Ontario and in *Gore's Landing and the Rice Lake Plains*, by Norma Martin, Catherine Milne and Donna S. McGillis (Heritage Gore's Landing, 1986). Henry Drayton was the kind of smug, successful lawyer who was often caricatured anonymously, most notably in *The Masques of Ottawa*, by "Domino" (Augustus Bridle) in 1921 and in *Bigwigs: Canadians Wise and Otherwise*, by R. T. L. (Charles Vining) in 1935.

Two of the many enjoyable histories of Winnipeg that I read were Christopher Dafoe's *Winnipeg, Heart of the Continent* (Winnipeg: Great Plains, 1998) and James H. Gray's *Red Lights on the Prairies* (Toronto: Macmillan, 1971). The best sources on the North-West Mounted Police were *The New West: Being the Official Reports to Parliament of the Activities of the Royal North-West Mounted Police Force from 1888–1889*, reprinted in the Coles Canadiana Collection in 1973, and *The Great Adventure: How the Mounties Conquered the West*, by David Cruise and Alison Griffiths (Toronto: Viking, 1996). Pauline's letter to Mrs. Higginbotham is in the Vancouver Public Library. Nellie McClung described her first encounter with Pauline, who subsequently became a friend, in her 1945 memoir, *The Stream Runs Fast: My Own Story* (Toronto: Allen).

Evelyn Johnson's 1913 letter to James Goulet came into the possession of Juanita Staples Brumpton in about 1942; a copy was kindly sent to me by Harry Brumpton of Windsor, Ontario.

Chapter 15

Women of Canada: Their Life and Work was compiled by the National Council of Women of Canada at the request of the Hon. Sydney Fisher, Minister of Agriculture, for distribution at the Paris International Exhibition in 1900. The material about Charles Wuerz draws on the detective work of Betty Keller for her 1981 biography, supplemented by material in the J. E. Wetherell Papers in the University of Toronto Thomas Fisher Rare Book Library. The fragment of a poem by Pauline about residential schools is quoted on page 148 of *Paddling Her Own Canoe* by Strong-Boag and Gerson.

I am particularly grateful to Carole Gerson and Gail Campbell for alerting me to the Mrs. Laura Wood material from the Public Archives of New Brunswick.

Chapter 16

Walter McRaye recorded his own life and partnership with Pauline in two boisterous memoirs, *Town Hall Tonight* (Toronto: Ryerson, 1929) and *Pauline Johnson and Her Friends* (Toronto: Ryerson, 1947), from which I drew extensively for this and subsequent chapters. He recalled reading Swinburne to Pauline in a letter to Lorne Pierce, written on March 20, 1943, that is in the Walter McRaye Collection in the William Ready Division of Archives and Research Collections at McMaster University.

Achille Fréchette's letter is quoted in James Doyle's *Annie Howells and Achille Fréchette* (University of Toronto Press, 1979). Pauline's letter to Miss King was sent to Peter Unwin by Miss King's daughter, Julia Hickey Sporka, who read an article by Peter about Pauline that appeared in *The Beaver* in November 1999; Peter kindly passed it on to me.

The Johnson–McRaye partnership's touring itineraries were a tangle of one-night stands and branch-line travel. I have relied on the research in local newspapers done by Betty Keller for her 1981 biography and for an article she wrote for the December 1986–January 1987 issue of *The Beaver*.

Getting to know the history and geography of the Kootenay area of British Columbia was one of the pleasures of writing this biography. Some of the books that proved useful were *The Silvery Slocan Heritage Tour Guidebook*, by Dan Nicholson, Jan McMurray, Robert N. Riley and Rodney Huculak (New Denver, BC: Word Publishing, 1998); R. G. Harvey's *Carving the Western Path: By River, Rail, and Road Through B.C.'s Southern Mountains* (Surrey, BC: Heritage House, 1998); and Robert D. Turner's *The S.S. Moyie: Memories of the Oldest Sternwheeler* (Victoria, BC: Sono Nis, 1991).

Information about the 1903 camping trip on Stony Lake comes from Bertha Jean (Thompson) Stevinson's memoirs of her friend Pauline. Mrs. Stevinson's son Harry, who lives with his wife, Isabel, in Ottawa, kindly showed me the inscribed copy of *Canadian Born* and lent me the five articles Jean wrote between 1931 and 1935 about her friend Pauline Johnson.

Chapter 17

Details about the CPR's passenger liners come from George Musk's *Canadian Pacific: The Story of the Famous Shipping Line* (Toronto: H. Rinehart and Winston, 1981). John A. Cherrington's wonderfully imaginative *Vancouver at the Dawn: A Turn-of-the-Century Portrait* (Madeira Park, BC: Harbour Publishing, 1997) included the anecdotes about Mr. and Mrs. Charles Henshaw. Betty Keller described Ernest Thompson Seton's interest in native rituals in *Black Wolf: The Life of Ernest Thompson Seton* (Vancouver: Douglas & McIntyre, 1984).

Books by Benson and Gillies already cited for Chapter 11 proved useful for Pauline's return to London twelve years later. The anecdote about Pauline's electrifying effect on Lord Cecil Manners appears on page 52 of Mrs. Foster's biography. Additional material for this chapter comes from *Seated with the Mighty: A Biography of Sir Gilbert Parker*, by John Coldwell Adams (Ottawa: Borealis, 1979); Donald B. Smith's biography of Grey Owl, *From the Land of Shadows: The Making of*

Grey Owl (Saskatoon: Western Producer Prairie Books, 1990); and *Lord Strathcona: A Biography of Donald Alexander Smith*, by Donna McDonald (Toronto: Dundurn, 1996).

Pauline's letters to "Little Divil" Archie Morton are in the Chiefswood Collection at the Woodland Cultural Centre Museum, Brantford.

Chapter 18

Pauline's letter about the Bridgewater fire is in the Trent University Archives, and her letter about the Chautauqua disaster is in the Thompson Seton Papers in the Philmont Museum and Seton Memorial Library in Cimarron, NM. Her correspondence with Prime Minister Laurier is in the Sir Wilfrid Laurier Papers at the National Archives of Canada. To learn about the Chautauqua movement, I read *Chautauqua in Canada*, by Sheilagh S. Jameson (Calgary: Glenbow-Alberta Institute, 1979), and *Chautauqua: A Center for Education, Religion, and the Arts in America*, by Theodore Morrison (University of Chicago Press, 1974).

Pauline's poignant comments on her advancing age were made in a letter to J. D. Logan, dated December 5, 1912, which is reproduced in Appendix 1 of John C. Adams's MA thesis, "English-Canadian Poetry and the Critics," Acadia University, 1955.

Chapter 19

Vancouver's colourful history has generated many lively books. I relied on Michael Kluckner's *Vancouver: The Way It Was* (North Vancouver: Whitecap Books, 1984); Bruce Macdonald's *Vancouver: A Visual History* (Vancouver: Talonbooks, 1992); *Saltwater City: An Illustrated History of the Chinese in Vancouver*, by Paul Yee (Vancouver: Douglas & McIntyre, 1988); and *Vancouver Past: Essays in Social History*, edited by Robert A. J. McDonald and Jean Barman (Vancouver: University of British Columbia Press, 1986).

Harry Stevinson lent me the book of columns written by his mother, Bertha Jean Thompson Stevinson, privately published as *Up and Down the Pacific Coast* in 1989. Much of the material in chapters

19 and 20 comes from Jean's articles written between 1931 and 1935 and printed in various Western Canadian newspapers on the anniversaries of Pauline's death.

A particularly interesting book about early attitudes to and treatments for breast cancer is *A Darker Ribbon: Breast Cancer, Women, and Their Doctors in the Twentieth Century*, by Ellen Leopold (Boston: Beacon Press, 1999).

The description of Chief Joe Capilano's funeral appeared in the *Daily Province*, Saturday, March 26, 1910.

Chapter 20

A letter to Lorne Pierce in the Queen's University Archives from a clever young writer named Beatrice Nasmyth is the source of the information about Pauline's feather boa and the raincoat row with Evelyn. Monica Newton, Beatrice Nasmyth's niece, told me a little more about the friendship between Pauline and her aunt, and about Pauline's corrections to the proofs of *Flint and Feather*. Charles Mair described his last visit to Pauline in "Pauline Johnson, an Appreciation" in *The Canadian Magazine*, July 1913, pp. 281–283.

Elizabeth Rogers's account of Pauline's cremation and burial, and information about Pauline's will, is lodged in the Vancouver City Archives. Both Marega's death mask of Pauline and Pauline's Indian costume, including the silver trade brooches, scalp, wampum belt, bear's claw necklace and George Johnson's dagger, are stored today in the Vancouver City Museum.

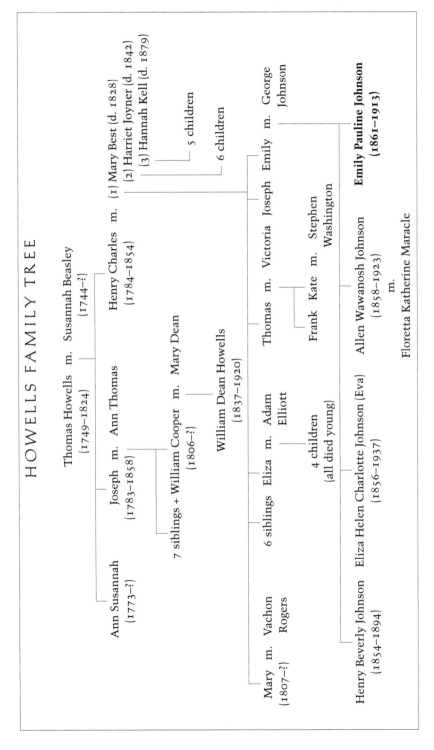

HOWELLS FAMILY TREE

Thomas Howells m. Susannah Beasley
(1749–1824)   (1744–?)

Ann Susannah   Joseph m. Ann Thomas   Henry Charles m. (1) Mary Best (d. 1828)
(1773–?)   (1783–1858)   (1784–1854)   (2) Harriet Joyner (d. 1842)
                                                                   (3) Hannah Kell (d. 1879)

7 siblings + William Cooper m. Mary Dean
                                 (1806–?)   5 children

                        William Dean Howells   6 children
                        (1837–1920)

Mary m. Vachon   6 siblings Eliza m. Adam   Thomas m. Victoria Joseph Emily m. George
(1807–?) Rogers   Elliott   Johnson

                                   4 children   Frank Kate m. Stephen
                                   (all died young)   Washington

Henry Beverly Johnson Eliza Helen Charlotte Johnson (Eva) Allen Wawanosh Johnson   **Emily Pauline Johnson**
(1854–1894)   (1856–1937)   (1858–1923)   **(1861–1913)**

                                                                m.

                                                      Floretta Katherine Maracle

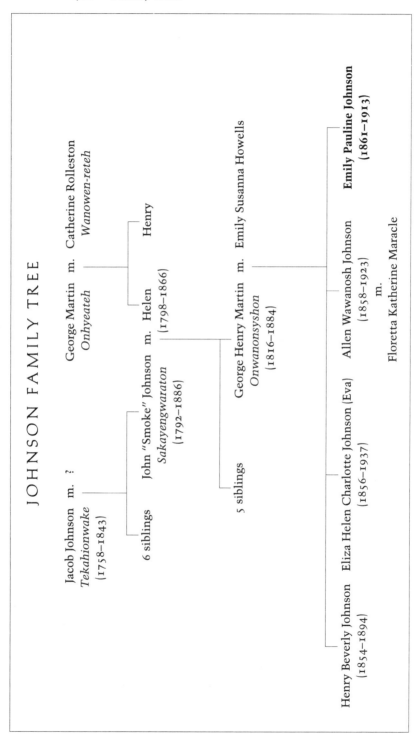

JOHNSON FAMILY TREE

ACKNOWLEDGEMENTS

P AULINE Johnson has intrigued me ever since I read Betty Keller's biography of her twenty years ago. When I began exploring the social history of Canada for my previous biographies, I kept coming across references from the late-nineteenth and early-twentieth centuries to the "Mohawk poet." She appeared to have captivated hearts everywhere during her lifetime, and her appeal resonated across the years. So when Phyllis Bruce suggested to me that there was room for another book about Pauline, I leapt at the idea. Coming to grips with this complex, talented woman has been a joy for me, enhanced by Phyllis's consistent support, encouragement and editorial suggestions.

The generosity of Pauline's previous biographers was impressive. At a long lunch in Vancouver two years ago, Carole Gerson and Veronica Strong-Boag shared insights and research, and pushed me to examine my own preconceptions. Carole provided me with material that I would not have found on my own. Sheila Johnston allowed me to use photographs that she had collected for her book, was always ready to discuss my project and communicated her own passion for "PJ" to me. Betty Keller explained to me how she had tracked Pauline's travels across Canada. This book would have been a much weaker biography without the graceful help I received from my predecessors.

I also owe a particular debt to two friends. The first is Dr. Sandy Campbell at the University of Ottawa, who knows far more about Canadian literature than I do and who gave me thoughtful feedback on every chapter. The second is Judith Moses, who not only read the manuscript but also ensured me a warm welcome at the Six Nations on the Grand River Reserve. Leona Moses, who knows Iroquois history intimately, and her husband, Bob, invited me to their home on the reserve and made sure I got my facts right about Pauline's Indian background. The help of the Moses family was invaluable.

Paula Whitlow at Chiefswood and Tom Hill, director of the Woodland Cultural Centre Museum, supported my project and provided useful suggestions and material. Chief Dan Maracle of the Tyendena'ga Reserve took time to show my husband and me round the Mohawk Church there. Dr. Olive Dickason, author of *Canada's First Nations: A History of Founding Peoples from Earliest Times*, gave me one of the best pieces of advice I heard: "Don't trust anything written more than twenty years ago about Canada's First Nations." Dr. Dickason also supplied suggestions and support throughout this project.

When I first arrived at the William Ready Division of Archives and Research Collections at McMaster University, archivist Carl Spadoni greeted me with a smile: "We've been waiting for you!" He and his staff went out of their way to ensure I had enough time to see all the Johnson and McRaye material. I am also grateful to the staff of museums, archives and libraries across Canada, particularly Elizabeth Hunter and Stacey McKellar at the Brant County Museum, Joan Seidl at the Vancouver City Museum, Bernadine Dodge at Trent University Library, George Henderson at Queen's University Library, Mrs. Dorrie Smith and Mrs. Doreen Nowak of the Rosseau Historical Society and Arlene Gehmacher at the Royal Ontario Museum.

In BC, I would like to thank Wendy Higashi at the Greenwood Museum, Sonya Strudwick at the Grand Forks Museum, Kelsey Hatlevik at the Rossland Museum, Babs Bourchier at the Rossland Miners Union Hall, Veronika Pellowski in Sandon and Elizabeth Scarlett at the Kaslo Historical Society Archives. Hillary Haggan kindly researched the Cope and Henshaw families for me, and Dr. Hamar Foster of the University of Victoria helped me on BC native bands.

In London, I was assisted by staff at the London Theatre Museum in Covent Garden and at the Kensington Public Library, where Caroline Starren was particularly helpful. My London research would not have been nearly so much fun without the companionship of my cousin

Colin Senior, who also slogged through electoral rolls for me to find out more about Portland Road and St. James's Square.

Living in Ottawa, I am lucky enough to be able to do much of my research in our two great repositories of national memory: the National Archives of Canada and the National Library of Canada. National Archivist Ian Wilson and National Librarian Roch Carrier make every visitor to their institutions welcome, and their staffs are a pleasure to work with. At the Parliamentary Library, librarians tracked down obscure titles for me with unfailing courtesy.

I would also like to thank the Office of Cultural Affairs at the City of Ottawa for its financial assistance, and for its continued support for local writers.

My telephone rang one hot July day in 2000, and a gruff voice asked, "Are you writing a book about Pauline Johnson?" The caller was Hugh MacMillan, a former archivist who had heard of a collection of letters written by Pauline to his distant relative Archibald Kains. Through Hugh's good offices, I was able to look at the letters, which were then owned by Kains's grandniece Joan Ritchie of New Jersey and in the possession of Susan MacMillan Kains. Since then, the letters have been donated to the National Archives, but Hugh and Susan allowed me to see copies of the letters at the point in my research when I was eager for new material. I cannot thank them enough.

Many other friends, acquaintances and strangers contributed to this biography, among them Harry and Isabel Stevinson, Marion McKenzie and Helen Elaine Woolley Diebel (who provided photographs of the 1903 camping trip), Joyce Lewis, Senator Landon Pearson, Mrs. Sara Sutcliffe, Harry Brumpton, Scott Calbeck, John and Deborah Bowen, Debbie Culbertson, Julia Hickey Sporka and Peter Unwin, Dr. Bill Williams for information about Pauline's illnesses, Dr. Norman Hillmer for historical background, Dr. Michael Peterman for Pauline's literary context, Dr. Clara Thomas for leads on the J. E. Wetherell correspondence, and Dr. Susan Bellingham at the University of Waterloo. Dr. Melanie Stevenson at McMaster University shared her research on the Johnson–McRaye performances at the Chautauquas. In Peterborough, Quentin Brown told me about Smily's chess set and Kathy Hooke explained the Mackenzie family to me.

When I tried to assess Pauline's legacy as a poet, I turned to Dr. Gordon Johnson at Trent University and Elizabeth Waterston, professor emeritus at the University of Guelph; their professional judgement helped me refine my own thinking.

At HarperCollins Publishers, I have enjoyed the help of a wondeful team of professionals. It was a real pleasure to work with not only Phyllis herself, but also associate editor Karen Hanson, typesetter Roy Nicol, copy editor and indexer Stephanie Fysh, jacket designer Scott Christie and publicist Shona Cook. Once again, freelance map-maker Jeanne Simpson knew exactly what I meant when I asked for "maps that tell a story," and went to extraordinary lengths to get details of trains and paddle-steamers correct.

As usual, my friends have lived this biography with me, with regular enquiries about Pauline's progress and intelligent questions that made me explore new angles. Sheila Williams, Sally McLean, Wendy Bryans, Maureen Boyd, Cathy Beehan, Kyle McRobie, Carol Bishop, Paddye Mann and Barbara Uteck reassured me once again that there is considerable public interest in how women in any century lived their lives. Wayne McAlear, Monic Charlebois, Precie da Silva, Violeta Hollmann-Bonales, Jillian Brant, Trinh Phan and Katie Plaunt provided the kind of practical help that allowed me to work without interruption. Ernest Hillen continued to be a source of wise editorial advice.

My parents, Robert and Elizabeth Gray, supported my research expeditions in England. My three sons allowed Pauline to preoccupy me and dominate dinner table conversation. My deepest gratitude goes to my husband, George Anderson, whose unfailing support included not only reading each chapter at least twice, but also driving up and down every lake in the Kootenays and listening to me recite "West wind blow from your prairie nest, / Blow from the mountains, blow from the west . . ." ad nauseam. Thank you.

A final word about language: what is acceptable in one time or place is offensive in another. Pauline and her contemporaries used terms such as "the red race," "palefaces," "savages," "half-breeds" and "pagan" which strike us today as racist and troubling. I have used such phrases only in direct quotations from the period; otherwise I have tried to find neutral and respectful words such as "Indians,"

"Métis" and "European settlers." I have avoided terms such as "Euro-Canadians," "Amerindians" and "First Nations" that would have been foreign to Pauline herself. But there are no hard-and-fast rules, and it is a lexicographic challenge to find a word for non-natives who were born in Canada. I hope readers will accept that I have striven for inclusive, impartial terminology. As Daniel Francis pointed out in his excellent *The Imaginary Indian*, it is part of our conflicted attitudes about our native peoples that "we lack a vocabulary with which to speak about these issues clearly."

PICTURE CREDITS

p. 82: NAC, C 2291

p. 84: BHS 780

p. 85: BHS 1662

p. 87: NAC, C 51848

p. 89: BHS 634; Photographer, J. Fraser Bryce

p. 93: William Ready Division of Archives and Research Collections, McMaster University

p. 99: Katharine Hooke, Peterborough

p. 105: BHS 563

p. 112: NAC, PA 132150; Photographer, Frank Micklethwaite

p. 129: NAC, C 56072

pp. 134–135: NAC, C 149034–149035

p. 151: William Ready Division of Archives and Research Collections, McMaster University

p. 159: VPL 9429; Photographer Cochran, Brantford

p. 162: NAC, PA 122594

p. 165: NLC, C 5350

p. 171: ROM, 85 Eth 192

p. 176: NAC, C 10109

p. 178: BHS 620; Photographer, Cochran, Brantford

p. 184: BHS 627; Photographer, Cochran, Brantford

p. 195: BHS 3789

p. 197: NAC, C 9485

p. 199: NAC, PA 41344

p. 208: PAA, B49

p. 209: PAA, B10595

p. 213: BHS 491

p. 218: Grand Forks Archives, PG181 BM 991-055-049

p. 234: BHS 540

p. 244: BHS 1306

p. 249: NAC, PA 63175

p. 254: NAC, PA 30212

p. 262: NAC, PA 27869

p. 268: PAA, OB540

p. 281: Courtesy of Sheila Johnston

p. 289: BHS 563a

p. 295: NAC, PA 29547

p. 296: Archives of British Columbia, HP 25606

p. 312: NAC, C 14100

p. 314: BHS 1653

p. 315: NAC, C 68847

p. 318: Courtesy of Steinway Bros, London

p. 321: Courtesy of Sheila Johnston

p. 323: CVA, P.41 N23 #1

p. 333: Courtesy of Sheila Johnston

p. 341: Courtesy of The Chautauqua Institution Archives, Chautauqua, NY

p. 342: Lorne Pierce Collection, Box 14, Folder 1, No. 29: Archives of Queen's University

p. 350: VPL, 12768

p. 351: CVA, IN. p.3 N13

p. 355: VPL, 5211

p. 356: Courtesy of Harry Stevinson

p. 358: Courtesy of Sheila Johnston

p. 360: BHS 1270

p. 377: Courtesy of Harry Stevinson

p. 379: BHS 249

p. 382: CVA, P.10 Port N200

p. 390: CVA, Port P.1422 N 742

p. 393: VPL, 7145

p. 401: BHS 630; Photographer, Cochran, Brantford

INDEX